Multinational Firms in Africa

Multinational Firms in Africa

Edited by
Carl Widstrand
With an introduction by
Samir Amin

African Institute for Economic Development and Planning, Dakar
Scandinavian Institute of African Studies, Uppsala
Uppsala 1975

ISBN 91-7106-093-6

Printed in Sweden by
Uppsala Offset Center AB, Uppsala 1975

Contents

Preface

Since 1963, the Scandinavian Institute of African Studies has organized a variety of international seminars. As a part of its function as a Scandinavian documentation and research centre on African problems, the Institute has sought to choose topics for these international seminars that would be of interest to academics as well as to planners, administrators and politicians. These topics have included refugee problems, boundary problems, problems of adult education, the role of mass media, co-operative development in East Africa and problems of land-locked countries in Africa. Scholars from abroad—primarily, of course, from Africa—have been invited to discuss their particular topics with Scandinavian specialists and other interested persons.

Another of our principle tasks over the years has been to promote and sustain the interest in African affairs among Scandinavians. Seminars comprise one way of doing so at an academic level. During these seminars, however, we have also attempted to offer "another point of view" on a variety of topics. The profile, strength and vigour of our institute depends, therefore, to a great extent on our being able to call upon a large number of Scandinavian Scholars with backgrounds and views widely differing from those held in other African studies establishments, in our discussions with experts from Africa and abroad.

We felt, however, that considerably more progress could be achieved towards sustaining the general interest in African affairs if we could pool our resources with African research and teaching institutions. During the preparatory work concerning a seminar on Multinational Corporations in Africa, we were interested to find that a seminar on a similar topic was being prepared by the *African Institute for Economic Development and Planning* (IDEP) in Dakar, Senegal, under its director, *Dr. Samir Amin.* A joint effort to provide accurate information and analysis on a variety of topics concerned with the operations of multinational firms in Africa was therefore suggested and a joint conference was held in Dakar on 25 September–5 October 1974, with forty participants from more than thirty, mainly African countries. The seminar was organized by the IDEP under the direction of *Dr. Jagdish Saigal* and *Dr. Norman Girvan.* Our institute provided seven resource persons for the seminar and undertook to publish the proceedings. Some of the papers presented at this "joint venture" are thus published in this volume.

I wish to record our institute's deep appreciation of the work by Dr. Samir Amin and Dr. Jagdish Saigal in the preparation of the conference and our thanks to the scientific, library and technical staff of the IDEP.

Uppsala in April 1975

Carl Widstrand

The Multinational Corporation in Africa: The International Capitalist System

Samir Amin

Towards a New Structural Crisis of the Capitalist System?

The previous structural crises and how they were surmounted

The capitalist mode of production is characterized by an inherent contradiction: the contradiction between the ever growing social nature of the productive forces and the persistently narrow nature of production relations. This contradiction has existed from its beginnings, so that it does not imply an impending "final breakdown". It has been surmounted for at least a century both by the expansion of the capitalist system and the renewal of its accumulation model. Marx reminds us that the capitalist mode is compelled to revolutionize production continually; it is therefore also compelled to revolutionize production relations continually, so as to adapt them to the requirements of the continuous development of the productive forces. The history of capitalism is therefore necessarily that of the process of adjustment of production relations to the requirements of the progress of productive forces.

It is not a continous history. It alternates between phases of expansion and phases of "structural crisis". In this way, it would seem that we can clearly distinguish four phases of expansion: 1815-40, 1850-70, 1890-1914, 1948-67 and four phases of structural crisis 1840-50, 1870-90, 1914-48 and the period after 1967.

Every phase of expansion is characterized by a particular accumulation model, a type of propelling industries, a specific context defining the methods of competition and the status of the firm, etc. Generally speaking, each phase corresponds to a certain stage of geographical expansion of the capitalist system, to a particular organization of international specialization in this context and more specifically to a distribution of the functions of its centre and its periphery, and finally to a certain balance (or imbalance) between the various central nation-States. We must add that these conditions together determine the type of class alliances which corresponds to the accumulation model and thereby the context of the class struggle and political life, as they also determine the reproduction model of the bourgeoisie, a necessary complement of that of capital reproduction (see below).

It will also be noted that from 1914 on one may speak of the decline of the system, and we will specify the nature and functioning of this decline both in the 1914-48 restructuration phase and in that of the subsequent phase of expansion 1948-67.

On the other hand, every phase of structural crisis constitutes a phase of "maladjustments and readjustments" (an apt expression used by Frank) in the transition from one accumulation model to another. The crisis implies a slowing down of growth and a sharpening of the class struggle.

The first phase of expansion (1815-40) marked the end of the Industrial Revolution which had begun in the last third of the 18th century, i.e., it came after the wars of the French Revolution and the Empire (1791-1815). The Industrial Revolution was based on the steam engine and the weaving loom. Its area of expansion was still practically limited to England, Belgium and the north-eastern quarter of France. The accumulation model was still to a great extent based on competition through which industry expanded to the detriment of handicrafts, while there was no keen competition among industries. Industry was still a strictly family enterprise producing for a local or a regional market; therefore, the confrontations with other industries of the same branch were limited. This accumulation model assigned a lesser rôle to the periphery, which had fulfilled decisive functions in the period prior to mercantilism.[1] The periphery was nevertheless still important, but henceforth as a supplier of raw materials, mainly American and Indian cotton, and as a buyer of part of the new industrial product—cotton prints.

At this first stage of the development of capitalism in its mature form, the emergence and the expansion of the capitalist mode of production depended on the class alliances of the new industrial bourgeoisie with the landowning classes. These alliances took various forms, that of an alliance with the renovated large agrarian estates in England, that of an alliance with the post-Revolution peasant landowners in France. Readers interested in this issue may consult our work on the relations between capitalism and agriculture.[2]

Of course, the long process which preceded the Industrial Revolution and its starting point took various forms in England, in France and in other European countries. Well before the English "Glorious Revolution" of 1688 and the French Revolution of 1789, the process of deterioration of the feudal relations of production, that of the constitution and development of mercantile capitalism, first in the Mediterranean region from the 13th to the 16th century, then in the Atlantic region from the 17th century, began preparing the ground for capitalism. It seems natural that under these conditions, the industrial revolution did not occur simultaneously in England, France, North America and on the rest of the European continent. It is therefore difficult to consider the first phase of the expansion of capitalism as happening simultaneously. The industrial revolution which began in the middle of the 18th century ended in England before 1815, specifically (as Frank observed), during the wars of 1790-1815, while it in fact developed in France, and sporadically in Germany and northern Italy, only between 1810 and 1840.

In any case, this process of expansion came to a halt in Western Europe (west of the Elbe, north of the Pyrenees and of the region of Florence) from the 1840s. The structural crisis culminated in the economic and political crisis of 1848. The forties witnessed the birth of the workers' movement (the English Chartism) in 1848; the Communist Manifesto announced the birth of Marxism. The evolutionary attempts in this period, however, proved a failure: the French workers' movement was crushed by the armies of peasant mercenaries mobilized by the bourgeoisie to this end; the confused movements led by the bourgeoisie and petty bourgeoisie of the less advanced regions of Germany and Italy were temporarily crushed, but had nevertheless began the unification process in these two nations.

The second phase of expansion of capitalism (1850-70) was based on the railway and the steel industry. The development of the productive forces necessarily led to the beginning of a socialization of production relations through arrangements for the association of individual owners of capital. It is true that these arrangements were known in the mercantilist era, but the limited liability company, the "société anonyme", reflects the accentuation of the inherent contradiction of the production mode and the solution to this contradiction in the context of capitalist relations. The railway extended the area of capitalist expansion. The unification of Germany and that of Italy were completed in this phase; Russia, the Austro-Hungarian Empire and Spain were integrated in the new European capitalist market. The abolition of serfdom in Russia (1861) accelerated the process of transformation of the old precapitalist Russian agriculture into a capitalist export agriculture. The definitive frontiers of the United States were established and the Civil War (1860-65) consolidated the predominance of capital in North America.

The international balance was altered. In place of the predominance of two Atlantic monarchies, England and France, in the West and of two decaying empires (Russia and Austria-Hungary) in the East, there was substituted a seven-fold balance: 4 advanced central capitalist nations (England, France, Germany and the United States), one semi-backward country (Italy) and two empires, multinational and backward but integrated into the new capitalist system (Russia, Austria-Hungary).

The functions of the periphery in this phase declined in terms of relative importance. The periphery certainly continued to supply cotton, but the new propelling industry (steel) obtained its raw materials from the centre itself.

This accumulation model came to an end by 1870. The crisis began with the sharpening of the class struggle marked by the premature Paris Commune. It was surmounted by the superseding of the laissez-faire policy of the fifties to the seventies (the only real period of capitalist liberalism), by the constitution of monopolies and by imperialist expansion. Electricity opened up new fields for industrial modernization, and shipping provided the market with its true world dimension. This phase of expansion of capitalism on a world level again attributed essential functions to the periphery: on the one hand the periphery supplied raw materials and agricultural produce, imported capital for the creation of infrastructures and bought manufactured products made necessary by the destruction of its handicrafts and the subjection of its agriculture to capital, but on the other hand, in addition to these exchanges and capital flows, there arose unequal exchange, that is, the unequal remuneration of labour power crystallized in "world goods".[3]

The unequal international specialization and the constitution of the contemporary periphery in these forms facilitated the swing of the European workers' movement towards revisionism, and the domination of the class as a whole by the labour aristocracy — in a word the social democracy of the 2nd International—while at the same time helping to reduce Marxism to an "economistic positivism", which showed that the working class was being imbued with the ideology of the dominant class.

International life was still characterized by the relative balance of the four major powers (the United States, Germany, England and France); and even the four backward or young powers (Italy, Japan, Russia and Austria-Hungary) had an important place. The first world conflict which inaugurated the period of the decline of capitalism sprang from this unstable equilibrium, the clash of imperialisms in the scramble for the periphery, imperial neo-protectionism, and the resultant coalitions.

Our present hindsight tempts us to see this relatively long period (1914-1948) as being one single period of structural crisis. The propelling industries between the two world wars were the same as they had been before 1914, the accumulation model was more or less the same and so were the methods of monopolistic competition. Nevertheless, as it went on, the crisis entailed profound changes in the international system. Europe was weakened by the First World War to the advantage of the United States. The Second World War finally ensured the triumph of North America. The period between these two world wars was not really a phase of autonomous expansion: the short boom which followed the reconstructions and the inflations of the first half of the twenties ended in a catastrophe in 1929, and the production level in 1938 was barely that of 1913.

One of the characteristics of this long phase of crisis was the redoubling of the class struggle in the centre and its extension to the world level through the nationalist, anti-imperialist movement. Between the precursory sign (the attempted Russian revolution, 1905) and the October revolution, the first breach in the capitalist system, there were only twelve years. Between 1917 and the beginning of the Chinese civil war which in 1950 ensured the first triumph of socialism at the periphery of the system, there were only 10 years.

Elsewhere, however, the revolution was crushed under the weight of the reformist social democracy. But the radical criticism of the reduction of marxism to positivist economism was still incomplete and Leninist bolshevism maintained some aspects of it, aspects which will later appear in our examination of the reason for the failure of the "popular front" attempts and the social significance of the fascism of that period.

The phase of expansion which opened in 1948 and ended 20 years later with the international monetary crisis, the French May and the "creeping Italian May" presented very particular features. The propelling industries of this period (which witnessed a high growth of the world economy, a growth which even surpassed that of the exceptional period 1890-1914 and contrasted with the near stagnation of 1914-48) were industries producing durable goods, particularly the motor car, and the "functional" urbanization accompanying it. The development of these industries began in the interwar period and the model of accumulation which they condition took a definitive form in the United States during the Second World War. The expansion which took place between 1948 and 1967 brought nothing new: it was all based on a "catching up" process due to the fact that Europe lagged behind the United States between 1914 and 1948. Europe and Japan did not set themselves any other target, and they were soon joined by Russia in this endeavour.

Herein lay the decay of capitalism. The "State monopoly capitalism" which first saw daylight during the crisis of the thirties, and the multinational corporations (of new types: conglomerates, etc. . . .) which began operation in the sixties, were not radically new forms of monopoly competition, but rather ways and means of prolonging the declining stage of the system, particularly by resorting to the State.

In the expansion phase 1948-1967, however, there was a change in the model of international specialization. The industrialization process through import substitution, which began during the Great Depression in some Latin American countries, and was accelerated during the war and in the fifties in America, in the Arab world and in Asia, began in Africa in the sixties. In this context the old imperial formulae were replaced by neo-colonial formulae. Development inequalities within the periphery grew worse and embryo "sub-imperialisms" appeared.

All these processes occurred side by side with the absolute predominance of the United States in the industrial, financial and military sphere. This period was characterized by a highly stratified international life. The dollar was accepted as a universal currency and "Atlanticism" was triumphant. In 1953, Russia's cold war policy yielded place to that of peaceful coexistence. The term "bipolar" world frequently used to describe the period is, in fact, somewhat misleading, for Russia played in this "bipolar" world the rôle of a close second after the United States. We should in fact speak of an almost unipolar world.

But from 1967 this balance began to totter, that is, well before Europe, Japan and, of course, Russia "caught up" with the United States. This is again a sign of decadence to which we will return. With today's hindsight, the 1948-67 period appears as the "time of illusions".

We shall now deal with the analysis of the contemporary crisis and the prospects it opens up. We think, however, that it would first be useful to survey the theoretical tools at the disposal of the socialist movement today for doing this, tools which have been considerably enriched during the last few years.

The contemporary crisis and the natural tendencies of the system to surmount it

To say that capitalism is declining does not mean that it will collapse by itself, as a result of the effect of some irresistible economic contradiction. This would be returning to the positivist economistic approach previously rejected.

In fact, we can already imagine the new industries which could constitute the basis of a renovated accumulation model: atomic and solar energy, space, genetics and synthetic food production; sea bed exploitation, etc. . . . One can also glimpse what the development of these new branches would imply with respect to the conditions of competition and the rôle of the State, the international division of labour, etc. . . .

It is therefore useful to consider the possible types of "balance" based on the development of these new branches so as to study subsequently how the social forces would operate to ensure the transition from the present situation to these "equilibrium states", what contradictions would have to be overcome and what, under these conditions, the weak links of the system are.

We will call these final equilibria the modalities of "1984" (referring to George Orwells's *1984*). Why? Because the picture of perfection in horror represented by George Orwell's world corresponds to the perfect rationality of the capitalist production mode and therefore to its natural trend. It reflects the "barbarian" side of the socialism or "barbarism" alternative envisaged by Marx and Engels in the 1848 Manifesto. 1984 reestablishes a perfect correspondence between the perfectly socialized productive forces and the production relations, perfectly dominated by commodity alienation.[4]

By what means has the inherent contradiction of the capitalist mode been surmounted so far? What fundamental trend of the latter is revealed by this story?

The contradiction between the ever-growing socialization of productive forces and the renewal of capitalist production relations has been surmounted by the continuous centralization of capital (which is thereby becoming more and more "abstract") and by the parallel gradual destruction of precapitalist modes. The individual bourgeois enterprise was replaced by the limited company and the latter by the monopoly. During the 1930 crisis, and ever since the State has been compelled to intervene actively in the process of reproduction, so as to support the monopolies and to absorb a share of the surplus which could no longer be absorbed by capitalist reproduction itself in the context of monopolistic competition. This has been clearly shown by Baran and Sweezy. Nevertheless, what has been called "State monopoly capitalism" is still ambiguous, for it is not a new phase, qualitatively different from that of the monopolies. State intervention as practised was only a means of sustaining the reproduction process of the monopolies. This intervention occurred during the 1914-48 period of structural crisis and continued in the subsequent phase of expansion.

On the other hand, we can easily see that the new industries imply a new status for the firm and modalities unknown to competition. In fact, in these fields it is difficult to see how the monopolies known to us, including the most powerful multinational corporations (the conglomerates) could intervene with the means at their disposal. They must be replaced to a very great extent by the State. If capitalism is to be perpetuated, it will reach an unprecedented level of centralization. The capitalist State would replace fragmented and competing capital: capital would become really abstract for the first time.

The survival of capitalism under these conditions is conditioned by the perpetuation of the capitalist ideology. Economism, that is, commodity alienation, has always been the content of this ideology. We have seen[5], however, that the extortion of the surplus in the capitalist mode was "opacified" by capital competition—the market—and the sale of labour power—itself a commodity. We have seen that for this reason the dominant factor in the capitalist mode was not the ideological but the economic factor, as opposed to the situation in the precapitalist modes and the Soviet mode. *1984,* with the centralization of capital, is close to the Soviet mode. The extortion of the surplus by the dominant State class again becomes transparent, and the ideological factor thereby acquires a dominant function in reproduction. The ideology corresponding to this new function is that analysed by Marcuse in his *One-Dimensional Man.* The totalitarian religious character of this ideology clearly reflects its dominant function.

Thus there is nothing cheerful in the final equilibrium reached: nothing less than the barbaric prospect of *1984*. Nevertheless, this prospect has some variants. For the sake of convenience, we will describe the two extreme types, any combination of the two also being possible. The prospect which we will call 1984 A would be characterized by the following international division of labour: the centre would reserve all new industries for itself and would throw cost out to the periphery all the "standard" industries, that is, those we know in our contemporary world (the "polluting" industries, to simplify things: iron and steel metallurgy, chemicals, light industries). We are not concerned here as to whether every central region would have the same function from this point of view.

The fact remains that the new industries only offer very limited employment opportunities: although they require a highly skilled and relatively numerous labour force during their installation stage; their subsequent operation, thanks to automation, requires hardly any manpower. In the 1984 A prospect, the citizens of the centre would therefore be engaged in parasitic activities which would undergo a massive development. To achieve this, the periphery would provide specifically agricultural produce and the "standard" industries intended for their maintenance. In other words, the masses of the periphery, proletarianized and exploited by the central capital (as a result of the control of technology monopolized by the centre) would produce the surplus consumed by the parasitic masses of the centre. This corresponds to a sort of extension of the South African model to the world level; that is why it does not seem to us that apartheid and the racialism it implies are "relics" of the past—they are on the contrary a requirement of this type of "advanced capitalism". It is necessarily a racialist model, because the ideological "justification" of the unequal exchange it implies (at the periphery, producers of surplus value; in the centre, their consumers) can only be of this type.

The goods produced under these conditions by the periphery for the centre are in fact, world goods, produced by the most modern means. One could not therefore claim that labour is less remunerated at the periphery on the pretext that the level of development of the productive forces is backward there. Nevertheless, we cannot compare the productivity in "standard" industries located in the periphery with that in the "new" industries concentrated in the centre. We have already dealt with these points in both *Le développement inégal* and *L'échange inégal et la loi de la valeur,* to which we refer the reader.

In this perspective, the "standard" industries would not be evenly distributed among all the regions of the periphery. On the contrary, they would be concentrated in some of them. This phenomenon, which is still at an embryonic stage and known as "sub-imperialism", would become general. The sub-imperialist countries would import capital and technology from the centre, export the products of the "standard" industries mainly to the centre and accessorily to the more deprived areas of the periphery, and in this way defray what they owed to the centre for the imported capital and technology. The concentration of "standard" industries in these countries, coupled with the high rate of exploitation of their proletariat, would enable the sub-imperialist bourgeoisies to benefit from a sufficient share of the surplus to ensure the economic and political balance of the system.

On the contrary, the prospect which we will call 1984 B excludes all international division of labour: like the standard industries, the new industries would all be concentrated in the centre, while the whole periphery would be really marginalized. This prospect would necessarily involve the genocide of the peoples of the present Third World, who have become completely useless and even dangerous for the reproduction of the capitalist system. Side by side with this, the centre would no doubt import a massive amount of unskilled manpower, accentuating a trend which is already visible. The unequal exchange would be internalized, as a result of the development of a systematic racialism with respect to the mass of immigrant workers.

These two different modalities of 1984 have a common characteristic: that of a simplified world, reduced to the capitalist mode of production. In 1984 we can no longer speak of social formations in the sense we did for the past and the present, nor of a world system, since the latter implies a diversity of modes of production.

The world of 1984 can be reduced to the capitalist mode on the world scale. This neither implies equality nor homogeneity, but the inequalities here are simply class inequalities within the capitalist mode: between bourgeoisie (henceforth State classes) and proletariat, between sections of the proletariat (on a racialist basis), between proletariat and parasites, just as the heterogeneity which reflects the uneven geographical concentration of classes merely accompanies the class differentiation and no longer expresses, as is still the case at present, the complex character of the formations in which dominant and dominated modes are interrelated, the latter modes being characterized by a retarded development of the productive forces.

Is the 1984 A prospect the most "natural"? Yes, in a way, because the uneven expansion of capitalism throughout the world has been a permanent trend of the system, the means by which it historically has surmounted its inherent contradiction. Mercantilism already implied a periphery which fulfilled decisive functions in the generation of capital. From the industrial revolution to the 1860s, however, wages in Europe were not better than those in India and were comparable with the real "income" of the slaves in America. The situation changed after 1870, with the gap widening even faster than that of productivities. The "external market" is therefore important for raising the profit rate, but as we have shown (*Le développement inégal*), it is not essential for the absorption of goods. Nevertheless, imperialism was the capitalist solution to the crisis of the years between 1870 and 1890 because it offered the monopolies a new and profitable field of action. The contradiction engendered by imperialism in turn led to the nationalist movements of the following period, 1914-48. The renewal of the class alliance between monopoly capital and the local bourgeoisies, which is the content of neo-imperialism characterized by the independence of the former colonies (from Egypt in 1922 to Africa south of the Sahara in 1960 through India and Southern Asia in the 1940s and 1950s), opened a new outlet to capital through import substitution industrialization. This outlet was highly profitable precisely because, as we have already seen, the wage gap was greater than that of productivities from one branch to another.

This very evolution was pregnant with political consequences, for—whether we like or not—it laid the basis for the reinforcement of racialism and fostered an ideology based on the "inequality" of peoples.

In the 1984 A assumption, this evolution would culminate in the strict equality of productivities, the total modernization of the productions of the new periphery, but side by side with this, the maintenance of a gap between real wages. Jaffe's intuition, according to which South Africa, under these conditions, is a sort of microcosm where the characteristics of the world of 1984 may already be found is a strong intuition, indeed. (Jaffe's mistake was to think that we are already in 1984, that the world system is already similar to South Africa, whereas productivities are in fact not yet equalized.)

These two extreme perspectives are probably somewhat of a caricature. If the system were to develop according to its own laws, without being challenged by series of revolutionary transformations, it would probably evolve towards a combination of both models, some standard industries being transferred from the centre to some sub-imperialist countries, and others being maintained in the centre and some areas of the periphery being gradually and genuinely marginalized, and even destroyed.

What factors would tip the scales in favour of A or B?

To answer this question, we must examine the significance of the transition from the present situation to that of the final balances described under the generic term of 1984. The accumulation model at present governing the capitalist system has collapsed, because the profitability of the propelling industries (motor cars and durable goods) on which it was based was handicapped: (1) by the huge mass of investments in infrastructure which support the expansion of the market for these commodities (urbanization, motorways, etc. . . .), (2) owing to the fact that a considerable portion of the surplus value generated in these industries is absorbed by the wastage of the accompanying tertiary services and of the sales services required by the forms of monopolistic competition governing these branches, (3) owing to the inadequate exploitation of the potentialities of the periphery, limited by the type of international division of labour implied by this model and (4) owing to the fact that this model is politically and ideologically viable only on the condition that a dual requirement of the working class of the centre be met: full employment and continuous increase in real wages, a requirement which makes the system less flexible in a case where a fall in the profit rate necessitated a difficult readjustment in terms of employment and wages.

Moreover, this accumulation model, for political and ideological reasons to which we shall return, was in crisis long before Europe and Japan caught up with the United States.

The following question may therefore be asked. The transition from the present accumulation model to the 1984 model implies extraordinarily massive investments in new industries. Who will finance these investments? The proletariat of the centre and/or that of the periphery?

In a situation such as this, in which all the illusions of "easy and sustained" growth crumble away, it is quite obvious that the frightened bourgeoisies will at first all attempt to get out of it by seeking to transfer to others the burden of facing the consequences. The stronger the bourgeoisie, the greater its economic, political and military resources, and the brighter its chances for success in creating a zone of influence on which to thrust the difficulties of the transition. A weak bourgeoisie, on the contrary, can be compelled to make its own proletariat bear more of the burden of transition. The strong will therefore incline towards the 1984 A horizon, the weak towards that of 1984 B. Therefore, the new period will first be characterized by a sharpening of the struggle between the central capitalisms for access to the Third World and to Eastern Europe. These are the battlefields on which is being fought the war which will decide the new international "balance".

We shall therefore examine successively in this context: (1) the nature of the inter-imperialist struggles on the battlefield of the Third World and the contradictions resulting from it (will the imperialist strategies be checked by the "nationalism" of the periphery?), (2) the nature of the Eastern European integration into the new world system and the contradictions arising from it in Russia and in the present satellite countries, (3) the nature of the social struggles in the centre which will result from the successes and failures of these strategies (where are the weak links, if any?).

Energy and raw materials crisis and the role of the periphery in the new world system

The present oil and raw material crisis must be placed in the above context. It will not be understood if these problems are examined separately; if for example (as is often done), the consequences a readjustment of relative prices will have on the various regions of the world are discussed without taking into account the crisis of the accumulation model. This is to take a stand on superficial grounds on which everything can be explained by apparently sensible arguments, the grounds on which those concerned manoeuvre according to their own strategy.

The very progress made by the Europe and the Japan of the "time of illusions" in catching up to the United States had led to a questioning of

American preponderance. In the immediate post-war period, the gap was such that the United States had, in every industry, a lead which gave them absolute superiority in term of competiveness; in other words, the productivity gap operated in their favour, because it was still greater than the wage gap. Little by little, however, this ratio was reversed, at least in a certain number of Japanese and German industries. The permanent surplus of the American balance of payments gave place to an opposite trend. Hence the United States lost the extra advantage which had operated in its favour and had enabled it to acquire strategic positions in Europe by buying up firms and modernizing them under its own direction. At the same time, the United States was no longer able to play the role of international policeman, because this expensive operation (i.e., the war in Vietnam) increased the deficit of its external balance. This is the reason why the crisis occurred in the field of the international monetary system and led to the fall of the dollar.[6]

Nevertheless, the United States was able to contemplate a major counteroffensive strategy which is now being implemented. This strategy was formulated, first in the sphere of ideological preparation ("zero growth", "the environment", neo-Malthusianism), then in the sphere of political preparation (the American-Russian pact, the peace in Viet Nam and the recognition of China), before it was launched in the actual economic sphere (the increase in the prices of oil, raw materials and agricultural produce).

Therefore, the ground was first prepared at the ideological and political level. The Club of Rome, constituted for this purpose, sounded the alarm and announced the generalized scarcity and depletion of raw materials, thus preparing the increase in the prices of energy and raw materials. The "environment" campaign was related to these preoccupations. By ending the war in southeast Asia, the United States improved the position of its external finance. Then like a thunderbolt came the announcement by the Shah of Iran of the increase in the oil price. It should be recalled here that this decision was taken before the Yom Kippur war.

From this point of view, the United States is in a better position than Europe and Japan. It is true that it depends on foreign countries for an appreciable percentage of its needs in fuel and raw materials. But it is also a large producer of oil and a wide variety of raw materials and agricultural produce. Compared with the United States, Europe and Japan are thus in a relatively poor position to consider a reconversion of their economy based on higher relative prices for energy, raw materials and agriculture. Indeed, we saw at once how the rise in the price of oil led to the recovery of the American balance and to that of the dollar.

The aims of this counteroffensive by the United States are multiple:

1. to weaken Europe and Japan and restore the situation prior to the international monetary crisis.

2. to win over the under-developed countries which, on the whole, also

benefit from this rise in the prices of oil and raw materials (we shall see later how this analysis must be qualified), and hence to snatch them from European and Japanese influence, thus placing the United States in the best possible position to develop the 1984 A strategy to its own benefit.

3. to seal the alliance with the USSR. In fact, this country, which is more self-sufficient than Europe and Japan, is also not much affected by the increase in raw materials prices; on the contrary, it is likely to benefit from it if its intention is to export more and more of these materials to the West in exchange for advanced technology. The USSR is thus compelled to play the role of "close second" to the American strategy.

It would be wrong to believe that this operation would be limited to oil, to connect it with the Middle East conflict and with the will of the Arabs to use the weapon of "black gold", etc. . . . even though this element has infact intervened.

The increase in the prices of raw materials in general should follow, particularly those of ores. But, in the American strategy, the same applies to agricultural products. Until now the United States has by subsidizing their producers, adopted a policy of low prices for agricultural products. This policy was feasible as long as the American balance of payments yielded a surplus, but it was costly for American capital. By abolishing these subsidies in order to allow prices to "adjust themselves to the demand", the United States, a large exporter of agricultural products, will improve its external situation.

Who will foot the bill for these adjustments? Who are the beneficiaries?

The first obvious beneficiaries are the multinational corporations, which are mainly American. The situation as regards the oil corporations, for instance, has been reversed: they used to be faced with a situation characterized by a high growth in demand (and therefore by the obligation to make heavy investments) and by low prices (and therefore small profits). The situation is now the opposite: with the super profits to be made in oil, these corporations can combine to finance the reconversion towards 1984, particularly in the field of atomic and solar energy, etc. . . .; that is, they will look for a place in the new leading sectors. The same applies to the multinational corporations dealing with other raw materials.

Generally speaking, by making Europe, Japan and the underdeveloped countries bear the burden of the crisis, the United States is cushioning its own reconversion towards 1984.

Do the Third World countries benefit from the operation? A serious detailed analysis must be made here, so as to avoid the fairly obvious dangers of blackmail and manipulation.

The underdeveloped countries as a whole are exporters of fuel and raw materials, and importers of manufactured goods and food products. The rise in the relative prices of the former in relation to the latter improves their external balance, even if this improvement is reduced by the opposite effect of higher prices for their imported food. This is quite clear and obvious, and all the statements about the so-called negative effects of this improvement in the terms of trade of the Third World are, to say the least, curious.

Nevertheless, the operation, as envisaged by the United States (we emphasize this point), is not in "the interest of the Third World", primarily because the imperialist strategic perspective is based on the unequal distribution of these profits among the countries of the Third World. The beneficiaries—their ruling classes—would in this context agree to play the rôle of sub-imperialisms: they would industrialize at an accelerated rate in the 1984 A perspective, thus offering capital the possibility of exploiting the potentialities of a cheap proletariat. The surplus which the centre would draw from this exploitation will quickly outgrow "profits" obtained at the stage of implementation of the new balance. It is very clear here that the operation aims at making the peoples of the Third World foot the bill for the reconversion towards 1984 A, through a capitalist alliance with the bourgeoisies of some countries in the Third World.

To this strategy must be opposed the possible counter-strategy of the peoples of the under-developed world. This certainly does not consist in doing the same thing with other partners (Europe and Japan), but: (1) in getting rid of the multinational corporations and replacing them by long-term State-to-State agreements, thus giving more autonomy to the underdeveloped States and enabling them to use the profits resulting from their higher export prices as they choose; (2) in rejecting the project of the new international division of labour (1984 A) and developing their economies on the basis of a maximum social and technological autonomy, the long-term State-to-State agreements being geared to that perspective; (3) in refusing the division of the Third World on the basis of "sub-imperialism"/"sub-colonies", and on the contrary accelerating the process of the constitution of large blocks with the prospect of an equal development of partners therein.

The requirements of this strategy, particularly in Africa and in the Middle East, will be studied subsequently, with respect to the European/French alternative and to the Soviet strategy.

Is the integration of Eastern Europe a way out of the crisis?

The USSR already presents all the characteristics of a subimperialism. In its relations with the developed countries of the West, it exports raw materials and imports advanced technology; in the relations it entertains with the Third

World, it exports "standard" manufactured goods (including arms) and imports raw materials. Moreover, the deficit resulting from the relations with the West is covered by the surplus obtained from its relations with the Third World.

Strictly speaking, the USSR is at the present time the only country clearly presenting these characteristics (together with South Africa). Those countries already termed "sub-imperialisms"—for instance, Brazil, India, Iran—are still far from this structure. From the strict economic point of view, they as yet export to the developed world only and in practice do not yet export to the under-developed world. But the logic of their growth policy will necessarily make them evolve in the indicated direction, and they already indicate that that is their political target.

Is there any possibility that the USSR will fulfil this function more and more, thereby offering an essential outlet (much larger than that of the Third World) to Western capital? In theory, yes, for it is already a well-formed society, with a large and disciplined proletariat and with still large peasant reserves, etc. . . . The projects for developing Siberia tend in this direction. As K. S. Karol humorously put it, since the late lamented comrade Stalin was no longer sending enthusiastic volunteers to Siberia, the system no longer knows what to do; it cannot implement effectively either the Chinese "labour-intensive" formulae, because they imply a real mass participation, nor truly Western formulae, since these require technology, organization and capital.

There are many signs which indicate that the USSR is a candidate for this rôle. It is being more and more proclaimed that closer relations must be established between the external market and the mechanisms of the national economy, that is, that the USSR wants to belong to the international capitalist system and not only to the international capitalist market. According to Agnelli, it is better to manufacture Fiat cars at Togliattigrad, where the proletariat is more disciplined and less costly, than at Turin.

But it would be wrong to stop here, for the USSR has three particularly essential characteristics: (1) it has a specific mode of production which cannot be reduced to the capitalist mode, (2) it has a world vocation, particularly a military vocation and (3) it entertains special relations with its zone of influence, in Eastern Europe. The Soviet mode, a *sui generis*[7] mode, is not the expression of the backwardness of the productive forces. On the contrary, although production relations here are class relations, they have reached a more advanced stage than in the West: here the total centralization of capital heralds 1984. That gives the political power a predominance it lacks in the capitalist mode. But the power of this dominant class as regards the external world requires the maintenance of the Soviet military power. This compels the USSR not only to refuse to specialize in the "standard" industries but also to develop the new industries (atomic, space, etc.). To achieve this, it must reserve for itself the maximum surplus generated by its proletariat, and this strictly limits the prospect of a large-scale installation of "standard" industries intended for the external market of the developed countries.

This is probably why the USSR is hesitating. That is why it will no doubt try to keep this process under its control, particularly by playing on the contradictions between the possible partners: the United States, Japan and Germany. One can see here the double blunder of the Soviet "opposition" of the Solzhenitsyn type, as shown by Karol. The opening to the West does not make the system a liberal one: firstly, because the "natural" prospect of capitalism is not the development of democracy but 1984; secondly, because this opening is based on the "discipline" of the Russian working class, unequal exchange and therefore, its continued oppression.

Europe, a weak link of the system?

The crisis has suddenly led to the break-up of Europe and put a stop, temporarily at least, to the construction of Europe at the very time when it seemed to be finally succeeding through the integration of Great Britain.

1948-67 had been the "time of illusions", in this case the illusion that the gradual constitution of an integrated Europe would enable it to catch up with the United States, thanks to the advantages of a market which would henceforth be a continental one. But the reality talked of was a different reality, that of the Europe of Nations, and of unequal nations. As always, the most powerful partner in this case, Germany—wanted to accelerate the movement. Italy, Belgium and the Netherlands accepted what Faire and Sebord aptly described as the choice of a "compradorization" supporting Germany. France, on the other hand, by manoeuvring between the maintenance of the pre-eminence of national institutions and policies and the acceptance of a limited supra-nationality—the policy of the "Europe of Nations"—sought to improve its position before the European fusion was completed. In its attempts to achieve this, it had important political and economic assets (the dependence of the franc areas).

The high growth rates of the late-comers of the "time of illusions" permitted the highest hopes. These hopes were justified by mechanical projections, a predilection of technocrats lacking social intelligence. Thus Herman Kahn amused himself by projecting these rates, predicting a glorious future for Europe and particularly for Southern Europe (France, Italy, Spain). This kind of exercise in fact never gives any information, because a small difference between two growth rates, if projected over a longer time, is enough to make this difference appear to reflect a qualitative change in the international balance. History shows that things never happen in this way, for the growing imbalance generates new contradictions which are not taken into consideration in the projection scheme. Once again, Kahn's exercise appeared at the very moment when the phase he was projecting indefinitely was coming to an end!

What are the contradictions involved?

The more advanced industrial capitalism of northern Europe had liquidated the vestiges of the mercantilist period. Agriculture in England had been definitely abandoned with the repeal of the Corn Laws in the middle of the 19th century and, thereby, the class alliance of capital with landed property had lost its real basis.[8] For Scandinavia, and particularly Sweden, the assumption has already been mentioned that the heterogeneity of the agrarian structurs and the early alliance between the leaders of the workers' movement and financial capital had facilitated a purer development of capitalism.

In Germany, Nazism had been the last phase of a policy of complex alliances, directed by large-scale capital, and designed to mobilize the peasants, petty traders, etc., against a revolutionary proletariat. Yet Nazism was at the same time eliminating the real basis of these alliances; its collapse, and the division of Germany after the war, saw the disappearance of this 19th-century heritage.

Society in northern Europe, with its simpler structure, requires for its own reproduction a fundamental social pact between capital and the working class. Thus, social democracy is *par excellence* the ideology of mature capitalism. It reacts in turn on the economic base, by ensuring, through full employment, social security and a negotiated but continuous increase in real wages as well as accelerated growth.

The system in North America is similar although still more favourable to capital domination. Drowned by the effects of the successive waves of migrants and by those of the conquest of the west, the workers' movement there had never managed to transcend the most elementary "economism" in order to reach the level of political autonomy, even a social-democrat autonomy. The conflicts rather occurred at another level: between dominant capital (the Republican party) and local interests (more or less in coalition in the Democratic party). With the progress of integration and accumulation, the alliance of the local interests lost its force, and ended in the present regime of a de facto single party. The State there must, nevertheless, adopt the equivalent of a social-democrat policy: this was the purport of Roosevelt's New Deal, and also of the "Great Society" invented by the "Democrat" Johnson and then taken over by the Republicans.

There is nothing similar in Southern Europe. Being weaker there, industrial capital was compelled to develop lasting class alliances with the remnants of mercantilism: in France and in Northern Italy with the small peasantry, in Spain and in Southern Italy with the latifundia, and everywhere with the urban petty bourgeoisie, the local notabilities, the commercial bourgeoisie, etc. This series of alliances drove the proletariat to a more radical opposition: the anarchism in the 19th century and the success of the Communist parties of the 3rd International bear witness to this fact.

The political life of Latin Europe has therefore been very different from that of northern Europe. It is characteristic that the expansion of the years between 1948 and 1967 was ensured by conservative and authoritarian governments (Francoism, Gaullism, Italian Christian Democracy). "Popular frontism" has been the counterpart of this type of regime. In this regime, the working class really threatened capitalism whenever it associated with power, as happened in France and Spain in 1936; from this angle, its presence in power had a quite different impact from that of the social-democrat governments in the north, which never constituted any danger to the social system (quite the opposite). But each time this participation in power only lasted for a short time and ended by a shift to the right: Francoism or Pétainism. The fact is that the parties of the working class were attempting the impossible: to snatch from the bourgeoisie its traditional allies (peasants, small traders, etc.) and this led to economic bankruptcy and to the return of the bourgeoisie to power, reclaiming these unstable allies from the popular fronts. The Germany of the Weimar republic had a similar history, which ended in Nazism.

Nevertheless, something changed during the expansion which took place between 1948 and 1967: the very process of growth sawed off the branch on which the traditional power of capital was based, since this process liquidated the peasantry, the small enterprise, etc. Capital tried to replace its traditional class alliances by dividing the working class, since it could not associate with it in the northern social-democratic way. The policy of very wide differentiation of wages, intended to win over the middle-grade personnel and technicians, was formulated for this purpose. The fact remains that this policy failed from the ideological point of view, as shown by day-to-day events in Italy and France from 1968 onwards. Capital was consequently compelled to maintain and renew the models of its traditional alliances: this was shown in its tolerance and support for the new bourgeoisie, which was growing rich from urban land speculation and from the parasitic tertiary sector (hence the failure of Chaban Delmas' social-democrat attempt in France).

This failure of social democratic integration made southern Europe a weak link in the crisis: firstly, because the class alliances in question limited the competitiveness of its capital with respect to that of the northern countries; secondly, because the fact of making the working class bear the burden of the crisis in itself caused an explosive situation in these countries with a revolutionary tradition. The frightened bourgeoisie then hesitated between an attempt to constitute an anti-American bloc together with some areas of the Third World (the present pro-Arab and Euro-African choices of the

French government) and submission, capitulation and acceptance of its "compradorization" (the choice of the "Centre democrate" and of the independents . . .).

Southern Europe is not the only weak link in the central capitalist system, although it seems to us that it is the most fragile. Will social democracy in northern Europe withstand the end of full employment? The wildcat strikes in Sweden and the emergence of a Marxist current in German social democracy already indicate the weaknesses of the system. If the so-called multinational capital in the United States can exploit the crisis for its own benefit, this will be to the detriment of the sectors of capital which are geared more to the home market. Minor though this contradiction may be so long as the working class does not intervene independently in the country's life, it is not negligible at the level of State political decision-making.

How can these shortcomings be used so as to open breaches towards a socialist transformation in the centre? The working class and its organizations now have a choice between a "defensive strategy" and an "offensive" strategy, as defined by Lucio Magri. The former, which consists in defending the "level of living" of the class, is ineffective in a situation of structural crisis. On the other hand, its possible success transfers the burden of re-adjustment to the periphery, accelerating the march towards 1984 A. The second, "offensive" strategy aims on the contrary at seizing the opportunity of the impending keen class struggles in order to abandon the economistic framework, to put forward the felt "need for Communism" (as shown by the crisis of the system of values, of education, the active criticism of the division of labour—at least in Italy and France) and at raising the working class, at a political level, to the rank of a hegemonic class. It is certainly too early to say how this strategy might progress. It already appears, however, that "popular frontism" and putting forward a programme of "economic revival" based on the priority development of collective consumption do not constitute effective means. "Frontism" assumes the absurd: that the working class can snatch from capital its surest allies: the parasitic sectors it sustains (land speculation, etc. . . .). The economic revival presupposes—this, moreover, is the diagnosis of the Communist parties—that the crisis is an ordinary recession and not a structural crisis. If that in fact were the case, collective consumptions could provide the means of a revival. But these consumptions (an additional cost for capital) could in no case facilitate the creation of new industries—on the contrary. As a justification for the diagnosis of the "ordinary" recession, it will certainly be recalled that the increase in the rate of unemployment is a modest one. This, too, is a major mistake. The crisis will not be a repetition of the one which occured in the thirties, because the forms of competition and of State intervention are not the same. That is why, in our opinion, this re-structuration crisis will be very long and will not entail a massive and sudden unemployment. Once again, it is a sign of the decline of the system: it is less and less flexible, less and less capable of rapid adjustments (even painful ones). That is also why the alternative, i.e., social democracy or fascism, is a false alternative. The latter is characteristic of the type seen in the 1930 crisis; today, it is rather—in the short or medium term—the prospect of an authoritarian neo-social democracy accompanied by selective repression, which is the means used by capital to delay the fundamental challenge to the system.

In a parallel way, inter-imperialist contradictions are bound to develop. The manifestations of this (already perceptible) will be blocs and wars by proxy between the countries of the periphery. It would be a serious mistake on the part of the socialist forces of the Third World to remain passive, to "adjust themselves" to the situation, to confine themselves to concluding tactical agreements with a particular bloc, etc., for these forces can also play a decisive rôle.

Once again: the tempest belt

The characteristic of the equilibrium described under the name of 1984 A is the existence of "sub-imperialism". Development in this direction already exists, although at an embryonic stage, and we can already distinguish at least two variants of this type of development. The first is quite simply characterized by the runaway industries of central capital benefiting from the existence of a cheap proletariat, as already found in Eastern Asia and in Mexico. The second is characterized by a more pronounced association of the local bourgeoisie and the concomitant creation of "standard" and integrated industrial complexes, as found in Brazil, India, etc.

Let us avoid quarrelling over words. The very term "sub-imperialism" has been criticized because it refers to imperialism and therefore to capital export, whereas "sub-imperialists" import capital but do not export it. So far as we are concerned, the phenomenon—no matter what it is called—indicates a specific structure with a definite place in the unequal international division of labour. The terms lumpen-Europeanization, or lumpen-development certainly give a better picture of the phenomenon than "sub-imperialism". It should also be recognized that this phenomenon is still quite embryonic and does not yet enter perceptibly into the foreign-relations structure of such countries as Brazil, India, etc. Should we fortherefore neglect to see what is taking place here and elsewhere?

The oil crisis suddenly reminded us of the importance of these possible developments. Not much imagination is needed to envisage a unified Arab world rich in oil royalties and hence able to industrialize through the massive import of Western technology and become an industrial workshop supplying cars to Europe and textile goods to other African countries. A second wave of Arab nationalism, maintained this time in the east by King Faisal, the emirates of the Gulf and Egyptian industry and in the west by Libyan and Algerian oil and the basic Maghreb industries, is clearly possible.

These are possible perspectives. But the game is far from being won. Here again, there are many contradictions, and the new equilibrium presupposes that they can be overcome without upsetting the system. Three series of contradictions are worth mentioning here.

The first and the most important are the contradictions occurring in the class struggle in the Arab world. The "time of illusions"—1948-67—was for the Arab world that of the "Nasserian" development model, inspired by the Soviet model, first transposed to Egypt and then extended to Syria and Iraq and renewed in Algeria. It was in Egypt that this model was most systematically applied, through the nationalization of the whole of industry and a radical agrarian reform, etc. It is also in Egypt that its limitations are most clearly noticeable. The alternatives are clear for Egypt today: either to give up the "attainments" of Nasserism, to accept a form of Arab unity in which the private capital of Saudi Arabia and of the Gulf would predominate, or to go beyond the "Nasserian" model. The violent and repeated struggle waged by the Egyptian proletariat and youth make it impossible to pre-judge the outcome. In Algeria, where the "technocratic" option benefits from the facilities afforded by petroleum, the game is not yet finished either, for in this country, this option is necessarily that of the country's "lumpen-Europeanization", based on the Turkish model. It puts a definite end to Algeria's integration into the Arab world and finally shelves "Arabization".

The second series of unsolved contradictions is that which currently exists and will long remain between the various sections of the Arab bourgoisie. Who will create the Arab unity which is necessary for the project to flourish? The emirs and kings of the desert or the bureaucracies of the densely populated countries? Will the latter accept being "compradorized" after having nursed hopes of achieving Arab unity under their own direction?

The third series of contradictions is that between the Arab world and other possible candidates. Israel has been used by the West since 1948 as a first-rate means of checking the development and the liberation of the Arab world. But this state has now lost its "raison d'être": if the Arab world can be integrated into the capitalist system as a "sub-imperialism", that is the end of the Zionist state's dream of fulfilling this function by submitting to its "peaceful" semi-protectorate the less industrialized and militarily weak Arab countries. The Yom Kippur war, in this respect, tolled the knell of Zionism, and the latter was quite aware of this when it realized "Kissinger's betrayal". But Israel still exists and nothing proves that the renewal of bourgeois Arab nationalism will have enough strength to deal a final blow to Zionism or to make the Arab peoples definitely accept it. Israel still remains the thorn in the flesh of Arab nationalism.

Hardly had Zionism begun to decline when Iranian sub-imperialism, with its obvious ambitions on the Gulf, loomed on the horizon.

The Arab world is surely not the only weak area in the periphery where we can see the difficulties of creating a 1984 A model. To southest Asia, where capitalism has been challenged since 1945, the sub-continent of India will perhaps be added. During the expansion years between 1948 and 1967, the Indian bourgoisie succeeded, by integrating their country more and more into the capitalist system, in widening its class basis through a series of agrarian reforms and by an acceleration of a dependent industrialization. The pursuit of this model may be hampered by the crisis, as already shown by the gloomy prospects regarding India's foreign balance. In that case, violent struggles are likely to take place in the context of a weakened bourgeoisie and State. Should we be disheartened by the failure of the sixties in Latin America, culminating in that of the Chilian "frontism"? Here again, it would be wrong to think that if the "miracle" of Brazilian sub-imperialism were to mark time, the situation would not become favourable to a new socialist break-through. Now, there are many reasons why this miracle is likely to stop at a certain ceiling. Based on an increasingly uneven internal income distribution (real wages have been reduced by 40% in 10 years) which created a market for durable industrial commodities (motor cars, etc.), commodities consumed by the local bourgeoisie and by the large number of the growing petty bourgeoisie, the miracle will soon require an opening of foreign markets. But in the atmosphere of competition sharpened by the crisis, this opening may be more difficult than the Brazilian bourgeoisie expected.

There will be a great temptation for the local bourgeoisies of the periphery to participate in the strategic game of the blocs. In the face of the primary threat, the American one, certain alliances may acquire a new meaning. The fact remains that the outcome of the class struggle in the metropolitan countries and in the periphery will decide the content of these alliances. The rapprochement begun between France and the Arab world, as well as the expressed will of the French to resist any American stranglehold over Africa, must be watched closely. There should not, however, be any illusions about a "right-wing" policy of this type. After all, it is the "paleo-colonial" French practice in Africa which often constitutes the best objective ally of American penetration, by facilitating Washington's demagogy towards the compradore bourgeoisies which are too weak to be more than one of the stakes. It is therefore important for another policy to be initiated, that of a front of the peoples of the Mediterranean region, of Africa and of the Middle East, a policy which requires a left-wing evolution on both shores of the Mediterranean.

Notes

[1] Frank and Amin, *Le développement inégal.*
[2] Amin, Samir, *La rente foncière et le capitalisme.*
[3] Amin, Samir, *L'Echange inégal et la lot de la valeur.*
[4] Amin, Samir, *Eloge du Socialisme.*
[5] Amin, Samir, *Le dévelopment inégal.*
[6] Amin, Samir, *Le développement inégal.*
[7] Amin, Samir, *Le développement inégal.*
[8] Amin, Samir, *La rente foncière.*

Norman Girvan

Economic Nationalists *v.* Multinational Corporations: Revolutionary or Evolutionary Change?

Towards a new international economic order?

Suddenly, it seems, the multinational corporations are on the defensive. In the space of a few short months the OPEC states have turned the tables on the giant oil companies and the Western nations and are now calling the shots on the price of the most important commodity entering into world trade. For once, countries in the Third World are actively controlling the terms of their trade with the industrialized world and the returns they get from the powerful multinational corporations, instead of the other way around. What is more, the OPEC action has inspired similar attempts from dozens of other Third World exporters of primary commodities. An influential US economist speaks ominously of "the threat from the Third World", warning that in addition to the OPEC action:

> the seven leading *bauxite* exporters have formed the International Bauxite Association (IBA). Immediately thereafter, Jamaica forced a six-fold increase in its earnings. Other members are now beginning to follow suit ...
>
> Six leading *phosphate* producers have tripled their prices, with further increases likely ...
>
> Four leading *copper* producers, through the Intergovernmental Council of Copper Exporting Countries (CIPEC) ... have announced that they will seize a greater share of the marketing of copper; expand the membership of CIPEC to increase their market power; and work directly with the producers of potentially substitutable metals to reduce the risks of cartelization to each....
>
> The *tin* producers, through the International Tin Agreement, are seeking a 42 percent increase in the guaranteed floor price maintained by its buffer stock. These countries maintained an effective produces cartel before World War II.
>
> The leading *coffee* producers, through a series of interlocking marketing companies and stockpile marketing arrangements, have seized control of world coffee prices. They were confident enough of their success to let expire the International Coffee Agreement, through which they had previously sought the help of consuming countries to block price reductions.
>
> Five of the leading *banana* producers, through the Organization of Banana Producing Countries, have levied sizeable taxes on banana exports to boost their returns.

> In addition, exporters of *iron ore* and *mercury* have been meeting regularly. The four major *tea* producers have sought too coordinate marketing and establish a floor price, and at least once reached agreement on production quotas. There are numerous other primary products—including tropical *timber,* natural *rubber, nickel, tungsten, cobalt, tantalum, papper* and *quinine*—where effective collusion among producing countries is distinctly possible . . .[1]

Nor does the new economic nationalism stop at attempts to control the prices upon which depend the export incomes and, through them, the economic livelihood of Third World nations. Action on prices is seen as only one component of a general strategy of securing control over marketing and ultimately production in the resource industries which sustain Third World economies. State participation in ownership—whether the percentage of equity held is 20, 51, 60 or 100—has in the space of the last few years become the order of the day for these industries in the Third World. National economic sovereignty, in short, is seen as inseparable from the objective of greater equality in international economic power-relations. An outgrowth of this is the development of direct government-to-government 'resource combination' projects within the Third World which seem to by-pass the multinational corporations. In the Caribbean three governments have agreed to develop aluminium production in which Trinidad will supply natural gas for power, Jamaica will furnish alumina and Guyana will provide both alumina and hydro-electric power. Similar projects are announced by the OPEC states almost daily. Apart from the OPEC action on oil prices, two recent events perhaps more than any other dramatise the apparently profound shifts taking place in international economic relations. One was the United Nations special session on raw materials, distinguished by the historic analysis of Algeria's President Boumedienne and marked by the passage—against the wishes of the West—of a resolution calling for a new international economic order. The other is the huge loans by Iran—allegedly an underdeveloped Third World country—to Britain and France, two of the leading industrial nations. The loans are to help these countries finance their balance-of-payments deficits, a problem normally regarded as a distinguishing feature of underdevelopment.

So is 'dependency' dead, or dying? Is 'economic imperialism' being decisively confronted? Is economic power slipping irretrievably from the grasp of the giant multinational corporations who will in the future have to share it on equal terms with national states in the Third World? Are we in fact witnessing revolutionary changes in the international economic system?

This paper offers some interpretive observations in answer to these questions. Definitive conclusions are out of the question, if only because of our proximity in time to the events as they unfold. We shall nevertheless advance certain views and show the factors which have led us to the interpretation they represent.

It is self-evident that we are in fact witnessing important and substantive changes in the structure and power-relationships of the international economic order which prevailed up until the end of the 1960s. I believe that the most important aspect of these changes is the rise in the international economic power of certain Third World states relative to that of Western industrialized states. But I shall also argue that it is important to distinguish Western industrialized *states* from the multinational companies which are based in those states and with whom they have traditionally been assumed to share a common, if not identical, interest. It will be suggested that the assumption of an identity of interest between Western states and Western multinational corporations should no longer be made. Indeed, a working hypothesis of this paper is that the rise in the relative economic power of some Third World states has been brought about—or at least, permitted—by factors engineered by the multinational firms.

We will argue that the solid achievements of the new economic nationalism do not in any way constitute a disengagement by these states from the system of internationalized capitalism. As a result the characteristic patterns of development and of income distribution implied by participation in that system are not being fundamentally altered. It will also be suggested that when one evaluates the process of strategy and counter-strategy being pursued by countries and companies, it will be seen that there has been no significant erosion in the power of internationalized capital, as represented by the multinational corporations. On the contrary, not only has the rise in the economic power of certain Third World states *vis-à-vis* Western states been permitted—if not actually planned—by the policies of the MNCs, but the new economic nationalism is also being turned by them to their advantage in the form of higher profits, reduced instability and more efficient long-term corporate planning. In the new international economic order now unfolding, certain Third World states can be accommodated as more equal 'children' in a family where unmistakeable and overall control is in the hands of a small elite corps of powerful multinational corporations. The quantitative and qualitative size, the resources and the power of these corporations are growing with extraordinary intensity and at a rate faster than any other component of the international economy.

Finally, we shall argue that these developments are having a 'perverse' effect: that side by side with a tendency for greater equality among states—a limited diffusion of international economic state-power, as it were—is a tendency for growing *in*equalities between groups of people. This development, which really represents an acceleration of trends already existing, takes place both among Third World countries and within them. It makes even more anomalous than before the practice of lumping all Third World countries together, and of lumping together all the people of any one Third

World country. In other words, the category 'Third World countries' now contains such wide heterogeneities as to lose its meaning altogether; 'Third World states' and 'financially poor states' are no longer interchangeable or identical; and the distinction between affluent people and poor people within 'Third World countries' has become more relevant than ever before. In short, we are in dire need of redefinitions, both analytical and terminological.

The transnationalized economy

When we speak of 'the multinational corporations', we mean far more than that category of business organizations whose main distinguishing feature is that they all happen to operate in more than one country. We mean a large and rapidly expanding *sector* of the *world* economy, characterized by a revolutionary new *system* of production and accumulation. The main features of this new system are diversified internationalized production under centralized control; massive size and huge financial resources of the basic institutional unit; technological dynamism and vanguardism; and high and continously growing concentration of economic power. In a very real sense this new system now dominates the world economy, whether 'developed', 'underdeveloped' or 'socialist'. Both quantitatively and qualititatively it is continually enlarging and intensifying its sphere of operation and control; attempting to absorb, subordinate or liquidate all other systems of production and accumulation. As a result, the expansion of this system is generating powerful tensions and contradictions—some of a traditional and familiar type, and others which appear to be altogether new. We will refer to this system as transnationalized capitalism, the specific contemporary phase of international capitalism which has emerged since World War II.

Quantitative indexes, we know, are not necessarily adequate measures of true economic significance or influence. But even the raw quantitative data speak loudly on the importance of the new transnationalized economy. The United Nations estimates value-added in this new sector of the world economy at $500 billion in 1971, amounting to *one-fifth* of total GNP of the non-socialist world[2] and exceeding the GNP of any one country except the United States. Furthermore, all observers are agreed that the share of this sector in the world economy is growing rapidly. At least since 1950 its annual rate of growth has been 'high and remarkably steady' at 10 percent, compared to 4 percent for non-internationalized output in the Western developed countries.[3] One apologist for the new system frankly envisages that within a generation some 400-500 MNCs will own something like two-thirds of the fixed assets of the world.[4]

The emergence and expansion of this new transnationalized economy is rapidly making a mockery of such traditional concepts as 'national' economy and the associated one of 'international' trade and finance. Even by conservative estimates, the value of internationalized production[5] now exceeds the value of international trade and the former has therefore displaced the latter as 'the main vehicle of international economic exchange'.[6] But so-called international trade itself consists to a growing extent merely of shipments among branches and affiliates of MNCs rather than arm's-length transactions. Such intra-firm transfers already account for about one-quarter of all British exports and imports;[7] the intra-firm shipments of American MNCs alone represented about 11 percent of total world exports in 1970,[8] and an estimated 33 percent of US manufactured exports consist of parent-to-affiliate shipments.[9] As one observer put it '. . . the direct activity of international companies (has) become the single most important link between industrial countries, even though the notion that this (is) still trade continues to be the basis for national economic policy and thinking'.[10] Overall, US multinationals are responsible for 62 percent of the exports and 35 percent of the imports of manufactured goods of that country;[11] domestically, they account for at least one-third of US economic activity.[12] It is also now accepted that American MNCs are by far the principal influence on the US balance-of-payments.[13] Furthermore MNCs generally have become the major actors on the international monetary scene to a degree which is frightening to many: at the end of 1971 they controlled no less than $268 billion in short-term liquid assets, 'movement of only a small proportion of which could produce' and has produced 'massive monetary crises'.[14]

What is important about the new transnationalized economy is not only its size and growing share in the global economy, but rather these in conjunction with the fact that it is characterized by a high and unprecedented concentration of raw economic power. Power in the transnationalized economy derives first of all from a number of characteristics of its basic institutional unit, the multinational corporation. The first of these is large size. It has become commonplace to compare the economic size of companies with that of countries, but repetition is nonetheless useful. The $36 billion-per-year turnover of the largest MNC—General Motors—is larger by far than the GNPs of the majority of member states of the United Nations, including such developed countries as Switzerland and Denmark. Of the 99 largest 'economies' in the world in 1970, 40 of them were multinationals.[15] Given the higher rate of growth of MNCs, their size relative to that of 'national' economics can only be expected to increase. The second characteristic giving rise to power is the wide spread of their activities, both over product lines and over countries. Among the 187 American MNCs selected for the famous Harvard Multinational Enterprise study, for example, the median enterprise produced 22 products, and the average firm operated in over 11 foreign countries.[16] Diversified production and global operation mean tremendous flexibility for management, and free the fortunes of the company from dependence on any one product or country. Third, these corporations operate on the very frontiers of technology. Compared to other companies they spend more on research and development, receive the bulk of government subsidies for technological development, and utilize more skilled and specialist manpower;[17] and it is they who introduce the bulk of new products and new processes into the mainstream of economic life. The fact that consumers and governments want—or have been conditioned to want—what these firms can deliver implies that tremendous leverage flows from their technological prowess.

A fourth characteristic of the MNCs that is crucial to the understanding of the power dimension is the centralization of authority in the global corporate headquarters. Recently two celebrated empirical studies of management practices in MNCs have appeared, one on either side of the North Atlantic.[18] Whatever their differences, both studies are agreed on one finding: in all such corporations, power in relation to overall strategic decision-making is concentrated in a small group of senior executives at the corporate head office. The key instrument in the service of this power is financial control. One consequence of this power is that large areas of global economic life—such as the distribution of production and employment among countries, the volume, value and direction of exports and imports, and the value and stability of national currencies—are falling increasingly under the control of a small number of committees of corporate managers. Another consequence is an increasingly uneven distribution of power and authority spatially across the globe. The late Stephen Hymer left us a vivid picture of where this development is leading us, a kind of corporate 1984, as it were. We can do no better than to quote him extensively:

> The modern multinational corporation has an eleborate vertical structure with many levels of intellectual work. The higher up the ladder, the higher the wages and status, the more abstract the level of planning, the longer the time horizons, the greater the scope for discretion and judgement. At bottom one supervises a few people, remains rooted in one spot, and deals with narrow specialities . . . operating activities (level III) spread themselves widely over the globe in response to the pull of men, markets and materials. Coordinating activities (level II), because of the need for white-collar workers, communications systems, and information, tend to concentrate in large cities . . . Level I activities, the general offices, tend to be even more concentrated than level II activities, for they must be located close to the capital market, the media, and the government . . . On the international level, the centralizing tendencies of multinational capital implies a world hierarchy of cities. High level decision-making will be centralized in a number of capitals—New York, Tokyo, London, Frankfurt, Paris, forming an inner ring between roughly the 40th and 50th parallel. These, along with Moscow and Peking, will be the major centers

> or radial points of strategic planning. Lesser cities throughout the world will deal with the day-to-day operations of specific local problems. These in turn will be arranged in a hierarchical fashion: the larger and more important ones will contain regional corporate headquarters, while the smaller ones will be confined lower level manufacturing activities.
>
> The new international economy will be characterized by a division of labor based on nationality . . . Day-to-day management in each country is left to the nationals of that country who, being intimately familiar with local conditions and practices, are able to deal with local problems and local government. These nationals remain rooted in one spot, while above them is a layer of people who move around from country to country, as bees among flowers, transmitting information from one subsidiary to another and from the lower levels to the general office at the apex of the corporate structure. In the nature of things, these people for the most part will be citizens of North Atlantic countries (and will be drawn from a small culturally homogenous group within the advanced world), since they will need to have the confidence of their superiors and be able to move easily in the higher management circles. Latin Americans, Asians and Africans will at best be able to aspire to a management position in the intermediate coordinating centers at the continental level. Very few will be able to get much higher than this, for the closer one gets to the top, the more important, is "a common cultural heritage." The majority will be little more than middlemen helping to organize their countries labor for sale abroad.[19]

Finally, power in the transnationalized economy also derives from the *collective* characteristics of the community of MNCs taken as a whole. In any one industry, for instance, production is dominated by a small number of giant corporations operating across the entire spatial spectrum of the world economy. The consequence is an enormous oligopolistic market power on a world scale; but since the corporations in any industry almost always fix their prices in sympathy with one another, what is oligopoly in form becomes monopoly in fact.

In addition there is the distinct tendency for growing concentration in industries which are technologically dynamic and/or capital-hungry, such as computers, transport equipment, and oil. All this must be seen in conjunction with the speed and frequency of mergers which produce giant world conglomerates, and of the formation of consortia for specific projects which blur the distinctions between allegedly 'competitive' firms. Such developments take place not only among firms from the same home country but also and increasingly among firms of different 'nationalities'. It is when we take the huge size, diversified production, technological dynamism and centralized global control of the individual corporation together with the collective market power of MNCs as a whole, that we begin to appreciate the enormous concentration of economic power represented by this large and growing sector of the world economy.

At the same time, this power generates reactions from and conflicts with those other capitalist groups—and other classes—which are increasingly threatened or subordinated by it. To some extent, these conflicts are manifested in the theme of 'The multinational corporation *v.* the nation-state'. In the underdeveloped world this issue has been an important one for decades: it is cast principally in terms of the subversion of national economic sovereignty which foreign ownership represents, and the set of reactions expressed broadly by the term 'economic nationalism'.[20] A relatively new phenomenon, however, is the emergence of this issue amongst countries such as Canada and Australia, which have most of the structural characteristics of economically developed countries but with predominantly foreign ownership in their manufacturing and natural-resource industries. Here the issue is posed in terms of the limited effectiveness of the traditional techniques of economic control and regulation in the context of what has been called a 'branch-plant economy'[21], as well as the degree of local processing and the fairness of export pricing in the natural-resource industries. The situation in these cases is complex and ambivalent, with labour generally suspicious of the power and intentions of foreign corporations but conditioned to believe that they are an indispensable means of securing higher living standards, while different segments of national capital make tactical alliances with or against different segments of foreign capital, depending on where they perceive their interests to lie. Here the nation-state is in a real sense buffeted between the powerful pull from the MNCs to adapt to the requirements of transnationalized capital by accepting a reduction in its sovereignty on the one hand, and on the other, pressures from opposing 'national' groups and classes who see it as the principal remaining means of defending their interests.

What is striking is the even more recent emergence of issues of this kind among the developed metropolitan countries such as Britain, France and the United States. These are the 'home countries' of many (in the case of the United States, most) of the MNCs and are traditionally considered to share common interests with corporations based within them. The fact is that the growth of the power exercised by MNC executives over the international distribution of jobs and income growth, over the direction and value of trade and monetary flows, and over advanced technology, have considerably strengthened their bargaining power and their leverage over even the most powerful of nation-states. Governments, which are subject to pressures from small- and medium-sized national capital and from labour, are uneasy at the shifting balance of power. Can the traditional 'loyalty' of multinationals to their home country and its government still be counted on?—even this is by no means clear. The Anglo-Dutch Shell Oil Co. has its commercial headquarters in London, but '. . . the British authorities know fully well that substantial interference (in Shell's foreign exchange transactions in order to protect Britain's exchange reserves) would result in the group moving its commercial centre of gravity to the Netherlands.'[22] The Anglo-Dutch Unilever is reported to assure itself of 'cooperation' from the British Government in a similar way[23]. In the United States, the labour movement has for years adopted the view that US-based multinationals acknowledge no national interest where the distribution of jobs is concerned: they are held responsible for the export of perhaps as many as 1.3 million American jobs to areas of cheap labour abroad.[24] And this development is in turn said to be at least partly responsible for the structural deterioration in the US trading position towards the end of the 1960s, which undermined the value of the dollar. To cap it all, the resulting speculation against the dollar which precipitated the devaluations of the early 1970s is ascribed in large part to the activities of US-based multinationals, who were seeking to protect the real value of their billions of dollars worth of liquid assets.[25]

In that sense we seem to be witnessing a process of *de*-nationalization of capital: a corollary of *trans*nationalization as corporations adopt a truly global view, selecting those investments which offer them the highest returns, wherever they may be; and favouring those governments which are most 'cooperative' and which 'offer them the biggest bribes'.[26] The change since the time when Lenin wrote his *Imperialism, the Highest Stage of Capitalism* in 1916 has been a profound one, and should by no means be underestimated. Up to the time of the First World War capital was international but corporations were (by and large) national. Capital exports took place mainly in the form of portfolio investments, financing more often than not locally-organized enterprises abroad in the production of primary products needed by the imperialist centres. Foreign markets were penetrated through commodity exports. In the imperialist centres, national, monopolistic, vertically-integrated corporations, closely allied with their governments, fought each other for access to the raw materials and the markets of the world. The important development since that time is the direct organization of production abroad by monopoly capital, providing itself directly with primary products and penetrating foreign markets more and more through foreign production rather than exports of finished goods. In the process, direct investment has displaced portfolio flows as the main form of capital export, and national companies have become world corporations. Destructive rivalries between national capitals, which twice in the first half of the 20th century generated world wars, are being replaced in large part by collusion, mutual market interpenetration and interlocking production and financial ties at the world level among MNCs of different 'nationalities'. Political imperialism has been replaced by neo-colonialism, the colony by the client-state. But even the client-state as such is becoming less necessary to transnationalized capital, as additional sources of leverage other than physical coercion or the threat of it are available to be deployed against governments, 'national' capital and labour: i.e., the huge financial resources, international flexibility and monopoly over advanced technology controlled by the multinational corporations. The power of transnational capital today is the power to withhold or relocate investments from a country, thereby threatening it with the spectre of economic stagnation and technogical retrogression. West Germany has no 'imperialist presence' abroad of the traditional kind, but the head of that country's largest commercial bank surveys the future with confidence:

> A prime necessity ... is the improvement of the investment climate in the developing countries themselves, as well as an improvement in the whole attitude towards private property and in particular towards business activity. ... In the longer term the necessary investment climate will be created by sheer force of circumstance, because automatically investment capital will flow to those countries providing the necessary conditions—and there are already a number of them. The others will undoubtedly learn the lesson and follow suit in their own interest.[27]

Exponents of the corporate ethic leave no doubt in the mind that the rise of the multinational corporation has, in their view, rendered the nation-state a technologically obsolete institution as a unit of economic decision-making or a reference-point for economic welfare. According to one, the nation-state should be considered as archaic, just as medieval institutions were at the time of the Rennaissance.[28] The managing director of Shell insists that the MNC can contribute '... much both to the immediate national interest and to the *more sovereign interest* of world economic development'.[29] Professor Raymond Vernon, director of Harvard's Multinational Enterprise Project, uses more academic and philosophical language, but the meaning is the same:

> It may be that, in the end, sovereign states will learn to live with a decline in their perceived economic power. But one marvels at the tenacity with which man seeks to maintain a sense of differentiation and identity, a feeling of control, even when the apparent cost of the identity and the control seems out of proportion to its value.[30]

In this view of the world, the concern for national economic sovereignty is regarded as some kind of 'traditional custom' surviving from a previous historical age, one which is quaint but fundamentally inimical to progress; in much the same way as the colonial powers in Africa regarded the "native's" attachment to village life as an anthropological curiosity which was inimical to his own welfare because it inhibited the spread of the money economy—i.e., colonial exploitation. Now it seems that governments in the developed countries, like colonized Africans, will have to be re-educated as to what is good for them.

Were Lenin alive today he would in all likelihood be less surprised at the transnationalization of capital since 1916 than at its growing success in incorporating the socialist world into its sphere of operations. Perhaps with some understatement, the United Nations report on MNCs noted that 'the centrally planned economies ... are more involved in the activities of (multinational) corporations than a cursory examination of the standard data might indicate'.[31] Equity participation by MNCs in these economies is obviously limited; even so, it does exist on a small scale in Romania and Hungary and on a growing scale in Yugoslavia, where up to 49 percent is allowed and where the constitution now protects such equity against expropriation. But the principal form of MNC involvement in the socialist world is through the sale of technology and co-production agreements. Anaconda, expropriated by Chile in 1971, signed in 1972 a $1,000 million agreement with the Soviet Union for the development of the latter's copper deposits, at the same time as the USSR proposed to help Chile develop its nationalized copper industry. By 1975 about one-half of Russia's passenger-car production will come from Fiat, under a co-production agreement;[32] and Soviet citizens are now drinking home-made Pepsi-Cola faster than it can be produced by the factory operating under license from the American company. As of January 1973 about *600* such co-production agreements were in force between multinationals and socialist countries;[33] every day, the list grows longer. Of former President Nixon it was often said that, whatever his domestic crimes, his foreign-policy achievements in securing detente with the Soviet Union and China were substantial and indeed revolutionary. It seems, however that the major beneficiaries of this 'revolution' are likely to be American MNCs. According to a recent report:

> Sino-American trade has already taken a great leap forward. (In 1973) it will probably exceed $800 million, up from $92 million in 1972. In only three years, the US has become China's second most important international trading partner, after Japan.
>
> *So far, the new link is proving to be a bonanza for US firms;* the Chinese import nearly 15 times as much from the US as they export. Among the biggest ticket items to date are some 4,000,000 tons of grain, ten Boeing 707 jetliners valued at $150 million, and eight ammonia plants to be built by M. W. Kellog Co. for $200 million. The Chinese are also anxious to do business with giant American oil companies such as Exxon, Mobil and Caltex, and makers of petroleum and drilling equipment, including US Steel International, Phillips Petroleum and Baker Oil tools ...
>
> ... In January (1973) the government disclosed that the Chinese were willing to seek 'deferred payment arrangements'—a euphemism for foreign credits—to pay for still more technology. This (indicates a) departure from China's previous policy (of) buying only what it could pay for in cash ...[34]

Evidently the celebrated Nixonian detente is nothing more than a means of facilitating the access of transnationalized capital to those areas of the world which had hitherto been closed to it.

We do not thereby mean to imply that the role and effects of MNCs in the socialist world are the same as they are in the capitalist bloc. A convincing case can certainly be made that, at least for the present, the socialist countries are adapting technological inputs from MNCs to their own internally-determined development process, rather than the other way around, as it is in the capitalist world. It is nevertheless the case that until recently the Soviet Union and China appeared to represent models of autonomous and self-reliant accumulation based entirely on technology which was either (i) internally-generated or (ii) universally known and freely available. The rapid growth of business between these countries and the largest and most technologically-advanced corporations has put an end to this model—whatever we might think of the merits or demerits of the 'socialist' pattern of absorbing technology from the multinationals. One important question relates to how far such relationships can develop before the socialist countries themselves become subject to an international division of labour programmed for the world by transnationalized capital. It is certainly the case that some observers are frankly stating that many MNCs may well prefer to deal with socialist countries than with many of those in the capitalist world—particularly the underdeveloped part of it.[35] Socialist countries are 'safer' and 'more stable': there is virtually no risk of expropriation, practically no strikes or labour unrest, little exchange risk since payment is made in cash or in kind, and they offer greater political stability than either the developed capitalist countries or the Third World. In short, the 'investment climate' in socialist countries is superior.

The meaning and consequences of Third World economic nationalism

The advance of capital has, historically, always been marked by tensions and conflict, by new contradictions generated just as old ones are transcended. In short, it is a process which is dialectical rather than linear; and the contemporary period is no exception. One of the principal contradictions had been that between international capital—i.e., imperialism—and various social classes in the so-called Third World. It is the response to that which constitutes that set of attitudes and actions expressed by the phenomenon of Third World economic nationalism, which has recently burst with such vigour upon the international scene.

It needs to be emphasized that the contradiction is not new, only the apparent success of the Third World offensive. From the outset, the securing of the non-capitalist areas of the world into the orbit of the international capitalist system was only accomplished through the violent subjugation of their peoples—i.e., the political imperialism and gunboat diplomacy of the nineteenth century. Conflicts between Third World states and MNCs involved in their natural-resource industries were evident as long ago as 1937/38, when expropriations of foreign oil companies took place in Bolivia and Mexico. Then as now, country-company conflict tended to crystallize around a number of fairly well-defined issues. These include (i) the issue of economic sovereignty posed by foreign ownership and decision-making in a major sector of the domestic economy, (ii) the state's share of the industry's surpluses, (iii) the extent of local processing of the raw material and production of by-products and inputs, and (iv) the existence of a foreign enclave physically, economically, and socially isolated from the national society and engaging in discriminatory or alien practices in relation to nationals.[36]

Behind these issues lie a variety of class interests and attitudes.[37] Imperialism is interested in the periphery principally as a source of primary products—food and industrial raw materials which can yield substantial profits at the same time as their supply helps to sustain the process of accumulation in the industrial-centre countries. Accordingly, imperialism could not lead to any substantial economic development in the periphery of the type enjoyed by the centre. One consequence of this is the continuous impoverishment of the mass of the population in the periphery—peasants, workers, underemployed and unemployed. This lays the basis for a *potential* alliance (not always realized) among these impoverished classes, directed against imperialism for the purpose of disengaging from the international division of labour it imposes and at the initiation of an autonomous development strategy geared to satisfying popular needs.

Another consequence of the imperialist impact is the exclusion of the possibility of the emergence of a powerful, independent national bourgeosie with a well-developed internal material base. Instead, a dependent 'comprador' bourgeoisie emerges, structurally attached to international capital and confined to such parasitic activities as commerce and real estate, and light manufacturing industry. Usually it is assumed that this bourgeoisie is an internal ally of international capital, and defends the latter; but in fact its objective position is rather one of ambivalence. Normally it is true that this class allies itself with foreign capital in order to protect its privileged position relative to the rest of the national population. But there is no reason to suppose that it is objectively satisfied with the weak, dependent and junior position it occupies in relation to international capital. On the contrary, where it perceives a configuration of international and domestic circumstances which provides the conditions for it to assert greater independence and to develop its material base internally, there is every reason for it to take advantage of such opportunities. These conditions are provided when (i) the nation-state possesses sources of leverage over international capital and the centre-countries, such as the supply of vital products; and (ii) a viable set of domestic class alliances can be constructed which range 'the nation as a whole' against international capital. It need hardly be added that, for such a project, the state machinery is an absolutely indispensable instrument used by such a class alliance in the struggle to secure greater surpluses from, and to redefine—if not necessarily revolutionize—the relationships with, international capital and the nation-states in the centre. The result is the phenomenon of 'economic nationalism' expressed in the form of conflict between MNCs in natural-resource industries and Third World governments.

It is precisely because such conditions were hardly met in the past that company-country conflicts have hitherto been so muted; and because they are now being provided in a significant number of Third World countries, that such conflicts are so widespread today. Let us remember that until the 1960s a large part of the Third World was under colonial rule, and the colonial state was of course in the direct service of imperialist capital. But even amongst the formally independent states, such as those in Latin America, the balance of power was tilted heavily in favour of the MNCs. A state which expropriated an imperialist firm could expect at the very least an economic blockade, as took place after the Mexican and Iranian oil nationalizations in 1938 and 1952; and in addition quite possibly a military intervention, as happened in Guatamala in 1954, Suez in 1956 and Cuba in 1961. In addition, production technology and marketing outlets in these industries were so tightly controlled by the MNCs as to make it difficult and costly for a state to attempt to defy them and operate a resource-based export industry successfully. Finally, the development of a sizeable and sophisticated bureaucratic class in these countries was not as well-advanced as it is today.

Developments since the early 1960s have changed much of this. First of all, Third World states now have at their disposal new and powerful sources of leverage in international economic relations. To begin with, the international political climate has changed with the rise of the non-aligned movement, the growth of the socialist bloc, and the influence of the United Nations Organization. One need not exaggerate the significance of this, however, as the recent case of Chile demonstrates the lengths to which an imperialist government will still go to preserve the political conditions necessary for the free operation of its corporations. The concrete sources of additional leverage arise out of two factors. One is the rise within the capitalist bloc of Western Europe and Japan, and the emergence of the Soviet Union and China, as well, as major economic powers. This has meant an increased competition among the major industrial nations for the natural resources of the Third World; this has also loosened the tight monopolistic control over production technology and markets exercised by the MNCs—especially those based in the United States. The other factor is the current (1972-74) shortages of many primary commodities, especially those of strategic importance in high-growth industries, such as petroleum, bauxite and phosphates. At the same time, in most Third World countries there has been the rapid development and maturation of a techno-bureaucratic class based on the state apparatus. Where this occurs together with the additional leverage represented by the possession of strategic export commodities, it creates possibilities which allow the techno-bureaucratic class, in alliance with the traditional comprador bourgeoisie, to attempt to transform itself into a class of state capitalists in a project for national industrialization and development, using the additional surpluses from the export industry, with the mass of the population more-or-less coerced or mobilized into the so-called 'struggle against imperialism'. Such countries as Iran, Saudi Arabia, Nigeria, Zaire, Zambia, Venezuela, Jamaica, Trinidad-Tobago, Guyana and possibly Algeria may fit this model to a greater or lesser degree.

But how far is this really a 'struggle against imperialism'? Furthermore, what is the nature of the changes which have been taking place and which we can expect from these developments? It is to these questions that we now turn our attention. Our contention here will be that these developments imply modifications in the international capitalist order, as regards the role, the relative power and the relative degree of development of different groups of nation-states, but without any fundamental change in the power of transnationalized capital and the pattern of unequal development characteristic of the international capitalist system.

We need first of all to reconcile the recent successes of Third World economic nationalism with the picture drawn earlier of the rapidly growing power of transnationalized capitalism in general. The apparent paradox can be easily resolved if we adopt a view which is (i) historical, (ii) sectoral and (iii) dialectical.

At the same time as the balance of bargaining power in Third World natural-resource industries has been shifting from the MNCs to host governments, the bases of dynamic incremental capital accumulation in international capitalism has been shifting to entirely new activities and geopolitical areas. It will be recalled that when the First World War brought to an end the great nineteenth-century boom in capital exports, the bulk of international investment was deployed in primary production in the periphery and the infrastructure needed to bring such products onto the world market.[38] Foreign investment in manufacturing was insignificant. Indeed, it was the growth of *national* manufacturing industries in Western Europe and subsequently the United States which made necessary—and profitable—international investment in food, raw materials and transport infrastructure. International investment in the periphery was not only necessary to support capital accumulation based on national manufacturing in the centre countries, it was also an important basis of incremental capital accumulation in its own right. But since 1945 the pattern has radically changed. The bulk of incremental international investment since then has been in manufacturing industry and among the industrial centre countries themselves.[39] This reflects the emergence of technology-intensive consumers' and producers' goods industries as the main bases of incremental capital accumulation in the contemporary period, and the growth of direct foreign investment by the large manufacturing corporations in the centre countries (for the purpose of mutual interpenetration of each other's markets) as the principal form of international capital flows. This, of course, is not to suggest that primary production and the periphery are in any way expendable to contemporary international capitalism—far from it. Raw materials from the periphery are just as essential as before—perhaps more so—in order to permit the process of accumulation in the industrial centre countries to continue. Nevertheless, the point is that the principal loci of incremental accumulation are technology-intensive manufacturing and service activities (such as information processing and transmission), and in the industrial centre-countries, and it is on these activities that the rapidly growing power of transnationalized capitalism chiefly rests.

The implications of this should be carefully considered. It means that international capitalism's interest in peripheral raw materials is more and more in a reliable and adequate supply of such materials, which permits the generation of more and more surplus-value *outside* of these industries; while its interest in these industries as sources of *direct* generation of surplus-value is relatively diminishing. This in turn creates possibilities for a new alliance with national state capitalism in the periphery for the provision of vital raw materials in return for a much increased share of the surpluses, and perspectives for national industrialization using technology from transnationalized capital. In other words, it creates possibilities for co-opting economic nationalism into the system of international capitalism, whose structure will have to be modified to permit the accommodation.

To be sure, this process will not be a smooth one, free from all kinds of tensions and contradictions. One of these is that the MNCs directly involved in the natural-resource industries are unlikely to take a broad view of the interests of international capital as a whole, and may, at least initially, resist the claims of peripheral state capitalism. Nonetheless, a distinct pattern has already emerged in which these corporations can and do accommodate to such claims without incurring significant short-term or long-term losses—and indeed, in some cases, turning them to their advantage. One of the strategies involved is to use the actions of producing-country cartels as a justification for raising 'down-stream' (finished-products) prices and thereby scoop up even greater profits at the refining end. There is considerable evidence that this has taken place in the case of petroleum, as the hugely increased revenues secured by the OPEC countries have been accompanied by astronomical profits by the multinational oil companies.[40] Indeed, in this-case there is a widespread conviction that the oil shortages of 1971-74, which permitted OPEC to exert so much leverage, were in fact engineered by the oil companies themselves in order to secure higher prices, and through that, the hugely increased surpluses they claim are necessary to fund expansion in the industry.[41] A similar process is taking place in the aluminium industry: the multinational aluminium companies are paying the higher taxes demanded by Jamaica and other bauxite-exporting countries after token protests, while at the same time calmly announcing that they expect record profits in 1974. These result from higher prices which are being secured because of the current state of excess demand in the aluminium industry—an excess demand which the companies themselves have probably been instrumental in bringing about.[42] The cases of oil and aluminium actually suggest the interesting possibility of conscious or *de facto* collusion between producing countries and the MNCs in securing higher prices from the final consumers.

In another case—that of bananas—the corporations seem to have succeeded in getting the best of both worlds, i.e., defeating the country-cartel's attempt to secure higher returns while at the same time raising downstream prices. In early 1974 seven Central and South American states formed a Union of Banana Exporting Countries (UBEC) and proceeded to raise export taxes against the opposition of the major US fruit companies. The companies retaliated by (i) raising banana prices to the consumer by more than enough to pay the higher taxes, and (ii) cutting production in and purchases from the countries concerned, eventually forcing the UBEC states to reduce or entirely remove the new taxes. The result:

> . . . in the end the big winner of the banana war may not be the seven members of the cartel but the two US fruit corporations. Only a year ago (1973) the two companies' profit per box of bananas was only 20 cents. But since the cartel boosted prices—and the companies retaliated by cutting back their purchases—the world price of bananas has increased by 40 percent. *And as a result of the shortage they helped create, the two companies are now making a profit of nearly 70 per cents a box.* All of which goes to prove that sometimes organizing a cartel is just plain bananas![43]

A second strategy is to secure the maximum financial benefits from equity participation by the Third World state.[44] This is done by negotiating favourable valuation and payment terms for the equity acquired by the state, expansion of the mixed enterprise using outside financing, and reduced taxation and foreign-exchange burdens. Through such devices an MNC can end up with a greater cashflow as a 49 percent shareholder (with the state owning 51 percent) than it did as a full owner: this was the case with the

Chileanization of Kennecot Copper in 1967 and the Zambianization of the copper mines in 1969. Closely associated with this is a third strategy: that of specialization in the supply of support services to state enterprises, such as management, purchasing and marketing. These can yield highly remunerative returns, since the fees are usually based on a percentage-of-sales basis. They also permit the MNC to retain a high degree of control over the state enterprise and indeed to regard it virtually as a member-affiliate of the multinational corporate family. As a Vice-President of Chase Manhattan Bank told a Conference of Industrialists and Financiers, sponsored by the UN's Economic Commission for Africa:

> Most successful (joint ventures) have been achieved without hard and fast requirements for certain rigid percentages of stock ownership. The important element is there be a meeting of minds at the beginning as to who does what—who manages and controls. Under these circumstances, a minority shareholder can in fact functionally not only manage but control the enterprise.[45]

A fourth strategy is for the MNCs concerned to diversify not only into the provision of support services but also into related industries. It is said that US oil companies should more properly be called 'Energy Corporations': besides their oil interests they control vast coal reserves, more than half the US uranium reserves and most of its natural-gas production.[46] Similarly, by the time Kennecott and Anaconda were expropriated by Chile, the former had acquired a substantial coal-mining interest and the latter was already a major aluminium producer. None of these strategies mean that country-company conflicts no longer exist. But they do mean that the MNCs involved in these industries have developed a fairly coherent and consistent formula for accommodating to economic nationalism and securing new alliances with the aspirant national bourgeoisies based on state capitalism in certain peripheral countries.

From the point of view of the wider interests of transnationalized capitalism, there are certain positive advantages to be gained if the Third World states progressively assume the functions of formal ownership and administration of the natural-resource industries. At first, stability of primary product supplies was secured by direct ownership of these industries in the periphery by MNCs. But the rise of economic nationalism has made foreign ownership and control an explosive issue: what was at first an asset has now become a liability. By ceding ownership to the Third World states, supplies may actually be made more reliable, since the ownership issue will have been defused. The point was made in the following way by US. Senator Frank Church, in hearings before the US Senate Sub-committee on Multinational Corporations, when he put the following question to the president of Reynolds Metals about that company's bauxite mines in the Caribbean:

> Would it have been possible for you to have contracted to secure that bauxite on a different basis than equity ownership, because it is that that is creating the highly intense nationalistic feeling? Is there a way for your industry and other industries that are involved in the extractive field to do business in foreign countries without securing the form of ownership of the minerals or the metals or the oil or whatever that arouses these highly nationalistic feelings? If there is, I would think it would be both in the interest of your company and in the interest of our Government. . . . We want to contrast our own pattern with the Japanese and Western Europeans to see what we can learn because we have to live with the political consequences of our acts and I would hate to see all of Latin America go the route chosen by Chile and by Cuba.[47]

Typical of the model Senator Church probably had in mind is the project for the construction of one of the world's largest gas liquefecation plants by the Algerian state company SONATRACH, in which the bulk of the production will be purchased by France, Belgium and West Germany upon completion in 1977.[48]

Third-world state ownership, moreover, makes the problem of dealing with the labour force a government responsibility, and removes the MNCs from the politically vulnerable position of being a 'foreign imperialistic exploiter' of indigenous labour. With ownership, the national governments also directly assume the risks of fluctuations in the international markets for the commodities concerned, a situation which could easily have adverse repercussions on them and benefit the consumers and the MNCs in the industry.[49] Such factors indicate that transnationalized capitalism is capable not only of accommodating to Third World economic nationalism but also of turning it to its advantage, by assigning it a specific role in the overall international system whose institutional structure has been suitably modified. From the point of view of Third World peoples, they show the importance of analyzing imperialism not only in terms of formal ownership forms but also in terms of the functions assigned to particular structures and the effects and consequences of the system as a totality.

In spite of the accommodations referred to above, important problems and contradictions generated by the new economic nationalism remain to be resolved. These can be analyzed with reference to the OPEC experience. This is not only the most important in its own right because of the sheer size of the financial flows involved, but it also represents a model upon which other Third World country-cartels are likely to base their own behaviour. It is not inconceivable, for example, that exporters of bauxite, iron ore, copper and other critical materials could arrive at a position similar to that of OPEC in the not-too-distant future. The most important problems arising, at least in the short run, are those which relate to the hugely increased financial power of the oil-producing states, occasioned by massive transfers of monetary assets to their account at the expense of the major consuming nations, mainly Western Europe and Japan.

This presents a formidable prospect so far as the equilibrium of international politico-economic power relationships is concerned. These states are expected to increase their monetary reserves by around $55 billion in 1974, perhaps as much as $75 billion in 1975, and could accumulate the astronomical sum of $1,200 billion of reserves by 1985.[50] At one level the problems appear to be merely technical, i.e., how to 'recycle' the 'petrodollars' received by OPEC into the accounts of deficit countries and the international economy generally so as to prevent economic collapse and worldwide depression.

From this strictly technical point of view a reasonably coherent pattern of dealing with the recycling problem is beginning to emerge. To begin with, the so-called conventional market mechanisms are handling a large part of the petrodollars: i.e., the OPEC countries are placing much of the funds with the largest multinational banks, mainly US and European, who are in turn lending them back to deficit countries. (One of the results of this is to strengthen the hold of US banks over Western European countries, thus reinforcing the reassertion of US economic dominance over Europe brought about by the rise in oil prices). To this must be added OPEC holdings of government securities in the developed countries. Another form of recycling is the large contributions by various OPEC states to the International Monetary Fund and the World Bank. This is similar to the use of the market mechanisms in that they involve chanelling the funds to deficit countries through the intermediation of international financial institutions not under the direct control of OPEC states. These forms can therefore be distinguished from another category, which by-passes international intermediation entirely—direct loans by OPEC states to institutions and governments in deficit countries, both developed and underdeveloped. Leading the way in this regard is Iran, which according to a recent tally, has pledged some $10 billion in over 12 countries;[51] followed by Saudi Arabia, which lent Japan some $1 billion in late 1974 on commercial terms. Such bilateral transactions include not only commercial lending and general aid but also massive deals for the purchase of capital goods, technology and military equipment, such as Iran's $1 billion advance payment to France for the purchase of nuclear reactors, and Saudi Arabia's deal with the United States. The purchase of technology with petrodollars is also being carried out through direct transactions between OPEC states and the large MNCs. Gulf Oil, for example, is reported to be investing over $1 billion in natural-gas liquefecation in a joint venture with the Nigerian government, which will itself contribute an even larger sum; similar joint ventures are planned by Saudi Arabia and Iran with Dow Chemicals and Marcona Steel.[52] In the longer term, such projects based on OPEC-MNC partnerships may well become one of the principal forms of petrodollar recycling. Recently, the director-general of the Kuwait Fund for Arab Economic Development is reported to have told a conference sponsored by the Banker's Trust Company that:

> The Arab oil countries want to use their surplus revenues to set up joint ventures with multinational firms to industrialize their own countries and are not interested in projects aimed at simply lending their funds to oil-consuming countries. ... Kuwait and other Arab countries are particularly anxious to encourage direct investment in their own countries and ... multinational firms offering such projects could be the main recipient of oil-producer investments.[53]

Associated with such partnerships is the emergence of another new phenomenon: that of direct equity investment by OPEC states in MNCs and Western enterprises generally. Iran's $100 million investment in Germany's Krupp Steel may be only the initial trickle of what could become a flood, for it is expected that the US stock market might absorb billions of petrodollars.[54]

It is evident that the process of 'recycling' involves far more important changes than those connoted by such an innocuous term. A whole new network of linkages—financial, commodity, technological and institutional—is being constructed between the OPEC states on the one hand, and the developed countries and the multinational corporations on the other. We can also assume that this pattern will form the model for other Third World countries which succeed in generating large surpluses through their primary-product exports. These new linkages are designed precisely to ensure that the international economic order can continue to function without any catastrophic dislocation: prognostications that the international monetary system is capable of handling the 'petrodollar problem', although with some strain, bear ample testimony to this.[55] In effect, success in recyling the petrodollars implies that the money eventually finds its way back into the international capitalist order and in particular into the cash-flow accounts of the major MNCs. In that sense, the substance of the system will remain intact. What is changing, however, is the nature of economic relationships and power-relations among governments, and between governments and MNCs.

The rapid emergence of a new network of ties between the OPEC states and the major industrial consuming countries signals a new set of relationships which are not only quantitatively greater, but also qualitatively different, from those that ruled in the past. They are based on far greater equality in power-relations than before; on a partnership between equals rather than that of a horse and its rider. Some might suggest that the huge reserves being accumulated by OPEC, which exceed those of Western European nations, will give the former an absolute superiority in economic power. Such a crude measure of economic power is nevertheless misleading, precisely because it is quantitative rather than qualitative. The industrial consumer countries possess the technology and the armaments that the OPEC states want to acquire, and to the extent that the former succeed in tieing up the latter's reserves in their own monetary and real assets, then they will have as much leverage over OPEC as OPEC has over them. Indeed, one implication of the new linkages is that there is emerging a growing reciprocity and mutuality of interest between the OPEC countries and the West. If the prospect of a worldwide depression was used by the Western countries as a means of trying to contain further OPEC price increases in early 1974, how much more so can it be used in the future, as the new forms of integration are consolidated?

Accompanying the diffusion of financial power to the OPEC countries is a longer-term process involving the diffusion to them of physical productive capacity, not only in light but also in heavy manufacturing industry. The growing list of projects in these countries for the establishment of petrochemicals and other chemical industries, steel, nuclear power, military equipment and other basic or heavy industry indicates concrete prospects allowing their industrialization to go beyond the limits of light manufacturing to which the majority of Third World countries have so far been limited. But this development should not be confused with an autonomous or indigenous industrialization strategy, for it is being based on advanced technology from the advanced industrial countries themselves, who will also purchase much of the output of the new industries. It therefore constitutes a new form of integration with the traditional centre countries: one that complements on the level of production the integration being established on the level of finance. Such an integration also allows the state bourgeoisies in the OPEC countries a much more developed and meaningful material base than before, and will permit the emergence of an economic structure bearing a closer (superficial) resemblance to that of the industrial centre countries. But the economic system will still be a dependent one, a component—although a vital one—of the wider international capitalist system. This new form of integration is also associated with a new structure of relationships between these states and the MNCs, which are the infrastructure of the system of transnationalized capitalism. Increasingly, these countries will purchase technology and goods from the largest and most technologically advanced MNCs, paying for them with surpluses generated either directly or indirectly by the activities of the oil MNCs, which transport, refine and market the oil produced by OPEC state enterprises or by joint ventures.

All this is of course to a certain extent an 'ideal' scenario: the actual course of events has not been as smooth as that implied by the apparent neatness of the new structure of relationships which seems to be evolving. Nor will the future process necessarily be much smoother. For one thing, the evolving equilibrium between OPEC states and the MNCs is not necessarily a stable one: already, the Organisation of Arab Petroleum Exporting Countries has signalled its intention to move into the 'downstream' and of the oil business,[56] thereby threatening the established position of the oil companies in areas such as oil-well drilling and refining. Indeed, in the long run there is no necessary reason why the new class of petroleum state capitalists should limit their international ambitions to the oil business alone. It is not inconceivable that, with their huge financial resources, they could wish to make a bid for their own place of near-equality in the overall system of international capitalism, as the Western Europeans and the Japanese were to do in the 1950s and 1960s, with all the accompanying tensions and strains which that provoked. Already, the mere financial power of the OPEC countries is alone causing grave anxieties to some powerful groups in the United States, and probably underlies the crude and abortive saber-rattling of Messrs. Ford and Kissinger in September 1974.[57] In the longer run, far-sighted analysts from the US, noting that country's growing dependence on raw materials imported from the periphery, refer to 'The Threat from the Third World'.[58] While the rhetoric of these groups tends to be couched in terms of universalistic or technocratic concerns, such as the need to 'curb inflation', to 'restore the operation of the laws (sic) of supply and demand' and to 'prevent a collapse of the world monetary system', it is the issue of power that really preoccupies them. As Vaughan Lewis puts it, 'the parameters of power relations and of behaviour patterns have been rudely disrupted, without their replacement by a new set which is clearly understood and respected by all'.[59]

Contradictions among the different bourgeoisies and power-groups provide only one reason why the new evolving system is not necessarily a stable one. Another and more potent reason is that the new order shows every sign of accentuating, rather than reducing, the contradiction generated by the process of increasing wealth accompanied by growing poverty on the world scale. In our final section, we turn our attention to a consideration of the meaning of the developments being discussed for the mass of the people in the underdeveloped countries of the Third World.

Equality and polarization. A global view

Recently the American magazine *Newsweek* carried a cover story on 'Iran's Push For Power'.[60] The Shah, it appears, uses his country's $20 billion-per-year oil revenues in some very interesting ways. In 1973 alone he spent $4 billion on arms purchases from the United States; in the first nine months of 1974 he had already ordered some 289 jet fighters, 500 attack helicopters, 700 tanks and six destroyers. He has also committed some $10 billion in aid, loans and investments to governments and institutions in twelve countries, in order to 'seek to expand his sphere of influence'. In addition, the revenues finance the 'opulent life-styles' of the royal family, the super-rich and the 'flourishing business class', all of whom 'frolic in striking splendor'. Of course, large sums are also being plowed into Iran's 'development': but in spite of this, both agriculture and industry are lagging and inefficient, the literacy rate for the population is only 30 percent, and 'Most of the populace still survives on a diet of bread and vegetable oil'. Perhaps this is one reason—along with his complete personal autocracy—why the Shah finds it necessary to maintain a secret police force which is one of the largest in the world. Its full-time personnel is estimated to number between 30,000 and 60,000, but perhaps as many as 3 million Iranians—some 12 percent of the adult population—are occasional informers. The organization is credited with holding as many as 50,000 political prisoners, and with carrying out at least 200 executions in the last four years alone. One wonders what these Iranians think of their country's success in redistributing the world's wealth from the rich countries to the poor.

The Shah's extremely centralized and personal rule may not be a characteristic shared by most of the other mineral-rich countries, but the picture of state affluence, based on mineral revenues, accompanied by continuing economic underdevelopment and class inequalities is by no means untypical. The same magazine also reports that:

> For every shiek who spent last summer in the cool mountain air and tolerant moral climate of nearby Beirut, thousands of uneducated and ill-cared for Saudies sweltered in slums of Jidda and Riyadh. And the gap between rich and poor is as great in such oil-producing non-Arab nations as Nigeria, Malaysia and Indonesia.[61]

As for many people outside of mineral-producing nation-states, the incidence of death by starvation is no longer a grim prospect but rather a grim reality. Perhaps as many as 200,000 Africans have died as a result of famine in Ethiopia and the Sahel; and in India, a neighbouring country of oil-rich Iran:

> In search of food, men are leaving their wives and children to fend for themselves. The Indian press reports cases of families committing suicide rather than die a lingering death from starvation, and of distraught fathers throwing small children into the rivers to drown. An official in the state of West Bengal estimates that 15 million people in rural areas are either living on one poor meal a day or starving. . . . But while some Indians are dying quietly, others are taking to violence . . .[62]

We have seen that Third World economic nationalism is succeeding in bringing about a diffusion of international economic power from the central developed countries to some raw-material producing Third World states. But this diffusion is accompanied by a contradictory, reverse movement—one of growing concentration of incomes and economic power on the world level.

The apparent paradox is easily reconciled if we adopt a global view, and one that is based on an analysis of classes rather than on countries as such.

Even before the recent successes of OPEC, it had become evident that for the countries of the underdeveloped periphery, the mere receipt of huge amounts of financial flows by the state did not necessarily lead to a process of self-sustaining development, structural transformation and general improvement in living standards for the mass of the population.[63] On the contrary, under certain conditions it can serve as an obstacle to the achievement of these objectives. On the purely economic level, an abundant and reliable flow of mineral revenues provides foreign exchange which props up an economic system which is structurally dependent on imports, and removes the pressure and incentives for changes which would orient the system along more self-centred lines. Food can be imported, so that agriculture can remain backward and inefficient without generating a foreign-exchange crisis: the same applies to manufactured goods, whether consumers, intermediate or capital. There is therefore no pressure or perceived need to develop and apply an indigenous technology for the utilization of indigenous materials in a productive system geared to satisfying the needs of the broad mass of the population. Thus the divergence analyzed by Thomas—that between the structure of resource use and the structure of demand—is unlikely to be narrowed in such a system.[64] We have seen that the considerable rise in revenues secured by raw-material producing states recently has increased their capacity to undertake large projects in basic or heavy industry. These are partly based on domestic resources and partly on imported raw materials, but in all cases they are based on imported technology and are geared to exporting to the markets of the central industrial countries, and they usually involve some form of partnership with the large multinational corporations. Thus they intensify integration with the centre rather than reduce it; the divergence between resource use and demand widens as the system expands. And the system is capable of expansion so long as production and/or prices of the mineral-exports grow, or accumulated foreign-exchange reserves hold out. Furthermore, this pattern of development is highly capital-intensive, and it does not normally involve any profound reorganization of the agricultural social economy. There is therefore no evidence that it can solve the problems of un- and under-employment, and of rural poverty, which is *the* fundamental condition for an improvement in living standards for the mass of the population in these countries.

What is more, mineral revenues serve to strengthen immensely the power of anti-popular political structures in these countries, which is the socio-political correlate of an economic system which excludes the mass of the population from effective participation in it. It is true that the nature of the political and social regimes in mineral-producing states appears to vary widely, from 'right-reactionary' (Iran, Saudi Arabia) to 'left-progressive'

(Algeria, Iraq), from 'parliamentary democratic' (Venezuela, Jamaica) to 'military dictatorship' (Nigeria, Indonesia), and so on. These differences correspond to the exact nature of the class alliance and the dominant political ideology in different countries. But they hide a reality which is much less heterogenous. In most cases the state plays an important and growing role in the economy, precisely because it is through state intermediation that mineral revenues are disposed of. The result is that a state or bureaucratic bourgeoisie is a powerful class whose strength is on the rise. The variety springs from the fact that in some countries this class shares power with a dominant (or subordinate) royal or landed group, or the military, or a 'revolutionary' petty bourgeoisie, and that in some cases it is the dominant economic class, while in others it remains junior to, and an adjunct of, the private capitalist class. Mineral revenues provide the state bourgeoisie with the material resources to undertake a project of national capitalist development which will strengthen its own material base and at the same time reproduce the structure of dependence and social inequality; they also provide this class with the resources to coerce or bribe the rest of the population into accepting the pattern. In that context, the objective role of economic nationalism is to serve as an alternative to socialism and a socialist pattern of development, rather than as a complement to the latter. Nevertheless, both the precise nature of the process of socio-political development in these countries and the resulting contradictions deserve more comprehensive and subtle analysis than we are able to undertake in this paper.

In the underdeveloped oil-consuming countries, the rise in oil prices is manifested as a foreign-exchange crisis which really represents an intensification of the balance-of-payments problem which is one of the most characteristic features of peripheral underdeveloped capitalism. The reflex reaction of the groups which control the state is, naturally, to seek ways and means of mounting a salvage operation by cutting imports and raising additional foreign exchange receipts. In countries which produce strategic commodities currently experiencing shortages—such as bauxite and phosphates—there are evident opportunities to turn what might have started as a defensive action into one which follows the OPEC example, not only in terms of raising taxes and prices through cartel-like actions but also in terms of undertaking development of new types of industries under the initiative of a state bourgeoisie, with all the economic and social consequences that that implies.

In a large number of underdeveloped countries, however—including countries having a large proportion of the world's population—such possibilities of raising fresh export receipts do not exist. Here the prospect must be for increasing foreign indebtedness and a reduced level of real imports, bringing about a contraction in the rate of economic growth. Who will bear the costs of adjustment in these countries?—the answer clearly can only be provided with reference to the structure and configuration of politico-economic power in these societies. Those who are strongest will pay the least, passing on the costs—in the forms of higher prices and taxes—to others who are weaker and less capable of defending themselves, i.e., labour, especially unorganized labour, the underemployed and the unemployed, and the peasants. Economic crisis and political contradictions in such countries, therefore, can only be heightened—the demise of the Selassie regime in Ethiopia is only the earliest manifestation of this. Again, we cannot pretend that these brief comments begin to adequately analyze developments and possible resolutions in this group of countries.

What we can say with some confidence is that those who wish to see, and struggle for, a more socially rational and just economic order for the peoples of the Third World, both on the national and international level, should be careful not to mistake the achievements of Third World economic nationalism for revolutionary change. The structure of the international capitalist order is being rapidly modified to permit the incorporation of a greater number of national bourgeoisies—the new ones being based on various peripheral states which have acquired leverage. In the process, some national bourgeoisies in the central industrial countries have had to countenance a relative decline in their power and status, as reflected in the greater equality in state-to-state relations between West Europe and Japan on the one hand and the OPEC countries on the other. But at the same time the power of big, transnationalized capitalism, as represented by the multinational corporations, has not been significantly affected; and indeed, new opportunities have been created for investment outlets and the sale of technology by them. The tendency for greater equality in power-relations between the developed countries and OPEC-type states is accompanied by one of growing polarization: between OPEC-type states and other states within the periphery, between the ruling class and the rest within OPEC-type states, and between the marginalized masses of the Third World on the one hand and the ruling classes of the whole world and the masses at the centre, on the other hand. Such evolutionary changes must be continually compared with genuinely revolutionary alternatives: i.e., alternatives which begin with the basic needs of the marginalized people of the world for material betterment and control over their own natural and social environment as the objective, of economic development and social change, rather than its derivative.

Notes

[1] Bergsten (1974) pp. 34-35.

[2] United Nations (1973) p. 13. This refers to value-added of MNCs both in home and host countries.

[3] Orville Freeman, President of Business International and former US Secretary of Agriculture, quoted by US Senate Committee on Finance (1973, 1) p. 3. The 10 percent figure refers to the rate of growth of production by MNCs.

[4] Sunkel (1973) p. 163, quoting A. Barber, "Emerging New Power: The World Corporation", *War/Peace Report,* October 1968, p. 7.

[5] I.e., 'production subject to foreign control or decision and measured by the sales of *foreign* affiliates of multinational corporations', United Nations (1973) p. 13. [Emphasis added.] This is less than the value of production of MNCs as a whole.

[6] Ibid.

[7] Stephenson (*1972*), *p. 4.*

[8] $35.6 billion out of a total of $309 billion. See US Senate Committee on Finance (1973, 2), pp. 275, 279.

[9] US Senate Committee on Finance (1973, 2) p. 275.

[10] Stephenson (1972) p. 4.

[11] US Senate Committee on Finance (1973, 1) p. 21.

[12] Vernon (1971) p. 13.

[13] Ibid., pp. 13–18.

[14] US Senate Committee on Finance (1973, 1) p. 6.

[15] Ibid., p. 8.

[16] Vernon (1971) pp. 11, 285. The author also notes that the 187 firms concerned are 'an extraordinary group, quite distinct in many respects from the rest of the US corporate economy' (p. 11).

[17] Ibid., p. 12.

[18] Brooke and Remmers (1979); Stopford and Wells (1972).

[19] Hymer (1973); see also Hymer (1972).

[20] See p. 37 ff.

[21] See, for example, Levitt (1971).

[22] Stephenson (1972) p. 128.

[23] Ibid., p. 51.

[24] On the most 'pessimistic' assumption that in the absence of production abroad by US MNCs, the market would have been supplied by US exports. US Senate Committee on Finance (1973, 1) p. 5.

[25] See, for example, comment in *The Wall Street Journal,* 20 August 1971, cited in Stephenson (1972) p. 123.

[26] A Conservative Party spokesman is reported to have said, during the 1970 British General Election, that '. . . some types of international industry go to those countries which offer them the biggest bribes and it will be necessary for the next Conservative Government to match these inducements'. Cited by Stephenson (1972) p. 49.

[27] Cited by Stephenson (1972) p. 12.

[28] A. Barber, "Emerging New Power: The World Corporation", *War/Peace Report,* October 1968, p. 7, cited by Sunkel (1973) p. 163.

[29] Cited by Stephenson (1972) p. 58. [Emphasis added.]

[30] Vernon (1972) p. 19.

[31] United Nations (1973) p. 21.

[32] Ibid, p. 22.

[33] Ibid.

[34] *Time,* 30 December 1973, p. 51. [Emphasis added.]

[35] See, for example, 'New era for multinationals', *Business Week,* July 6, 1974, pp. 73-74. The magazine quotes C. Fred Bergston as remarking that '. . . ironically, the multinationals probably will find that it's safer to operate in Communist countries than in some others'.

[36] See, for example, Girvan (1970), and Mikesell (1971).

[37] For a useful discussion of class categories and class structure in the social formations of peripheral capitalism, see Amin (1972).

[38] See, for example, Ashworth (1952). Admittedly, this generalization holds most strongly where the United States, Canada and Australia are regarded as part of the nineteenth-century 'periphery', which in a very important sense they were.

[39] See, for example, United Nations (1973) p. 8-12. Some two-thirds of international direct investment were located in the developed market economies and manufacturing was the largest single sector, constituting 40 percent of the total.

[40] See, for example, "Putting The Heat on Big Oil", *Newsweek,* February 4, 1974, pp. 36-38.

[41] Ibid. Also Leonard Silk, 'Multinational Morals', *International Herald Tribune,* March 8, 1974. It is also felt that the oil companies' allies in engineering the energy crisis were the US Government which, following the dollar crises of 1971-73, wished to reassert US economic dominance over oil-dependent Western Europe and Japan) and the giant US automobile companies (who wished to gain political leverage over the environmentalist lobby). For the first see Amin (1974). The point about the automobile companies was suggested in conversation by Mrs. Kari Levitt.

[42] In 1970-71 the international aluminium industry suffered from excess capacity due to over-expansion in the late 1960s. In early 1972 the leading aluminium multinationals took the lead in establishing the International Primary Aluminium Institute, which monitors production, inventories and expansion plans throughout the capitalist world. Since that time the excess capacity has gradually been replaced by excess demand, and the companies are reporting high profits for 1974.

[43] From 'Cartels: Just Bananas', *Newsweek,* August 26, 1974, p. 38 [Emphasis added.] See also 'Multinationals: A banana brouhaha over higher prices', *Business Week,* July 6, 1974, p. 42.

[44] See, for example, Semonin (1971) and Girvan (1972).

[45] Semonin (1971) p. 14.

[46] *Newsweek,* February 4, 1974, p. 36.

[47] United States Senate (1973, 3) pp. 80, 82.

[48] 'Algeria to Build World's Largest Gas Plant', *Newsweek,* September 16, 1974, p. 51. In this connection see also Quandt (1972), and 'Shortages: Risky Race for Minerals', *Time,* January 28, 1974, pp. 48-49.

[49] See, for example, Moran (1971-72). In this connection it should be noted that by October 1974 sources in the United States were predicting a fall in oil prices within two years, though not to the 1973 levels.

[50] 'Recycling the Petrodollars', *Newsweek,* October 14, 1974, p. 41; 'Oil: The US Talks Tough', *Newsweek,* October 7, 1974, p. 16.

[51] 'The Master Builder of Iran', *Newsweek,* October 14, 1974, p. 27.

[52] 'Gulf Oil to Tap Nigeria's Natural-Gas Resources', *Newsweek,* May 27, 1974, p. 36; 'Saudi Arabia to Make Cheap Steel', *Newsweek,* April 15, 1974, p. 36; 'Dow Chemical to take part in $500 million joint venture in Iran', *The Financial Times,* August 9, 1974, p. 18.

[53] 'Priority Use of Oil Money in Development, Arab Says', *International Herald Tribune,* September 18, 1974, p. 9.

[54] *Newsweek,* October 14, 1974, p. 43.

[55] 'Recycling the Petrodollars', *Newsweek,* October 14, 1974, pp. 41-43.

[56] 'Arab Drive For Bigger Oil Profits Continues', *Newsweek,* May 27, 1974, p. 36.

[57] 'Oil: The US Talks Tough', *Newsweek,* October 7, 1974, pp. 15-18; 'Coping with the Oil Cartel', *Newsweek,* October 14, 1974, pp. 25-26.

[58] Bergston, (1973). See also 'Shortages: Risky Race for Minerals', *Time,* January 28, 1974, pp. 48-49.

[59] Comment at Society for International Development, Round Table on the Energy Crisis, Abidjan, August 11, 1974.

[60] 'The Master Builder of Iran', *Newsweek,* October 14, 1974, pp. 27-33. The quotations and information in the rest of this paragraph are based on this article.

[61] From 'Winners and Losers', *Newsweek,* September 30, 1974, p. 41.

[62] From 'Time of Famine in India', *Newsweek,* October 7, 1974, p. 29.

[63] For an analysis of this see Girvan (1970).

[64] See Thomas (1974) esp. ch. 2.

References

Amin, Samir, *Contemporary Peripheral Social Formations, Unequal Development and the Problems of Transition.* IDEP Reproduction, 1972.

—, *Towards a New Structural Crisis in the World Capitalist System?* (Chapter 1 in this book).

Ashfield, Michael, 'Look to the Third World', *The Financial Times,* May 21, 1974.

Ashworth, W. W., *A Short History of the International Economy.* London, 1952.

Bergston, C. Fred, "The New Era in World Commodity Markets", *Challenge,* September/October 1974, pp. 34-42.

—, 'The Threat from the Third World', *Foreign Policy,* No. 11 summer 1973.

—, 'The Threat is Real', *Foreign Policy,* No. 14, Spring 1974.

Brooke, Michael Z. and Remmers, H. Lee, *The Strategy of Multinational Enterprise.* New York, 1970.

Girvan, Norman, 'Multinational Corporations and Dependent Underdevelopment in Mineral-Export Economies', *Social and Economic Studies,* December 1970.

Hymer, Stephen, *Notes on the United Nations Reports on* "Multinational Corporations in World Development". United Nations, Geneva, November 6, 1973 (Mimeo).

—, 'Multinational Corporations and the Law of Uneven Development', in J. Bhagwati (ed.), *Economics and World Order.* New York, 1972.

Lenin, V. I., *Imperialism, The Highest Stage of Capitalism.* Various editions.

Midesell, Raymond, (ed. & contrib.), *Foreign Investment In the Petroleum and Mineral Industries.* Baltimore, 1971.

Moran, Theodore, 'New Deal Or Raw Deal in Raw Materials', *Foreign Policy,* No. 5, Winter 1971-72.

Quandt, William B., 'Can We do Business With Radical Nationalists? (1) Algeria: Yes'. *Foreign Policy* No. 7, Summer 1972.

Semonin, Paul, *Nationalization and Management in Zambia.* IDEP Reproduction, 1971.

Stephenson, Hugh, *The Coming Clash: The Impact of the International Corporation on the Nation State.* London: Weidenfeld and Nicolson, 1972.

Stopford, John M. and Wells, Louis T. Jr., *Managing the Multinational Enterprise.* New York, 1972.

Sunkel, Osvaldo, "Transnational Capitalism and National Disintegration in Latin America", in Norman Girvan (ed.), *Dependence and Underdevelopment in the New World and the Old,* Special Number, Social and Economic Studies, Vol. 22, No. 1, March 1973.

Thomas, Clive Y., *Dependence and Transformation: The Economics of the Transition to Socialism.* New York, 1974.

United Nations, *Multinational Corporations in World Development.* New York, 1973.
United States Senate Committee on Finance, *The Multination Corporation and the World Economy.* Washington, 1973.
United States Senate Committee on Finance, *Implications of Multinational Firms for World Trade and Investment and for US Trade and Labor.* Washington, 1973.
United States Senate Committee On Foreign Relations, Subcommittee On Multinational Corporations, *Hearings: 93rd Congress, 1st Session. On Overseas Private Investment Corporation (OPIC): July-August 1973.* Washington, 1973.
Vernon, Raymond, *Sovereignty at Bay: The Multinational Spread of US Enterprises.* New York, 1973.
—, *The Economic and Political Consequences of Multinational Enterprise: An Anthology.* Boston, 1972.

The Multinational Corporation in Africa: Case Studies

Helge Hveem

The Extent and Type of Direct Foreign Investment in Africa

Purpose

The patterns of direct foreign investments in Africa are closely linked to the evolution of the international capitalist economy and the growth of the multinational corporation. It is not possible to explain, nor even merely describe these patterns without reference to dominance theory and to the historical integration of Africa into the imperialist economies.

We do not propose to discuss at any length the theory of domination at the international level in the present context.[1] It is doubtless true that direct investments—the establishment of production or sales affiliates by a center-based corporation outside its 'home country'—represent a central part of the international political economy. Made on the basis of monopolistic advantage or according to some other motive or driving force, they represent an important tool in the spread of international capitalism. At the same time, they form the structure of international capitalism—and with the increasing East-West industrial cooperation, even the Socialist world to some extent—in a world-wide 'division of labor' characterized by highly unequal distribution of power and consequently also of wealth and development.

The purpose of this paper is thus to describe the extent and type of direct investments and the corresponding corporate structure in Africa and to show how they reflect the 'international division of labor'. We shall *not* assume the task of showing how foreign direct investments operate at the micro level, in the process of (under)development or in the process of 'unequal development', as described by Stephen Hymer and Samir Amin,[2] as this issue is taken up by other contributions to the present volume. Nor do we propose, at the present stage, to analyze the historical background. Our own understanding of this subject is based upon works by Amin, Hobsbawm and others.[3]

Throughout this essay, the operational definition of direct investments is that of the IMF and the OECD: investments in a wholly-owned subsidiary or subsidiary-controlled firm in a foreign country or purchase of minority holdings in a foreign-based firm in which the investor takes a substantial interest in the day-to-day operations and the control of the object of investment.

On the political economy of direct investments

Direct investments represented 23.5 percent of total capital exports to underdeveloped countries by the DAC (OECD) countries in 1970-71, as opposed to an average of 21.6 percent for 1960-61.[4] The real impact of direct investments, however, is much greater than these percentages reveal. The most important reasons for this are—as has been described above—(i) that investments aim at the creation of a permanent structure in the form of a production outfit, which is done in order to maximize direct on-the-spot control over the object of investment, and (ii) that the superordinate goal of the investment is to maximize the accumulation capacity of the investor. Export credits, loans, public aid, portfolio investments, etc., obviously also share the goal of maximum accumulation, but not the same range and degree of control of opportunity. Moreover, the stocks of investments accumulated over the years and the production and thus renewed constant accumulation capacity they represent most probably far exceed other forms of capital export. Furthermore, foreign investment holders increasingly finance their operations from liquid assets, not new investments from the mother company. The overriding impact of direct investment, however, should not lead us to overlook the impact in terms of control which can be reached through, e.g., export credits, which in particular the Japanese and the Soviet industries are using and which even the largest direct investors have successfully used to obtain large profits.

Direct investment is a way of penetrating and establishing control over another social unit by means of capital export. It usually takes the form of establishing a wholly-owned subsidiary firm, the large multinational corporations obviously being the investor. In other words, direct investment is a mechanism used by the corporation to penetrate foreign markets and obtain their resources. The fact that direct investment is a tool of the corporate headquarters and not one type of financial flow which analytically can be distinguished from the analysis of the corporation seems to be overlooked or at least misrepresented in the recent UN study on multilateral corporations.[5]

Direct investment as a form of penetration abroad dates back to at least the period of early free trade, in the first part of the 19th century. The first foreign production subsidiary that resembles the present pattern of investment through the corporation is reported to have been the plant set up by the Belgian firm Cockrill in Prussia in 1815.[6] Both American and European investments were well under way by the end of the 19th century, taking over the position until then held by the old mercantilist trading companies. A majority of the corporations now controlling the stock of investments in the world, including Africa, are based on 'pioneer investments' initiated before 1930.[7] Corporations practically never die. Investments do die, but only in their separate parts—and often not forever. They may reappear, perhaps in new forms, such as the present situation, where Western investors are currently moving on a large scale into Eastern Europe, after an interlude of Socialist disinvestment of the Western pre-World War II investments in that region.

The particular reasons for making a particular investment may be many and may vary from one case to another. In the classical theories of Hobson, Lenin and others,[8] export of capital in the form of direct investment (and in other forms) to underdeveloped areas was explained as a consequence of the falling rate of profit due to a narrowing market at home. Investments were then made in order to conquer new markets, so as to maintain or increase the rate of accumulation.

Another motive, leading to expansion long before direct investments began to be used on a large scale, was the need for raw materials for an expanding capitalist industry which could not meet the requirements of a growing demand and a rapidly developing technology with domestic resources alone.

Historically, most of the direct investments in underdeveloped areas seem to be due either to one of these two factors, or to a combination of both (as when, e.g., a manufacturing plant was set up to process some raw material on the spot). As direct investments have grown and become part of an increasingly complex and geographically as well as sectorially widespread organizational structure, the motives behind investments may also have multiplied. In a decision to maintain an investment, to reinvest in order to increase the stock, or to make a new investment, one or several of the following motives may be decisive:

take advantage of a monopolistic position: in technology, whenever you have developed a new product which may become a market leader, or in terms of exploiting control over a market;

minimize risks by spreading the investment geographically and diversify production (the insurance principle);

take advantage of economies of scale, or create such an advantage;

take advantage of lower production costs in the periphery;

check competitors, either in the global or in the local market, by preventing them from gaining an advantage (which you possess, or would want to possess yourself);

jump tariffs or other barriers;

remove less profitable or otherwise 'noisy' production from your own country or area;

gamble purely and simply in a short-run drive to see whether an operation may yield profits.

These motives are not all at the same level of explanation. The overall aim is to grow (in income, power, prestige, visible size, etc.) through the processes of accumulation and penetration of control. The conquest of markets, raw materials and the search for more profitable outlets are strategic concerns; the other motives mentioned have more of a tactical nature in the attempt to realize these strategic concerns.

Murray argues that several factors, notably the need for integrated communication and easy access to infrastructural and other facilities, act as a pull-back restraint on investments in the periphery: investments tend to be concentrated to the already-established investment areas, to the 'nodes' of the international capitalist economy, that is, the advanced centers.[9]

On the other hand, Hymer offers a concept of how the need for restraint may be eased and perhaps completely dealt with.[10] In order to sustain growth, the corporation needs to develop a specialized production apparatus, where every single part operates as efficiently (and cheaply) as possible, according to its particular speciality. The organization becomes highly differentiated and subdivided into a great variety of tasks, product lines and firms. In order to function efficiently, elaborate organs of integration at higher levels and vertical communication networks from the top to the bottom are required. Decision-making and control opportunities become highly unevenly distributed: they are confined to the top echelons. The formula is a double movement: expand and spread the productive functions at the bottom, concentrate control and accumulation opportunities to the top.

This 'new international division of labor'[11]—by which the structure of the international economy increasingly becomes that of the multinational corporation—is built on older structures shaped during expansionism, imperialism and colonialism. The structure is constantly changing: new forms of control are developed; new centers of power are created according to the evolution of the power struggle between contenders for the top position(s). What remains constant is the hierarchical structure: emperors may fall and their mechanisms of control may wear out, but the imperial structure remains.

At present we are in the midst of—if not already past—the most revolutionary element of another major period of qualitative change: the revolution in technology and information and the ascendance of these factors—simultaneously both superior means of control and accumulation, and increasingly the actual centers of control and accumulation themselves—to the top of the global hierarchical structure. The major vehicles behind this, the most recent revolution on a global scale, are

the establishment of 'the technological basis for a major advance in the conquest of the material world and the beginnings of a truly cosmopolitan production';[12]

the creation of highly sophisticated, highly specialized, highly efficient means of sorting, communicating, and controlling information on a global scale—the emergence of information on information as the decisive means of control;

the formidable growth and superior efficiency of the multinational corporation in organizing the use of technology and information, creating and recreating an even more efficient hierarchical structure on a global scale.

Such an outline of the historical development of this structure, necessarily only a rough sketch in a short paper, points to the cumulative character of the dominance system. This 'law of cumulative hierarchy' means that the present structure (and any past or future one) is the result of a process of accumulating control opportunities, where new ways and/or actors of control are superimposed, or superimpose themselves on existing ways and/or actors. The structure becomes a set of control layers, the more recent ones imposed on the older ones, but without abandoning subordinate layers. This structure is a growing organism, a process of vertical extension of control. Nevertheless, old forms of control may be indispensable to the efficient functioning of the structure in various geographical and social spaces.

The unequal accumulation of value, where those operating at superior levels in the production hierarchy can take a larger share of the (surplus) value than those working at lower levels, is supported by monopolistic structures of control, demand-supply structures of the market, the pull of location forces, size (as indicated by the importance commonly attached to economies of scale) and—obviously—the further use of power as the ability to blackmail or otherwise force others to give up surplus value. All of these forces—as well as important and often decisive control mechanisms outside the system of production and distribution as such (e.g., the military apparatus)—will often, although not always, work in the same direction, as the close coordination of state and corporate interests shows (e.g., in the military-industrial complexes), thus giving rise to competing accumulation between various power centers.

Monopoly and location on a global scale are indicated by concentration—the share of a sector/activity of production/distribution. A list of world-wide activities and some data on their concentration by regions gives at least a superficial picture of the geographical mapping of the structure (cf. Table 1).

These are the aggregate (regional) patterns of distribution. Obviously, the geographical location of activities need not correspond to actual control over, nor possession of, the value created by these activities. 'Sectors of activity' are increasingly vertically integrated—which simply means that the center increasingly possesses or otherwise controls value located and created in the periphery. This seems particularly true of the bauxite-aluminum

Table 1. *Shares of world activities at different levels of the production process*
(In percentages)

Sector of activity	Shares of world activities OECD	CMEA	UDC's
R & D	85	13	2
Services:			
Sea transport	81[1]	9	10
Tourism	80	–	–
Trade (total world)[2]	72	11	17
Production:			
Manufactured goods[3]	62	32	6
Energy (crude oil)[3]	33	7	60
Minerals[3]	52	25	23
Food[3]	40	30	30

[1]Includes registrations in Liberia, Panama, etc., the 'convenience flag' states.

[2]Data from UN Statistical Yearbook, 1971.

[3]Pierre Jalee, Le Tiers Monde dans l'economic mondiale, Paris, Francois Maspero, 1968.

sector, which is highly monopolistic in character. Two large corporations, Alcan and Alcoa, control more than half of world production and distribution at all levels and are world 'price leaders' within their sector.

In the case of aluminum, monopolistic control would seem to override or direct such factors as location concerns and the 'free paly' of supply-demand forces. Thus, the completely vertically integrated production and distribution structure which this sector approximates would seem the most efficient control structure. But is this necessarily true? Is the nationalization of mines and energy supplies—such as those now taking place in the copper and petroleum sectors and which remove metropolitan on-the-spot control of lower levels of production (extraction)—a threat and thus a counter-strategy to the domination structure?

We would contend that this is not necessarily so. In fact, it may be argued that the direct penetration of the periphery, establishing some form of direct control over it, may be both more costly (and thus dis-accumulative) and at the same time not more efficient as a way of having the periphery assume its proper place in the production hierarchy than working through indirect means of control. As long as production is an *integrated process,* i.e., occurs for a market and needs marketing transport and services, as long as it needs technology and information and management, and as long as these 'factors' are monopolized at higher levels of control and accumulation, then the state of dependency may remain, despite the assumption of self-control over the actual extraction-production.[13] This is the 'new international division of labor' by domination via the global structure—different from the 'old' direct control through organized vertical integration of all components of production and distribution. The two coexist in the present world, and vertical integration is still a major policy of the corporations. But it is possible to envisage the 'new' structure replacing the 'old' one and that such a development is in the interests of the center.

It is in such a perspective that we should analyze the role of direct investments. This may still work as a 'vanguard' mechanism of penetration, just as it used to be when, for example, corporations integrated vertically in raw materials. Furthermore, it may still be necessary in order to capture and/or maintain a monopoly in a local market, or to have full control over the operations on the spot. This is why most corporations still seem to favor a fully-owned subsidiary rather than a joint venture or some other form of shared control operation: minority share, etc.

As is well known, however—and often because they are met by 'host country' governments' desires for taking over or sharing in the control over firms—corporations are forced to change from total ownership to some other form of control involving less nominal control. The question then remains: can the same degree of control effectively be maintained by the foreign investor by using means of control other than full ownership, e.g., technology, marketing organization, etc.? This is what research has begun to ask[14] and what African governments must ask themselves.

Size and patterns of direct investments in Africa

Size. At the end of 1967, the stock of direct investments in Africa controlled by investors of the DAC countries amounted to close to 6.6 billion US dollars (excluding South Africa, but including Rhodesia and Portuguese colonies). This was 6.3 percent of the total world investments of DAC countries in that year. The stock of investments in all the underdeveloped areas amounted to 32 percent of world investments.[15]

According to OECD figures and estimates, the stock of DAC-based investments in Africa in 1972 was 9.4 billion, an increase of about 43 percent over 1967. The total world stock of foreign direct investments was about 165 billion dollars for the year 1971, an increase over 1967 of 60 percent growth in the foreign investments of the capitalist metropoles. Thus, the aggregate investments in Africa grew slower than world investments. The relative 'decline' of Africa as an investment area would seem to be due to the relative decline in the economic strength of the old colonial powers, notably the UK.

But it may also partly be due to the fact that the accumulated investments in Africa already represent a sufficient degree of penetration of the African economies. In comparison, Japan seems to have invested relatively more in Africa over the period covered than she invested in the world as a whole.

As one surveys the investment patterns for each individual African nation, however, the picture gets more complex (Table 2). Not surprisingly, the single biggest investment market is Nigeria, with an estimated stock of foreign investment in 1972 of 2.1 billion US dollars. Nigeria nearly doubled its stock of foreign investments from 1967 to 1971, making it the fifth most important foreign investment object in the underdeveloped world (following Brazil, Venezuela, Mexico and Argentina). 22 percent of all foreign investments in Africa were registered in Nigeria, as apposed to 17 percent in 1967.

Other major African 'host countries' for foreign investments are Libya, Zambia and Zaire. Among them, widely different trends in investment policies appeared between 1967 and 1972. While Zambia (after the Mulingushi declaration in 1969) and Zaire (its 1967 partial nationalization of the copper industry being recorded in the 1967 data) followed a policy of a moderate nationalization and disinvestment, Libya continued to receive huge amounts of foreign investments in her oil sector, increasing her share of the total stock of foreign investments in Africa from 9 to 16.5 percent.

Libya's pattern was the opposite of Algeria's, which is the African disinvestor. From 1967 to 1972 Algeria reduced foreign investments by 64 percent in her drive to take national (state) control over the economy. From a position of relatively strong domination of foreign capital upon assumption of political independence, she has been able to change to a position of moderate dependency—from penetration and exploitation to a degree of cooperation with foreign capital.[16] After the nationalization measures adopted during recent years, Libya now seems to be following the Algerian pattern.

Apart from these few cases—Nigeria as the 'liberal' or 'interesting' (from the investor's point of view) African 'host country', Algeria as the most restrictive one, while Zambia, and recently also Libya, Mauretania and to a certain extent even Zaire are in-between cases of moderate restriction—there have been no dramatic changes in the pattern of foreign investments in Africa. That countries like Botswana, Lesotho, Gambia and Malawi show large increases in foreign investment during this period is probably due to the fact that they were relatively 'uninteresting' investment areas for the center countries until recently; due to their small internal markets and lack of natural resources, they are likely to remain so, with the exception of mineral-rich Botswana. Obviously, this does not mean that, e.g., Lesotho and Swaziland are not highly penetrated areas: South African investments, and British or American South Africa-based capital, are not recorded in the data we employ.

Dependency and 'spheres of interest'. By and large, metropolitan investments in Africa, as measured by their shares in the total world investments of the capitalist developed countries, are not great. Nevertheless, seen from the point of view of the African countries, metropolitan investments represent—in size and in the opportunity to exercise power which they imply—an effective penetration of their economy. This is one way of describing the unequal (economic) dependency between the center and the African periphery.

The degree of penetration can only be measured in very rough and approximative terms. One such measure would be the share of foreign investments in the GNP of a country. It would give an idea of which foreign power centers enjoy what degree of (potential) control over the African countries, in spite of the methodological weakness inherent in combining a cumulative variable (stock of investments) with an 'instant' one (GNP of one year).[17]

Employing this measure, Goux and Landeau divided 'host countries' into five categories: 'colonies', 'protectorates', 'condominia', 'countries on the road to annexation', and 'independents'. 'Colonies' were those countries in which the direct investments of one metropolitan country (e.g., the United States) represented 30 percent or more of the GNP of that country, 'independents' those where the corresponding percentage was below 1. According to the Goux-Landeau scale, there were three French 'colonies' (Gabon, PR of Congo, and Mauritania), two British (Swaziland and Zambia), two US (Liberia and Libya) and one Belgian (Zaire) in Africa in 1967. Only the UAR and Lesotho fully qualified as 'independents', while Mali, Sudan and Ethiopia were rather close to doing so. There were no changes in this respect from 1967 to 1971, except that Lesotho seems to be 'on the road to annexation'[18] and Congo PR is moving towards a 'protectorate' status (see Table 3). We do not have access to the country-by-country breakdown of investment data on the 'home country' part of the structure for 1971 or 1972, but it seems clear that Zambia 'decolonized' from the UK during that period (foreign investments as a percentage of GNP being reduced from 36 to 19), while Zaire probably reduced its 'colonial' type of dependency on Belgium without reducing its overall dependency on investments from the capitalist developed countries. Libya, as has already been pointed out, did not start to 'decolonize' US penetration until after 1972, increasing her foreign investments/GNP ratio to 48 percent from 1967 to 1971. Algeria, where French investments in 1967 represented 17 percent of the GNP, moved from being a 'protectorate' of France into a 'condominium' type of relationship (4 percent ratio), an observation that would seem to be rather close to that of Akkache.[19]

Table 3 also shows the pattern of monopoly position when monopoly is measured at the level of the nation; it means that one single metropolitan country accounts for a major share of the foreign investments in one particular peripheral country. The share which in reality corresponds to a monopoly position is determined by several factors, some of which were mentioned above, such as technological leads and the overall political, military and economic relationship which exists between the investing metropole and the 'host country'. It would, however, be safe to conclude from our analysis and from what we know of the historical background of African-metropolitan relations that a monopoly position is held when one investing country controls 70 percent or more of the foreign investments in the country. This would seem particularly true when the investing country is a metropole, i.e., a big (economic) power, and at the same time has a long tradition of colonial rule over the peripheral country. The only country that would not seem to qualify for a monopoly position according to these conditions is Belgium, which lacks the power base enjoyed by the Big Three, and which probably for that reason has since 1967 seen her grip on her favorite colony, Zaire, taken over by the big powers. And possibly in Italy's position in Somalia also has been counterbalanced by the policy of nationalization adopted by the present Somali government and to some extent by Soviet Russian influence in that country.

According to our definition of a 'national monopoly', France had a monopoly position in 1967 in 12 African countries, i.e., in 2/3 of the former French colonies, and was close to having a monopoly in two additional countries. 7 out of 12 were highly penetrated by foreign investments, if 'high penetration' is defined by a case where the stock of foreign investments represents 18 percent or more of the GNP (18 percent being the average for Africa as a whole). The UK occupied a similar position in 8 African countries (9 if Rhodesia is included), and 4 of these countries were highly penetrated. The United States had a monopoly in Libya and the UAR, but the latter is clearly *not* penetrated by US investments: Liberia is a much clearer candidate, being particularly penetrated, indeed, and with medium-power Sweden as the next largest investor.

These figures show that metropolitan 'spheres of interest' policies still play an important role in the context of Africa. Such policies are pursued not only in the field of direct investments, but in trade[20] and public aid, as well as in political and military relations, all of which show 'spheres of interest' structures highly consistent with the patterns of direct investment.

This does not mean, however, that the metropolitan interests have been stabilized in a permanent division of Africa. Both because these interests meet opposition from independence-oriented African governments and because the relationship between the metropoles is constantly changing (as, e.g., the US-European relations bear witness to), competition for the markets and the resources of Africa will always remain. In certain countries, metropoles may be able to achieve a cartel-like cooperation. In Guinea, groups of US, French, British, German, Japanese and Swiss corporations jointly run the mining sector (in the Boké mine, as a joint venture with the Guinean government). In Togo there also exists a joint US-French operation of the phosphate sector, which after 1973 has been subject to intervention by the Togolese government. In most countries, the national petroleum market has been divided between the big oil companies, both US-based and Shell/BP. In the manufacturing and 'service' sectors, however, competition at the level of the national market seems to be more prominent. And with the present and future race for raw materials and the widening contradiction between the United States and the greater European capitals, competition is likely to increase in the mining and petroleum sectors, as well. The extent and degree of competition, however, may depend largely on the extent to which the United States decides to challenge the established European 'supremacy' in capital exports to Africa in the future, and that may largely depend on which needs the United States seeks to find in Africa's raw materials and the 'preventive' interest she may take in controlling the supply of such resources—petroleum and minerals—to her metropolitan competitors in Europe and Japan. In 1967, the United States had only 2.3 percent of its total world investments in Africa, while accounting for 20.8 percent of all foreign investments in Africa. France had 28.8 percent of its stock of foreign investments in Africa in 1967 and the UK 11.4 percent; this accounted for 26.3 and 30.0 percent, respectively, of the total foreign investments in Africa that year. Half of the total US investments in Africa were in petroleum production and most of that half in Libya. Libyan-US relations after the moves against US oil companies from 1970 on have thus been quite important to the evolution of US investments in Africa at the present time. But the US stake in Africa may be moving from Libya to Nigeria, Zaire and a few of the other relatively large markets and/or resource-rich countries. Gulf Oil is reported to be negotiating with the Nigerian government on a venture that would eventually supply liquefied gas to the United States and that would involve investments of 1 billion US dollars.[21]

Economic penetration. From a methodological point of view, a better measure of economic penetration through direct investments may be to calculate the turnover of the activity established by direct investments. Objections of a methodological and theoretical nature may nevertheless be raised against such a measure, as well. Moreover, such a measure is difficult to assess, because we lack information which will have to be calculated at the level of the firm.

When assessing the value of the production of foreign investment, a rough estimate may be made by multiplying the book value of the investment by a constant factor. This factor has been chosen as 3 in some,[22] as 2 in other studies.[23] The measure would give an indication of the depth to which the foreign investments have penetrated the peripheral economy and account for the local accumulation process. In order to arrive at a 'moderate' measure, we have chosen a factor of 2.0. In the real world, actual turnover will probably vary between a factor of 5 (perhaps far more in the highly favorable production of crude petroleum in the Middle East) to less than 1 in an unproductive sector and/or area (as when investments are 'lying idle'). The results obtained must therefore be interpreted with great care and with a considerable margin for variations, as well as possible errors.

The measure arrived at is simply the ratio of stock of foreign investments/GNP employed above, multiplied by 2. This means that the patterns we recorded and described above are repeated, but that we in addition are able to give an indication of the 'instant (and recurrent) penetration' of the African economy by foreign capital by estimating its share of the annual national product.

As Table 5 shows—provided that our estimate is a fairly accurate one—a number of African countries are highly dependent on foreign capital for their annual production output and its growth. Gabon and Liberia seem particularly dependent: they represent fully-controlled bases of foreign production in Africa. According to the same estimate, Mauritania, Congo PR, Swaziland, Zaire and Guinea had more than 50 percent of their national product operated by foreign capital (although Congo had reduced the share considerably from 1967). In an additional 11 countries, including Angola (12 with Rhodesia), foreign-controlled production accounted for more than 25 percent of the GNP.

The investment goal: types of investment and the international division of labor

Close to 30 percent of the stock of foreign investments in Africa in 1967 was in the petroleum production sector, and close to 20 percent in mining and smelting. The sectorial breakdown for 1972 (or 1971) is not available to us, but it seems reasonable to assume that the share of total stock of investment in these two sectors increased rather than decreased in the years after 1967.

If investments in agriculture are added to those of the two sectors just mentioned, 56.5 percent of the stock of foreign investments in Africa in 1967 was in raw material extraction. The corresponding percentage of investments in manufacturing and petroleum refining, the two main processing sectors, was 23.4 or exactly half of this. The rest, about 20 percent, was spread onto various sectors usually referred to as 'service sectors'. Dealing with such activities as petroleum marketing, trade and transport of both processed and unprocessed goods, they represent supporting activities for the two main types of productive activity: the extractive and the processing types. (See Table 4.)

These two general types of production may be looked at from two different perspectives. Firstly, they fit in rather well with the differentiation of investment strategies, as made above: raw materials are extracted for consumption and further processing in the center markets; processing in the periphery aims at the local market in the African periphery.

Secondly, the extractive-processing dichotomy reflects, even if only in very rough terms, the international division of labor. Processing represents by and large a higher level of production (as the simple distinction between petroleum extraction and refining indicates), because it gives better accumulation opportunities, more socio-economic 'spin-offs', i.e., better development prospects. This clearly is a rule-of-thumb approximation. The recent price increases for crude petroleum have accumulated more profits for various Arab governments (if not development to their peoples) than have exports of semi-manufactures and manufactures from Hong Kong or Mexico. Moreover, the development effect on industrialization is a question of, among other things, what type of industry it is, whether it stimulates, assists, and in turn benefits from the development efforts of other sectors as an 'industrializing industry',[24] and to what extent its benefits accrue to the workers, the local population, and the nation.

Nevertheless, something may be derived from an application of the simple processing-extractive dichotomy to investment statistics. It may give a profile of the type of productive activity in which a firm, a community, or a country is engaged, and an indication of the position it occupies in the international system. High concentration on raw materials extraction means a low position in the system—with the possible exception (after 1973) of countries specializing in petroleum production.

Compared to other regions of the underdeveloped world, Africa ranks low (cf. Table 6). It has a profile similar to that of the Middle East, but a lower share of petroleum production, thus on the whole ranking lower than the Middle East in terms of accumulation and opportunities for self-control. A quick glance at the export income statistics of the individual countries for the last year will substantiate this point: African countries are at the lower end of the international 'division of labor'.

One central element in the explanation of this is the economic structure which was imposed upon most of Africa during colonial times: the export enclave and monocultural production. As Table 5 shows, there is no perfect correlation between the degree of foreign penetration of the economy at the present time and the degree of monoculture. But there are very clear indications of such a relationship in the case of the typical monocultural economies: the mineral extractive ones.

12 African countries earned 60 percent or more of their total export income

from one product in 1965. For two of these, Burundi and Mauritius, we have sufficient data on direct investments. Of the remaining 10, 8 were also among the most penetrated countries, and 6 of them had most of their stock of foreign investments concentrated in the most important export sector: Libya, Zambia, Liberia, Algeria, Senegal and Sierra Leone. These represent the core extractive areas of foreign investment in Africa. Algeria, Zambia and recently also Libya are on the road to disinvesting, and at least Algeria has embarked upon a major campaign to increase its processing capacity, both in absolute and relative terms. So far, however, all of them still remain monocultural export economies with the problems, and for some (e.g., the petroleum exporters), the present advantages which that means.

In Table 7 we have made an attempt to compare the composition of the national GDP with the types of productive activity in which foreign investments are held. This may give an idea of the extent to which foreign investments have penetrated the important parts of the national economy.

This table shows great variations from country to country. In cases like Botswana, Lesotho, Ethiopia, and Sudan, there is little correspondence between the importance which a type of activity may have to the GDP and the priorities of foreign investors. In practically all of the typical extractive economies, however, the correspondence is very obvious. Metropolitan investments in the extraction of African resources have shaped the economies of the present African countries.

It is a widely accepted view that it is necessary to distinguish between growth and development and that one may find 'growth without development'. Looking at growth data and assuming that economic growth may be a prerequisite for development (even if they do not as a rule coincide), comparison of the growth of foreign investments and the growth in the GDP of African countries may be useful. Thus, we calculated the (rank) correlation coefficient between the two growth rates (growth in GDP 1969-72 and growth in foreign investments 1967-72) for all African countries. The coefficient was 15, which would seem to imply that there is no particular correspondence between the two. In other words, new foreign investment does not seem to be related to a growth in the (domestic national) product. More empirical investigations, however, will be needed before we may draw safer conclusions on this point.

A firm-by-firm or a country-by-country analysis of productive profiles would give more relevant information for deeling with policies for disentangling the African economies from the present structure. Africa's integration into the unequal 'division of labor' is illustrated in the, e.g., petroleum branch. In 1967, the ratio of foreign investments in petroleum production (extraction) to investments in the three other petroleum sectors (refining, marketing and transport) was 21 in the case of Nigeria, 14 for Gabon, 51/2 for Libya and 51/2 for Algeria. Similar illustrations of inequality are found in the case of the 'mining economies', if investment in mining and smelting are compared to those in, e.g., manufacturing.[25] Sierra Leone, Zambia, Guinea, Togo and Liberia then obtain ratios ranging from 15 (Liberia) to 9 (Togo). Mauritania, however, represented the extreme case: 92 percent of all foreign investments were in the mining sector (iron ore and, since 1966, some copper), as opposed to 0.4 percent in manufacturing. Moreover, practically the whole of the mining sector was controlled by one firm, MIFERMA. This firm alone accounted for 1/3 of the gross national product of Mauritania, and so far its production has been based completely on exports, which represented 80 percent of Mauritania's total export—it was a veritable state-within-a-state. In December 1974, the Mauritanian government announced that MIFERMA would be nationalized against indemnization with 'petrodollars' borrowed from neighboring Arab countries. The direction and real meaning of this decision, in terms of prospects for mass-based political changes and Mauritanian development, are, however, not yet clear as this goes to press.[26]

MIFERMA, however, is not a unique case. LAMCO of Liberia, the Liberian-American-Swedish Minerals Co., is larger than MIFERMA in both absolute terms and relative to the size of the 'host country' economy. Involving a total investment exceeding 200 million US dollars (62.5 percent of the shares being in foreign hands), it represents another example of the integration of an African export enclave into the international (metropolitan, i.e., US) capitalist system.

The single biggest corporate holding in the African extractive business (excluding South Africa) is BP/Shell's investment in the Nigerian petroleum production. In 1967 it alone amounted to at least 7 percent of the stock of foreign investment in Africa. Taking an interest in the vast potential Nigerian market and to some extent also urged by the Nigerian government, the two sister companies started to build a refining industry in Nigeria and now control most of the present refining capacity, together with the state National Oil Corporation. Nevertheless, the export of crude petroleum, and (increasingly) also of natural gas, dominates the Nigerian petroleum activity.

Considering the extractive business in Africa as a whole, the pattern of a 'spheres of interest' partition of the business among the national metropoles seems to a large extent to be confirmed at the level of the firm, as well. There are, however, a number of important exceptions, where corporations have merged across national boundaries; this obviously reflects the process of internationalization of capital.

We have already mentioned LAMCO of Liberia, Boké of Guinea and Togo's phosphate production, where US and European corporations cooperate. Other examples of US-European corporate corporation are found in Ghana's bauxite, in Gabon's petroleum and mining, in Angola, etc. In a number of other cases, European capitals have cooperated. Some of these international merges are expressions of cartel policies of longstanding tradition, such as in the petroleum and bauxite sectors. Others may be uneasy local 'peace treaties' or simply 'ceasefire agreements' and may break down at any moment, leading to the reemergence of tough competition. Whether and when are questions which must be related to the overall political developments in US-European relations and the extent to which the corporate leaders will follow state policies in that respect, to the availability of raw materials at any given time, and to future development in the market concerned.

Foreign investors may perhaps forget about their own quarrels to the extent that 'host country' governments challenge their control of African resources and thereby the position of African production in the international 'division of labor'. Such a prospect, however, seems increasingly to be met by another strategy: that of making a new deal with the local governments in a joint-venture operation of production. Developments have shown that foreign investors may profit from such a strategy.[27]

The manufacturing sector in Africa and the multinational corporations

Foreign investments in manufacturing account for more than 50 percent of the total stock of foreign investments in Gambia, Swaziland, Chad, Somalia and Burundi. Considering the low share which the manufacturing sector occupies in the GDP of these countries, this is a rather surprising list. Nevertheless, the size of foreign investments in these countries is small. Furthermore, the type of manufacturing established by foreign investors in these countries should also be noted: in Chad, the 2/3 share of foreign investments falls on cotton ginning and textile works (both joint ventures), a brewery, sugar and flour mills, assembly plants for bicycles and transistor radios, brick and tile factories.[28] These activities do not represent a high level of processing. On the other hand, it should not be concluded *a priori* that the development effect of these activities is negative (meaning underdevelopment) even in terms of the national economy. To the people of Chad an assembly plant for bicycles may be as important, or rather, more important, than an assembly plant for automobiles.

The overall processing level of foreign-controlled manufacturing in Nigeria is not very much higher than that of Chad. During recent years, this has been changing, as the Nigerian government has initiated industrialization programs, including high-processing industries.

A note should be added here about processing level: we are primarily discussing it in terms of the international system and its hierarchisation in a structure of unequal division of labor—not in terms of development theory. A high processing level obviously may mean capital—and technology-intensive production with little spin-off in terms of labor opportunity, the learning of skills, taxes to the state, etc. In short, development prospects do not necessarily increase to the extent that the processing level increases. What determines the development process is whether the planning and the growth of the industry result in a positive transformation of the four elements of underdevelopment, all of which are characteristic of most African countries:

1. Foreign penetration and a resultant external dependency;
2. Disintegration or 'disarticulation'[29] of the economy;
3. Mass poverty, a low living standard for the great majority of the people and a lack of resources (capital means of production, energy, skills, etc.) at the level of the national economy;
4. Gross inequalities between the rich few and the great majority of poor within the country, in an economic, cultural and political sense. In the present context, we are almost exclusively dealing with the first element, which, however, is closely linked to the three others.

Exhaustive surveys of foreign corporate activities in Africa still remain to be done. They are needed to fill in numerous gaps in the analysis which a survey of investments represents. These surveys are difficult to carry out because corporate headquarters practice the same strategy towards researchers that they pursue with respect to subsidiaries or firms at the lower echelons of the corporate hierarchy: they give some but not all the information the others would like to possess; the rest is for headquarters only. Or: the researcher may be even worse off than the manager of the subsidiary.[30]

The most comprehensive statistical survey of the world's multinational corporations ever carried out is the Harvard Business School study.[31] It covers 187 US-based and 214 corporations based outside the United States, with a total of more than 25,000 subsidiaries around the world. The study does not give information on the individual corporation, only data in aggregate form. This and a number of other 'non-information gaps' considerably reduces its value. Furthermore, if used without being placed in a context of domination-theory—which is attempted here—it may be a highly misleading and even dangerous exercise in 'pure empiricism'. Although of limited value, it may nevertheless be useful as a source of information at the aggregate level and as a guide in further research.

On the average, US corporations had 2.5 percent of their total number of subsidiaries in Africa, as opposed to 2.3 percent of their world stock of investments, non-US corporations 8.9 percent and 9 percent, respectively (excluding Rhodesia).[32] The average size of the subsidiaries in Africa (size measured by the book value of investments) is rather similar to the world average. This is primarily due to the large size of the subsidiaries in the extractive sectors, and does not seem to hold true for the manufacturing sector. This may be illustrated by comparing sales to the number of subsidiaries: while 5.3 percent of the total number of subsidiaries of the non-US manufacturing corporations were placed in Africa (according to the Harvard study), only 2.4 percent of the world sales of these corporations were realized in Africa. Their headquarters probably can be counted among the strongest supporters of economic integration schemes among African countries (provided these countries maintain an open-door policy towards non-African investors after integration).[33]

A closer look at corporate penetration according to the type of manufacturing in which investment has been made shows great variations (Table 8). Comparatively more subsidiaries in Africa are found in petroleum (close to 16 percent of all the subsidiaries in the world in that industry), food (9.4 percent), and wood (7.3), much less in the more sophisticated industries like chemicals (4.8), electric products (4.0), or precision goods (none). This pattern is in accordance with the observations made above on the basis of investment patterns, and it confirms the 'international division of labor'.

Another way of illustrating this pattern is to show the extent to which investment in Africa is determined by the technology-intensity of the investing corporation. Again, we have only aggregate data, but they are sufficiently indicative of the pattern which we have suggested. Those corporations which use a relatively large share of their sales on research and development are also relatively less inclined to set up a subsidiary in Africa (or any other underdeveloped area). While 30 percent of all the non-US corporations surveyed spent 4 percent or more of their annual sales on R & D, less than 20 percent of them had subsidiaries in Africa. The technology-intensive corporations were most inclined to invest in the larger African markets: Nigeria, Algeria, etc.[34]

Of much greater importance, however, is the question of what foreign corporations spend on R & D in Africa and to what extent this benefits the local industry. Available information indicates that there is *very little if any R & D activity in the subsidiaries of foreign corporations in Africa.* New technological information is highly centralized and protected: it is confined to headquarters or research laboratories directly under headquarters control. The technology which is 'trickled down' to a periphery-based subsidiary primarily takes the form of a finished product to be sold directly on the market or assembled on the spot from its pre-fabricated parts, most of them probably developed and produced in some other (foreign) affiliate of the corporation. And it arrives at the periphery only after having gone through the international 'product cycle' by which new products are made according to the perceived needs of the most sophisticated consumers in rich markets and then, after reaching economies of scale production, are 'cycled' down to poorer markets.[35]

Several ways of transferring technology to a periphery economy short of through the wholly-owned subsidiary or the joint venture are open to the corporation: licensing agreements, delivery of 'turnkey' factories, ordinary export of technological items, etc. In order to maintain control over the use of the technology, the corporations most often protect their products through international patenting. Studies of the role of foreign technology in a number of underdeveloped countries, notably in Latin America, indicate that the patent proprietor—and the corporations presently own at least 80 percent of all patents originating in the advanced capitalist countries and probably close to 100 percent of all foreign patents being registered in underdeveloped countries[36]—in several ways may create problems for the development of a technology-importing country. Strategies which they use range from preventing a patent from being put into production locally, and putting clauses on patents which prevent products locally preduced from being exported, to transfer pricing practices which charge undue and often exorbitant prices for the technology.[37] A recent study of transfer of technology to Ethiopia, after giving a detailed survey of the problems that country faces through the operations of foreign firms, concludes that the costs involved in the transfer of technology amounts to 3 percent of the GDP, to over one-third of export proceeds and to little more than half of the net value added in the modern manufacturing sector.[38] Ethiopia may—as the report in fact concludes—represent an extreme case, but it nevertheless reflects the position of an underdeveloped country—the largest among the so-called least developed countries. More case studies would show to what extent the Ethiopian pattern is true for other African countries. Since patenting as well as other forms of restricted transfer of technology very often follow direct investments, it may well be so. On the other hand, and as the stock of foreign investments in Ethiopia is relatively low, foreign transfers of technology in this case may represent an *additional* and perhaps dominant form of penetration and in fact may illustrate how the foreign corporations may exercise their power and accumulate profits even if direct financial control has not been established.

The industrial patents registered in Africa are in many cases 100 percent owned by foreign corporations (cf. Table 9). This means that they hold a key to the industrial development of the continent. Their control over technology and the information necessary to use it, *and* to put a product on the market, etc., is in fact what we referred to in the initial parts of our paper as the new means of power. If corporations loosen their control as a shareholder by changing to a joint venture or a minority-holding position, they may still maintain both sufficient control and a satisfactory profit by taking advantage of their monopoly on technology. This is a fact which calls for urgent considerations of counter-strategies by African governments and for a critical evaluation of the role which foreign technology plays in the process of underdevelopment or development in Africa.

Still, corporations seem to maintain even the financial control over their African operations through majority ownership. 81 percent of the US and 72 percent of the non-US corporations had a more than 51 percent share of the book value capital of their African subsidiaries in 1971, against a world average of 78 and 71 percent, respectively. The 50-50 joint venture ownership was established in 6 percent of the US and 7 percent of the non-US African subsidiaries, while a minority interest was held only in 13 and 20 percent, respectively, of the affiliated.[39]

At the same time, the manufacturing corporations continue their primary goal for investments in the periphery: that of capturing the market. 95 percent of the US and 94 percent of the non-US manufacturing corporations operating in Africa had the local country as their principal market in 1971. The percentage was 100 for Nigeria (a total of 48 subsidiaries) and Zambia (35), while 31 percent of the reporting subsidiaries in French-speaking Africa (38) had external markets as their most important client, most probably neighbouring African countries,[40] or (for the Maghreb countries) their (French) parent companies. On the average, 93 percent of the foreign subsidiaries in Africa sold their products primarily to customers outside the corporation, but the corresponding percentage for Maghreb subsidiaries was 73.[41] This means that the practice of sub-contracting African subsidiaries to produce for other affiliates higher up in the corporate structure—another way of practicing the unequal division of labor—does not seem to be very widespread in Africa. *The African pattern is mostly that of being the last link in the 'product cycle'.*

Conclusions

The purpose of the present paper has been to describe the extent and type of foreign direct investments—as one among several means of penetration which the centers of the international capitalist system may employ in taking control over and/or realizing accumulation—in a periphery area, Africa. Patterns of investment have been analyzed in broad terms, primarily by aggregate figures. Further analysis must devote more concrete studies to the level of the single investment, the firm.

We have deliberately avoided attempts to theorize to any great extent on the patterns we have described. Some suggestions, in the form of hypotheses, and some observations, based on the facts at hand, have been made. They relate primarily to the high degree of foreign penetration, a state of penetratedness in which most African countries find themselves at present, and the actual or potential adverse effects it may have on a strategy of development and independence. The crucial question of development and of how foreign investments may prevent it (instead perpetuating the process of underdevelopment) or assist it, has not been sufficiently dealt with. That would go for beyond the purpose set for the present contribution—and we have occasion to deal with this question in other contexts. We have, however, shown that foreign investments in Africa largely retain the African economies in a position of dependency on an unequal international division of labor, and in 'spheres of interest' of the metropoles, in themselves aspects of underdevelopment. We have shown that a growth in foreign investments in Africa during the period 1967-72—as indicated by the low correlation between the two growth rates—does not seem to have contributed to a corresponding growth in the GDP. We have presented evidence that the transfer of technology through the multinational corporations does not necessarily support the process of autonomous industrialization, but on the contrary leads to exploitation of locally-accumulated capital, of natural resources, and of the labor force.

A few African countries have started to disinvest foreign holdings. Much research will be needed in order to assess the extent to which they have succeeded in really changing their own position in the 'division of labor' and of entering a process of development. We have pointed out some factors which may represent obstacles in that respect: continued control over the market, monopoly on technology, the fact that many African leaderships are 'bridgeheads' for foreign interests, of foreign investments, or—if one could get the corporations to agree on such a scheme—for an agreement of gradual disinvestment, as Hirschman has suggested.[42] Such strategies, however, must be worked out consciously and with due recognition of the problems involved in carrying them out.

A short-term strategy may be to set up, unilaterally or (if possible) in agreement with the corporations, a code of conduct for their operations in Africa. Certain instances put great faith in such a device.[43] It should be stated very clearly, however, that it is totally unrealistic to expect great changes through such a formal regulation of the activities of the corporations. In fact, there is a danger that their activities, even when they contain aspects which are detrimental to the interests of the people of underdeveloped countries, will become legalized by such a code. Thus, is never the case that this can or should be seen as a substitute for more radical measures, such as strict regulations of, e.g., the transfer of technology, a disinvestment strategy, or complete and real nationalization of not only the capital assets, but of the management, technical equipment and R & D, marketing, etc., of the foreign-owned firm.

In the end, the question becomes one of how far underdeveloped countries, working from a position of having been subordinated to the economies of the metropoles of the world and also being subject to constant reproduction of structures of domination, can become independent and develop on their own terms and at the same time remain integrated in the present world economy. Even if they succeed in, e.g., raising and stabilizing prices on raw materials, they may still remain largely underdeveloped to the extent they remain an export economy of an enclave type. Due to their continual need for export earnings to finance development projects—and their attempts to avoid or escape strong dependence on foreign capital for the financing of such projects—they will have to continue exporting to the markets of center countries. Moreover, they will need to import technology (at least for the foreseeable future) from those same countries.

The question is on what terms and to which extent. As a general observation, underdeveloped countries and not least the African one, need the markets, assistance and capital of the center countries. At the same time, they must gradually dissociate themselves from those countries and their agencies, notably the multinational corporations. Only by associating more with each other and on relying more on themselves can development be achieved. This holds true for the extractive sector, where producer associations[44] are needed, and for the processing one, where there is an urgent need for a conscious strategy of industrialization and cooperation on planning, research and development, market sharing, etc., between underdeveloped countries.

Notes

[1] See Helge Hveem, "The Global Dominance System", *Journal of Peace Research,* no. 4, 1974, and *The Technocapital Structure and the Global Dominance System,* mimeo, paper presented at the ECPR Workshop, Strasbourg, 28 March-2 April 1974.

[2] Stephen Hymer, "Multinational Corporations and the Law of Unequal Development", in J. D. Bhagwati, ed., *Economics and World Order,* New York, The World Law Fund, 1972, and Samir Amir, *Le développement inégal,* Paris, Les Editions de Minuit, 1973.

[3] Amin, ibid., Eric J. Hobsbawm, *Industry and Empire,* London, Weidenfeld and Nicholson, 1968; Roger Owen and Bob Sutcliffe, eds., *Studies in the Theory of Imperialism,* London, Longmans, 1972; Dieter Senghaas, Hrsg., *Imperialismus und Structurelle Gewalt,* Frankfurt am Main, Suhrkamp Verlag, 1972; Walter Rodney, *How Europe Underdeveloped Africa,* London/Dar es Salaam, Bogle L'Ouverture Publications/Tanzania Publishing House, 1972.

[4] United Nations, *Multinational Corporations in World Development,* New York, 1973.

[5] Ibid., p. 5.

[6] Lawrence G. Franko, *The Other Multinationals:* The International Firms of Continental Europe, 1870-1970, Geneva, CEI, forthcoming.

[7] J. W. Vaupel and J. P. Curhan, *The World's Multinational Enterprises,* Geneva, Centre d'Etudes Industrielles (CEI), 1974.

[8] J. A. Hobson, *Imperialism,* 1902, and V. I. Lenin, *Imperialism, The Latest Stage of Capitalism,* 1917.

[9] Robin Murray, "Underdevelopment, International Firms, and the International Division of Labor", in Jan Tinbergen, ed., *Towards a New World Economy,* Rotterdam, Rotterdam University Press, 1972.

[10] Stephen Hymer, *Some Empirical Features of United States' Investment Abroad,* mimeo, Economic Growth Center, Yale University, August 1970.

[11] For further development of these ideas, see Hveem, *The Global Dominance System.*

[12] Hymer, in Tinbergen, op.cit.

[13] Zaire's nationalization of her copper industry is probably a case in point. Taking over the majority share of the Union Minière du Haut Katanga, the Congolese government, in order to secure exports and marketing outlets, let the former majority holders and certain other foreign interests take charge of these parts of the business.

[14] Cf. Sayre P. Schatz. "Crude Private Neo-Imperialism", *Journal of Modern African Studies,* no. 4, 1969; Giovanni Arrighi, "International Corporations, Labor Aristocracies and Economic Development in Tropical Africa", in Robert I. Rhodes, ed., *Imperialism and Underdevelopment,* N.Y., 1970.

[15] The data on direct investments used in the present paper are taken from OECD, Development Assistance Directorate, *Stock of Private Direct Investments by DAC Countries in Developing Countries,* end 1967, Paris, 1972; investment data for 1971 and 1972 have been obtained from the OECD headquarters in Paris.

[16] Ahmed Akkache, *Capitaux étrangers et libération économique: l'expérience algerienne,* Paris, Francois Maspero, 1971.

[17] Gabrielle Winai-Ström, *Multinational Corporations in Lesotho,* paper presented at the ECPR Workshop, Strasbourg 28 March-2 April, 1974.

[18] Christian Goux and Jean-François Landeau, *Le peril americain,* Paris, Calmann-Levy, 1971.

[19] Op. cit.

[20] Michael Barratt-Brown, "Imperialism in Our Era", in *Spheres of Interest in the Age of Imperialism,* The Spokesman, nos. 24/25, 1972-73.

[21] *US News and World Report,* 8 April 1974.

[22] Paul A. Samuelsson, *Economics,* N.Y.; Paul Baran, *The Political Economy of Growth,* N.Y., Monthly Review Press, 1962.

[23] UN, *Multinational Corporations and World Development,* p. 159, derived the estimate of this factor as follows: the ratio of foreign sales to book value of foreign direct investment has been estimated from 1970 United States data on gross sales of majority-owned foreign affiliates and book value of United States foreign direct investment. "Gross sales of majority-owned foreign affiliates" (approximately $157 billion) includes transactions between foreign affiliates and parent corporations (approximately $20.3 billion) and inter-foreign affiliate sales (approximately $28.1 billion), which together account for about 30 percent of gross foreign affiliate sales. The book value of United States foreign direct investment in 1970 amounted to $78.1 billion. The resulting ratio of gross sales to book value is 2:1. This ratio has been used to estimate the international production of non-United States foreign affiliates.

[24] Gerard Destanne de Bernis, "Industries industrialisantes et contenu d'une politique d'integration regionale", *Economie Appliquée* (3-4), 1966.

[25] This is an inaccurate measure, not comparable to the ratio between petroleum extraction and the other petroleum sectors, as manufacturing normally would represent a variety of production branches, not only those directly related to the processing of extracted minerals (and perhaps as a rule not at all related to mineral processing).

[26] Francois de Chassey, *Le Monde Diplomatique,* July 1973, For an account of the nationalization, see Vincent de Burctel in *Le Monde Diplomatique,* January 1975.

[27] Schatz, op. cit.; for a less critical view on the joint venture form, see Lawrence G. Franko, *Joint Ventures in Developing Countries: Mystique and Reality,* Geneva, CEI, March 1973, mimeo.

[28] OECD, *Stock of Private Direct Investments by DAC Countries in Developing Countries:* Country Notes, DD-217, mimeo, pp. 21-99.

[29] Amin, op. cit.

[30] An example of a corporate case study which gives inside information about the operations of a corporation is Claes Brundenius, "The Anatomy of Imperialism: Multinational Mining Corporations in Peru", *Journal of Peace Research* no. 3, 1972.

[31] The study is directed by Professor Raymond Vernon and was initiated in 1965. The European center of the Harvard study is the Centre d'Etudes Industrielles in Geneva.

[32] Vaupel and Curhan, op. cit. In these and other figures on subsidiaries, UAR and Libya are not included.

[33] Studies of the Central American Common Market show that US multinational corporations benefited most from the economic integration, among other things because it increased economics of scale.

[34] Vaupel and Curhan, op. cit., Table 29.1.1, pp. 499-503.

[35] R. Vernon, "International Investment and International Trade in the Product Cycle", *Quarterly Journal of Economics,* Vol. 88 (May 1966).

[36] *The Role of the Patent System in the Transfer of Technology to Developing Countries,* UNCTAD, TD/B/AC.11/19, 1974.

[37] Cf. Constantine Vaitsos, "Considerations on Technological Requirements in Developing Countries", UNIDO, ID/WG 130/2, 21 April 1972; and UNCTAD, op. cit.

[38] "Major issues arising from the transfer of technology. A case study of Ethiopia". Report by the UNCTAD Secretariat, TD/B/AC.11/21, p. 61.

[39] Calculated from Vaupel and Curhan, op, cit., pp. 270-73.

[40] Ibid, p. 379.

[41] Ibid, p. 402.

[42] Albert O. Hirschman, "How to Divest in Latin America and Why", *Essays in International Finance,* no. 76, Princeton University, Nov. 1969.

[43] This is an idea put forth in the UN study by Dr. Raoul Prebisch and others.

[44] Helge Hveem, "Anti-Domination Strategies and the 'Opecisation' of Raw Materials", International Peace Research Institute, Oslo, February 1974, draft mimeo.

Table 2. *Stock of foreign (private) direct investments in Africa, 1967 and 1972, and growth trends*
(mill. US $)

	Stock end 1967	1967 percentage of total in A.	Stock end 1972	1972 percentage of total	Perc. growth 67–72
Equatorial Guinea	...	...	...	...	...
Botswana	3	0.0	35	0.4	1 300
Gambia	2	0.0	5	0.1	117
Ghana	260	4.0	360	3.8	38
Kenya	172	2.6	235	2.5	37
Lesotho	0.5	0.0	2	0.0	300
Malawi	30	0.5	55	0.6	83
Mauritius	...	...	...	...	...
Nigeria	1 109	16.8	2 100	22.3	89
Sierra Leone	68	1.0	75	0.8	10
Sudan	37	0.6	35	0.4	–5
Swaziland	29	0.4	35	0.4	21
Tanzania	60	0.9	65	0.7	8
Uganda	48	0.7	30	0.3	–38
Zambia	421	6.4	300	3.2	–29
Anglophone Africa	*2 239*	*34.0*	*3 332*	*35.5*	*49*
Algeria	703	10.7	250	2.7	–64
Marocco	179	2.7	250	2.7	39
Tunisia	135	2.0	200	2.1	48
Cameroon	150	2.3	210	2.2	40
CAR	37	0.6	50	0.5	37
Chad	18	0.3	20	0.2	12
Congo PR	90	1.4	100	1.0	11
Dahomey	18	0.3	25	0.3	40
Gabon	265	4.0	375	4.0	41
Guinea	93	1.4	175	1.9	88
Ivory Coast	202	3.1	340	3.6	69
Madagascar	72	1.1	95	1.0	31
Mali	7	0.1	8	0.1	23
Mauretania	101	1.5	150	1.6	48
Niger	23	0.4	35	0.4	50
Senegal	154	2.3	210	2.2	37
Togo	42	0.6	65	0.7	53
Upper Volta	16	0.2	18	0.2	11
Burundi	14	0.2	18	0.2	27
Rwanda	15	0.2	17	0.2	12
Zaire	481	7.3	620	6.6	20
Francophone Africa	*2 815*	*42.7*	*3 231*	*34.4*	*15*
Angola	193	2.9	290	3.1	50
Guinea-Bissau	...	...	...	...	...
Mozambique	102	1.6	125	1.3	22
Ethiopia	50	0.8	70	0.7	39
Liberia	300	4.5	360	3.8	20
Libya	578	8.8	1 560	16.6	170
Somalia	13	0.2	15	0.2	19
UAR	58	0.9	100	1.1	72
Other Africa	*1 294*	*19.7*	*2 520*	*26.8*	*95*
Rhodesia	237	3.6	315	3.4	33
South Africa R	...	...	...	...	...
'Racist Africa'	*237*	*3.6*	*315*	*3.5*	*33*
Grand Total	**6 586**	**100.0**	**9 398**	**100.0**	**42.7**

Table 3. *Dependency and direct investments*

	Stock of foreign direct investments/GNP of country, 1967	1971	Share of metropolitan countries in the stock of foreign direct investments in Africa, 1967, %					
Equatorial Guinea	...	...						
Botswana	4	10	UK	88.0	Neth	12.0		
Gambia	10	6	UK	87.0	US	4.3		
Ghana	15	15	UK	59.1	US	24.6		
Kenya	15	11	UK	78.8	US	8.7		
Lesotho	1	2	UK	60.0	US	20.0		
Malawi	14	9	UK	92.7	US	6.7		
Mauritius	...	...	...					
Nigeria	21	22	UK	53.8	US	16.4	Neth	14.5
Sierra Leone	18	13	UK	84.4	US	13.2		
Sudan	2	2	UK	74.9	Neth	13.6		
Swaziland	39	44	UK	96.6	US	3.4		
Tanzania	7	4	UK	46.7	Ital	18.2	Denm	12.9
Uganda	7	4	UK	48.1	Cana	31.3	US	4.2
Zambia	36	19	UK	79.6	US	19.2		
'Anglophone Africa'	*17*	*15*						
Algeria	23	4	Fran	71.7	US	16.4		
Morocco	7	6	Fran	45.2	US	19.5	Ital	15.6
Tunisia	14	10	Fran	39.2	Ital	28.5	Swed	10.5
Cameron	19	17	Fran	75.1	UK	11.9		
CAR	19	19	Fran	91.8	US	4.1		
Chad	7	6	Fran	80.4	Neth	8.4		
Congo PR	72	33	Fran	83.4	Belg	6.1		
Dahomey	10	8	Fran	57.0	Ital	25.7		
Gabon	147	103	Fran	73.4	US	10.9		
Guinea	30	39	US	38.5	Fran	23.1	Swit	20.5
Ivory Coast	19	17	Fran	80.0	US	3.7		
Madagascar	10	9	Fran	76.5	US	8.3		
Mali	2	2	Fran	76.9	US	7.7		
Mauretania	65	73	Fran	68.8	UK	16.2		
Niger	8	6	Fran	95.7	US	2.1		
Senegal	19	20	Fran	87.4	US	4.4		
Togo	21	21	Fran	56.6	US	30.7		
Upper Volta	6	5	Fran	75.3	UK	12.3		
Burundi	10	8	Belg	84.5	Cana	7.1		
Rwanda	16	7	Belg	86.8	Ital	6.6		
Zaire	36	32	Belg	87.8	Neth	4.4		
'Francophone Africa'	*21*	*14*						
Angola	...	13	UK	48.6	Port	28.5	US	17.6
Guinea-Bissau	...	...						
Mozambique	...	5	UK	50.1	Port	37.2		
Ethiopia	3	3	Fran	43.7	US	23.9	UK	15.9
Liberia	125	100	US	57.8	Swed	21.7		
Libya	37	48	US	77.7	UK	10.9		
Somalia	10	7	Ital	83.3	US	7.9		
UAR	1	1	US	70.7	Ital	26.7		
'Other Africa'	*11*	*13*						
Rhodesia	22	18	UK	88.3	US	4.2		
South Africa R	...	...	...					
'Racist Africa'								

Table 4. (See pp. 86–87).

Table 5.

	Est. value of production of foreign investments 1967 Volume	Perc. of GNP	Income from exports of most important product/total export income, 1965 Percentage (Sector)	Percentage of total foreign investments to one (most important) sec.
Equatorial Guinea	...	...		
Botswana	6	8		40.0 Manufact.
Gambia	4	20	50.5 Ground nuts	56.5 Manufact.
Ghana	520	30	71.5 Cocoa	30.9 Mine & smelt.
Kenya	344	30	30.0 Coffee	32.4 Manufact.
Lesotho	1	2		60.0 Petr. mark.
Malawi	60	28	37.7 Tobacco	39.3 Agriculture
Mauritius	...	...	95.6 Sugar	
Nigeria	2 218	42	25.4 Crude petr.	65.5 Petr. prod.
Sierra Leone	136	36	64.2 Diamonds	75.6 Mine & smelt.
Sudan	74	4	46.5 Cotton	36.0 Manufact.
Swaziland	58	78		51.7 Manufact.
Tanzania	120	14	23.2 Sisal	40.4 Manufact.
Uganda	96	14	48.5 Coffee	38.5 Manufact.
Zambia	842	72	91.5 Copper	82.4 Mine & smelt.
'Anglophone Africa'	*4 477*	*34*		*31.0 Petr. prod.*
Algeria	1 406	46	61.3 Crude petr.	80.6 Petr. prod.
Morocco	358	14	26.6 Phosphates	30.1 Manufact.
Tunisia	270	28	19.9 Phosphates	38.4 Manufact.
Cameroon	300	38	27.1 Coffee	46.4 Manufact.
CAR	74	38	54.0 Diamonds	35.3 Manufact.
Chad	36	14	77.5 Cotton	67.4 Manufact.
Congo PR	180	144	38.9 Wood	54.2 Agriculture
Dahomey	36	20	51.3 Palm oil	36.9 Manufact.
Gabon	530	294	33.2 Timber	46.6 Petr. prod.
Guinea	186	60		34.5 Agriculture
Ivory Coast	404	38	37.8 Coffee	34.5 Agriculture
Madagascar	144	20	31.3 Coffee	21.1 Manufact.
Mali	14	4	33.0 Livestock	38.5 Petr. mark.
Mauretania	202	130	55.0 Fish	92.5 Mine & smelt.
Nigeria	46	16	49.0 Ground nuts	33.9 Manufact.
Senegal	308	38	70.9 Ground nuts	30.2 Manufact.
Togo	84	42	32.9 Phosphates	68.6 Mine & smelt.
Upper Volta	32	12	56.9 Livestock	26.5 Mine & smelt.
Burundi	28	20	82.5	57.8 Manufact.
Rwanda	30	32	53.9 Coffee	47.4 Manufact.
Zaire	962	72	68.2 Copper	41.1 Manufact.
'Francophone Africa'	*5 630*	*42*		*26.6 Petr. prod.*
Angola	386	...	46.8 Coffee	48.6 Transport.
Guinea-Bissau	...	...	17.8 Cotton	
Mozambique	204	...	17.8 Cotton	36.2 Manufact.
Ethiopia	100	6	66.5 Coffee	43.7 Transport
Liberia	600	250	73.3 Iron ore	62.0 Mine & smelt.
Libya	1 156	72	99.4 Crude petr.	77.7 Petr. prod.
Somalia	26	20	45.6 Bananas	52.4 Manufact.
UAR	116	2	55.6 Cotton	60.3 Petr. prod.
'Other Africa'	*2 588*	*22*		*39.6 Petr. prod.*
Rhodesia	237	44	33.0 Tobacco	49.1 Manufact.
South Africa R	...	...	12.9 Diamonds	

Table 4: *Foreign direct investments in African countries* (by sector stocks end 1967, percentages)

	Petroleum production	Petroleum refining	Petroleum marketing	Petroleum transport	Mining and smelting	Agriculture	Manufacturing	Trade	Public utilities	Transport	Banking	Tourism	Other
Equatorial Guinea													
Botswana	0	0	20.0	0	20.0	0	40.0	0	0	0	20.0	0	0
Gambia	0	0	13.0	0	0	0	56.5	21.7	0	0	8.7	0	0
Ghana	0	7.7	9.2	0	30.9	0.6	26.5	20.9	0	0	3.8	0	0.4
Kenya	0	7.5	5.8	0	0	21.4	32.4	16.9	0	0.6	4.9	4.4	6.2
Lesotho	0	0	60.0	0	0	0	0	0	0	0	40.0	0	0
Malawi	0	0	13.3	0	0	39.3	9.0	10.0	0	0	6.7	0	21.7
Mauritius													
Nigeria	65.5	1.3	1.8	0	1.4	0.5	14.8	9.9	0	0	2.4	0	2.4
Sierra Leone	0	0	5.1	0	85.6	0	8.5	8.7	0	0	1.5	0	0.6
Sudan	0	32.7	8.2	0	1.4	0	36.0	9.5	0	5.5	6.8	0	0
Swaziland	0	0	6.9	0	37.9	0	51.7	0	0	0	3.5	0	0
Tanzania	0	11.6	9.9	0	0	34.4	40.4	0	0	0	0	0	3.6
Uganda	0	0	16.7	0	18.8	8.3	38.5	3.1	0	0	12.5	0	2.1
Zambia	0	0	1.9	0	82.4	1.8	7.8	3.3	0	0.2	0.7	1.0	0.9
'Anglophone Africa'	*31.0*	*2.8*	*3.9*	*0*	*26.0*	*4.0*	*17.3*	*9.5*	*0*	*0.2*	*2.7*	*0.5*	*2.3*
Algeria	80.6	4.1	0	18.3	0	0	4.0	0.4	0	0	0.1	0.6	0
Morocco	0.6	8.9	10.0	0	21.8	0	30.1	6.3	0	2.8	5.0	10.0	4.5
Tunisia	12.6	8.9	7.8	7.4	5.9	0	38.4	3.7	0	3.7	3.0	5.7	3.0
Cameron	0	0	8.7	0	12.0	24.6	46.4	4.4	1.7	0	2.3	0	0
CAR	0	0	8.2	0	5.5	34.4	35.3	2.7	11.2	0	2.7	0	0
Chad	0	0	11.2	0	0	15.7	67.4	2.8	0	0	2.8	0	0
Congo PR	1.1	0	6.1	0	22.2	54.2	9.8	3.7	0	0	3.0	0	0
Dahomey	0	0	27.9	0	0	13.4	36.9	14.0	0	0	7.8	0	0
Gabon	46.6	2.4	0.9	0	34.7	6.1	1.6	3.0	3.9	0	0.8	0	0
Guinea	0	0	1.0	0	88.3	0	8.6	2.2	0	0	0	0	0
Ivory Coast	0	7.6	4.7	0	6.0	34.5	31.0	5.5	8.2	0	2.5	0	0
Madagascar	0	19.3	13.8	0	6.9	13.3	21.1	5.5	7.6	5.5	6.9	0	0

Mali	0	0	38.5	0	0	0	30.8	15.4	0	0	15.4	0	0
Mauretania	0	0	0.7	0	92.4	5.4	0.4	0.4	0.6	0	0.1	0	0
Niger	0	0	8.6	0	23.8	12.9	35.9	6.4	10.3	0	2.2	0	0
Senegal	0	5.9	3.6	0	18.5	31.1	30.2	3.9	4.6	0	1.8	0	0.7
Togo	0	0	10.6	0	68.6	2.6	5.4	9.4	0	0	3.3	0	0
Upper Volta	0	0	24.7	0	0	18.8	26.5	12.4	13.6	0	3.1	0	0
Burundi	0	0	10.6	0	3.5	7.0	57.8	7.0	7.0	0	7.0	0	0
Rwanda	0	0	6.6	0	26.3	0	47.4	6.6	6.6	0	6.6	0	0
Zaire	0	2.1	1.7	0	13.1	14.6	41.1	7.3	2.1	15.6	2.5	0	0
'Francophone Africa'	*26.6*	*4.2*	*5.2*	*0*	*15.4*	*12.2*	*22.9*	*4.1*	*2.4*	*3.3*	*2.1*	*1.1*	*0.5*
Angola	11.4	1.6	1.6	6.2	18.9	1.6	8.2	1.0	0	48.6	1.0	0	0
Guinea-Bissau													
Mozambique	6.9	7.8	5.9	9.4	11.7	5.9	36.2	9.4	2.9	0	3.9	0	0
Ethiopia	0	0	9.9	0	0	6.0	35.8	2.6	0	43.7	2.0	0	0
Liberia	0	2.0	1.0	0	62.0	19.5	4.3	9.5	0	0	1.7	0	0
Libya	77.7	12.6	1.4	0	0	0	2.4	1.9	0	0.7	1.0	0	2.3
Somalia	0	0	11.9	0	15.9	0	52.4	0	0	19.8	0	0	0
UAR	60.3	8.6	17.2	0	0	0	3.5	5.2	0	0	0	5.2	0
'Other Africa'	*39.6*	*7.3*	*2.8*	*1.7*	*18.2*	*5.5*	*8.2*	*4.3*	*0.2*	*9.5*	*1.4*	*0.2*	*1.0*
Rhodesia	0	8.4	7.2	0	10.7	3.7	49.1	4.7	0	1.0	2.1	0	13.1
South Africa R													
Grand Total	**29.6**	**4.4**	**3.9**	**1.6**	**19.4**	**7.5**	**18.8**	**6.0**	**1.0**	**3.4**	**2.1**	**0.7**	**1.7**

Table 6. *Production profiles of the underdeveloped regions according to the distribution of foreign investments on types of productive activity, 1967* (percentages)

	Africa	Asia	Latin America	Middle East	All
Processing activities (manufacturing and petroleum refining)	23.4	41.5	41.7	23.3	36.3
Extractive activities (petroleum production, mining and smelting and agriculture)	56.4	28.9	28.5	47.7	36.9
(Petroleum production only)	(29.5)	(5.0)	(14.2)	(47.4)	(19.0)
'Service' activities (transport, petroleum marketing, trade, public utilities, banking, tourism and other)	20.2	29.6	29.8	29.0	26.8
	100.0	100.0	100.0	100.0	100.0

Table 7. *Gross domestic product and stock of foreign direct investments by type of economic activity, 1967 (68)* (percentages)

	Processing		Extractive		'Services'		Other	
	GDP	INV	GDP	INV	GDP	INV	GDP	INV
Equatorial Guinea	...	...	...	...	...	...	...	...
Botswana	6	60	43	20	17	20	30	0
Gambia	...	57	...	0	...	43	...	0
Ghana	...	34	...	32	...	34	...	0
Kenya	11	40	35	21	22	33	25	6
Lesotho	1	0	64	0	8	100	22	0
Malawi	8	9	34	40	17	30	36	22
Mauritius	13	...	23	...	26	...	24	...
Nigeria	5	16	59	67	22	14	9	2
Sierra Leone	5	9	50	76	23	15	14	1
Sudan	9	69	41	1	34	30	16	0
Swaziland	13	52	48	38	17	10	17	0
Tanzania	8	52	41	34	24	10	19	4
Uganda	7	39	54	27	20	32	19	2
Zambia	11	8	46	84	24	7	15	1
Algeria	...	8	...	81	...	11	...	0
Morocco	13	39	43	22	26	34	18	5
Tunisia	13	47	21	19	27	31	25	3
Cameroon	...	46	70	37	18	17	11	0
CAR	...	35	...	40	...	25	...	0
Chad	...	67	...	16	...	17	...	0
Congo PR	...	10	...	78	...	13	...	0
Dahomey	5	37	41	13	30	50	18	0
Gabon	4	4	43	87	35	9	17	0
Guinea	...	9	...	88	...	3	...	0
Ivory Coast	7	39	34	41	32	21	9	0
Madagascar	11	40	33	20	25	39	27	0
Mali	...	31	...	0	...	69	...	0
Mauretania	...	0	...	98	...	2	...	0
Niger	6	34	59	37	21	28	13	0
Senegal	...	36	...	50	...	14	...	1
Togo	10	5	52	71	20	23	11	0
Upper Volta	5	27	46	20	18	54	15	0
Burundi	...	58	...	11	...	32	...	0
Rwanda	...	47	...	26	...	26	...	0
Zaire	16	43	27	28	20	29	34	0
Angola	...	10	...	32	...	58	...	0
Guinea-Bissau	...	...	...	...	...	...	...	...
Mozambique	...	44	...	25	...	32	...	0
Ethiopia	9	36	56	6	18	58	16	0
Liberia	4	6	55	82	22	12	20	0
Libya	2	15	61	78	17	5	16	2
Somalia	...	52	...	16	...	32	...	0
UAR	...	12	...	60	...	28	...	0
Rhodesia	19	58	26	14	25	15	24	13
South Africa R	24	...	23	...	27	...	25	...

Note. The GDP percentages do not add to 100% because import duties are in many cases not included in the reported industrial groups.

Table 8. *Percentage breakdown of number of manufacturing subsidiaries of non-US-based parent systems by subsidiary's country classified by principal industry-group of subsidiary*

Principal Industry-group of Subsidiary as of 1.1.71	Latin-America	Africa[1]	British Africa	French Africa	South Africa and Rhodesia
Food and Tobacco	9.1	9.4	8.1	0.6	14.9
Textiles and Apparel	14.3	9.3	5.7	0.4	5.8
Wood, Furniture, Paper	5.8	7.3	5.3	1.5	9.6
Chemicals	14.5	4.8	3.3	1.1	5.6
Petroleum	4.6	15.7	3.1	10.8	3.6
Rubber and Tires	6.5	4.6	4.6	0.0	12.9
Primary Metals	9.4	5.2	2.4	2.1	9.7
Fabr. Metal + Non-El. Mach.	11.1	4.3	2.6	1.2	5.6
Electric and Electron.	12.0	4.0	2.1	1.9	6.0
Transportation Equipment	19.0	6.0	3.2	2.0	8.5
Precision goods	5.2	0.0	0.0	0.0	5.1
Other	8.0	6.6	4.8	1.2	3.3

[1]UAR, Libya, South Africa and Rhodesia not included.

Table 9. *Patents granted during 1971, patents in force at the end of 1971 and patents granted to foreigners.*

Country	No. of patents in force end 1971	No. of patents granted in 1971	% of patents granted in 1971 held by foreigners	USA	W. Germ.	UK	France	EEC	Switz.	Japan	USSR	Comecon
Gambia	24	16	100.0	50.0	37.5	6.2	—	43.7	6.2	—	—	—
Ghana	...	98	100.0	26.5	17.3	25.5	1.0	51.0	6.1	1.0	—	9.1
Kenya[3]	1402	122	99.2	25.6	18.2	29.7	0.8	52.8	7.4	1.6	—	—
Malawi	803	5	100.0	20.0	—	20.0	2.7[2]	40.0	5.4[2]	—	—	—
Mauritius	64	3	100.0	33.3	—	33.3	33.3	66.7	5.0[4]	—	—	10.0[4]
Sierra Leone	...	22	100.0	27.3	22.7	27.3	—	54.5	13.6	4.5	—	—
Uganda	1612	83	100.0	22.9	15.6	33.7	—	53.0	6.0	1.2	—	—
Zambia	1710	115	99.1	28.9	0.8	19.2	7.0	33.3	2.6	2.6	—	—
Algeria	1949[1]	369[2]	99.2[2]	22.4[2]	4.6[2]	3.6[2]	2.4[2]	49.5[2]	12.0[2]	0.2[2]	3.3[2]	8.3[2]
Morocco	3375	337	92.9	15.3	10.2	5.1	40.2	65.8	6.3	0.6	2.5	4.4
Tunisia	...	150	98.0	21.8	8.1	6.8	29.2	57.8	12.9	0.6	0.6	2.7
OAMPI[5]	2838	470	96.8	17.1	5.7	6.3	37.5	56.7	16.9	1.3	—	0.8
Burundi	58	5	100.0	40.0	20.0	—	—	40.0	20.0	—	—	—
Rwanda	51	9	100.0	11.1	11.1	22.2	11.1	55.5	22.2	—	—	—
Somalia	...	5	100.0	60.0	—	—	—	40.0	—	—	—	—
Egypt	...	156	98.1	26.1	13.1	3.9	6.5	34.6	9.1	1.3	11.1	21.5
Rhodesia	3263	377	98.2	...	...	...	...	...	...	...	...	...
S. Africa	28187	7027	70.2[2]	31.9[2]	14.0[2]	20.0[2]	5.3[2]	46.5[2]	7.9[2]	2.8[2]	0.0[2]	0.3[2]

(—means the number is zero, blank means not current, . . . means data not available.)

Slurce: Industrial Property, *Monthly review of the World Intellectual Property Organization.* December 1972, Annex, Chart 1a and Chart 1b

[1] Including patents or certificates of addition
[2] Patent applications and percentages of total applications, patents granted are n.a.
[3] Patents are not originally issued in Kenya but only registered on the basis of patents previously granted in the United Kingdom
[4] Values are from 1972.
[5] The African and Malagasy Industrial Property Office.

Reginald Herbold Green[1]

The Peripheral African Economy and the MNC:

Free trade for planned capitalism, a new and sharper division of labour, greater income and greater dependence, structural change and widening inequality, and notes toward alternative patterns

> So far nobody has produced an alternative to the (MNC World) vision . . . a depressingly feudal vision of Western workers living off the backs of workers in the poor countries with multinationals, as the bailiffs for the rich. But what other possibilities are there?
>
> Michael Ashfield[2]

> A truly liberated nation is a self-reliant nation, one which has freed itself from economic and cultural dependence on other nations, and is therefore able to develop itself in free and equal co-operation with other members of the world community.
>
> Mwalimu J. K. Nyerere[3]

> That tree that grows
> There splendidly alone . . .
> Is Africa, your Africa. It puts forth new shoots
> With patience and stubborness puts forth new shoots.
> Slowly its fruits grow to have
> The harsh, strong taste of liberty.
>
> David Diop

The study of multinational corporation penetration of, operations in, and relations with African economies is often confused by inadequate analysis based on dubious fundamental assumptions. Three of the latter are:

1. the MNC *is* the inevitable wave of the future;
2. the MNC is a *diabolis ex machina* (or a *deus ex machina*) which will worsen (or solve) all African political economic problems;
3. the proper study of African—MNC relationships from the African side is how to "respond" and "react" to the MNCs.

The first assumption is hardly self-evident: China *does* exist; the Socialist European pattern of relations with MNCs is quantitatively different from that of small capitalist or developing economy politics; even Canada and Australia are reasserting their political economic sovereignty to some degree. Nevertheless, if a small political economic unit *believes* that an MNC world is inevitable, its actions are likely to validate the assumption so far as its own MNC relationships are concerned.

The second assumption is a gross oversimplification. It is peculiarly anti-Marxian, and anti-historical in general, because it combines both conspiratorial and single, uncontradicted force elements. It is anti-empirical because there is plenty of evidence that degrees of penetration and exact positive and negative results vary from country to country and case to case. When coupled with the first assumption, it leads either to febrile anarchic resistance, passive fatalistic acceptance, or exuberant welcome of any and all MNC initiatives.

The third proposition, like the first pair, is grossly Eurocentric. It denies the possibility of independent African aims. It is an intellectually neo-colonial approach, however anti-capitalist or paternalistically "pro-African" it may be. It is the opposite of liberation.

This is *not* to say that an African state can act as if it were completely separate from the world system. It is not to deny that tactics do depend on estimating probable external constraints and reactions to African measures and how the African states can loosen the constraints and meet (or use) the reactions. The essential point is to start from the premise of African aims for the benefit of Africans and to formulate strategies and policies from that starting point—*not* to start from external trends, realities, and aims in order to formulate a pattern of African tactical responses whose aims are thus, at best, mirror images (whether literal, inverted, or distorted) of those items to which they are reacting.

This study considers six clusters of issues:

1. certain key analytical operating premises in respect of the political economy of MNC—African relationships;
2. the essential characteristics of MNCs from the point of view of the African unit dealing with them;
3. the MNCs' nature as the modern standard-bearer of planned capitalism (including state capitalism) and free trade;
4. the potentialities and limitations of MNCs as instruments for altering the global division of labour and of income;
5. the logical hierarchy of dependence and domination centred on ownership and control of knowledge and the power to create it which lies at the heart of the logic of the MNC worldview and the implications of such a

hierarchy for both global and national structures of production and of income distribution;

6. notes toward an alternative strategy of use of international economic opportunities in the service of African economic liberation.

II

Some of the above premises may appear trite. Nevertheless, in practice, failure to accept (or at any rate to internalize) them seems to lie at the root of numerous policy errors and analytical confusions. African—MNC relations are not zero-sum games (using that term in its mathematical sense). Rarely will the result of a continued or changed relationship be to leave the direct economic product (let alone the total direct and indirect political, economic, and social product) the same and alter only its distribution between the African polity and the MNC. It is quite possible for both parties to gain or for both to lose. In creating new relationships (as opposed to altering past ones) there is everything to be said for seeking out positive-sum games, so that the debate is over the sharing of the surplus, not over who is to lose!

Any viable *new* relationship must have an acceptable cost/benefit ratio to both parties. Knowing something about the other party's cost and benefit estimates is vital to being able to push (negotiate) him closer to his minimum acceptable level and to choosing changes which have high benefits to the African party relative to their costs to the MNC. When changing entrenched unequal relationships, the calculations are rather different. Unless a great efficiency gain is likely, the former (present) exploitative party must lose.

One implication here is that the substitution of joint ventures for regulation of foreign private firms does *not* necessarily injure the African parties even if it is welcomed by the European parties. If the regulation and the uncertainty surrounding it were to seriously damage productive efficiency and its development, then a new form of relationship could be beneficial to both parties.

Second, national economies are not homogenous wholes nor is there necessarily any dominant power group making individual relationship decisions on the basis of national economic gain (as measured by, say, GNP). Especially in capitalist systems, individual economic unit decisions (and especially the decisions of its economic units when operating abroad) are taken on the basis of benefits to individual firm or group interests subject to fairly loose national interest constraints at the macro and sectoral levels.

This sheds light on the colonial gains and losses argument. French concessionaires gained (some made serious errors of judgement or procedure and lost, but that is not unusual) in the initial era of French penetration of the Congo but it is hard to argue the same for the French economy as a whole.

Nevertheless, such a statement is less than no evidence against the proposition that great economic (as well as social, political, and physical) damage was done to the economy of the "French" Congo as a territorial unit and to the vast majority of the people directly or indirectly affected. A small colporteur class of clerks, foremen and sub-traders probably gained economically, so that the non-homogeneity is as real in the penetrated as in the penetrating economy.[4]

Unfortunately, the implications for current African—MNC relationships are distinctly unsatisfactory. To the extent that a European-oriented elite in the government bureaucracy, manipulative political parties, and associated local businessmen dependent on government favour and foreign business support take decisions designed to benefit their own groups, there is no guarantee that these decisions will further African interests taken as a whole.

This is *not* merely to say that class interests diverge. It is to say rather more—that in a neocolonial situation the interests of a privileged enclave elite are likely to be complementary to those of foreign economic (or for that matter political or military) interests and not to those of other classes in their own country.[5] It is idle to talk of alternative strategies based on African mass interests or even African national-economy interests without a careful analysis of the domestic power structure and the effects of the alternative strategy on their interests. A nationalistic bourgeois strategy is *not* impossible in principle; given, however, the weakness, dependence, and existing transnational interest linkages in many African states, there must be grave doubts as to whether such a strategy is practicable.[6]

Third, the same individual contractual relationship means very different things in different contexts. For example, China's exports of carved ivory (a luxury consumer good), pig bristles (a byproduct raw material), and soy beans (an agricultural raw material), are significant absolutely and as a proportion of its total exports. The same can be said of wood carvings, hides and skins, and coffee in the case of Tanzania. This does *not* mean that the degrees of external dependence of the two economies are similar.

Similarly, it is possible to interpret certain Chinese factory purchase—erection—testing—training package deals as turnkey purchases plus technical consultancy contracts. Do such contracts have the same meaning in respect of—say—a fertilizer plant in China and in Senegal? Surely *not*, because in one case the foreign relationship is limited as to scope, size, and direction and in the other it is part of a system of penetration and domination which embraces virtually the entire modern directly productive and public service sectors.

Fourth, even the same sets of relationships have different meanings in different historic and sociopolitical contexts. If the present Tanzania pattern of 100% public sector productive units, joint ventures, and managerial/technical/sale contracts is looked at as an isolated snapshot one can say that it illustrates a high level of dependence, although one lower than that of most other African states. If one adds another snapshot of the same institutions and relationships in 1967 and a resumé of the evolving strategic commitment to a self-reliant transformation to participatory socialism, a rather deeper and more detailed analysis is possible as to direction of change and increasing (or decreasing) congruence between the relationships actually existing and the direction of their change, and the stated political, economic, and socio-political commitment.

The differences—and they are very real ones—among Kenya, Zambia, and Tanzania would be underestimated on the single-snapshot basis. They would be much more clearly seen in the context of historic change patterns and of the political and economic goal context to which they related (whether by dominating or responding to it). This premise illustrates the absurdity of arguing that because the USSR has used foreign capital, knowledge and management inputs formed into *de facto* joint ventures both in the New Economic Policy period and again during the past five years, one can therefore define the USSR as a capitalist-inclined, dependent economy. Similarly, it means that much further analysis is needed to defend the proposition that the present Egyptian welcome to foreign capital and capitalists will be akin either to the NEP or the present Soviet contracts and not to the Mahamet Ali foreign involvement period in Egypt or the foreign takeover of the Chilean economy at the close of the 19th century. Is Egypt really strong enough politically, socially, ideologically, and economically to avoid being dominated by its "guests"?

Fifth, the belief in powerlessness is self-fulfilling. (The inverse is, whether fortunately or no, not generally valid.) If those negotiating or planning for an African state believe that there are no (or very limited) ways to reduce unilateral external dependence, to reverse past unequal bargains, to negotiate mutually advantageous external economic relationships, these beliefs will prove true. No serious efforts to determine, seek, and achieve the limits of the possible, and to do so in a way which push the limits outward, will be made.

This is not a trivial point. No one believed that the British government could be forced to accept responsibility for the pensions of her ex-colonial offices until Tanzania unilaterally shifted the obligation. It was in 1967 standard wisdom that bank nationalization in Africa would lead to chaos, corruption and collapse. Tanzania refused to accept that premise and proved it false. Until 1970 (and to a lingering extent until 1973), it was "clear" that a producer's cartel (like OPEC) could have only a marginal impact on world prices for raw materials or on their sharing between producer states and international companies. Who would contend that today or insist that petroleum was a unique case?

Changes in unequal relationships in favour of African states and a successive shift in the pattern of new relationships toward greater interdependence and fairer division of gains will not come by chance, an invisible hand, or appeals to goodwill or charity. They will only come through careful assessment by African states of their own needs and potentials, and through their concentration and deployment of what power they have to achieve changes.

Sixth, the search for an alternative strategy does not imply that every African state as now structured can pursue such a strategy, much less that it will, nor that all African elite groups would benefit from such action. The preconditions for radical change from within an initially externally-oriented, dependent, hierarchical class structure are very complex—some African states appear to possess them (e.g., Guinea-Bissau, Mozambique, Tanzania); for others, it is likely that revolution is needed (e.g., Ethiopia).

Seventh, an establishment can be the servant of radical change under two somewhat different sets of conditions. The first is that the establishment is personally committed to radical change, whether because it is in its own interests (e.g., in Sao Paulo during 1950-1965) or because its vision is broader than personal self-interest (e.g., at least a significant part of the Chinese establishment). Second, there may be adequate external checks (whether from private industrialists in—say—Nigeria or from organized mass political groups in—say—Tanzania) for the establishment to find it necessary to work to achieve radical change, whether this is self-evidently in its own interests or not.[7]

This applies to radical change in the broad sense, e.g., to industrialization (which can be radical structural change) as much as to a transition to greater egalitarianism or to socialism. The two conditions are not separate: the longer the establishment is constrained to act in a given way the more likely it is to internalize the values consistent with that course of action and the greater the success of educational efforts to secure commitment by at least a part of the establishment, and the less the tightness and omnipresence of checks needed. In a situation in which major establishment deviation from radical change is foreclosed by outside checks, individually committed members of the establishment will find it easier to formulate, propose, and secure adoption of the instruments of such change and passive resisters will find blocking such initiatives much harder and more dangerous to their own positions.[8]

Radical change is likely to be viewed sceptically by most managerial and civil service establishment figures, unless the case for it (or their personal commitment to it) is very strong. Such change involves immediate disturbances, costs, and inconveniences which the administrator or manager—unlike the political or economic entrepreneur—is likely to overestimate. Such inertia is both different from, and narrower than, the defence of the status quo as a system beneficial to oneself, a defence which underpins the neo-colonial reality in many African states by making the groups of the African establishment its most numerous and effective defenders.

III

The basis of the multinational corporation's strength is knowledge. It is ownership (whether *de jure* or *de facto*) of, ability to use, ready facilities for procuring, and (for the strongest) the power to create knowledge which are integral to being a successful multinational corporation. Neither breadth of activities geographically nor sectorally is enough, nor is volume of physical assets owned. Flexibility and adaptability are indeed distinguishing characteristics, but these flow from the basic role of knowledge because knowledge (including the capacity to procure or create additional or new knowledge) is the most flexible of all assets.[9]

This assertion does not contradict the premise that ownership is basic. It merely asserts that ultimately the ownership of knowledge, at least when organized into strong units, can dominate the ownership of fixed assets embodying, or institutions using, selected portions of that knowledge. It is equally not a contradiction of the aspects of micro-economic theory relating to distinctions between competitive and oligopolistic markets. The more sellers there are of any particular type of knowledge and the easier it is for the fixed-asset and institution owner to build up his own "knowledge asset stock", the more competitive the market. A cleaning or a catering firm is not able to extract monopoly profits from its clients (although it may from its employees) because access to its specialized knowledge is too widely available. A computer manufacturer—renter—servicer, however, is in a very different position. That industry illustrates a further proposition—technological knowledge alone without knowledge as to application and marketing is inadequate. On the purely scientific—technological front a case can be made that Control Data and Univac are superior to IBM; in terms of a marketable package of knowledge IBM is very clearly far ahead.

The price which can be obtained for any particular knowledge package depends not only on how many (and how separate) the sellers are but on how disparate buyer and seller knowledge levels are, how vital the missing parts of the knowledge package are to the buyer, and how well the buyer knows the sellers' costs and the alternative sources of supply (in itself a form of knowledge and case). Nigeria—seeking to build up a national propertied bourgeois as well as a national technical capacity—has stressed moving toward substantial or even majority scattered private Nigerian holdings of shares combined with training of citizens. Tanzania, because of its commitment to a transition to socialism, stresses rapid general progress toward the fifth case with the sixth transitional and the fourth an increasingly common target. The shift from five to four represents the gaining of experience and with it certain aspects of knowledge previously in the management package.

Chad is in a weaker position to seek case six (let alone stage four) than the Cameroon or the Congo because of its far more limited array of knowledge and its lesser bargaining power. It may of course get case five simply because the ownership risk is unattractive to MNCs, but that is a somewhat unfortunate reason for acquisition of asset ownership and risk. Similarly, Ghana can insist on at least case four in respect of brewing or distilling but not yet in respect of aluminium smelting (for technical and marketing reasons).

IV

MNCs are the major standard-bearers of planned capitalism, including free trade and orderly (but not non-existent) competition. Proponents see them as "Up Dating Adam Smith"[13] and meeting the needs of a new age.[14]

> The structure of a multinational corporation is a modern concept designed to meet the requirements of a modern age; the nation state is a very old-fashioned idea and badly adapted to serve the needs of our present world.

Even their critics—and those who find this vision of an anti-Marxian "withering away of the state" as highly overstated[15]—see them as at the core of expansion, co-ordination, and allocation of productive forces.[16]

Almost equally prevalent is the view that the key arena for MNC upgrading of efficiency and expansion of production over the next thirty years will be the present poor countries (or a selected handful of them blessed with acquiescent labour forces, production-minded governments, and relatively large internal markets and natural resource bases). To cite an admittedly extreme view—but one which is the policy line of *The Economist*[17]:

> The manufacturing age of the rich countries is coming to a close. During the 1950's and 1960's continental Europe has thrived on increasing its manufacturing production, partly because it has drawn in cheaper labour from its south. In the next two decades manufacturing industry is going to move south to that cheaper labour instead. By the late 1980's the normal way of manufacturing both soft and durable goods, up to and including motor cars, will be for the computer at the multinational corporation's head office in California or Japan or the European confederation to talk by satellite to the computer in its manufacturing plants in what are now underdeveloped countries—controlling

their accounting systems, logistic systems, production flow, and sending package programmes to teach semi-skilled labour techniques to masses of workers on the spot. All signs suggest that these knowledge-based multinational corporations will be mainly incorporated within the company law systems of the three noncommunist superpowers. [If England does not reorganize itself fast it will] compete with the Pakistanis and Algerians for some of the contracts to make gewgaws at the Euramerican or Japanese computers' command . . .

The same theme has been explored in great depth in recent books by L. Turner (who is somewhat ambivalent on its desirability)[18] and N. Macrae (who has no such doubts)[19] and has appeared as an element in much recent work on MNCs, including that by those who see the MNC as an antagonistic or ambivalent force.[20]

Planned capitalism is used here in the Galbraithan[21] sense of the planned as opposed to the cut-throat competitive sector. A large corporation seeks to minimize both uncertainty and factors not under its control. It deliberately seeks to collect as much data as possible and test alternative operating strategies against most probable, less favourable, and more favourable external event patterns. Indeed, an MNC planning system is very often larger and its planning process more sophisticated than that of any African country.

Nevertheless, the MNC is *not* concerned with the welfare of any national economic unit (except as a constraint) nor with the general social, production, and income distribution consequences of its actions.[22] If Africa can produce a raw or processed input for its industrial economy plants more cheaply, an MNC will seek an end to protection of an inefficient European industry. Similarly, if sisal twine can be produced more economically in Tanzania than Europe, the more alert members of the industry (even if of less than MNC stature) will wish to move to Tanzania and either break the *de facto* European marketing cartel or have their quotas shifted from the European to Tanzanian plants. Similarly, if paying far higher than normal wages and salaries to citizens will buy choice of employees, labour peace, and local middle level management loyality the MNC will often pay them with very little (and possibly purely *pro forma*) government or trade union pressure.[23]

Conversely, the MNC will not take into account gains to the economy from backward, forward, or lateral linkages unless it can capture them. These may be the most valuable effects of a project to the African state. For example, a mine and infrastructure to export thermal coal which allows low marginal cost coal for reconverting thermal power plants and locomotives and building a coal chemical industry might be very valuable to several African political economic units (e.g., Tanzania, Botswana, Zambia), even if the direct return on the coal mining and infrastructure investment were low. But the power, rail, and (perhaps) chemical gains would not accrue to the MNC and so could not significantly affect its decision. The high-wage policy—however justified for the MNC and however well within its ability to pay—can also be harmful. It distorts income distribution, drags up wages in sectors whose productivity (or revenue base for public services) will not support them; "buys loyalty" all too fully and too well by creating citizen groups with highly vested interests in defending many of the MNC's interests as their own.[24]

To assert that MNCs are the standard-bearers of free trade may seem somewhat contradictory, but only if one believes that free trade and perfect competition are inseparable. In fact, a more basic and more consistent historical meaning of free trade has been the right of the economically strong to use their economic power free from the erection of special governmental devices to protect the economically weak. To that extent the MNCs *are* the heirs of Adam Smith and not—as is sometimes argued—of the mercantilist tradition.[25]

MNCs are hardly prone to engaging in cutthroat competition (except by accident) but they do have a real (if implicit) code of competitive conduct quite capable of driving the truly inefficient to the verge of bankruptcy and of significant swings in relative positions among relatively efficient firms, including formerly weaker ones which sharply raise efficiency. So long as this code is followed, competition is accepted; when devices of a grossly monopolistic nature are used to damage an efficient competitor, then, *and only then*, does the large firm go to court for redress.

These propositions flow from the MNCs' nature as standard-bearers of planned capitalism (or of planned socialist participation in the basically capitalist international economic system).[26] No planner wants constraints irrelevant to his goals imposed on him and any sensible planner wants some freedom to compete against other planning units within a code of conduct which bans "dirty tricks" or conduct likely to cause generalized chaos. For example, unless a national planner sees income distribution and poverty eradication as among his goals, he will be sharply critical of any attempt to impose them as constraints on his attempts to increase national product and control inflation (*vide* Senhor Delfim Neto, the former Brazilian Finance Minister). An MNC will *not* welcome locational constraints within a common market. A rational planner will, however, accept a constraint if it is either inevitable *or* offers a new resource (*vide* again that Senhor Delfim Neto was willing to talk of rural poverty elimination when the World Bank suggested cheap funds could be made available for that purpose *and no other*). If acceptance of a regional allocation scheme is a prerequisite to entry and entry will be profitable, an MNC will accept the constraint.[27]

Britain's 19th-century policy is relevant. The imperialism of free trade via pre-colonial neo-colonialism in West Africa and Southeast Asia and post-colonial neo-colonialism in Former Spanish America was seen as more profitable to the mercantile and industrial interests as a whole than colonialism. Backing "friendly" states (e.g., the Fanti against Ashanti), punitive wars to enforce trade (e.g., the first two Burmese wars), prevention of reconquest of American Colonies (enforced by the British Fleet, not President Monroe) all backed this strategy. It was abandoned where one or more of three constraints arose: neo-colonial states became unable to provide trade facilities (e.g., West Africa), settled colonization was practicable (e.g., South Africa), or pre-emptive French, German, or Leopoldian colonization blocked the free trade via dependent states option.

The MNC parallel is similar in its main features. MNCs would *prefer* a world free from all trade barriers. This they know is unattainable. As a first detente they ignore barriers in fields not of much concern to them—to date most agriculture and first-stage processing.[28]

Nevertheless, the marginally adjusted first best is not usually practicable. As a second best, MNCs seek large regional free-trading areas plus reduction of tariffs to zero on intraindustrial economy trade and on industrial economy imports from poor countries if the production of these imports in poor countries is of interest to the MNCs directly or their lower cost will benefit MNC manufacturing profits.

Finally, *if* a single developing economy clearly is inward-looking, planning on a protected-market basis, *and* has a large enough market for a product to make production interesting, then an MNC will be willing to operate in that framework rather than being pre-empted out. Brazil and Kenya are examples of this *faute de mieux* strategy, albeit in both cases the MNCs clearly seek to open up broader free-trading areas in smaller, weaker, political economic units adjacent to, and served from, their satellitic sub-centres.

From the point of view of African political economic units, several points emerge:

a. since MNCs seek to maximize gains within the constraints a national framework imposes, it is critical to know national minimum frame requirements before dealing with MNCs;

b. some strategies—e.g., planned regional economic integration—can further both national and MNC interests *but* must be pursued with care to avoid MNC pre-emption of the strategy to serve only its own interests;

c. "free trade" has never been the weapon of the weak. The analysts of economic catching-up who worked from the point of view of the economy which had to catch up have always believed state intervention essential. This is true of conservatives, liberal democrats, bourgeois champions and radical socialists alike. The pure "free trade" goal of the MNCs is inimical to African interests and great care must be taken before accepting particular pieces of it. E.g., unilateral free trade on *all* products from Africa *to* industrial economies would be valuable; free trade on raw or semi-processed exports but *not* manufactures made from them would be structurally and dynamically harmful.[29]

Controlled competition also has implications. First, it is unusual for more than one MNC to enter a free-trading area (national or regional) unless two or more can operate profitably. This constraint is not universally followed—the larger the market or the smaller the MNC, the more numerous the exceptions. It does *not*, apparently, apply to seeking to establishing a plant—formal or informal agreements on which firms will approach which countries seem less common (although one operated in respect of tyre plants in East Africa) and bargaining (i.e., reducing initial demands) one which requires time, effort, money, skilled personnel, and applied experience to acquire). Presumably, it is self-evident that on all of these points African states (and even more so, individual African-owned firms) are usually in a very weak position.

From the point of view of an African state, any foreign corporate seller of knowledge (whether alone or as part of a package deal including other elements) is effectively an MNC. It does not matter whether the MNC is engaged in one line of activity or many, is a private or a state corporation, is large or small. This is true even if the MNC in question has quite limited and minor interests outside its home base, e.g., Eastern Airlines in respect of its technical and managerial advisory services contract with East African Airways *is* an MNC *vis-à-vis* EAAC and the East African states, even if not for most other purposes. This is not to suggest that differences among MNCs are irrelevant to the nature of their impact on African states nor to any alternative strategy formulation. Quite the contrary.

There are two broad "grades" of MNCs—those which can produce new knowledge and those which are basically limited to acquiring and organizing existing knowledge. The distinction is not complete—any MNC generates some new organizational, marketing, and management knowledge itself. Similarly, while a second-grade MNC cannot produce advanced technical knowledge, a first-grade MNC in many of its operations and probably in almost all of its relationships with Africa will be using existing knowledge largely available to second-grade MNCs.

The first-grade MNCs' charges are usually higher (in part to cover knowledge-creation overheads) and the number of competitors at that level lower. Therefore, a second-grade MNC is likely to be a better bargain for an African government or firm so long as it is technically competent at knowledge procurement and organization. Even more important is avoiding hiring a first-grade MNC to perform a knowledge creation role and allowing it to do a second-grade one—especially when it collects the knowledge from the African country. This is not unusual—for management consulting firms it appears to be very common indeed! The size of an MNC is not necessarily relevant to how well it can do any particular job. Experience in comparable settings and similar tasks is likely to be more critical.

A moderate-sized MNC with poor-country experience has three relevant pluses in African terms. It is small enough not to be a totally dominant partner in negotiations. It has relevant experience. Finally, it tends to cost less than a first-grade European (much less North American) MNC. Nevertheless, state-owned MNCs, whether from capitalist countries (e.g., Italy's ENI) or from socialist ones (e.g., the Rumanian metals and minerals group of state concerns), are not likely to behave very differently from other MNCs.

The broader the range of knowledge possessed by an MNC, the more relationships it is capable of and interested in developing with any one African state. This is *not* self-evidently an advantage. True, economies of scale in negotiation and experience in bargaining tactics and reaction patterns can be achieved. Yet the more sectors of an African economy any one MNC controls, the stronger it is *vis-à-vis* the host government; and the more its own profit are derived from a state, the more it will deploy its own power in order to resist change.[10]

A broad spectrum of relations is possible between an African government or firm and any MNC. The two extremes—an auction sale of goods to a company which happens to be an MNC and a corporate government—can usefully be excluded because the first raises few problems *unique* to the nature of the buyer and the second is rather unlikely; no MNC large enough to play such a role would consider it prudent.[11] The relevant relationship classes include:

1. single specialist contracts of limited duration (e.g., textile capacity development engineering and design study);
2. multiple specialist contracts, each one of limited extent and duration (e.g., a series of studies of different aspects of the textile industry, including domestic marketing, export marketing, development of uniform accounting procedures);
3. an ongoing specialist consultancy role (e.g., a package of studies on organization and efficiency of different parastatal and government units envisaged—by the consultant, at least—as continuing more or less indefinitely);[12]
4. an ongoing specialist service contract (e.g., an export marketing contract for an intermediate or manufactured export, the supply of technical maintenance and repair personnel for complex equipment);
5. a general managerial role (e.g., managing agent for a sugar estate with responsibilities ranging from personnel procurement to capacity development planning and overseeing);
6. a combination of general (or conceivably, but rarely, partial) management with minority ownership in a joint venture (e.g., managing and technical agency agreements plus 40% ownership of a cigarette company);

7. general management and majority or total ownership (the classic MNC penetration pattern, although now being eroded in favour of joint ventures).

Which pattern is appropriate will vary from mode of production to mode of production, time to time, country to country and case to secure the right of establishment is not considered cutthroat competition. Thus, there will not be effective competition among locally based MNC subsidiaries (except in the very largest of developing-economy markets), except in peripheral commodities. Competition from imports produced by other MNCs is within the conduct code, but is not very helpful to the African economy deliberately using partial closing of the economy to secure structural change and reduce dependence!

Second, exports will be sought by MNCs from their lowest cost units with subsidized or marginal cost "dumping" from others discouraged or banned. MNCs oppose export subsidies and certainly they seek to concentrate exports on low-cost, *not* high-surplus capacity plants.[30] For African economies, this is unlikely to be a helpful restriction. Exchange rates appropriate for the basic traditional exports may justify export subsidies for manufacturing.[31] Because it usually pays to build plants with capacities well in excess of current demand and because minimum sizes for economic plants in many lines of manufacturing lead to initial excess capacity, "dumping" moderately above marginal variable cost *is* a sound policy for many African manufacturing sectors.

V

Given the increasing importance of MNCs, the greater attention they are likely to pay to poor countries as production bases and markets, and the basic nature of MNCs, what is their potential for altering the global division of labour and income through promoting structural change in poor countries?

The traditional view has tended to be that very little in the way of structural change of redistribution of production and that a worsening of global income distribution would result.[32]

The case of Katanga—where the Union Miners group has been involved for fifty years and for forty played a dominant enough role to be decisive in economic change—suggests that the traditional view is quite wrong for at least some countries and regions in Africa. The group's activities did not simply create a limited mining enclave and raise the incomes of a few workers. They produced an array of industries, including nuclei chemical and engineering ones as well as building and mass market consumer goods. Changes in the food market created changes in domestic market agriculture. The copper industry was, in fact, a genuine and pervasive growth pole.[33]

Even cases cited as demonstrating the limits of foreign investment in leading to structural change demonstrate that the underlying problem is usually distortion of income distribution (including external drain) and a resultant trap at low output levels.[34] In fact, the polishing, packaging, and printing type of pseudo-industry consisting of the sky-high tariff-protected miniature plant is *not* what MNCs want—there is too much bother for too small a unit from their point of view.

To suggest that the MNC—far more than the traditional trading company or small consumer goods manufacturer—does have the power to, and, on occasion, a perceived interest in altering national and global production structures is not to suggest that its alterations are optimal or even necessarily desirable. There is a slightly odd tendency for traditional radical critics to be overwhelmed by the evidence that MNCs really do intend to make twine and automobiles, radios and blouses in poor countries for export as well as national sale and to conclude from this "major upsurge" of industrial capitalism that at present the poor economies are in a stage in which capitalism is a creative ideology in standard marxist terms.[35]

That, too, is an oversimplification for several reasons:

a. MNCs represent foreign capital and capitalists with all the resultant resource drain and reinvestment uncertainties;

b. only mass market consumer goods based on local raw materials (and income redistribution to enlarge the market), capital goods industries, or genuinely high value-added export-oriented manufacturing can generate self-substainable structural shifts;

c. MNCs are most unlikely to be active in all, as opposed to a selected handful of poor economies;

d. the internal income redistribution effects of a small, highly efficient sector are likely to create serious structural barriers to broader change;

e. the nature of the MNC is such that while it may well act in ways increasing output per capita (after remittances) and altering production structures, it is more likely (at least if left to its own planning) to increase rather than to reduce dependence;

f. in certain critical fields MNCs have either negligible or inappropriate knowledge.

The first of these points requires little elaboration except to underline that the broader a group's field of operations, the less certain it is that investible surpluses gained in one country will be reinvested in it. This situation is made worse when capitalists are imported as well as capital, so that overall day-to-day management and especially decision-taking remains in foreign hands. In that case the level of national managerial and entrepreneurial capacity will be decreased because the MNC presence is likely to have more smother than spread effects on locally-based firms.[36]

Not all manufacturing industry nor all large-scale primary product extraction leads to a continuing, as opposed to a "fossilized"[37] shift in production patterns and average national productive forces per capita. Unless production and use linkages to local suppliers and buyers and income generation linkages creating local market expansion in consumer and investor unit hands exist in some strength, the process will lead only to a new and higher plateau, not to a transformation of the economy.[38] Manufactured goods exports with significant local value added and mass market consumer goods with high local raw material content form the minimum package for structural transformation led by an integrated, self-regenerating, industrial sector.

The typical African first stage of easy import substitution plants does *not* represent such a package because it usually has low value added, high import content, and dependence on incomes generated by the primary product export sector.[39] It obscures rather than reduces the degree of dependence. Whether it is a sensible way of moving to a more vectorally integrated set of raw material through finished product industries[40] is an open question; it sometimes has been the prelude to such development but fairly rarely.

MNCs' search for optimal allocation of their own resources and for free trade will cause selective development by country as well as by sector. A number of their regional choices are becoming clear: Abidjan, Nairobi, potentially Mauritius, probably the Egyptian Canal Zone, Algeria (if it wants them), Singapore, Iran, Sao Paulo, perhaps Venezuela. There are, and will be more, exceptional cases in which an otherwise unattractive country has such favourable resource potential it can attract a vector in *that* field (almost certainly dominantly for export), e.g., probably Liberia (integrated steel works). This would not help a majority of African countries. It is not preferable to be a dependency of a regional market rather than a global, unless regional spread and linkage effects are much stronger.[41] That requires co-ordinated regional planning and location policy which MNCs accept only when they cannot evade or alter it. It is not part of MNC global development strategy. To preserve a chance of selling to the "left out" countries, the MNCs favour concessional aid, that is "leave it to IDA".

MNCs are opponents of low-wage syndromes on grounds of self-interest. They do provide a push toward a necessary raising of wage levels to allow the settled, family-present, stable labour necessary for building a modern urban productive sector. Unfortunately, they go further than this and pay higher wages partly as a matter of public relations with governments and unions, partly to have free choice of available labour. Combined with their capital/labour ratios and technological requirements, this tends to create a small, stable, compact "labour petty bourgois". This subclass both sees its interests as linked to the MNCs and imposes an unfortunate demonstration effect on the rest of the medium- and large-scale directly productive and public service sectors. Zambia is an extreme example of this with its dominance of copper made self-perpetuating by the wage-level doubling for the whole modern sector resulting from its demonstration or spread effect.[42]

At middle and senior (subsidiary) managerial level the problem is even more acute. Unless a strict rationing system is enforced, the MNC can buy the best local talent, both in the sense of bidding them away from governments and domestic firms and in that of socializing them into the margins of the international managerial elite.[43] The resulting life styles and attitudes are not consistent with mass-need oriented, geographically generalized, rural emphasis development. This problem is all the more acute if the MNC pays domestic managers a rate for the job equal to that paid to expatriates.

None of the foregoing criticisms suggest that MNCs will be unable to raise purely productive efficiency or domestic output *per capita* in many poor countries nor that this will not lead to structural change and a greater body of semi-skilled, skilled and junior managerial labour. Nevertheless—even ignoring the major problems of (probably perverse) geographic, class, and sectoral income distribution shifts—the nature of MNCs suggests that *external dependence is likely to be increased.*

Because the MNCs' basic asset is knowledge, which the African state is often not in a position to recreate rapidly itself or buy from another source, a new strand of the standard concentrated external dependence argument[44] is created by the simple existence of the MNC relationship. If, in addition, key physical inputs come from, and major export volumes go to, foreign markets, then unless the African state knows how to find and deal directly with alternative suppliers and buyers, its dependence is almost total. To hold a coffee or cotton auction *is* within the capacity of many African states; to market a manufactured consumer good (e.g., tinned beef, roasted and tinned cashew nuts, instant coffee) is *not.*[45] Similar problems arise in securing specialized inputs. Dependence is at a higher level of productive forces—absolutely and *per capita,* territorial and national—but it is no less concentrated or pervasive.

MNC knowledge is not universal in scope. It is particularly weak in labour-intensive, low production cost, modern technology.[46] The bias to capital intensity notable in MNCs is a transplanting of technology appropriate to their previous bases of operation.[47] It has not been worth their while to develop new technologies or to engage in more than marginal adaptation. This weakness is particularly serious in construction, in small-scale domestic-market oriented manufacturing and in public services.

Possibly this is temporary. Japanese firms have more experience in working with small, labour-intensive suppliers and may attempt to transplant this experience. There are cases of similar programmes in Latin American, e.g., Sears Roebuck in Mexico. Such a pattern would improve income distribution effects and build up local linkages and domestic managerial and entrepreneurial capacity. With a combination of state incentives (cost support for local supplier development) and constraints (minimum percentage of purchases from local units), MNCs might find it worthwhile to apply more research effort in this area.

A more basic, and less easily fillable, gap relates to what might be viewed as almost the *paradigmal rural African problem.* This combines uncertain rainfall, mediocre soil, low unit value crops, scattered population, meagre input levels for both physical (e.g., seed, fertilizer) and knowledge (e.g., extension, new techniques) items, and resultant constant minimum level of cash income and recurrent near-famine conditions. It is almost incredible that MNCs will concentrate resources on this problem, but for any African government reponsive to mass needs it must rank at the top of priority and urgency lists.

These are inherent limitations in use of (or dependence on) MNCs. They are by no means the only difficulties nor even the ones likely to appear most immediate in any particular African—MNC negotiation.[48] Such micro problems include:

a. transfer pricing—i.e., ensuring that prices paid and charged by the local unit are fair to it and to the African economy;

b. market rigging—i.e., creating artificial output and price levels which may seriously impair the welfare of the host country;

c. failure to citizenize operating knowledge—i.e., not training citizens and building up knowledge-use units (e.g., testing, marketing, and adaptive research sections) even to the extent desirable from the point of view of cost efficiency;

d. overcharging for specific services and chunks of knowledge or tieing unneeded services and personnel into the package;

e. special restrictions (e.g., as to exports) on use of knowledge bought or rented;

f. because negotiating is a form of knowledge whose effectiveness depends on possessing data about the substance of the transaction, the knowledge buyer is inevitably at a disadvantage. Only if the buyer is larger and can exert pressures in other ways can he balance this initial disadvantage.[49]

These issues are very real and require at least a paper each to treat adequately. They are, however, not unique to deals with MNCs and are relevant in respect of *particular* cases after a framework for determining overall relationships has been set, not in determining the framework.

VI

MNCs will not abolish the international economic class system of nations. They will alter the centre-periphery hierarchy and strengthen the middle class: e.g., those chosen as regional sub-centres.

The twin concepts of a "Quatorze Monde"[50] (or "Extreme Periphery") and International Middle Class[51] are relevant in illustrating that a simple dichotomy of centre/periphery with the socialist world outside the system is not a universally useful analytical tool. The smaller capitalist industrial economies (e.g., Finland), the industrialized European socialist economies, certain semi-industrialized "aspirants" (e.g., South Africa, Mexico, Singapore), and at least two of the oil boom states (Iran, Venezuela) are not easily handled in a dichotomous model. The hierarchies posited here for MNC functional and geographic organization are not intended as all-purpose tools but as useful for analytical organization of data and trends.

From the vantage point of an MNC headquarters there are five main levels of economic activity:

a. raw material production and processing;

b. industries characterized by relatively simple and slowly changing technology and by viability at production unit sizes allowing establishment on a domestic market base in countries;

c. complex industries characterized by more advanced, but fairly standard, technology and usually by market size requirements met by only a handful of poor economies;

d. frontier technology industries with a very high rate of technical and technological change and usually multinational market requirements for viability;

e. central knowledge creation, organization, management, consultancy and control operations.

The first (lowest) group concern MNCs only in cases in which a high technology is needed to win the raw material and/or significant opportunity for profiting from market organization and manufacturing demands control over primary production (e.g., aluminium and—in the past—petroleum). The second group concerns MNCs only in special cases because it is too open to entry. Too many units own or can acquire relevant knowledge for ownership to be very attractive except in the largest markets. Management, technical, and consultancy agreements on the other hand are very likely (with or without joint ventures) because they offer high returns on low investment outlay and with little risk. Broad-market consumer goods (e.g., textiles, cigarettes), simple consumer durables (e.g., radios, fans), construction materials (e.g., cement, glass, sheet metal and rods), and final stage assembly and packaging (e.g., light bulb, pharmaceutical, and vehicle "manufacturing" as normally found in Africa)[52] fall into this category.

In the third group are an array of industries which have been the backbone of industrial development and still dominate output. Metal production and basic fabrication (e.g., integrated iron and steel), standard machinery manufacture (e.g., lathes, textile machinery), automobiles, consumer durables (e.g., refrigerators), basic chemicals (e.g., petrochemical, plastic, coal, chemical, pharmaceutical, integrated fertilizer) fall here. This is the swing area both as to MNCs' views on optimal location and appropriate (or necessary) ownership and control patterns.

Computers (and related data processing devices), jet aircraft (and engines), atomic energy, and anti-pollution devices fall in the fourth category. It is closely related to the fifth because the much greater flow of, and much greater likelihood of a monopoly over, knowledge make it logically closer and creates a reinforcing probability of a much higher rate of cash flowback, at least after an initial lag. The fifth category is the core of the MNC system. Even if its knowledge creation units may be spread among several companies, they are likely to be concentrated in or near the head office and one or two principal sub-head offices.

No industry is permanently in classes two, three, or four. Jet aircraft may drop from four to three over the next decade, as automobiles already have. A burst of innovation in a formally class three industry can raise it to class four—the photographic equipment industry represented such a phenomenon in the early days of Polaroid.

The emerging logic of the MNC (a logic which a number are already explicitly stating) will involve withdrawing from full ownership of fixed assets and operating units in the first two classes and taking a selective attitude in the third.[53] Licenses, purchase and sale agreements, management contracts and joint ventures will replace the wholly-owned subsidiaries. Whether this is a devious plot to deceive,[54] a logical evolution of MNC needs, or a defensive course imposed by economic nationalism is debatable. Enthusiasts for all three positions exist. On the whole, the first is the least generally applicable (though numerous individual cases can be found). Reaction to constraints is certainly the way in which both MNCs and African governments usually perceive the process.[55]

Even if the MNCs should have begun a shift to selling knowledge and buying or marketing outputs instead of running 100% subsidiaries and even if the logic of resource allocation (in MNC profit terms) dictated relocation of production toward Africa, it is doubtful that MNCs would have begun to move in these directions without pressure. Now that they have started, some seem to be acting ahead of pressures, either to meet constraints they think will arise or because they have found their old patterns were not optimal for them.[56]

This functional hierarchy will lead to a geographic one:

a. countries with small markets and low *per capita* incomes lacking key raw materials will not secure any significant MNC involvement (unless paid for by technical assistance) e.g., Chad, Burundi, Dahomey, Equatorial Guinea, Guinea-Bissau;

b. countries as in "a" but with key raw materials will secure investment and knowledge for extraction and—if they are alert and aggressive and can offer a

labour forces, and pro-MNC governments will have a chance of securing gradethree industries, e.g., Nigeria, Kenya, Egypt, Algeria, and Mauritius (for export), perhaps Cameroon and Ivory Coast.

c. countries with moderate domestic markets (or participating in regional arrangements) will be able to secure grade two industries, e.g., Senegal, Congo, Ghana, Tanzania;

d. countries with relatively large domestic markets, well-trained urban labour forces, and pro-MNC governments will have a chance of securing grade-three industries, e.g., Nigeria, Kenya, Egypt, Algeria, and Mauritius (for export), perhaps Cameroon and Ivory Coast.

That is as far as one can expect African countries to advance in this class structure in the next two decades. South Africa might be an exception—after all, it already has two perfectly genuine MNC groups based in it (the Oppenheimer and the Rupert groups)—but the transition to independent African rule (however it takes place and over whatever length of time) will delay this.

Class "d" are secondary sub-centres or the lower middle class members of an MNC world. The upper middle class would have substantial class three and four activities and bits and pieces of class five, e.g., Brazil, Singapore, Spain, the UK. The upper class would (apart from sectors related to special raw material bases, consumer goods for particular tastes, and commodities not readily transportable) concentrate on production classes four and five, e.g., Sweden, the USA, Japan, Switzerland. The USSR is hard to place because of knowledge application weaknesses. By preference it would be upper class, treating the CMEA group and the poor countries as its MNC penetration unit; in practice it is in the upper middle class. China is *not* classifiable because it will not take part in an MNC world order and its dealings with it are restricted to the margins of its own and the MNCs' systems.

VII

Any alternative strategy—unless it is complete isolation—requires negotiation with MNCs. That is a matter of complexity in which a good deal is at stake. Nevertheless, it falls outside this study because it follows after determining the basic framework to be employed.[57] The task of formulating an alternative strategy is not aided by the fact that many critics attack features which are secondary and subject to alteration rather than considering basic strengths and weaknesses. Neither root and branch assaults by those all too ready to accept unnecessarily unequal terms[58] nor confusion of particular, removable weaknesses and basic limitations[59] is productive.

No alternative strategy can be defined without reference to the objectives of the African state pursuing it. If an African state is dominated by interest groups (foreign or domestic) who see their welfare as best served by closer integration into the international economic system, then its logical strategy *is* one of seeking to exert pressure and offer concessions adequate to achieve lower middle class national economic status. That involves close relations with—and heavy dependence on—MNCs.

Given the nature of the Kenyan elite, this is the strategy their government should pursue. It is more doubtfully appropriate for Nigeria, which has the resources to adopt a more independent strategy, a much less coherent national elite, and a rather stronger national entrepreneurial bourgeois, or for Egypt, which has more populist and protosocialist strands in its elite and power structure and greater chances of playing a key role in a loose regional alternative strategy. For really poor and small states like Rwanda, Somalia, and Upper Volta there can be no real payoff, because—to paraphrase Joan Robinson—no MNC will find it worth its while to devote significant knowledge and finance to exploiting them. For states with a commitment to a transition to socialism, e.g., Tanzania, Guinea-Bissau, Mozambique, Guinea, possibly Somalia, Algeria, Egypt, Zambia, potentially Ethiopia and Malagasy, the strategy outlined is clearly inappropriate, because the transition would block the strategy, the strategy would block the transition, or the two would cause each other's joint failure.

The recent UN Group of Eminent persons study[60]—predictably—falls between a critique of surface weaknesses and a basic strategic rethinking, but much nearer the former. Half composed of MNCs and their supporters, the GEP was—like the Pearson Commission—unlikely to do more than refine conventional wisdom and make half proposals for a few less threatening (to the MNCs and their home bases) strategic changes.

The main practical proposals, such as removing barriers to MNC exports from developing countries to industrial economies, avoiding double taxation, policing the worst abuses of transfer pricing, and increasing the role of joint ventures with a later phase-out of MNC investment are *precisely* what the earlier analysis suggests MNCs will wish done. The proposals as to safety, pollution, and labour standards are less clearcut but do, in a sense, fall into the realm of creating standards for orderly competition. The more radical words on international anti-trust and international regulation or incorporation in general are presumably not taken as serious possibilities. The views expressed on "renegotiation" of grossly unequal arrangements versus "retroactive measures" and the combination of a pious affirmation of the right to nationalize subject to "fair" compensation are more reactionary than present standards of MNC conduct! It is not surprising that shrewder MNCs and the more sophisticated financial press have taken a broadly favourable view, while less subtle companies and capitalist apologists have been stridently critical.[61]

Just as Pearson was a manifesto for the "sensible" use of aid to integrate the LDCs into the international economic system with only minor alterations to the latter,[62] so the present report is a manifesto for the building of an MNC world with a more decent role in it for poor countries. That can hardly constitute a foundation for developing a workable strategy for an African government with a genuine mass base seeking to set a framework in which relationships with MNCs would be accepted and continued only to the extent they furthered national development.

The following strategy notes assume a government which gives a high priority to meeting mass needs as perceived by the broad spectrum of workers and peasants. That presupposes at least some two-way participation and communication channels, a commitment to lessening inequality of consumption power, to access to public services, and to absolute poverty eradication. In practice it includes—at a minimum—commitment to a dominant domestically-owned productive sector with nationally set guidelines for individual firm operations and perhaps a commitment to a transition to socialism. On an operational level it will imply a belief in radical structural transformations followed by consolidation measures and a self-confident and assertive attitude in respect of foreign firms and governments.

An immediate question is whether ownership of fixed assets and local subsidiaries is relevant. The optimistic (or naive) argument that majority ownership automatically gives real control is now about as discredited as the equally optimistic (or naive) view that formal political independence automatically confers effective political sovereignty. Nevertheless, over-reaction to the limits of "flag independence" led to a too-pessimistic view that political neo-colonialism was inevitable; to assert that ownership is meaningless or harmful is also to overstate.[63]

If the key characteristic of MNCs is possession of knowledge, the main aim must be to secure use of, control over, and capacity to reproduce and adapt that knowledge. The second and third steps require accumulation and application of local African experience in applying and operating (not just regulating) the knowledge and its technological, technical, and institutional embodiments.

In some instances (e.g., major financial institutions) the spread effects (in the case cited, macro credit control and micro credit allocation in terms of national planning objectives) are so critical, and so separate from the immediate interests of the firm, that immediate effective control is vital. In such cases even critics of majority ownership often advocate selective 100% ownership.

Two arguments for broader full ownership and for joint ventures in addition to increasing the reality of economic sovereignty can be noted briefly. *First,* if proper attention is paid to project selection and contract negotiation (but not otherwise), an average return on investment of 25% can be obtained. In reducing external drain and bolstering domestic investible surplus mobilization, that is hardly minor. *Second,* if a general transition to socialism is envisaged, a large foreign majority owned productive sub-sector is a rather evident contradiction.

Full public-sector ownership of all large productive units is not a practical first step—China took at least six years (and perhaps fourteen) and the USSR at least twelve to reach that point. The real question is whether a limited 100% sub-sector with a large regulated private sector is as good as a 100% sub-sector, plus a joint-venture (in transition to 100%), sub-sector plus a much smaller regulated private sub-sector.[64]

Because of real practical limits to control without ownership, the answer is almost certainly no.[65] The attitudes inherent in control and being controlled—especially in African government/MNC cases—are not conducive to determining joint interests, planning positive initiatives, and achieving desired targets. Borrowing, foreign currency use, expatriate employment, dividends, etc., can (and must) be controlled (for publicly-owned as well as MNC units), but use of local credit facilities, maximizing foreign exchange balance gains, and developing local personnel committed to national (*not* MNC) values and aims seem quite unlikely to be secured via the quasi-adversory controller/controlled relationship.

MNCs and their employees *do* have different attitudes to controllers and partners and to minority and majority partners. Information supplied and attitudes to problem-solving are—or can be made to be—radically different. Minority public participation in joint ventures is normally a mis-allocation; it obtains little more control than that obtained by a statutory government director on all company boards.

Because the key to MNC power (as well as usefulness) is knowledge, the key elements in a strategy must relate to balancing and then replacing MNC knowledge inputs. One element in building knowledge must be high-level education. Because operating knowledge (and its reproduction) is embodied in people, medium-term quantitative high-level manpower plans are possible both at production unit and national level. Nor are they impossible to implement. For example, the high-level manpower position in Tanzania moved from 500 citizens to 4,500 expatriates in 1961 to 5,000/5,000 in 1971 and probably 7,500-8,000 citizens to 4,500 expatriates in 1974. By 1981 (the 15 year plan target for basically complete citizenization) the figures seem likely to be 20,000 citizens to 1,000-2,000 expatriates. In the case of one large MNC unit, which has not greatly altered scale or technology since 1961, expatriates declined from 358 in 1961 to 251 in 1966, 79 in 1971, 23 in 1973 and perhaps 15 in 1974.

In addition to formal training, relevant experience in a relevant framework is needed. Control is *not* a relevant framework for management experience;

coordinated planning with a joint venture *can* be. The framework needed includes a commitment to national objectives—something no MNC majority owned subsidiary can possibly have. The dangers of citizen high-level manpower becoming so socialized into the MNC system as to become "plus royaliste que le roi" are very real. Worker participation, wage and fringe benefit control, joint annual and investment budget planning, agreed targets in respect of non-firm goals (e.g., location, adult education, support for local component producers) are all easier to agree with a minority partner / manager than to impose creatively and effectively on a majority owner.

Knowledge and experience must also be built up directly in the areas in which MNCs have little to offer. Applied research in respect of entrenched rural poverty, arid land agriculture, modern intermediate technology (especially in construction and in component manufacture), new patterns of services making much greater use of "para" personnel (quickly trained, low salarial, numerous, close to workers and peasants served) in a wide variety of fields (e.g., health, education, agricultural extension, construction, book-keeping and finance) as part of an integrated system which neither ignores not overemphasizes its high-technology units, nutrition and diet (e.g., can edible protein be extracted cheaply from cottonseed[66] and how can soy bean protein be made an accepted addition to eating patterns?)[67] is needed *by*, as well as for, poor countries. Some research should be "contracted" to international and bilateral non-profit bodies but as much as possible, within a few years the bulk of it, should be done by poor-country personnel in poor countries, whether on a national or a regional basis. "Applied experiments" or "pilot projects" should *from the start* be dominantly citizen-staffed *at all levels.*[68]

Other knowledge beyond day-to-day operation and training personnel to do it must be secured from MNCs to make phasing out real. The general manager of a $100 million a year chemical producer in a large poor country who said his MNC had cut down to three Americans but retained total control over financial, technical, product development, and investment decisions is a warning. Ensuring a complete transfer of technology and knowledge plus the ability at least to adapt it is more critical than price. Certainly that reading of the Japanese and Soviet experiences seems the most reasonable one.[69] Once ownership and control to this extent has passed, no regard need be paid to licencing and patent laws at home nor to most export limitations. Something can be done *now* by total refusal to register or protect foreign trade-marks, get-ups and (probably) copyrights, and by substituting compulsory registration cum automatic fixed-fee licencing for standard patent laws. Nevertheless, the real effect of such legislation will be limited (except in the trade-mark case where a 100% tax on trade-mark royalties in respect of *domestic* sales could well be added to the refusal to register or protect) until more knowledge has actually changed hands.[70]

Once knowledge (including experience in applying it) has been *developed,* it must be steadily *deployed.* Joint ventures are candidates for phasing out, first in respect of general management and of areas which maximize the need for transfer price checking. Renegotiation should be pursued regularly (obtaining contracts with automatic review clauses to facilitate this) and selective controls built up on the basis of analysis of data acquired as an owner.

These *are* practicable lines of action. Tanzania has phased out several joint ventures,[71] renegotiated down cost and coverage of numerous contracts,[72] moved to end two major sole export selling arrangements,[73] asserted and enforced a *de facto* right to renegotiate backed by its *de jure* right to nationalize,[74] fed investment data into credit, foreign exchange, price control and annual planning operations. In none of these can total success be claimed but the trend is forward and the results quite significant (especially when contrasted to the 1961-66 period of *de facto* acceptance of foreign private dominance cum fragmentary governmental control in the large-scale productive sector). Tanzania certainly had few knowledge, personnel or financial advantages over other African states—commitment and a belief that radical change could be secured, combined with a willingness to plan and follow through on the micro level in an orderly and sustained fashion seem to be the distinguishing characteristics. This process can be seen as one of making majority ownership of local assets a step toward meaningful national control based on acquired knowledge. It is difficult to see it working without the initial ownership base—especially because ownership seems to be a precondition for African governments to give sustained, creative attention to joint areas of need and interest with productive sector units, including allocating them adequate flows of citizen middle- and high-level manpower.

Ownership and knowledge acquisition are basic operating tools of implementing a strategy; they *cannot define its goals.* For the African state requiring an alternative strategy these include:

1. Attainment of a radically less unequal income distribution eliminating the most glaring urban/rural, educational level, and class anomalies;[75]
2. Sustained progress toward ending absolute poverty in personal consumption capacity and access to public services;
3. An integrated assault on entrenched rural poverty;
4. Primary attention to identifying and meeting mass needs, including consumption goods and public services;[76]
5. Attainment of a better balance between national and sectoral production and use structures;
6. Greater flexibility in resource use based on greater knowledge (itself the most flexible of resources) and a greater coherence between domestic supply (production) and demand (use);[77]

7. A more defensible international economic position based on higher national economic integration and flexibility, providing greater power to secure less unequal bargains;

8. A ratio of domestic to foreign involvement (in personnel, knowledge, and finances) adequate to ensure that effective national control is maintainable.

From these objectives several guidelines follow:

a. MNCs cannot safely be used as central investors or managers of the production sector but at most of particular firms and subsectors;

b. while MNC relationships as a group may well continue for a long time, any particular joint venture or contact should be phased down and out as rapidly as possible;

c. because of the limits on the total size of MNC involvement consistent with continued national control, care should be taken not to use MNC links where other alternatives are available;

d. when dealing with large MNCs it is desirable to avoid a situation in which their total interests in any African country are genuinely critical to them, because that will increase the amount of power they deploy to resist change;

e. the areas in which MNCs are most likely to be useful are those involving new (to the African state) technology for significant (in national terms) new productive units or new external marketing patterns;

f. before actually beginning to negotiate, the *first* question is whether MNCs really have anything to offer, the *second,* whether local knowledge really is unavailable, the *third,* whether an MNC link is the only way of securing foreign knowledge. The second question, if put seriously, will often produce the answer that local knowledge *is* available or could be developed rapidly if local institutions were given contracts allowing them to secure direct-hire and technical assistance personnel. For example, in import and wholesale commerce, price control, banking, and domestic textile distribution, sound consultancy studies have been carried out by Tanzanian teams. In the first case implementation is nearly complete and has proven successful, whereas a very expensive McKinsey consultancy study proved a nearly unmitigated disaster;

g. Relations (at both case and sector level) should be seen both against a background of national goals and in a dynamic context contrasting past changes and projected trends with the present in evaluating any present or proposed relationship.

Notes

[1] At the time this paper was written, Dr. Green, now with the Institute of Development Studies at the University of Sussex, was Honorary Professor of Economics at the University of Dar es Salaam and Economic Advisor to The Tanzania Treasury. The analysis and views expressed in the paper are his personal responsibility and are not necessarily those of The Treasury or of SIDA.

[2] "Look To The Third World", *Financial Times,* 21 May 1974.

[3] Opening Speech, Seminar on Education in Africa, Dag Hammarskjold Foundation and Institute of Development Studies, University of Dar es Salaam, 20 May 1974.

[4] For a much fuller analysis see S. Amin and C. Coquery-Vidrovitch, *Histoire économique du Congo, 1880-1968,* Editions Anthropos, Paris, 1969.

[5] Cf., for example, G. Arrighi, "International Corporations, Labor Aristocracies, and Economic Development in Tropical Africa", in R. Rhodes (editor), *Imperialism and Underdevelopment,* Monthly Review, New York, 1970.

[6] For a clear statement by an African statesman see J. K. Nyerere, "Economic Nationalism", in *Freedom and Socialism,* Oxford, Dar es Salaam, 1968. For a fuller argument by the author see "Economic Independence and Economic Co-operation", in D. Ghai (editor), *Economic Independence in Africa,* East African Literature Bureau, Nairobi, 1973.

[7] This is not a particularly easy exercise to carry out. To quote President Nyerere:

> Tanzania is attempting to achieve change by deliberate policy, and to maintain stability by involving all the people in both the direction and process of change. We are under no illusions about the difficulty of the task we have undertaken. With few socialists we are trying to build socialism; with few people conscious of the basic requirements of democracy, we are trying to achieve change by democratic means; with few technicians we are trying to effect a fundamental transformation of our economy. And with an educational elite whose whole teaching encouraged motives of individualistic advancement, we are trying to create an egalitarian society.

("Stability and Change In Africa", in *Freedom and Development,* Oxford, Dar es Salaam, 1973, p. 112.)

[8] It is nevertheless fairly easy to disguise conservative or reactionary motivations under the guise of being *plus radicale que les radicales.* This has been a possible motivation of several university student, parliamentary, and journalistic critiques of specific Tanzanian policies. The claim was hardship for the poor but the measures criticized did not touch the poor and the complainants were those whose expectations of gain in the future were reduced by them. E.g., S. Msuya, "Are We Really Serious About Removing Inequality", *Daily News,* 24 October 1972.

[9] For a parallel assessment see E. Penrose, 'Ownership and Control': "Multi-national Corporations in Less Developed Countries", in G. K. Helleiner (editor), *The Third World And International Economic Change,* Cambridge, forthcoming.

[10] Thus the degree of resistance to full or partial nationalization in Tanzania has normally been relatively low. The MNCs affected simply did not consider their Tanzanian interests as large enough to make a major issue. The contrary case of the British Banks almost certainly turned on their (not entirely unjustified) fear that if Tanzania "got away with it" other developing economies might follow its example.

[11] Even ITT seems to stick to rather puerile attempts to "destabilize" governments so far as direct political action goes. And ITT is rather atypical. Anaconda and Kennecott Copper did more harm to Chile by economic boycott tactics. Their aim was limited to securing what they considered equitable compensation; whether this came from the Allende government or a successor was probably a matter of indifference. (This is *not* intended as an endorsement of Anaconda or Kennecott.)

[12] Any consultancy contract can be organized so that it throws up new issues which "justify" another contract. Similarly, any consultancy firm using basically second-level personnel and depending for 99% of its facts and 90% of its proposals on what it can glean from the African country's own employees (citizen or expatriate) and reports will inevitably come across new areas in which it thinks it can "sell" itself. Since consultancy firms are among the worst of MNCs at citizenizing, the "need" for the foreign consultants will be "greater" as time passes if the African state allows this game to be played.

[13] S. Rolfe, *Interplay*, Vol. 2, November 1968.

[14] G. Ball, "The Promise of the Multinational Corporation", *Fortune*, Vol. 75, No. 6, June 1967, p. 80.

[15] Cf., e.g., S. H. Hymer and R. Rowthorn, "Multinational Corporations And International Oligopoly", in C. P. Kindleberger (editor), *The International Corporation*, MIT, Cambridge Mass., 1970.

[16] Cf., e.g., Arrighi, op. cit.

[17] 10 July 1971.

[18] *Multinationals and the Third World*, Allen Lane, London, 1974.

[19] *The Next Forty Years*, Economist Booklets, London, 1974.

[20] Cf., e.g., Hymer and Rowthorn, op. cit.; Arrighi, op. cit.; Penrose, op. cit.; A. Emmanuel, "Current Myths of Development", *New Left Review*, 85, May-June, 1974.

[21] *The New Industrial State*, Houghton Mifflin, Boston, 1967.

[22] This is discussed in more detail in Hymer and Rowthorn, op. cit., as are the related issues of non-coordination in respect of Keynesian-type macro-problems in an MNC-dominated economy.

[23] Zambian copper is a case. The companies quite openly sought to insure that copper miners' primary loyalty was to them. They openly boasted (via African middle level managers and academicians) that they were successfully socializing African foremen and managers into the life styles, values, clubs, consumption patterns, etc., of their expatriate fellows. A more insidious form of corruption of an African state is hard to imagine, whatever the companies' intentions may have been.

[24] Cf. D. Seers, "The Mechanism of an Open Petroleum Economy", *Social and Economic Studies*, March 1964.

[25] Cf. J. Gallagher and R. Robinson, "The Imperialism of Free Trade", *Economic History Review*, N.S. No. 6, Dec. 1953.

[26] There is no genuine socialist international economic parallel system. Increasingly, socialist countries of Europe participate in the capitalist international economic system in ways very hard to distinguish from the middle-level capitalist powers. China's participation is quite different but its relations with other poor countries are not substantial enough to define a counter system. Cf. R. H. Green, "The International Economic System and Development: Some Limitations of a Special Case", Economic Research Bureau, University of Dar es Salaam, March 1970.

[27] For a fuller exposition see R. H. Green. "Economic Cooperation and Economic Co-operation", op. cit., and "East African Economic Integration: Benefits, Costs, Priorities", in *Integration and Regional Plan Coordination in East Africa*, Dag Hammarskjold Foundation, Uppsala, forthcoming.

[28] If enough incentives are given, MNCs will enter large-scale agriculture. For example, Volkswagen is to build up a huge cattle-ranching scheme in the interior of Brazil for beef exports to Germany.

[29] This is a standard danger of improved terms and access for primary products. They can distort internal benefit/cost ratios in such a way as to deter structural change.

[30] For example, in 1967-68 Unilever switched supplies of detergents and fats to Tanzania from its Kenya plant to Malaysian and UK plants even though the Kenya plant was under capacity and there was next to no difference in price cif. Dar es Salaam.

[31] Cf., e.g., N. Kaldor, "International Trade and Economic Development", in *Journal of Modern African Studies,* Vol. 2, No. 4, 1964.

[32] Cf., e.g., M. Barratt-Brown, *After Imperialism,* Heinemann, London, 1963.

[33] For a detailed exposition see J. La Croix, *Industrialisation au Congo,* Mouton, Paris, 1967.

[34] Cf., e.g., J. Rweyemamu, *Underdevelopment and Industrialization in Tanzania: A Study of Perverse Capitalist Industrial Development,* Oxford, Nairobi, 1973.

[35] Cf., e.g., W. Warren, "Imperialism and Capitalist Industrialization", in *New Left Review,* September-October 1973.

[36] For a fuller discussion of this problem see K. Griffin, *Underdevelopment in Spanish America,* MIT, Cambridge Mass., 1969. An extreme case is Chile, where foreign firms borrowed from Chilean banks to buy up a previously Chilean-owned large-scale productive sector, ending by buying up the banks themselves in the same way.

[37] The concept is developed by Hla Myint in respect of a once for all agricultural export shift but is equally applicable to industry. See "The Gains from Trade and the Backward Countries", *Review of Economic Studies,* No. 2, 1954-55 and "An Interpretation of Economic Backwardness", *Oxford Economic Papers,* June 1954.

[38] See C. Thomas, "Industrialization and the Transformation of Africa", pp. 325–360, this volume and La Croix, op. cit.

[39] Cf. J. Rweyemamu, op. cit., R. M. Green and Ann Seidman, *Unity or Poverty? The Economics of Pan Africanism,* Penguin, 1967; R. H. Green, "Reflections on Economic Strategy, Structure, Implementation, and Necessity: Ghana and the Ivory Coast: 1957-67", in P. Foster and A. Zolberg, *Ghana and the Ivory Coast: Perspectives on Modernization,* University of Chicago, 1971.

[40] For an elaboration of the conçeptual strategy of vectoral integration from a raw material through intermediate stages to an array of finished products see Myint, "Infant Industry Arguments for Assistance to Industries in the Setting of Dynamic Trade Theory", in R. Harrodd and D. Hague (editors), *International Trade Theory in a Developing World,* Macmillan, London, 1963. See also C. Thomas, *Dependence and Transformation: The Economics of Transition to Socialism,* Monthly Review (New York), 1974.

[41] Cf., e.g., R. Green, "East African Economic Integration . . .", op. cit. and P. Robsen, *Economic Integration in Africa,* Allen and Unwin, London, 1968, especially sections on the East African Common Market.

[42] Cf. Arrighi, op. cit., and J. Saul and Arrighi, "Socialism and Economic Development in Tropical Africa", in *Journal of Modern African Studies,* Vol. 6, No. 2, 1968.

[43] Cf. Saul and Arrighi, op. cit.; Saul, "The Political Aspects of Economic Independence", in D. Ghai, op. cit.; "Towards Socialism in Tanzania—a Postscript" (A debate among I. G. Shivji, T. Szentes, W. Rodney, J. Saul), in L. Cliffe and J. Saul (editors), *Socialism in Tanzania,* Vol. 2, East African Publishing House, Nairobi, 1973.

[44] Cf. Green and Seidman, *Unity or Poverty?,* op. cit.—Part II.

[45] There are alternatives. For example, one could envisage shelling, roasting, vacuum packing, and labelling cashew nuts under orders from several national cooperative federations (e.g., those of Scandinavia) and chain stores. This would provide much higher local value added in Tanzania, probably reduce marketing costs globally (as well as to Tanzania), increase Tanzania's freedom of bargaining room and outlets. It would, however, take knowledge of three types—technical to operate the increased processing, quality control to be sure the exact European appearance as well as taste standards were met, and marketing to locate and negotiate deals with the prospective buyers.

[46] Cf. G. K. Helleiner, "Beyond Growth Rates and Plan Volumes—Planning for Africa in the 1970s", in *JMAS,* Vol. 10, No. 3, 1972.

[47] For a fuller discussion see J. Gouverneur, *Productivity and Factor Proportions in Less Developed Countries: The Case of Industrial Firms in The Congo,* Oxford University, 1971.

[48] For fuller details of the immediate issues of this type see E. Penrose, op. cit., and A. Maizels, "A New International Strategy for Primary Commodities", in G. K. Helleiner (editor), *The Third World and International Economic Change,* forthcoming.

[49] One way of course is to be a government and to act like one—an advantage not open to an African private sector firm. For a fuller discussion see R. H. Green, "Political Independence and the National Economy: An Essay on the Political Economy of Decolonization", in C. Allen and R. Johnson (editors), *African Perspectives,* Cambridge University Press, 1970.

[50] Cf. Barbara Ward, "First, second, third and fourth worlds", *Economist,* 18 May 1974; R. H. Green, "Aspects of the World Monetary and Resource Transfer System 1974: A View from the Periphery", in Helleiner, op. cit.

[51] Cf. I. Wallerstein, "Dependence In An Interdependent World: The Limited Possibilities Of Transformation Within The Capitalist World Economy", *African Studies Review,* April 1974.

[52] These very often are cases in which the *net import cost* of the inputs, personnel, capital goods for producing locally *exceeds* the fob prices of the finished product. For a fuller analysis and exposé see S. B. Linder, *Trade and Trade Policy for Development,* Praeger, New York, 1967.

[53] This is evident from behaviour in Tanzania. A number of first- and second-stage MNCs have actively sought to reduce their ownership share (in one case by selling out but retaining marketing monopoly arrangements).

[54] Cf., e.g., Shivje, op. cit., and "We Become Helpful to Those Who Claim To Help Us"/"Capital Imports Negligible and Training Clauses Carefully Ignored", *Daily News,* 6-7 September 1973. MNCs rarely claim to "help". Tanzania wishes to *minimize* MNC equity capital imports because of their expenses, and training clause performance seems dependent more on intelligent overseeing of the management (e.g., in two cases the expatriate component in relatively constant size and technology firms fell from 358 in 1961 to 15 odd in 1974 in one case and from 60 odd in 1969 to about a dozen in 1974 in the other) than on anything else. Thus the titles seem to contain certain confusions of thought and misidentification of dominant contradictions.

[55] Szentes, op. cit., and *The Political Economy of Underdevelopment,* Budapest, Academie Kiado, 1971, argues this forcefully.

[56] The same nearsightedness was true in respect of appropriate wage levels and organizational patterns for labour treated solely from an expatriate firm's profit point of view. Cf. R. H. Green, "Wage Levels, Employment, Productivity and Consumption", in J. R. Sheffield (editor), *Education, Employment and Rural Development,* East African Publishing House, Nairobi, 1967.

[57] For a masterful exposition of points to consider in actual cases of negotiation see E. Penrose, op. cit. Also D. Seers, "Big companies and small countries: A Practical Proposal", *Kyklos,* 4, 1963.

[58] For example, see the submission of G. K. Kahama of Tanzania, whose contracts and MNC relations are the main target of the Shivje papers cited. Whatever criticisms of lack of perspective, confusion of concept, and overstatement can be made of Shivje's writings, the situation they portray is not a satisfactory one nor one remotely resembling the crusading posture of the submission.

[59] For a fuller criticism of this tendency see R. H. Green, "Relevance, Efficiency, Romanticism, and Confusion in Tanzanian Planning and Management", in A. Rweyemamu (editor), *Problems of Public Sector Management in Africa,* Dag Hammarskjold Foundation, Uppsala, forthcoming.

[60] (E/5500/Add.1-New York-1974).

[61] Compare "Nanny knows worst", *Economist,* 15 June 1974 and A. H. Hermann, "Thoughts on multinationals", *Financial Times,* 16 July 1974.

[62] Cf. R. H. Green, "Anatomy of Two Assessments—Pearson, Jackson and Development Partnership", in *The African Review,* Vol. 1, No. 2, (Dept. of Political Science, University of Dar es Salaam), 1971 and "Columbia Declaration" signed by majority of participants at Columbia University International Conference on the Pearson Report, published in B. Ward et al. (editors), *The Widening Gap,* Columbia University, New York, 1971.

[63] Cf. R. H. Green, "Political Independence and the National Economy" op. cit., and "Economic Independence and Economic Co-operation", op cit., for a fuller exposition.

[64] For a trenchant presentation of the case for control plus selective 100% ownership cum direct management and against a significant joint venture/management contract sector see E. Penrose, op. cit.

[65] The arguments in this section are based on eight years' experience in dealing with MNC (and other) firms both in compensation and associated agreement negotiations and subsequent ongoing operation planning and evaluation from the Tanzania government's side of the table. For fuller presentation on the Tanzania parastatal sector see R. H. Green, "Foreign Resources and the Parastatal Sector", IDEP/ET/CS/2367-X, Seminar on the Use of Foreign Funds in the Development of the East African Countries (Dar es Salaam, April-May 1972) and "The Parastatal Corporation As An Element In The Quest For National Development: Tanzania 1967-1972", IDEP/ET/CS/2365-26, Seminar on The Role of Public Sector in the Economic Development of Africa (Cairo, May-June, 1972).

[66] Pilot plants exist in Texas and in India. The problem is separation of gossypol, which is poisonous to people. The secondary problem is that the resultant flour is tasteless and non-bakable.

[67] For example, in Tanzania there is very considerable evidence that soy bean growing is an attractive proposition in several areas. Doubtless the beans (or oil and cake from them) could be exported, but given the national protein shortage it would be an unhappy admission that nutrition/diet research and experimentation had failed.

[68] Cf. Helleiner, "Beyond Growth Rates . . .", op. cit.; J. Loxley, "Technical Assistance, High Level Manpower Training, and Ideology in Tanzania" and R. H. Green "Technical Assistance and Tanzanian Administration", in Y. A. Tandon (editor), *Technical Assistance Administration in East Africa,* Dag Hammarskjold Foundation, Uppsala, 1973.

[69] This is the provisional conclusion resulting from a series of interlocking research projects at the Institute of Development Studies at the University of Sussex in relation to Russian industrialization (Cf. Sixth Annual Report-IDS).

[70] For detailed discussin see E. Penrose, op. cit., "International Patenting and the Less Developed Countries", Economic Research Bureau, University of Dar es Salaam, 1972.

[71] E.g., British American Tobacco, Tanganyika Portland Cement.

[72] E.g., Kilombero Sugar on acquisition of control from the IFC-CDC-NOFC shareholders. The new management contract—unlike the old—was heavily linked to output expansion and profitability. It would have cost about one-fourth as much had the previous production and loss record remained unchanged. In practice the Managing Agents received about the same total remuneration, but the 20-25% increase in output and turnaround from massive losses to moderate profits needed to achieve this presumably owe something to the form of the contracts as does their suddenly enhanced citizenization programme which was both required by the new contract and seen as a way of reducing costs and raising profits and thus the profit element in their fee.

[73] E.g., Mitchell Cotts (pyrethrum extract) and Brooke Bond-Liebig (tinned meat and byproducts). Both cases also involve ending a joint venture's ownership side, as well.

[74] E.g., the 1967 purchase of 50% of the petroleum refinery on deferred payment terms with the funding arranged by the ENI group as opposed to the immediate cash payment option which was actually provided in the original agreement.

[75] Cf. R. H. Green, "Toward Ujamaa and Kujitegemea: Notes on Income Distribution and Poverty Eradication Planning and Practice in Tanzania", IDS, Sussex, Communications Series, forthcoming. For a more general and global approach, see M. Ahluwalia, H. Chenery, R. Jolly, et. al. (editors), *Redistribution with Growth: An Approach to Policy,* Oxford, 1974.

[76] This is an area in which Chinese and Soviet priorities have differed markedly. China has given first priority to mass consumer necessities rather than either to GDP growth or heavy industry. The USSR placed absolutely overriding priority, during the parallel period in its history, on heavy industry leading to maximum defence capacity.

[77] Cf., e.g., J. Rweyemamu, op. cit., R. H. Green, "Political Independence and the National Economy . . .", op. cit. and *Stages in Economic Development: Changes in the Structure of Production, Demand and International Trade,* Bank of Sudan, Khartoum, 1968 (also Yale Economic Growth Center Paper 149, 1970).

Lars Bondestam

Notes on Foreign Investments in Ethiopia

Historical review

The fact that Ethiopia remained uncolonized for a long period of time puts her in a different position than the rest of Africa relative to the industrialized countries. This constitutional independence implied that foreign economic influence and subsequent economic dependence on Europe were delayed and have therefore not yet reached the level found in most other African countries. This does not mean that foreign interests were absent, but that they previously had only little influence on the economic development of Ethiopia. The European powers actually outmanoeuvred each other in their attempts at colonization, so that it was not until 1935 that one of them gained a temporary control over certain parts of the country.

Nevertheless, ever since the beginning of the 19th century foreigners were to be found in all sectors of the non-subsistency economy, particularly Arabs, Greeks and Armenians, who dominated the trade and large-scale business. It was not until the end of that century that foreigners came as representatives of European companies. Emperor Menelik was in need of modern arms to defend his country. Thus, he paradoxically encouraged European investments in order to increase exports, and for the money he obtained, he primarily bought weapons from Europe in order to fight the Europeans more effectively.

Foreigners had held land on more or less the same terms as Ethiopians—a system that continued until 1910, when a decree was issued prohibiting the sale and distribution of land to foreigners. Those who already held land were nevertheless entitled to keep it and to dispose it freely. Foreign land ownership implied foreign plantations. Thus, commercial cultivation of tobacco was in the hands of Italians, Frenchmen and Greeks. With the opening of river communications between south-western Ethiopia and the Sudan, the demand for coffee in the Sudan caused a rapid increase in exports and a growing commercialization of the coffee production in this part of Ethiopia. The main producers were members of the Ethiopian aristocracy, who cooperated with the coffee export companies, predominantly Greek firms with headquarters in Khartoum. With the construction of the Addis

Ababa-Djibouti railway in the beginning of this century, coffee production in Hararge in eastern Ethiopia suddenly became very profitable and several Belgian, British and French plantations sprang up. In 1912, for example, two Belgian companies, Société Générale de Culture and Société Générale des Plantations d'Abyssinie, established themselves as large coffee growers. Commercial production of cotton had also started in this area and important concessions were granted to a Franco-Belgian company.

With Emperor Menelik's occupation of western Ethiopia in the mid-1880s, several European companies and individuals showed on interest in starting mining in this part of the country. Two valuable gold concessions were granted, the more important being granted to a Belgian company, Mines d'or du Wollega. In 1910 the Deutsches Syndikat für Abessinien took over the concession. Italian companies also received concessions, including Sindicato Italiano d'Oltre Mareb and Société Minière des Concessions Prasso en Abyssinie, the latter with headquarters in Paris. Emperor Menelik, and later to some degree Emperor Haile Selassie, willingly granted concessions to foreign companies at such a rate that they lost control over the exploitation of gold and other minerals. The availability of minerals attracted many foreign firms and the Government was eventually forced to introduce mining legislation. In 1931 decrees were issued, proclaiming all alluvial minerals to be State property. As we shall see, this did not mean that foreign companies were thenceforth to be denied mining concessions in Ethiopia.

The first step towards the establishment of a banking system in Ethiopia took place in 1903, when Emperor Menelik requested Britain for economic support to continue the construction of the Addis Ababa-Djibouti railway, which had been started by French entrepreneurs. Two years later, the National Bank of Egypt obtained a 50-year concession in Ethiopia. Shares of the new bank were offered for public subscription in New York, in major capitals in Europe and in Addis Ababa. No other bank was to be allowed to establish in Ethiopia; the bank was the sole issuer of bank notes; all government funds were to be deposited with the bank; it was given preference in the issue of loans, etc. Ethiopian representation in the board of governors was limited to two persons only, and not more than 7% of the share capital was subscribed by Ethiopians. Opposition against the foreign dominance and the monopolistic position of the bank was not lacking, which may explain its liquidation in 1931. Other banks nevertheless emerged during this time, although probably with a somewhat different function. The first development bank, Société Nationale d'Ethiopie pour le Développement de l'Agriculture et du Commerce, was founded as early as 1908. It was reorganized twenty years later, with a French group holding 60% of the share capital and the French government the remaining 40%. In 1915, two other foreign banks established branches in Ethiopia, namely Banque de l'Indochine and Compagnie de l'Afrique Orientale.

The above examples have been cited in order to show that the lack of formal colonization was no guarantee for economic independence. European capital was indeed present in Ethiopia, although—as already mentioned—its influence on the broad masses was negligible, if we exclude the indirect effect it had by making it possible for the Emperor to purchase arms and munitions, with which he supplied his huge armies for the defence of the country.

The main reason for the Italian annexation of Ethiopia in 1935 was an increasing demand for raw materials. Mussolini's economic policy aimed at a high degree of self-sufficiency. This demanded larger areas for the production of raw goods and the exploitation of resources which were not available in Italy but many of which were abundant in Ethiopia. The economic programme ultimately led to territorial expansion and consequently to imperialist ventures. In the *New York Times* of August 8, 1935, one could read:

> Italy's primary hopes of profit in Ethiopia are based on development of products that would affect its trade with North and South America—cotton and coffee. Whatever may be the outcome of its expectations in gaining gold, iron ore, platinum, copper and other minerals, Italy has reason to believe that cotton and coffee will compensate it for the billions of lire expended in East Africa. Italy's imports of cotton average 740 million lire yearly, mostly paid to the US, and of coffee about 185 million—a total of nearly 1,000 million lire representing 13.5 per cent of Italy's total imports.

Some of this cotton, which was imported from the USA, was manufactured in Italy and reexported as ready-made articles to its colony, Eritrea. A better solution would be to control not only the manufacturing of textiles, but also the production of raw cotton—within Ethiopia.

Moreover, both industry and plantations in Eritrea were in need of labour. Despite migration to Eritrea from northern Ethiopia and from Italy, the Italian companies repeatedly faced difficulties in finding a sufficient number of labourers (a majority of the Eritreans were tied to agriculture and only a fraction of this labour force could be spared for non-agricultural activities), particularly when this movement of people northwards was hampered by regulations issued by the Ethiopian authorities. This factor might at times have had a braking effect on the rate of growth of the Eritrean industry. The abundance of manpower in the south was under these circumstances an additional reason to extend the economic control to Ethiopia.

The Italian plans never materialized: some plantations and a few small industries were established, but efforts were at first primarily concentrated on the construction of an infrastructure in Ethiopia as a base for a further exploitation, and no large-scale Italian company invested in the new colony. In 1941 the Italian intentions were drastically blocked by the British reappearance on the scene. Nevertheless, the behaviour of the British advisers did not indicate any immediate British interest in an economic colonization of Ethiopia. The industrial development during the 1940s was limited to a few Greek, Lebanese, Armenian and Italian investments. Although the new Ethiopian government after 1941 welcomed foreign capital, it met with little success. The European countries were exhausted after the war and American interests were focused on Europe: between 1945 and 1957 only 11% of US economic and military aid went to the underdeveloped countries, of which only a fraction reached Africa (except the commencement of military aid to Ethiopia in 1953). Out of total direct American investments abroad in 1950 less than one percent was made in Africa (exc. South Africa). Despite the fact that Ethiopia had been opened up by 6000 kms of Italian-built roads, and harbours had been improved, the country remained comparatively isolated from the world market. A very small portion of the population was in the money economy and most trade in the country was characterized by barter during the 1940s and 50s. A feudal mode of production was still dominant in many parts of the country; wage-labour was an almost unknown concept outside a few industrial pocket zones; and the market for manufactured goods was therefore extremely small.

The Emergence of a Modern State

Ethiopia's strategic position in the Horn of Africa and the fact that it was one of the few independent states in Africa made it attractive for American political, military and economic interests, whose possibilities of gaining a foothold in the rest of Africa were very limited. Moreover, the USA had a "tradition of interest" in Ethiopia. As early as the beginning of this century, American delegations were sent there to investigate its resources. Just after the First World War a delegation stated that:

> Abyssinia is able to supply hides, skins, coffee and articles of lesser importance such as honey, beeswax, ivory, civet, etc. The mineral resources are the richest—gold, silver, copper, iron, coal, sulphur, oil and potash. The presence of oil seems assured while potash is abundant near the Italian frontier. The Virginia-Carolina Chemical Company and the Anglo-American Oil Company are materially interested in Abyssinia. It would seem better to be on the ground when those underdeveloped resources were proved actually to exist in commercial abundance—and not wait until the European powers have established themselves to our exclusion. As a precautionary measure as well as a means of investigation, a legation would be of utmost importance. (*The National Archives of the United States*, M-412, p. 15.)

An agreement had been signed in 1942 between Britain and Ethiopia, giving the former great privileges in Ethiopia's internal affairs as well as in its international relations. A rapid decline in Britain's impact on Ethiopian policy, however, led to a new agreement between the two, less than three years later, which definitely put an end to British control in Ethiopia. The USA had obviously foreseen this outcome of the British-Ethiopian relations and was on hand a few months before the new treaty was signed. An American economic commission showed up, was received by the Emperor, and the first US-loan was granted to Ethiopia. In January 1945 the Emperor met President Roosevelt and the principles for an economic assistance were decided upon.

It would certainly have been possible to initiate economic growth with the available manpower and land resources in Ethiopia. Instead, a wide road to progress was chosen—via foreign capital and Western technology. It all happened very quickly: from being an undeveloped country with a weak and undeveloped state administration after the Italian occupation, the profile of Ethiopia's economic structure had drastically changed two decades later—at least for some 15-20% of the population. Developments during this period led straight to an increasing economic dependence on the USA, Europe and later Japan, and to a consequent vicious circle of underdevelopment.

About 85% of Ethiopia's population live by agriculture. Almost two-thirds of the total population live outside the money economy—their purchasing power is close to zero. Of the remaining one-third, only a fraction live above a level which allows the regular purchase of manufactured goods other than clothes, simple household equipment, etc. Due to a process of underdevelopment in certain rural areas (land concentration and eviction of tenants and small peasants) a relative surplus of labour has been created. This reserve army of labour is found in the plantations and in the towns. Their number does not stand in any reasonable relation to the supply of work. The symptoms are unemployment, underemployment and underpaid labour.

The export products are produced by a relatively small segment of the population. Much of the capital is either spent on imported luxury and consumption goods, primarily consumed by the upper levels of the society, or invested in non-productive activities, e.g., the private service sector. Moreover, most government funds are spent on the upkeep of an overdimensioned military and police corps and an overpopulated state bureaucracy where corruption was rampant, according to investigations made by the governments of 1974. In order to feed an upper and a growing middle class on a relatively costly level, Ethiopia more and more came to depend on the import of capital. In 1971/72, capital expenditures were to 58% covered by external assistance and loans. This increasing economic dependence strengthens the bargaining power of those who can offer this capital, i.e., the aid agencies, the credit givers and the potential investors.

Private investors are attracted by a set of advantages. In 1963 an Investment Decree was promulgated in order to encourage capital investments in the country—local as well as foreign. Among the advantages may be mentioned exemption from taxes during the first five years of operation, exemption from import duties, etc. Special agreements have been signed with individual governments, among others the American and West German governments. By these agreements, foreign investors are protected against inconvertibility, expropriation and risks arising from wars, rebellion, revolution and the like. Foreign investors are also allowed to remit profits to the country of origin and the repatriation of investment funds are provided for as well. From the legal point of view, the investment climate in Ethiopia is favourable. Yet, as we shall see, from the economic point of view it is not—at least not when production aims at internal consumption.

In order to understand the role of foreign investments in Ethiopia, a brief picture of the growth of the modern sector of the economy will be given. Production in large industries (defined as industries with more than five employees) grew by 15% yearly during the second half of the 1960s—a rapid relative growth but small in absolute figures. Only 80,000 people worked within the industry sector in 1970, which corresponded to 0.6% of the total economically active population, or 5% of the economically active urban population. The number of employees increased by 3.3% yearly between 1967 and 1970, to be compared with the population growth of those urban areas (where industries are concentrated), which was 7-8%. This means that unemployment is rapidly increasing in the large towns, absolutely as well as relatively. Whereas the Labour Exchange Offices in the three largest industry towns (Addis Ababa, Asmara and Dire Dawa) could find jobs for 22% of the registrants in 1968, they could find jobs for only 9% three years later. Whereas the number of employees per industry decreased by 3.5% yearly, the productivity, measured in gross value of production per employee, increased by 11.3% yearly. This development is logical: a high degree of dependence on imported capital implies an import of advanced technology. Industrial production has primarily grown through the introduction of advanced machinery, which is handled by skilled or semi-skilled labourers (the labour-intensive textile and leather industries constitute exceptions). An average wage increase of 4.7% yearly is primarily the result of the fact that a comparatively privileged labour force, usually with some education or vocational training, more and more replaces the unskilled labourers. Wages for this latter group have remained more or less constant during the entire decade.

The implications are not particularly "Ethiopian", but well-known wherever private capital dominates the economy. A slow increase in the number of wage labourers, and very low wages paid to those who are lucky enough to find a job, mean that the market for manufactured goods is extremely small. The reigning view in the development planning—supported by foreign advisers at all levels of the planning hierarchy—is that the only way out of this vicious circle is more foreign capital. In practice, they refuse to accept the fact that the high rate of unemployment, the low purchasing power and the low industry production are interlinked and functions of the profit-oriented economy—and that this economy behaves according to fluctuations in the world economy as a whole.

Concentrating on the two largest industry sectors, food and textiles, which had two-thirds of the total gross value of production in 1969/70, we find that 60% of total investments were made in these two sectors (36.5% in foods and 23.3% in textiles). As much as 70% of gross value-added in modern industries was found in these two sectors (40.2% and 29.5% respectively).

Characteristic for the food and textile industry is that none of its products can be manufactured further. This light industry is, together with the production of raw materials (in this case, cattle breeding and cotton), an isolated unit and does not contribute to a development of other sectors. This definitely does not mean that an import-substituting industry of this type is in itself development-obstructive, but encouraging investments within this light industry leaves less domestic capital for other sectors of the economy, thus hampering the industrial growth. Moreover, when the purchasing power is limited to a minority in the towns and when only a fraction of the ready-made products can be exported (as is the case for Ethiopia), the demand for

Table 1. *Some data about the 479 largest Ethiopian industries in 1969/70, for which data are available*
(values in million Eth$)

Industry	Fixed assets	Value-added at market price	Number of employees	Paid-up capital[1] local	Paid-up capital[1] foreign
Food & beverages	134.8	94.5	11,230	45.4	53.5
Textiles	86.0	69.2	21,610	31.9	45.6
Others	148.4	71.2	16,060	107.0	39.2
Total	369.2	234.9	48,900	184.3	138.3

[1] Only 263 industries.
Source: *Annual Survey of Manufacturing Industry for 1969/70*. Min. of Commerce, Industry and Tourism, and Central Statistical Office, Addis Ababa, June 1972.

consumption goods will already be satisfied at a comparatively low production volume and a continuous growth is hampered even within this sector. The fact that some of the textile industries produce at half capacity and that the yearly new investments in the food and textile industries decreased by 30% in the last four years of the 1960s may be interpreted as signs of a coming stagnation in the growth of these two sectors.

From Table 1 we can conclude that about 43% of the total paid-up capital is foreign; 54% in food, 59% in textiles and only 27% in other industries. The foreign control over the Ethiopian industry is, however, far larger than these figures indicate. Since the technology is monopolized by those enterprises which invest in Ethiopia it automatically gives them not only technological but also administrative control over a majority of the largest industries in the country—whether they have invested directly in those industries or not. Thus, as we shall see, not even 100% state-owned companies can avoid foreign influence. Moreover, foreign bank capital borrowing, with which industry capital is allied, and licensed production of certain items (e.g., Pepsi-Cola and tobacco) are instrumental in the foreign check on Ethiopia's industrial development.

In addition to the foreign-based industries, there are certain Italian, Greek, Lebanese and Armenian factories, transport firms, trade companies, etc.—some may have imported capital for investments and may send some or all of their profits abroad, but usually do not have any investments in other countries. They are often private local investors of foreign nationalities, neither controlled by mother companies abroad nor having responsibilities to large shareholders outside Ethiopia. These industries are in most cases defined as "foreign" in Table 1.

Foreign Investments in Ethiopia

The presence in Ethiopia of foreign companies, some of which are multinational, will be exemplified by the following. The distribution of petroleum products is done by the four companies Shell, Agip, Total and Mobil. The American company Tenneco has a concession on the exploitation of oil and gas in an area in south-eastern Ethiopia. Whitestone and Louisiana Land & Exploration Co. have a similar concession in eastern Ethiopia. An agreement has been signed with the Royal Dutch Shell Group, according to which they will explore for oil in a 26,800 sq. km. off-shore area at the Red Sea coast. Ethiopian-American Coffee Co., in which American companies own 70% of the shares, has one of the largest coffee plantations in the country. International Industrial Development Consultant Inc. (US) has interests in forest exploitation. 50% of the shares in the first large paper factory were owned by Parsons and Whittemore (US) but have since been sold to the Ethiopian Government and to IFC. Ethiopian Airlines is in practice a daughter company of TWA. There are also a few other world-renowned American companies with major shares in Ethiopian companies, but none of them is particularly large in Ethiopia. Their interest at this stage is less that of making profits than of following developments and being on the spot "if anything happens" (some of these companies have tasks of more of a political than of an economic nature).

Among consultant firms could be mentioned Stanford Research Institute and Opportunities Industrialization Centre, both of which have started activities in Ethiopia with an aim to investigating the investment climate there. American companies also receive regular financial support from USAID (since 1967) in order to explore investment opportunities through study trips to Ethiopia. Actually, it is hardly possible to distinguish American companies from assistance agencies such as USAID and IBRD. Their interests are closely linked and these two agencies, probably together with a few others, should therefore logically be included in an enumeration of foreign commercial interests in Ethiopia. They do not invest directly, but the impression they give is that their task is to prepare the ground for a penetration of American business capital. Moreover, they tie more local capital into so-called development projects than pure companies do. This means that given the dependence on foreign capital through 'aid', local capital, which would otherwise have been available for investing in improvements for the Ethiopian people, is very often 'lost' in development-alienated projects. It might be of interest to note here that the question of foreign loans became a very hot issue in the Ethiopian Parliament during its "radical period" in 1974. Many of the MPs complained about the biased allocation of loans, and one of them once exclaimed, while discussing a new IDA-loan of US $21.4 million, that "in the past the country has borrowed about Eth $811 million. This sum alone could have made all Ethiopians millionaires instead of borrowers." Later the same year, when the USA threatened to withdraw its aid from Ethiopia, a spokesman for the military government stated at a press conference that Ethiopia could do without the American money, which anyway always had gone to the "reactionary government" (before March 1974), and never been used for the welfare of the Ethiopian people.

Among British investments may be mentioned Mitchell Cotts Ltd., which has the largest share in one of the largest cotton plantations in the country, and which, together with International Packers (Chicago and London) has invested in slaughter-houses. Smith and Nephew Associated Cos. (London) has 50% of the share capital in Ethiopian Drug Manufacturing Company.

Japanese capital has come fairly late to Ethiopia, but is now advancing. In addition to various investments in the textile industry—discussed below—

the Nippon Mining Co. has made investments in copper mining in Eritrea in northern Ethiopia (the same company has a monopoly on copper in Angola and is expanding in Zaire). Nippon has 49% of the shares and the Ethiopian Government the remaining 51%. A condition for the Japanese investment was that the Ethiopian Government arrange the loan and stand as the sole guarantor. In practice this means that Nippon brings the technology to Ethiopia and returns to Japan with the copper—at a rate considerably below the world market price. In March 1974 a guerilla group blew up the copper mine and production was interrupted. It had not yet recommenced one year later. Nippon is (or at least was) also investigating the possibilities of mining copper in western Ethiopia.

Here are four examples of foreign investments within various sectors of the Ethiopian economy. First, the sugar industry, which is monopolized by a Dutch company and the second largest industry in Ethiopia, will be presented as one of the most striking example of the destructive effects of foreign capital in Ethiopia. Secondly, the complex ownership pattern of the textile industries will be elaborated on. The increasingly important agricultural export is the third example, and finally, a foreign concession will be discussed, which differs from other investments in the sense that it has not led to any production and which thereby hampers the growth of an important sector, namely the potash industry.

The sugar industry[1]

HVA (Handels Vereniging Amsterdam) is a Dutch company, previously very active in Indonesia and which has now moved into Africa. It administers two large sugar plantation southeast of Addis Ababa. HVA-Ethiopia is a joint venture in which HVA (Holland) has the major share and the Ethiopian Government 10%. The company has in practice a monopoly on sugar production in Ethiopia. The primary purpose of this sugar industry was to substitute the import of sugar. This goal has been attained and Ethiopia is now self-supporting in sugar.

Nevertheless, a study of this local sugar production reveals since 1954, when the first plantation was started, HVA-Ethiopia has not had any noticeable positive effect on the country's balance of payment. It is even possible that the net effect has been an outflow of capital compared to a hypothetical situation in which Ethiopia had imported all the sugar now consumed in the country. Moreover, taxes on locally produced sugar are much lower than on imported sugar (explained by the fact that profits are inversely proportional to taxes). This implies that if Ethiopia had imported all the sugar that was consumed in 1970/71, the state revenues that year would have been higher by Eth $9.5 million. The company is one of the largest employers in the country, but has kept the number of labourers more or less constant during the last decade, despite an increase in production. In eight years, the productivity, measured in tons per man-year, has increased by almost 50%. The capital-intensive investments have meant an outflow of capital from the country—at the expense of more employment opportunities in Ethiopia.

Though productivity has increased, wages have not. Huge reserves of manpower are utilized to a limited extent, which has made possible a minimization of wages. Although a doubling of the low-paid labourers' wages would mean a reduction of profits by not more than some 20%, wages have been kept at a minimum level, which is about Eth $1-2 per day (after strikes and demonstrations in 1974, however, wages increased). Out of total emoluments of about Eth $10 million in 1971, 90% of the wage-earners earned 33%, which totalled less than the salaries to the 2% best paid (who received 37%). Repeated demands by Dutch shareholders for increased profits have several times forced HVA-Ethiopia to increase the price of its sugar, and to follow this by requests to the Government to impose heavier taxes on imported sugar. The price has now reached such a level that sugar has become a luxury for an increasing number of Ethiopians. This may explain why the growth of sugar consumption has decreased from 8-9% yearly up to 1966 to about 4% since then. After the last price increase in 1972 the consumption in fact decreased by 2.1% compared to the previous year. This remarkable development was counteracted by the new government in 1974, by imposing price controls on sugar.

To summarize, local production of sugar has not contributed to an improvement of Ethiopia's balance of payment, and it has implied a relative decrease in state revenues. The retail price has increased by some 30% in a decade, whereas wages have remained more or less constant. It is possible to prove, with mathematical exactness, a direct correlation between level of profits, retail price of sugar, and sugar consumption *per capita*. With increasing retail price, profits go up and consumption goes down. A retailer earns five times more than the harvester per kilo of sugar, the total capital outflow from the country amounts to 7-8 times the total wages paid out to the labourers, etc.

The textile industries

The textile industry in Ethiopia is a complicated interlacing of foreign interests. The biggest factory, Cotton Company of Ethiopia, is 50%-owned by a Japanese union of companies, Sabean Utility Corporation (SUC), which also has a share in the Fibre Company of Ethiopia. In the same factory we find the powerful Indian company, Birla Brothers Ltd. Co. (BBLC), which also has 41% of the shares in the Indo-Ethiopian Textiles Share Co. (in addition, 13% of the shares are held by Indian citizens). The director of BBLC is simultaneously both responsible for the operation of the state-owned Bahr Dar Textile Mills and the director of one of the largest distribution firms in textiles, namely the Indian Shantilal and Co. Ethiopia Ltd. Moreover, BBLC is partly associated with the Indian firm, Messrs Duncan Brothers and Co. Ltd., which has 50% of the shares in National Textiles. Three Japanese companies, Toyo Rayon Co., Sakai Textile Manufacturing Co., and Mitsuisiu Shoji Kaisha Ltd., with interests in the above-mentioned SUC, own half of the share capital in Ethio-Japanese Synthetic Textiles.

To these textile industries, which are all to be found in the neighbourhood of Addis Abeba and in Dire Dawa, we should add the Italian-dominated textile industries in Asmara, namely Manufattura Sacchi (89% Italian), Barattolo Cotton Mills (100% Italian), Industrial Maglieria Asmara, Ethiopian Textile Industries Co. (60% Italian) and Ethio-Fabrics (86% Italian).

It goes without saying that it is extremely difficult for the Ethiopian authorities to exert any efficient control over this complicated network of foreign interests in Ethiopia.

The textile industry is, as a sector, the largest employer, with more than 20,000 labourers. As we have seen above, almost 60% of the paid-up capital is foreign, mainly Indian, Japanese and Italian. It is not an exaggeration to say that no part of this industry is not wholly or partly controlled by foreigners or foreign companies: most of the local capital—whether public or private—is tied to factories with foreign directors. As we have seen, even the 100% state-owned Bahr Dar Textile Mills has an Indian as one of its directors. No one has attempted to estimate the number of weavers who have lost both job and income after large-scale production took over some of the market for clothes, but since handicraft and domestic small-scale industry have a much lower productivity than large-scale industry, one may draw the conclusion that more people have lost than 'gained' (i.e., own-account weavers versus wage labourers).

It is worth repeating that the textile industry is only linked backwards to the production of raw cotton, and not linked to the rest of the economy. Therefore, it does not have any stimulating effect on industrialization as a whole. It is a closed entity with little further possibility for growth. This does not mean that there should be no textile industry in a country such as Ethiopia, but when it has no development effect and is, together with the cotton plantations, controlled by foreign interests, one may justifiably question the priority this industry has received. This is particularly true for one of the largest industries, Ethio-Japanese Synthetic Textiles, which imports the raw material (plastic) to make synthetic clothes. It is doubtful whether Ethiopia is the right place for such an industry, and if this is the right type of industry in a country like Ethiopia.

The textile industries are, and must be, labour-intensive. It is a well-known fact that this is the main reason why MNCs prefer to establish these industries in countries where wages are comparatively low. Contrary to other industries in Ethiopia, women are preferred to men as labourers in all but one of the textile industries (despite the fact that traditional weavers are often men). The reason is that the wage demands of women are less pronounced than those of men and wages constitute a large part of the production costs in labour-intensive industries, it is important that these costs be kept at a lower level, so that women are used as labourers. Moreover, women were traditionally thought to be less prone to labour disputes and therefore less of a threat in factories which depend on large numbers of unskilled workers. Strikes among the textile workers in 1971 and 1974 showed, however, that this assumption was wrong.

Export of agricultural products

For the industrialized countries it pays better to move the production of food to regions where land is abundant and labour is cheap. Most of the arable land in Ethiopia is not utilized. This land is of two types: either State Domains, which usually demand irrigation for cultivation and which can be granted as concessions to private investors, or privately owned land, which for various reasons (land speculation, lack of technology or capital, difficulties in finding local markets, etc.) is kept idle. Large areas in Ethiopia are waiting for capital and technology to start producing food for an increasing demand in the 'centre of the world'. Due to inadequate infrastructure a foreign exploitation of these resources has been delayed. But various important roads are now opening up the country more effectively than during the short period of Italian occupation.

A new road linking Addis Ababa with the port town of Assab on the Red Sea coast, constructed by a German entrepreneur (Trapp & Co.), gives and will give plantation owners along the large Awash River, running parallel with the road, opportunities to sell their produce both to the market in Addis Ababa and for export. The above-mentioned HVA-Ethiopia, is one of them. Among others may be mentioned the British company, Mitchell Cotts, producing cotton for the above-mentioned textile industries. A Japanese firm has shown interest in establishing itself here in order to produce, for example, alfalfa as animal feed for export to Japan. The Japanese firm did not, however, obtain the concession. Instead, a newly established Italian plantation, MAESCO, is producing alfalfa for export—to Japan. This production of animal feed for export takes place in a region where people were starting to death and tens of thousands of cattle, camels, sheep and goats were lost in 1973, partly due to the lack of rain, but primarily due to the fact that these people (and their domestic animals) had been evicted from their best grazing lands (which they had used for centuries) by the establishment of commercial plantations. This cynicism later became more or less a criminal offense when MAESCO started to breed cattle and sheep—also for export.

Another example is a huge area, called Setit Humera, in north-western Ethiopia, where sesame seeds and other agricultural products are grown for export. No specific foreign investment is involved in this production yet. Nevertheless, the IBRD, through the Ethiopian development bank (Agricultural and Industrial Development Bank of Ethiopia—AID Bank) takes part in the development of the area. Logically, the region, which has been very isolated previously, is now being linked via a highway with the world market.

A similar development may be found in southern Ethiopia, but in this region the interest is entirely focused on cattle-breeding. USAID has here started large-scale ranching for the local people, called the National Development Range Project. In order to facilitate and improve trade with Kenya, a road leading between Addis Ababa and Nairobi is under construction by an Israeli firm (Solel Boneh) with German capital. The project area is located along this road. American companies have registered as potential investors in cattle-breeding in this particular area, for the production and export of meat and hides & skins. Another project, Southern Rangelands Livestock Development Project, covering the southern part of Ethiopia (160,000 sq. kms), is planned as well—but with IBRD-capital. It is not known whether the 1973-74 famine in this region has affected the plans.

The last example will be a long but expressive interview with the director of American Foods Share Co., Robert Zwarthruis.[2] The firm is owned by two Swedish shipping companies, Salénrederierna and Johnsonlinjen. The interview is here translated and presented without comments:

> American Foods sells fruits and vegetables through its own offices in Sweden, Norway, Denmark and Finland and in collaboration with companies virtually all over Europe. Our greatest stake is in Ethiopia, but we are also trying countries such as Ivory Coast, Egypt, Kenya, Zambia, Uganda. In South America our interest is focused on Mexico and Venezuela. We don't go to an underdeveloped country because we believe that we should help that country. Anyone who says that "We go to Ethiopia or Morocco in order to help those poor things" is lying. We just have to accept this. We go to an underdeveloped country for one simple reason. Israel has become a very strong producer of exactly the same goods as we have. Israel exports through a state company and sets its own prices.
>
> If we are to be able to compete with them we have to do it on the same price-conditions, and this we cannot do if we buy goods from North America as we

did earlier. We need a continuous supply and this we get if we go to countries like Ethiopia and Egypt, which do not have any local market for these products.

The only ones we have any contact with in, for example, Ethiopia is the official authorities. We sign a contract and we do not care about the rest. We have tried to understand the situation there, but we did not succeed very well. I don't think Ethiopia constitutes an exception in this case. We have never regarded it as an advantage to invest in an underdeveloped country. It isn't. I tell you frankly—you cannot trust them.

We take home our investments every year. When the season is over the money is at home. And depending on the outcome of the season, one stakes on the coming year.

The increase has been enormous. We double every year in Ethiopia. They have a good product and the only real problem is that the resistance group (the Eritrean guerilla—author's note) is very active although not very much is published about it in the papers. One gets stuck in barricades about once an hour and it has happened that truck transports have been stopped. But if you give them 10-15 dollars they will let you through. Another factor of uncertainty is that the Emperor is so old. One doesn't know what will happen to him.

The only thing we really stick to, from the moral point of view, presuming it has any meaning to talk about morals in affairs, is that we keep a very good price in comparison with the prices in America or in Italy, and that we always pay straight to the bank of producing country, not to, for example, an account in Sweden. We haven't had much contacts or any problems with trade unions in the supplying countries. There was one case, the wellknown Cesar Chavez-case, agricultural labourer in California and the boycott of salad. They asked us to support the boycott but we refused. We would do the same thing if they asked us in Ethiopia or Uganda. We buy where we get the best goods at the best price—that is decisive for us.

We are now searching for the ideal country in Africa. We believe it is on the west coast of Africa, where the climate is better and where it is politically calmer. We expect to be able to export large quantities to Japan and America. We believe that Africa is going to become the world's biggest producer of vegetables, not only to Europe but also to America. If you demand 10% yield on the capital in Sweden, it should be 20-25% in Africa. The political risks imply that once you have succeeded in building up an organization for export, it may be nationalized. There is no country where you can be safe today.

The potash concession

Non-mineral resources in Ethiopia are limited, with the exception of salt and potash—both abundant in the Danakil desert in the north-east. According to the Third Five-Year Development Plan (1968-1973), potash production was planned to increase to a value of some Eth $45 millions in 1972/73, corresponding to more than 10% of Ethiopia's total exports that year. This would have meant a great deal for the trade balance, but so far production has not started.

According to a study made in 1968[3], the potash reserves are supposed to be about 160 million tons. The top of the potash horizon is to be found at 45-80 meters, but according to other sources even higher. The production costs would amount to about US $25 per ton. Investments for exploitation are estimated to about US $67 million (34 million for the project and 33 million for the infrastructure). Full production could be achieved by the third year of operations. Even when depreciation is subtracted, there would be a gross profit as early as the fifth year. The gross profit would later stabilize at US $11-12 million annually.

The centre of potash production is Saskatchewan in Canada. High inland freights from Saskatchewan to the coast mean that Ethiopian potash is cheaper than Canadian potash. When comparing transportation costs to Bombay—India being the probably biggest importer of potash in the world—it is only US $8 per ton from the mines in Ethiopia, but US $21 from Saskatchewan. In fact, transportation costs are even lower from Ethiopia than from Canada to harbours in USA. One may well ask why the Ethiopian potash is not mined.

In 1957 Parsons and Co. (USA) joined another firm to study possibilities for the exploitation of the Ethiopian potash. The company later obtained concessions on the mines, which implied a monopoly on potash mining in Ethiopia. Nevertheless, the same company has a concession on the Saskatchewan mines in Canada. By extending their activities and producing potash in Ethiopia, they would cause the world market price of potash to fall, thereby affecting the profitability of the mines in Canada. Ethiopians who have studied the matter are of the opinion that it is for this very reason that Parsons and Co. let the mines in Ethiopia lie idle. India pays a high price for imported potash. The Indian Government has therefore asked the Ethiopian Government to take over the concession. According to an Ethiopian official in the Ministry of Mines, "The Indian Government is willing to pay any price to start potash production in Ethiopia to be exported to India", but the arm of the Ethiopian Government is being twisted: breaking the contract with Parsons and Co. might threaten Ethiopia's trade relations with USA (to which 50% of all exports go).

The Parsons and Co.-concession is probably of a very special type of MNC-activity in an underdeveloped country. By withholding production, the world market price of potash can be kept high—to the advantage of the American company, but to the disadvantage of Ethiopia, who loses a potential income from exports, and of India, who must pay an unreasonably high price for potash.

Conclusion

From what has been said above, we can draw at least three general conclusions:

a. the modern sector of the Ethiopian economy has grown rapidly during the last two decades, when measured in relative terms (growth expressed in percentages), but is still small when measured in absolute terms (total production, or total production in relation to the so-called traditional sector of the economy).

b. foreign-owned companies, among which we find some multinational, control the major part of the modern sector. But since this sector is comparatively small, it follows that foreign capital still plays a relatively limited role in Ethiopia, at least in comparison with most other Third World countries (this refers to the *direct* effects of the presence of foreign capital, whereas the situation is, of course, somewhat different when analysing the *indirect* effects on the conditions of the Ethiopian people).

c. the Ethiopian people do not benefit from the growth of the modern sector of the economy. On the contrary, several examples could be given to show that growth in Ethiopia has always been followed by underdevelopment (it should be noted that the latest famine in Ethiopia is an accentuation of a normal situation, and not an isolated occurrence—a fact which this year has been stressed even in the Ethiopian Parliament and by government authorities).

An old economic system, which one might call "feudal", was not replaced but temporarily complemented by a growing presence of capitalism. This growth of a modern economy expanded more rapidly than the political consciousness, and a confrontation occurred between the two systems. The established system hampered the growth of the establishing one. The weaker resisted too long and is now being artificially eradicated. This political development is logical and has therefore been expected by everyone.

Due to a rapid increase in world market prices of raw products and food in 1973-74, the balance of trade became positive for the first time in 15 years. During Ethiopia's introductory period of economic transformation, the country was richer than ever before: total monetary resources stood at over Eth $1,000 million in June 1974. On the other hand, no important investments were made, and by the end of the year, over 70 foreign firms had applied to the National Bank for the repatriation of their investment funds. During the first half of the year, strikes flourished all over the country. They were forbidden, but were then replaced by slow-downs (this has been confirmed for at least some industries and plantations), with the same effect: production declined. A stagnation in the economy should, however, be seen as a short-term effect of the political turmoil of 1974.

The growth of the modern sector has during the last two decades been rather spontaneous. With a new political platform, an economic "take-off" may become a possibility in the long run—not to be confused with "development for 30 million people". The technology is in Europe, Japan and North America, but the capital is moving to the oil-producing countries. Five conditions for a growth of agricultural export are now fulfilled: (i) technology available in the advanced capitalist countries, (ii) surplus of capital in the oil-producing, particularly the neighbouring Arab, countries, (iii) abundance of fertile land and manpower in Ethiopia, (iv) a new political platform in Ethiopia, which may become adapted to the demands of a modern economy, and (v) increasing food demand in the industrialised countries.

Despite all the factors that point towards an increasing dependence on the industrialized countries in the future, there also exist possibilities for a fairly strong and less dependent state capitalism. The recent wave of "Ethiopian socialism", infused by a large portion of nationalism, and manifested in the nationalization of banks and insurance companies (January 1975), in combination with the prospects for ever-increasing export earnings (and expected decrease in import of luxury goods—Tanzanian model), particularly if Ethiopia itself should become an oil-producing country, may lead to such a development.

Notes

[1] This is a summary of a chapter in L. Bondestam, *People and Capitalism in the Awash Valley—Ethiopia,* prepared for the Seminar on the Emergence of Agrarian Capitalism in Africa South of the Sahara, Dakar, December 1973. A manager of HVA obtained a copy in January 1974 and promised an official of the Ethiopian government to comment on it. One year later, no comment had been given. After it was reprinted in *Journal of Modern African Studies,* Sept. 1974, an HVA spokesman gave the following comment in *African Development,* Nov. 1974: "... much of Bondestam's criticism is now irrelevant at a time of high sugar prices. The price HVA was selling sugar at, $69 per quintal at the beginning of 1974, actually meant that sugar was being sold at a loss on the local market and that the company and Ethiopia would have made a good profit if its production had all been exported. The company's costs (fertilisers, plastic bags, etc.) have rocketed this year and yet it has kept the selling price down." Since the facts given in the paper have so far not been denied by HVA, one must assume they are correct.

In order not to receive a wrong impression of the actual situation from the comment above, it is worth adding that from 1971 to 1973 HVA's legal export of sugar increased from 14.000 to 32.000 tons due to a doubling of the world market price during this period. Due to a continuous rise in sugar price during 1974, illegal sugar export commenced and rocketed. The rapidly increasing legal and illegal export was not balanced by a comparable increase in production and consequently local consumption of sugar declined, due to a lack of sugar on the domestic market.

[2] The interview was referred to in *SIDA-rapport,* No. 8, Stockholm 1972.

[3] *Dallol potash project, a review and reappraisal,* a study by Mackay & Schnellmann Ltd, London, December 1968.

Jan Jelmert Jørgensen

Multinational Corporations and the Indigenization of the Kenyan Economy[1]

The process of de-indigenization of the Kenyan economy in the colonial period and the subsequent post-independence attempts to indigenize or Africanize the economy can be analysed at three distinct levels: the structure of the economy; control over individual production and distribution firms; and the racial division of labour within each firm. In this paper I shall examine the role of multinational corporations in the de-indigenization and indigenization processes, using the three-level analytical framework presented in Figure 1.

Analytical level		*Operational measures*
I.	The structure of the economy. Inter-sectoral integration and the integration of the economy as a whole within the vertical international division of labour.	Input-output analysis, inter-sector relationships, and composition of external trade (raw materials *v.* processed goods).
II.	Control of units of production and distribution within economic sectors and sub-sectors.	Racial identity of owners of individual firms within each sector or sub-sector.
III.	Division of labour by race within individual firms.	Racial identity of employees in high-level positions within each firm, especially managerial, sales, accounting and technical positions.

Figure 1. *Three-level framework for analysis of indigenization or de-indigenization in the Kenyan economy*

Kenya became structurally integrated into the world economy in the nineteenth and twentieth centuries. During the colonial phase the structure of the domestic economy was transformed to produce agricultural goods needed by the external economy and to import consumer goods and machinery from the external economy. Under pressure from European settlers, the colonial regime relegated the African population to a subservient role as labourers for non-African enterprises. Thus de-indigenization took place at all three levels of the economy. During this period the foreign firms in banking, agriculture and commerce accommodated themselves to the settler economy, thus acquiescing in the subjugation of Africans at levels II and III, while participating directly in the process of de-indigenization at level I.

Since political independence in 1964, the urban African political and commercial elite has replaced the European settlers as the *comprador* class allied with multinational corporations. Hitherto the post-independence political regime has pursued an Africanization policy which is limited to the racial division of labour within firms and, to a lesser extent, the Africanization of ownership of firms (levels III and II, respectively). The regime's Africanization policy does not deal with the structure of the economy, an omission or non-decision which benefits the multinational corporations. Thus the post-independence phase has been characterized by continued de-indigenization at the structural level (level I), combined with increasing indigenization of ownership of firms and employment (levels II and III).

The colonial phase: the political economy of de-indigenization

Foreign control of the Kenyan economy began with the incorporation of the coastal strip into the nascent international mercantilist/capitalist system in the fifteenth and sixteenth centuries. After almost four hundred years of intermittent battles fought by the Portuguese, English, Arabs, Germans, Galla and Swahili for control of the various towns and forts along the shores of the Indian Ocean, the coastal strip passed into the hands of the Sultan of Zanzibar under British protection in the nineteenth century. Through the imperialism of free trade, the coast of what is now Kenya became integrated with the British economy in the mid-nineteenth century, well before the arrival of the first British firms on the mainland and well before the onset of formal colonial rule.[2]

Trade between the coast and the interior of East Africa was pioneered by Africans, such as the Nyamwezi traders of what is now Tanzania and the Kamba caravans of Kenya, and by Arab traders.[3] Exports consisted of ivory, skins and hides, and slaves for French sugar plantations in the Indian Ocean islands and for the Americas. Imports were more varied, consisting of cotton cloth, brass and iron goods, beads, wire and tobacco. Trade within the interior, consisting of grains, beans, other foodstuffs, cattle, salt and iron tools, was largely controlled by the Africans themselves, such as the Kikuyu traders of Mahiga.[4]

Thus the first British firms to become successfully involved in trade with the interior, such as Smith-Mackenzie,[5] were relative late-comers, although their involvement with the coastal trade had secondary effects on trade in the interior.

Whereas earlier traders had only been involved in transportation and distribution, delegating the production and collection of goods for export to Africans living in the interior, the British firms quickly became involved in re-organizing production as well.[6] British firms and British settler-planters established copra and sisal plantations along the coast and later coffee and finally tea plantations further inland at higher elevations. The British firms were interested not merely in making a profit but also in finding new markets for manufactured goods from Britain and in finding cheap sources of raw materials for British firms with whom they were connected by trade or ownership.[7] Moreover, the political and moral movement to replace the slave trade with "legitimate commerce" at the end of the nineteenth century necessitated the discovery of viable exports other than slaves and ivory to pay for the growing volume of imports[8] and the construction of railways for the transportation of exports as well as the transportation of troops required to suppress the trade in slaves. In terms of economic motives, the replacement of the slave trade with legitimate commerce also enhanced the British firms' competitive position *vis-à-vis* Arab and coastal rivals who had become overly dependent on the slave trade, and the building of railways enhanced manufacturing interests in Great Britain.[9]

Even so, African producers in Kenya held their own up until World War I. Prior to the construction of the railway from Mombasa on the Indian Ocean coast to Kisumu on Lake Victoria in 1902, African producers accounted for virtually all exports from the interior. These exports consisted of slaves, ivory, hides and skins. African producers accounted for at least 70 percent of exports in 1911-12, including all of the simsim crop, Kenya's major export at the time, and three-fifths of the maize crop carried by the railways in that year.[10] But with the maturation of sisal and coffee plantations in the early 1920s, European-owned plantation agriculture replaced African-controlled production as the "foundation" of Kenya's economy, the former accounting for half of the colony's exports in 1929.[11] Faced with increasing political and administrative interference and economic pressure to make African labour available for the European planters and settlers, African production of goods for export entered into an *absolute* decline in 1925.[12] By 1928, the African producers' share in total exports had fallen below 20 percent, consisting mainly of hides and skins.[13] The share of European plantation crops in total exports remained at approximately half up until World War II, although the composition changed from primarily coffee and sisal to include tea in the 1930s as the second most important export. Coffee plantations were largely run by independent European settler-planters, whereas the establishment of the vast tea plantations around Kericho and Eldoret in the Highlands involved "large London interests"[14] such as Brooke Bond.

Between 1902 and 1929 the political economy of Kenya was further transformed by the influx of approximately 2000 European settlers and their families.[15] These Europeans, mainly British but also Boers and others, exercised political influence far out of proportion to their numbers during the course of Kenya's colonial period and sought vigorously to establish a white-settler regime in Kenya and to stifle any signs of independent economic activity among Africans which might endanger the supply of African labour for European farms and plantations or which might engender competition in the supply of agricultural produce for the domestic and export markets.[16]

Three levels of de-indigenization, 1902-1952

The decline of African control of the Kenyan economy, or de-indigenization of the economy, occurred simultaneously at various levels of economic activity. At the structural level, Kenya entered the vertical international division of labour through trade with the outside world, so that Kenyans laboured to produce raw materials or labour (slaves) needed by the external economy and in turn consumed manufactured goods and machinery imported from the external economy. Over the course of the nineteenth and twentieth centuries a larger and larger proportion of the African population was diverted from production solely for domestic consumption to satisfy their own needs (use-value) to production largely or solely for export to satisfy the needs of the external economy (exchange-value) or to production to satisfy the needs of resident aliens such as the Europeans, Asians and Arabs (also exchange-value). It is in this sense of transforming the structure of the economy to meet the needs of the external economy and resident aliens that I speak of the de-indigenization of the structure of the Kenyan economy (level I).

At the level of control of units of production and units of distribution in the form of ownership of farms, firms and other commercial entities (level II), the decline in African control began with the loss of control over trade with the outside world, a loss which predated the arrival of British firms in the interior. Next, control over trade between the interior and the coast slipped from the hands of the Kamba and Swahili into the hands of Arabs, Asians and Europeans. Finally, control over internal trade, or the more lucrative portions of it, shifted from African to European and Asian control. Likewise, African control over units of production and over production itself was abrogated by the emergence of European plantation agriculture and by the arrival of European settlers. The demands of European planters and settlers for control of the means of production—African labour, African land and private and public capital—through control of the colonial administrative apparatus gradually reduced Africans from independent producers and traders to the status of labourers for European and Asian firms and for public works to benefit these same firms. Legal sanctions were invoked to deprive Africans of land and to force tenants or squatters who remained behind to work at least 180 days in the year for their European masters.[17] Those Africans who chose not to work for European firms or the European colonial administration were only allowed to engage in subsistence agriculture on ever-shrinking "Native Reserves". By 1937 the amount of land *reserved* for European alienation plus land deemed *suitable* for alienation to Europeans totalled 119,357 square kilometres (29.5 million acres), whereas the amount of land in Native Reserves totalled only 124,768 sq. km. (30.8 million acres), despite the fact that Europeans comprised less than one percent of the population and Africans almost 98 percent of the population.[18]

At the level of racial division of labour within firms (level III), Africans ceased to be independent producers of goods for trade except for production of foodstuffs and other goods *within* the Native Reserves for consumption within the same area, and were coerced into becoming labourers for Europeans and Asians.[19] Europeans controlled the colonial administrative apparatus, financial institutions, the larger import-export firms, shipping, mining (gold and soda ash), plantations, large farms, large-scale food processing firms (breweries, bacon factories, co-operative creameries, canneries), and the larger commercial firms in urban areas. Asians controlled smaller import-export firms, most of the retail shops in cities and towns, financial institutions serving the Asian community, and small-scale manufacturing (aluminium pots, soap, vegetable oils, saw mills). In addition, Asians filled most of the positions of artisans and clerks in European and Asian firms and in the colonial administration. Africans controlled petty trade, subsistence farming and subsistence pastoral agriculture within the Native Reserves or worked as labourers for Europeans and Asians. Very few Africans were employers rather than employees.[20] In 1937, the great majority of employed Africans, 58.1 percent out of a total 182,900 regular employees, were to be found in agriculture, working for European farmers and planters.[21] A further 15.4 percent of regularly employed Africans were to be found in government employment on the railway, in the military, police or prison staff, or in other government departments. Domestic servants accounted for 9.5 percent of African employment; mining, 3.5 percent; and other employment in timber, construction, lighterage, missions, etc., 13.5 percent.

European settlers and the politics of de-indigenization

During the period 1902-52, under pressure from the European settlers, the economy of Kenya was transformed into an economy of "labour reserves", to use Samir Amin's terminology.[22] Africans were driven off land reserved for European planters and settlers and segregated into Native Reserves, where they were kept at a level of subsistence existence to form a pool of labourers available for employment by European farms and firms and by the colonial government, thus artificially "solving" any problems of low wages or labour shortages. The goals and strategy of the settlers were described in 1912 by the Provincial Commissioner for Nairobi:

> . . . The Settlers particularly those with South African experience . . . are bent on a process of denationalizing the native tribes for what they imagine to be their own ends, the belief being that a large landless native population will be forced into the labour market.[23]

Moreover, the white settlers were extremely suspicious of any attempts by the colonial administration to further even rudimentary programmes of development in the Native Reserves, such as education and health or introduction of cash crops, for fear of any consequent reduction in the supply of cheap labour to the white farms and plantations.[24] The hostile attitude of a large segment of the European population towards any policies which benefited Africans was deplored by a few of the colonial administrators, especially those who bore the wrath of the settlers when attempts were made to better conditions in the reserves:

> There is, as we all know, an unfortunate tendency amongst the unthinking part of the white public, and even amongst the thinking part, when they have immediate interests to serve, to look upon the native of the country as having only one use in life, i.e., to work for the White. When the native does not come up to expectations in this respect the European officials serving in the Reserves are blamed and abused. The ordinary public does not attempt to try and understand the native point of view. It refuses to allow that he has any right to cultivate his land except perhaps for his immediate food requirements. And this public views any policy as having as its object the betterment of natives as strongly inimical to white interests, because so they say, it tends to keep the natives out of the labour market, or induces them to ask for higher wages. . .[25]

By the 1920s, this ideology was so deeply ingrained among the European settlers and planters that the Governor of Kenya, Robert Thorne Coryndon, found it necessary to defend the colonial agricultural policies within the Native Reserves directly in terms of their effect on the supply of labour to white settlers:

> . . . I do not believe for a moment that the Government's policy of encouraging the production of native grown crops in the reserves will have any adverse effect upon the supply of voluntary labour outside the reserves, if the measures and safeguards I have already indicated are taken and observed.[26]

Increasingly, the ideology of European settlers made itself felt on the policies of the colonial government in Kenya. Africans were barred from *individual ownership of land* in the Native Reserves in a landmark judicial case in 1921.[27] Without recognition of individual ownership of land, Africans were in effect barred from using land as security in borrowing money from banks and wholesalers. Furthermore, within the capitalist legal framework imposed on Kenya by colonial rule, the absence of individual ownership of land left land in Native Reserves open to future alienation to non-Africans by administrative fiat with no question of compensation being allowed.[28]

Pressure from European settlers led to an *unequal distribution of tax burdens and government services* among Africans and Europeans. Africans received the bulk of the tax burden; Europeans, the bulk of the government services.[29] The Africans bore the bulk of the tax burden through poll taxes, hut taxes and high customs duties on imported cotton piece goods. By contrast, European settlers successfully resisted the imposition of income tax up till 1938. The bulk of government health, education and agricultural services supported by government revenues went to European settlers. Similarly, railway extensions were situated to develop European settler areas rather than African peasant agriculture.[30] On the other hand, the rail freight structure fell disproportionately on tropical exports produced by African peasants (and some European plantations) in Uganda and Tanganyika and effectively subsidized the temperate-climate agricultural produce of the European settlers.

In addition, Africans were barred from *wholesale trade* in agricultural produce under the provisions of the Marketing of Native Produce Ordinance of 1935, which prohibited "non-established" (i.e., African) traders from buying or selling specified produce within a three-mile radius of "established" (i.e., European or Asian) trading centres.[31] This measure not only gave European and Asian traders a virtual monopoly on the buying of African produce but could also be used informally to bar Africans from producing cash crops, such as maize, which competed with produce from European settlers' farms, since it left marketing in the hands of non-Africans, who could simply refuse to buy from Africans or could set artificially low prices to discourage African producers.

African peasant farmers also came into conflict with European planters and settlers over the *cultivation of cash crops for export,* notably coffee. Under pressure from the European growers, the colonial regime *denied Africans the right to grow coffee* throughout the 1920s and 1930s by denying Africans licenses to grow coffee under the Coffee Plantations Registration Ordinance of 1918.[32] Similarly, under the guise of protecting the crop from disease, Africans were denied the opportunity to cultivate *pyrethrum,* a high-value flower whose extract is a powerful insecticide. This crop became a mainstay of the European farmers' profits from 1937 onwards.[33]

Throughout the colonial period Africans were placed under severe *credit restrictions.* These assumed renewed importance following World War II, when African servicemen returned from overseas duties with ambitions of starting their own businesses. Under the Credit to Africans (Control) Ordinance of 1948, which replaced earlier such measures, debts incurred by Africans to non-Africans were not enforceable in court if they exceeded 200 shillings (US $28), a limit later raised to 2,000 shillings (US $280), still a sum hardly adequate for financing or stocking even a small shop. The effect of the ordinance was to prohibit lending to Africans by non-Africans, not only by banks but also by non-African wholesalers. The only exceptions allowed were to specified individual Africans who obtained exempted status through application to their district commissioner.[34] Thus aspiring African businessmen were placed under the watchful supervision of the District Commissioner, who was in turn vulnerable to pressures from European settlers and other non-African business interests who opposed any independent economic activity on the part of Africans.

Yet another form of restriction on African entry into trade in urban areas was the *legal framework of trade licenses,* which was designed to protect European and Asian shopkeepers from competition by African hawkers and petty traders.[35] In addition, there were other laws designed to protect large European and Asian merchants and landowners from competition by small European and Asian entrepreneurs, particularly in real estate.[36]

In *education,* the policy of the colonial government was not designed to train Africans in the skills required for business or artisanship, much less for managerial posts. In the words of the Director of Education in 1924:

> The policy on native education at present is really summed in these three items, discipline, physical training, and industry ... Mere literary education is not going to do that [i.e., give African artisans skills for use in the village], and the whole policy of the village schools is therefore connected with the development of village life through village industry ... The object of the Education Department is the production of good citizens, and *not* in the wholesale production of artisans, and for that reason the industries inserted in the curriculum of these central schools are *to divert* the education of the Africans from too much literary education *rather than turn out fully fledged industrial artisans.* It has always been recognised by the Education Department that

> these boys *cannot* become fully fledged carpenters in the short time that they are at these central schools.[37]

Thus industrial training was designed to be mediocre and incomplete, so as to prevent the emergence of African artisans who could compete with Asian and European artisans and to ensure the continued supply of unskilled African labour. On the eve of World War II the educational policy of the Kenyan colonial regime had not departed significantly from these goals with respect to Africans. The largest expenditure on African education went to an industrial training centre. The total number of Africans in school represented only 2.5 percent of the total African population in 1937, whereas the total number of Europeans in school represented 18.7 percent of the total European population.[38] The government expenditure per pupil in government schools was Shs. 107 per annum in African schools and Shs. 568 per annum in European schools. To sum up, the purpose of African education was to perpetuate the racial domestic division of labour by training semi-literate labourers for European enterprises.

Finally, in addition to these restrictions and adverse policies which blocked African entry into business and promoted the de-indigenization of the economy, the crude *counter-measures taken by the colonial regime during the so-called* Mau-Mau *Emergency* from 1952 onwards resulted in the padlocking of many urban African businesses which had succeeded in overcoming all previous barriers to entry. Not only were their shops closed, but many African businessmen were placed in detention or forced to hide in exile in the forests.[39] Furthermore, the ban on hawking during the Emergency resulted in control of the wood-carving and curio trade passing from the hands of Africans into the hands of Asians and Europeans.[40]

Summing up, the measures which promoted the de-indigenization of the Kenyan economy in the period 1902-52 included the following policies and restrictions within an ideological climate which justified the permanent relegation of Africans to the status of labourers for European and Asian employers within the domestic division of labour: (1) the barring of Africans from individual ownership of land in 1921; (2) the unequal distribution of tax burdens and government services among Africans and Europeans; (3) the barring of Africans from wholesale trade in agricultural produce in 1935; (4) denial of Africans' right to grow cash crops such as coffee in 1918-37 and pyrethrum from 1935 onwards; (5) severe credit restrictions for Africans; (6) the legal framework of trade licensing which discriminated against African petty traders and hawkers; (7) an educational policy designed to perpetuate the racial basis of the domestic division of labour in which the African's only role was that of subsistence farmer and unskilled or semi-skilled labourer for non-American firms; and (8) the special restrictions imposed during the Mau-Mau Emergency, including the banning of hawkers, the closing of many African businesses in urban areas, and the wholesale detention of leading Africans, especially Kikuyu. This list of restrictive policies is by no means exhaustive but serves as a sufficient counter-argument to scholars[41] who virtually ignore historical factors which have excluded Africans from business and other areas of economic enterprise in Kenya and as a counterargument to scholarship which concentrates almost exclusively on ahistorical models of entrepreneurship in explaining the lack of African participation in the Kenyan economy outside the lowest rungs of the vertical division of labour.

As one African businessman aptly caricatured European expectations of Africans in the colonial period: "We Africans couldn't own land, couldn't borrow money. We were supposed to wander around happily in a state of nature."[42] The official policy was finally shaken by the Mau-Mau Emergency and the rise of African nationalism. By the mid-1950s such tentative steps as the establishment of the African Traders Small Loan Fund[43] demonstrated the beginning of the colonial administration's grudging recognition of the African's right to operate independent distribution firms.

Foreign firms and the de-indigenization of the Kenyan economy

What, then, was the role of the foreign firms, especially the European multinational firms, in the de-indigenization of the Kenyan economy in the colonial period? Among directors of multinational corporations[44] it is now fashionable to shift the blame for past discrimination suffered by the Kenyan Africans onto the European "settlers and their government".[45] While it is largely true, as the previous section demonstrated, that "the settlers did everything possible to hold back the Africans",[46] it is equally true that the European firms operating in Kenya found such an environment quite congenial to their operations, just as these same firms today find the apartheid regime in South Africa a congenial environment.

Moreover, the European firms were more important than European settlers as the intermediary which de-indigenized the structure of the Kenyan economy and integrated Kenya into the vertical international division of labour as a producer of raw materials and buyer of manufactured goods and machinery.[47] From the viewpoint of the European firms in banking, shipping, trade and manufacturing it was of secondary importance whether production of raw materials needed by Europe was controlled by African peasants or the Kenyan economy from its pre-capitalistic *undeveloped* pattern, responsive only to domestic needs and limited by primitive technology, to a capitalistic *underdeveloped* structure employing industrial technology to meet the needs of the external economy.[48] Under pressure from British commercial interests, productive forces were to be developed in

Kenya but in a manner distorted by the demands of powerful economic interests in Britain.[49] The British firm was the midwife of dependence and underdevelopment in Kenya.

The incorporation of the Kenyan economy into the international capitalist system under the aegis of British commercial interests consigned Kenya to the rôle of a producer of raw materials for the needs of British industry. The secondary question remained: the form which this production should take and who should be in charge of production at the local level. In parts of West Africa the secondary question boiled down to whether plantations or African peasants were the cheapest and most efficient producers of agricultural raw materials. In Kenya the secondary question boiled down to a choice among European settlers, European plantations, or African peasants, with political as well as economic considerations coming into the picture for each separate crop. As Brett points out, commercial interests in Britain had no sentimental reasons for favouring European settlers over African peasants:

> . . . commercial interests would not necessarily back settler claims if it was clear that peasant production would be more efficient and would leave a larger percentage of the final price of the crop in their hands than would the more sophisticated settler producers.[50]

Thanks to their disproportionate political strength both in Kenya and among allies in Britain, European settlers pressured the colonial regime into undertaking the previously-mentioned policies which restricted African enterprise and boosted European enterprise, thereby clouding the issue of which form of production was more efficient.

Nonetheless, the multinational firms adapted themselves to this situation. Whereas multinational firms in West Africa such as the United Africa Company (UAC/Unilever), G. B. Ollivant (now Unilever), John Holt (now Lonrho), Société Commerciale de l'Ouest Africaine (SCOA), Compagnie Française de l'Afrique de l'Ouest (CFAO) and Union Trading Company (UTC) adapted themselves to an African peasant economy, buying African-produced cash crops and selling to the Africans manufactured goods from Europe, the multinational firms in Kenya such as Gailey and Roberts (UAC/Unilever), Mackenzie (Inchcape), Dalgety (now Inchcape), Mitchell Cotts, Tancot (now Lonrho), and African Explosives and Chemical Industries (now Twiga Chemicals, jointly owned by ICI and de Beers) adapted themselves to a European settler economy, marketing crops from European farms and plantations and importing fertilizers and machinery for the European enterprises.

While multinational corporations were directly instrumental in the de-indigenization of the Kenyan economy at level I and acquiesced in the de-indigenization of the control of agricultural production at level II, they also participated directly in de-indigenization in other sectors at level II and benefited from de-indigenization at level III. Certainly the European firms which operated plantations and mines in Kenya could only have viewed favourably the colonial regime's efforts to provide cheap African labour and to block Africans from cultivating cash crops such as coffee, tea and pyrethrum. Moreover, the British commercial banks operating in Kenya did not view the credit restrictions imposed on Africans as having deprived the banks of any important potential business. The banks were content with the status quo of having Africans as customers only in the role of depositors and restricting lending to European firms and European settlers.

The extent of the multinational firms' adaptation to the political climate in Kenya with respect to the racial division of labour within firms (level III) can be illustrated by the extent of Africanization of top positions in Kenya and Ghana, respectively, for two of the firms which operate in both countries and for which data are available. In Ghana the multinational firms adapted themselves to a peasant economy and accordingly began the process of Africanizing managerial positions fairly early; in Kenya the multinational firms adapted themselves to a settler economy and delayed Africanization of managerial positions until after political independence, or rather until Africans won the political struggle against European settlers.

The two firms which illustrate this are Barclays Bank and Unilever. In 1973 Barclays Bank of Ghana had 24 full-scale branches (as opposed to sub-branches and agencies). On the basis of the names of the managers of these branches, it appears that 13 of the managers were Ghanaian, 10 British, and one unascertainable.[51] By contrast, in Kenya in the same year, Barclays Bank International had 26 full-scale branches, of which only 7 were managed by Africans, 5 by Asians, and 14 by British managers. In other words, in Kenya only about one-fourth of the managers of Barclays branches were African, whereas in Ghana over one-half of the managers of Barclays branches were African.

For Unilever data is available on senior management, i.e., those earning at least UK £5,000 per annum.[52] In Ghana in 1963, 42 per cent of senior management of Unilever subsidiaries were Ghanaian; by 1973, this figure had risen to 61 per cent. In East Africa (most of Unilever's East African subsidiaries are located in Kenya) in 1963, only 7 percent of senior management were citizens of the East African states; by 1973 this figure had climbed to 50 percent. Of course, not all the citizen managers are African; some are European and Asian Kenyan citizens, for example.

Of course, this contrast is due not only to the adaptation of the multinational firms to the respective political economies of Kenya and Ghana, but also reflects the consequences of the colonial educational policies in the two nations, which had resulted in a greater scarcity of educated and experienced Africans available for management posts in Kenya, as compared to Ghana.

Nonetheless, even among the multinational firms one can find strong opposition to further indigenization at the level of racial division of labour within firms. In the words of one European director living in Kenya:

> Let us be frank. Kenya's economy is run by 6,000 Europeans, and we are fortunate to have an African government content to leave it that way.[53]

Thus the attitudes attributed to the European settlers can also be found among the directors and managers of European multinational corporations in Kenya.

Finally, the attempt to blame European settlers for the de-indigenization of the Kenyan economy ignores a curious paradox. At the structural level the European settlers pursued a policy of economic nationalism and self-reliance which ran counter to the large British firms' interest in transforming the Kenyan economy into an exporter of raw materials and importer of manufactured goods. While the European settlers opposed economic self-sufficiency on the part of African peasants because of the need for a reserve of cheap labour, they themselves wanted maximum self-sufficiency in the production of foodstuffs and other consumer goods for the entire East African market; in other words, they wanted to produce locally the same goods which the British firms wished to export to Kenya. Moreover, in the long run the settlers wished to extend their control of the economy to the processing of raw materials in Kenya. As Brett observed:

> . . . the Kenyan settlers, though in most respects opposed to the advancement of African interests, were in a very real sense economic nationalists when conflicts arose between broader Kenyan and British interests. They were willing and able to press for policies committed to building up internal rather than export markets, and even for protection for industrialization despite what they saw to be the opposition of British manufacturing interests.[54]
>
> . . . In British colonies based on peasant production the whole developmental effort was generally devoted to export production. The resulting tendency for means of communication, marketing arrangements, and other elements in the infrastructure, to be totally geared in this direction is a common and justified criticism of the nature of the assumptions on which policy was based. But in East Africa, however limited and costly the experiment, the presence of the settlers did lead to a much higher degree of development of the local market, which was to play a much more positive role after the Second World War . . .[55]

Therefore, if one is willing to count European settlers among the indigenous population of Kenya, one can then say that the settlers favoured a higher degree of indigenization of the Kenyan economy at the structural level than did the multinational firms.

The post-independence phase: the political economy of indigenization

From a normative perspective indigenization should encompass more than the mere replacement of the European colonial-elite by a new African elite in positions of power in the Kenyan government and economy. Indigenization in its broader sense means the creation of an economy responsive to the human needs of the members of that society and controlled by members of that society. At the structural level indigenization entails production for domestic needs rather than for external needs, indigenous technology and indigenous patterns of consumption rather than imported ones, integration of the various sectors and sub-sectors of the economy, and increased self-reliance. Moreover, indigenization entails not merely a re-orientation of the economy for the benefit of a small urbanized elite among the indigenous population but rather re-orientation for the benefit of the African majority consisting of peasant growers, pastoralists, agricultural labourers, urban workers, and petty traders, of both sexes.

Indigenization *v.* de-indigenization at the structural level since 1964

The indigenization of the Kenyan economy since independence in 1964 would have required integration of the various sectors and sub-sectors of the economy to increase self-reliance and decrease dependence on the import of foreign technology, foreign machinery, foreign intermediate goods and components, and foreign consumption patterns on the one hand and decreased dependence on the export of agricultural raw materials and of minerals on the other. Unfortunately, on the basis of trade statistics it appears that the trend since independence has been towards de-indigenization rather than indigenization. Kenya was more dependent on the traditional vertical international division of labour in 1971 than in 1964. Over this period the sum of the value of exported raw materials plus the value of imported processed goods increased more rapidly than the sum of the value of imported raw materials plus the value of exported processed goods.[56] This trend towards increased de-indigenization at the structural level reflects the fact that Kenya's industrialization drive in the 1960s based largely on import-substitution within MNCs, which has led to increased imports of semi-processed materials and components and increased imports of foreign machinery and technology that more than offset the anticipated savings in imports of consumer goods.[57] The Kenyan economy has become more structurally dependent since independence.

As has been observed by Langdon,[58] it is in the interest of the multinational corporations to operate within an environment of a structurally dependent economy for the sake of transfer pricing involving raw materials, intermediate goods, machinery and technology. A European banker resident in Kenya indicated to me that such transfer pricing was widespread among multinational corporations operating in Kenya. In a fully-integrated self-reliant economy there would be little need for multinational corporations and furthermore less opportunity for foreign firms to manipulate pricing and profits.

Nonetheless, there is little prospect that the government of Kenya is about to embark on any policy of self-reliance or any policy which would seriously alter the structure of the Kenyan economy from its present state of fragmentation among sectors and subservient position within the vertical international division of labour, since the present structure serves well those who now control it, namely the urban African elite and the foreign firms. The regime is prepared to control the more blatant practices of the foreign firms by hiring a Swiss superintendence firm to monitor the prices of imported goods and by continuing the settler economy pattern of delegating control of most exported commodities to state marketing boards rather than to foreign firms, although the number of exceptions is increasing.

Indigenization at levels II and III since 1964

While indigenization of the structure of the Kenyan economy may be a dormant issue within the current political framwork, much more attention has been focused on the other two levels: ownership of firms and the racial division of labour within firms. Indeed, attention to the issues of Africanization of ownership of units of production, distribution and finance and Africanization of jobs within foreign firms has all but precluded attention at the official level to the wider problem of the economic structure of Kenya.[59] I have limited discussion of indigenization at levels II and III to the more important sectors of the Kenyan economy, namely banking, agriculture, manufacturing, and trade, and have grouped the discussion accordingly.

Banking

Banking, although comprising only a small proportion of Kenya's gross domestic product, is strategically important in determining the allocation of investment and thereby the allocation of control within other sectors of the economy. The fact that multinational corporations are not a new phenomenon in Kenya may be illustrated by the fact that the predecessor of the National and Grindlays Bank (the so-named National Bank of India, although it was British) opened its first branch in Kenya at Mombasa in 1896.[60] During the next twenty years it was joined by two other British banks, the forerunners of Standard Bank and Barclays Bank.[61] By 1926, the banking network of these three British banks reflected the European settler control of agriculture and European control of trade, in that bank branches were located in the major towns of the settler "White Highlands" (Nakuru, Eldoret, Nyeri, Kitale and Nanyuki) as well as the three major trading centres of Mombasa, Nairobi and Kisumu.[62] The banking network did not change noticeably thereafter until the 1950s.

The 1950s and 1960s saw the rapid expansion of the rural networks of the three British banks to a peak of 177 branches from the modest network of 16 branches in 1926. At the same time a number of new banks entered the urban areas: Algemene Bank Nederland, Bank of India, Bank of Baroda, Habib Bank, Ottoman Bank and Commercial Bank of Africa (linked to Bank of America). The 1970s saw a further influx of foreign banks from America and Japan, as well as the establishment of the first indigenous Kenyan commercial bank, the National Bank of Kenya; the start of a bank for co-operative societies, the Cooperative Bank of Kenya; and the splitting of National and Grindlays into two banks with varying degrees of government participation. Virtually all of the National and Grindlays network in Kenya was taken over by Kenya Commercial Bank, in which the Kenya Goverment held 60 percent of the shares and the chairmanship of the Board of Directors, while National and Gridlays retained 40 percent of the shares plus control of daily management through a management contract. Two of the largest urban branches were taken over by Grindlays Bank International (Kenya) Ltd., a merchant bank owned 60 percent by National and Grindlays and 40 percent by the Kenyan Government.

Nevertheless, despite these changes, the three commercial banks managed by British multinational banks continued to account for approximately 80 percent of total commercial bank deposits as late as 1973.[63]

On the lending side, the bulk of the advances of the "big three" British banks in the colonial period went to European firms, European settlers, and the European colonial government. The types of activities financed by these loans included the financing of imports, the financing of marketing and export of agricultural commodities, general loans to European farmers, the holding of government securities, and (increasingly after World War II) the financing of manufacturing subsidiaries established by foreign firms. Africans were simply not in the picture on the lending side. As late as May 1967 loans to Kenyan Africans and Kenyan African firms accounted for only 2.6 percent of the total loans and advances of all the commercial banks operating in Kenya,[64] despite the fact that Africans comprise over 97 percent of the population.

The reasons for the lack of lending to Africans were and still are manifold. First of all, the above-mentioned policies of the colonial regime, notably the lack of individual title to land and the restrictions on credit to Africans, made the African a poor credit risk in commercial terms. The lack of title to land left the African with little to offer as security for a loan. Secondly, the banks viewed Africans as potential depositors rather than as potential borrowers. Given the small size of African firms, they were poor business prospects in terms of the cost of administering small loans within a banking system in which 11 or 12 percent was the accepted maximum rate of interest on advances. In the period after 1956, the initial experience of the commercial banks with defaults by African farmers combined with the political sensitivity of having a powerful European bank foreclose and arrange for the auctioning of a relatively poor African farmer's land, left the European lending officiers of the commercial banks with the almost racist view that "Africans have a different mentality about repaying loans—they don't see it an obligation."[65] Thirdly, the British style of banking relies heavily on social interaction between bank officers and customers outside of banking hours. As one London officer of a British bank defended the bank's large proportion of loans to British individuals and firms in Kenya, "You need to get to know a man a bit before you can trust him." Because of the racial compartmentalization of social life in Kenya, the Africans were, until recently, cut off from social contact with banking officials. Thus a pattern developed in which British banks lent to British firms and settlers; Asian banks lent to Asian firms; and since there were no African banks, no one lent to African firms. Even within the European community the British banks continue to favour British firms. This tendency is illustrated by the fact that even in the 1960s new British investment in Kenya was on the average financed 78 percent by local borrowing and only 22 percent by inflow of foreign capital; whereas Indian, Japanese and American investors were only able to finance 22-40 percent of new investment through local borrowing.[66] The major source of local borrowing by the British firms was, of course, the British banks operating in Kenya. Fourthly, once the non-African commercial banks had committed themselves to lending to non-African customers rather than to Africans, they developed a vested interest in the success of their customers. This interest, it is alleged by Africans, extended to supporting the European and Asian firms in conflicts with the growing demands of African nationalism. The bank could not be a neutral observer in the question of Africanization of European farms or Asian shops, they argue, if loans to these non-African firms comprised a substantial part of the assets of the non-African commercial banks.[67]

The standard commercial operating procedure of the banks in Kenya has also contributed to uneven development between urban and rural areas. The rapid expansion of the network of rural branches by the "big three" banks in the 1950s and 1960s was designed to soak up savings in rural areas (at 3% interest) to lend to the banks' customers in urban areas (at 7-11% interest). The great majority of savings account customers in rural areas were Africans, while the major borrowers in urban areas were the multinational corporations and the colonial regime. There was a net flow of capital from rural to urban areas. The claim by the banks that the rural branches were often unprofitable is undoubtedly true since a bank branch earns money on loans rather than deposits. Since some of these rural branches even today have a ratio of advances (loans) to deposits in the range of 12 to 15 percent, it is hardly surprising that they are unprofitable when viewed in isolation from the remainder of the bank network. Yet these so-called "unprofitable" rural branches were not operated as a philanthropic service to Africans looking for a safe place to deposit savings. The "unprofitable" rural branches contributed a vital part of the pool of funds available for lending to European firms in the urban areas. For the commercial bank which made the most data available to the author, the rural branches accounted for one-third of the bank's total deposits, but only for one-fifth of the bank's total advances (loans).[68] The median advances/deposits ratio for this bank's rural branches was 28 percent; the median advances/deposits ratio for urban branches, 58 percent. Similarly, despite government exhortations to increase the proportion of loans for agricultural purposes, loans to agriculture as a percentage of total loans by all commercial banks has gradually declined over the last five years to a 1973 level of 10.5 percent.[69] The officials of one bank argued that such statistics as these are highly misleading, since a large portion of the money lent in urban areas filters back to the rural areas either in the form of rural development projects administered from Nairobi, or in the form of employment on projects such as plantations controlled by foreign firms based in Nairobi, or in the form of imports of agricultural tools and chemicals and consumer goods by European and Asian firms in Mombasa. Yet this argument that a form of "trickle-down" effect ultimately benefits the *rural Africans* who comprise 90 percent of Kenya's population neglects the fact that *control* of the allocation of funds and the administration of funds is centered in urban areas in the hands of non-African firms and, more recently, in the hands of urban-based African civil servants. Another factor which works to the disadvantage of rural-area development is the practice by urban Africans of using land owned by themselves or relatives in rural areas as collateral to borrow money ostensibly for farm improvements but actually for the purpose of financing businesses in urban areas.

The government's indigenization policy in the banking sector has mainly been limited to level III, Africanization of high-level positions in foreign banks. At level II, control of individual firms, the government has bought shares in the banking network of one of the "big three" (as already mentioned), has established a state-owned National Bank of Kenya to replace the East African Currency Board, and has established the Cooperative Bank of Kenya. The Cooperative Bank of Kenya could conceivably be an instrument of change at the structural level; however, in the period January-April, 1974 its operations merely reinforced the old pattern, since it received deposits from cooperatives and in turn lent money to the commercial and merchant banks to lend to multinational corporations, on the basis of the argument that there were not sufficient viable investment opportunities in rural areas. The government has made some attempts to encourage banks to lend more to rural areas in general and to agriculture in particular, but without much success. One wonders whether such encouragement is more for consumption by newspapers than a genuine attempt to influence banks' lending policies. Finally, the Central Bank of Kenya has imposed some limitations on the amount of local borrowing by foreign-owned firms, but interviews with banks indicated that dispensation was not difficult to obtain and that in times of credit restrictions banks were more than willing to exploit loopholes in the law for the benefit of their multinational customers. In conclusion to this section it is sobering to note that eight years after independence the proportion of commercial bank loans going to African borrowers (excluding government and parastatal bodies) was still only 14.1 percent of total loans by commercial banks.[70]

Agriculture

In agriculture control of units of production has been shifting from European settlers to Africans. Yet the unequal distribution of land among Africans has emerged as an explosive issue, especially in the highlands. Rather than breaking up the old European farms, which averaged 880 hectares (2,150 acres),[71] and embarking on land reform, the Kenyan political elite (with financial assistance from the United Kingdom) chose instead to transfer the farms largely intact to African owners. The white settler farms are being Africanized in terms of ownership, but the settler mentality in terms of attitudes towards income distribution and domestic division of labour continues under the new African management. At present in Kenya one finds at the one extreme large African (and European) farms averaging 850 hectares, and at the other extreme, the vast majority of African farms (*shambas*) which range in size from 0.2 to 12 hectares (half acre to 30 acres).[72]

While Africanization of control of coffee and pyrethrum production has gained momentum in the period 1962-70, with African small holdings now accounting for most of the acreage under these two crops, there has been resistance on the part of foreign firms to shifting tea and pineapple production from plantations to peasant agriculture or out-grower schemes owned by Africans, allegedly on grounds of quality control. Moreover, multinational firms, with encouragement from the Kenyan government, continue to establish new plantations in such crops as cotton and flowers for export to Europe. In the case of an enormous new cotton plantation in the Tana River area, the foreign firm has been granted permission to sell the cotton directly on the world market, while African peasant cultivators of cotton must sell their output at a lower price to the Lint Marketing Board, which thereby in effect taxes African-controlled production but not European-controlled production.

Through the Industrial Court the government has allied itself with multinational firms in keeping agricultural wages extremely low to attract foreign investment. For example, on a Danish-owned plantation the workers went on strike for higher pay and better working and living conditions. Unskilled labourers who formed the bulk of the 4,000 person labour force on the farm earned only Shs. 3/25 (US $0.46) per day.[73] The Industrial Court intervened in the dispute and awarded the labourers an increase of 25 percent over two years, or not quite enough to keep pace with inflation, and, although admitting that the company housing for workers was substandard, granted the firm an indefinite extension in the deadline for improving the housing on the grounds that the company was still establishing itself.

Except for coffee processing (controlled by the Coffee Marketing Board), small-scale maize milling, and a few African-owned sawmills, agricultural processing is still in the hands of foreign firms or resident Europeans and Asians. Moreover, control of technology and control of imports of agricultural machinery is vested in the old established trading firms such as Gailey and Roberts (Unilever), Mackenzie (Inchcape), Metal Box Company, Mitchell-Cotts, and newcomers such as Lonrho. As in the case of the European commercial banks, many of the importers of agricultural processing machinery prefer to deal with customers with whom they also have social contact. A European director of the Kenya subsidiary of a firm involved in selling food processing technology and machinery indicated that the firm made no effort to seek African customers or to develop links with potential African food processors and could only recall two past orders from African firms, which were not followed up by re-orders. Nor had the foreign subsidiary made any attempts to follow up the lack of re-orders by the African firms, arguing that such advisory services were too expensive and beyond the commercial role of the subsidiary. By contrast, the parent firm in the United Kingdom does give advisory services not only to British food processors but also to African firms from nations where this multinational does not have a subsidiary.

The importation of agricultural inputs such as fertilizers, insecticides, and medicine for livestock is also controlled by foreign firms. Recently these firms have established "manufacturing" subsidiaries in Kenya which do little more than mix imported chemicals, add local water and repackage the agrichemicals for domestic sale. As one executive of a large UK chemical firm noted, "Shipping water is expensive so we try to emulate the Coca-Cola example of shipping only the secret ingredients, letting the local firm add water, mix and package the product." He also observed that much of Kenya's import substitution was actually import substitution within foreign firms who now allowed subsidiaries to assemble and package what formerly had been imported pre-packaged. The ultimate source of the machinery and materials, as well as control of the process (including marketing) remained in the hands of the parent multinational corporation and its local subsidiary. Moreover, the involvement of multinational firms in "agri-business" in Kenya buttresses the bias towards large-scale farms which are more capital-intensive and import-intensive than peasant holdings. In 1970 the gross domestic product in the monetary agricultural sector (as opposed to the subsistence agricultural sector) was estimated at K£73 million.[74] In the same period the total value of imported material inputs to the agricultural sector was estimated at K£12 million, consisting of fertilizers, agricultural chemicals, livestock drugs, fuel, spares for machinery and manufactured feeds.[75] Viewed from another perspective, the total value of material inputs in the agricultural sector in 1970 (K£13.7 million) roughly equalled the total wage bill in the monetary agricultural sector (K£14.2 million).[76]

Manufacturing

Manufacturing contributes 20 percent to Kenya's monetary gross domestic product.[77] The Kenya government has given high priority to industrialization, with little concern for ownership of firms in this sector. As a result, much of the new manufacturing activity in Kenya has centered on the last link in the processing chain: mixing of imported chemicals, or assembly of imported components, and repackaging of bulk imports—all characteristic of import-substitution within the firm. As of 1967, predominantly or totally foreign-owned firms contributed 71.4 percent of total value-added in the manufacturing sector in Kenya.[78] It must be recalled that of the remaining 28.6 percent value-added contributed by predominantly domestically-owned firms, many of these are owned by non-African Kenyan citizens of European or Asian origin and very few by Africans or by para-statal firms.

Although the government-owned Industrial and Commercial Development Corporation (ICDC) has bought shares in a number of manufacturing subsidiaries of multinational corporations, it is often content to have a minority or even token share-holding in foreign firms (e.g., only 8.4 percent in Metal Box Company of Kenya), and almost always leaves management in the hands of the foreign firm. From the foreign firm's viewpoint such joint-ventures have several advantages. Minority government ownership of shares is a sign of government approval which can be used in negotiations with trade unions. The foreign firm can in effect wave the national flag and accuse the trade union of letting down the government. In other circumstances joint-ventures lead to the government taking a less than stern view of the company's price rises. No doubt multinational corporations see minority government participation as a form of vaccination against the risk of later nationalization. Other aspects of joint-ventures are discussed below in connection with interviews with African businessmen.

Trading sector

In the trading sector the government has been pre-occupied with Africanization of retail trade at the level of ownership of shops in the three-level indigenization scheme. The main target of indigenization of retail-distribution control is the Asian-owned shop, particularly shops owned by non-citizen Asians. Twice a year the authorities publish a new list of shops which have been denied renewal of trade licenses and the owners served with quit notices. These shops must then be sold to citizens, usually African citizens. The procedure in Kenya is more gradual than in Amin's Uganda with regard to the expulsion of non-citizen Asians, but the goal is the same.

Retail trade is the type of business which Africans can easily take over with a minimum of experience and capital. Moreover, Asian non-citizens, having been betrayed by the British government in 1968 over the issue of British passports and entry rights to Britain, are bereft of political power and are unable to oppose Africanization of their shops and their eventual expulsion.

At the same time, while ICDC has not been particularly active in the indigenization of control of manufacturing firms, it has pursued a more vigorous policy of indigenization in the field of wholesale trade and in the field of transport through its subsidiaries Kenya National Trading Corporation and Kenatco Transport.

Interviews with African businessmen in the trading sector on their opinion of ICDC's role in promoting indigenization of the economy at the level of ownership of firms and the level of Africanization of key positions within firms brought forth a wide range of opinions. Some felt it was wrong for ICDC to enter into joint ventures with foreign firms in fields in which there was or could be competition between the foreign firm and the African-owned businesses. Others favoured ICDC participation in joint ventures but wanted to see ICDC take a more active role in managing the firms. Still others saw ICDC participation as a potential barrier to the pace of Africanization of management and technical positions within such firms. In other words, they feared the government would be more lenient with such firms in pushing Africanization. Interestingly enough, the more successful African businessmen, generally those with the most powerful political connections, felt that the ICDC should not buy shares in foreign subsidiaries in Kenya but should instead make loans available to African businessmen to buy the shares. These same businessmen also argued that the time had come for ICDC's subsidiary in wholesale trade, KNTC, to embark on a path of total or partial divestment, either by dissolving the KNTC and selling the scheduled commodities solely through private African wholesalers or by turning over some product lines to private African wholesalers.

Implementation of the government's Africanization policy has centered on ownership of retail shops and on Africanization of top-level employment within foreign firms. Even in these areas there was much criticism on the part of the African businessmen who maintained that the pace was too slow. They were especially critical of the experience criteria set by foreign firms in advertising high-level positions in management, sales and technical fields. They argued that foreign firms could best afford to give educated Africans the needed practical experience on the job. On the other hand, the interviewed African businessmen themselves sometimes employed non-Africans in positions such as the firm's accountant or distributor, defending such actions on the grounds that they were unable to afford the time or risk involved in using inexperienced African graduates or inexperienced African salesmen. Again, returning to the social circle aspect of indigenization, one African manufacturer of office supplies argued that he had to employ an Asian distributor, since most of the office supply stores in Kenya are owned by Asians. Similarly, a European paint manufacturer found that he could get an edge over his competitors in the building and construction market by employing a citizen Asian, since most of the major contracting firms in Kenya are Asian-owned. A European distributor of food processing machinery formally abolished the position of sales-manager after attempts to Africanize the post foundered, partially because the buyers were European- and Asian-owned firms.

Given such a vicious circle of social barriers to entry into distribution, the Africanization Committee of the Kenya National Chamber of Commerce and Industry has been lobbying the government to simply decree that manufacturers must appoint African distributors for their products and that foreign manufacturers be forbidden to operate distribution networks. The committee points out that the success of Africans in handling wholesale cigarette and beer distribution demonstrates the ability of Africans to handle large volumes of business. Furthermore, they argue, success in such fields as wholesale distribution will give Africans the experience needed to enter manufacturing. They cite as examples the case of A. Wahome, who diversified from being a tobacco and cigarette wholesaler to starting a bicycle plant in Nakuru, and the case of Njenge Karume, who diversified from being a beer distributor in the Kiambu area to a whole range of business activities, including pharmaceuticals.

The Africanization Committee's proposal moved a step closer to realization when Dr. Kiano, Minister for Commerce and Industry, announced at the Chamber of Commerce and Industry's annual meeting on 27th March 1974 that henceforth foreign-owned manufacturing firms would no longer be allowed to distribute their own products and that the distribution would have to be handed over to citizen firms by the end of April.[79] Interviews with directors of foreign firms revealed that they were generally angry over the announcement. Some argued that the decree was primarily directed at manufacturers of consumer goods such as soap and that manufacturers of industrial goods such as paint, machinery, tin cans, packaging materials, and industrial chemicals should be exempt, using the familiar arguments of expertise, experience, and the fact that industrial customers were Europeans and Asians rather than Africans. Others were prepared to wait out the announcement, preferring to dismiss it as little more than a piece of election-year rhetoric. Finally, some accepted the announcement as inevitable and argued only that the implementation, particularly in industrial goods, should be spaced out over five years.

When the April deadline rapidly passed without any sign of implementation of Dr. Kiano's distribution proposals, the African businessmen began to fear that the foreign manufacturers were winning in behind-the-scenes lobbying. One important African businessman even alleged that the government officials had been bribed to delay and postpone implementation. During this period I encountered only one instance of increased Africanization of distribution of goods manufactured under control of foreign firms as a result of Kenyan government intervention. This was an alleged attempt by the Kenyan and Ugandan governments to transfer Kenyan distribution of the products of a chemical firm in Uganda from the British firm which had the management contract to a relative of the president of Kenya. If true, this form of Africanization by nepotism was hardly what the original Africanization group within the Kenya National Chamber of Commerce and Industry had in mind.

Even though the Africanization Committee may have lost this round, it is obvious that within a few years wholesale distribution of manufactured goods will be largely Africanized, starting with consumer goods, just as Africanization of wholesale distribution has occurred in varying degrees in other anglophone African states such as Tanzania, Uganda, Nigeria and Ghana. Yet the question remains as to whether such Africanization of wholesale distribution will have any spill-over effects in the increased indigenization in the manufacturing sector at level II or in increased indigenization at the structural level of the economy. Clearly the short-run spill-over effect will be negative in both areas. Since production of consumer goods and industrial goods in Kenya is dominated by firms controlled by multinational corporations, Africanization of distribution of consumer goods and industrial goods will make the African commercial class even more dependent on foreign firms than at present. The African distributors will have a vested interest in continuation of Kenya's structural dependence and in continued foreign control of that particular sub-sector of manufacturing. In the past decade, when African wholesalers linked to foreign firms have branched into manufacturing, they have entered new fields rather than infringing on the manufacturing domain of their multinational patrons. Moreover, they entered manufacturing in the new field under the auspices of still other foreign firms who provide them with imported technology, imported machinery, imported components and semi-processed raw materials, and imported consumption patterns. Thus the pattern of multinational corporation paternalism has been transferred from the wholesale sector to the manufacturing sector.

Interviews with African businessmen indicated that they themselves would be content with such a dependent patron-client relationship *vis-à-vis* multinational corporations. One of the most nationalistic of the African businessmen, when asked what he himself most wanted, replied that he wished to become the sole agent for a Swiss insurance firm. Furthermore, interviews with Africans already in manufacturing revealed that they were just as reluctant as the multinational corporations in seeking out local inputs, in employing African distributors, and in establishing labour-intensive forms of manufacturing. In general all the interviewed African businessmen had good political connections (as did the multinational corporations) or were themselves former civil servants of high rank, and in general they longed to work in cooperation with multinational corporations rather than embarking on their own paths towards a more autonomous, more self-reliant pattern of development. In other words, the African businessmen could be said to have a "*comprador* class" mentality.

Multinational corporations and the politics of "political insurance"

Multinational corporations are not reactionary dinosaurs doomed to extinction through lack of adaptability, but are rather remarkably adaptable organizations capable of bending with the current political environment to protect the long-term interests of the organization and its stockholders. In Kenya multinational corporations were willing to accept and even encourage certain forms of indigenization. At the structural level foreign firms were willing to engage in import-substitution within the firm. That is, the firm was willing to establish so-called "manufacturing" subsidiaries within Kenya to handle the final stages of assembly and packaging in order to protect the firm's share of the market and in order to anticipate indigenization of the trading sector. The local subsidiary of the multinational corporation in effect retreated to higher ground in the vertical international division of labour in order to survive. The manufacturing subsidiary may indeed be "little more than a tin shack", as one London director described his firm's manufacturing unit in Kenya, but on the Kenyan scale such a tin shack may have a powerful competitive advantage over potential indigenously-owned rivals through its integration with the parent firm. Import substitution within the firm is one form of "political insurance" employed by multinational corporations to protect long-term interests.

Joint participation with government and with local shareholders is another form of "political insurance". Minority shareholding by the Kenyan government and by African Kenyan citizens is seen by the foreign firm as a form of vaccination against future nationalization. Moreover, in the future joint participation will extend to minority shareholding by the multinational corporation itself combined with control through management contracts or technological expertise and patents. Today, for example, most of the shares of East African Breweries are held by East African firms and individuals. Yet by being the largest single shareholder, with only 10 percent of the total shares, and by maintaining licensing agreements and a supply of engineers, a British multinational firm controls the future expansion and technology of East African Breweries. Similarly, in the case of banking it appears that the partial nationalization of the branches of one of the "big three" combined with a management contract for the British parent bank was initiated by the British bank itself in anticipation of pressures for nationalization. A similar measure merging the branches of the other two banks of the "big three" under a new firm with majority government interest was blocked by back-benchers in the Kenyan Parliament, who viewed the proposal as an effort to prevent the establishment of a 100 percent Kenyan-owned commercial bank and as an effort to continue foreign control of daily management of banking in Kenya through management contracts. Another reason given by back-benchers for opposing the partial nationalization of these banks was that the terms of compensation were far too favourable to the foreign firms.

A third form of political insurance is the strategy of Africanization at level III through appointment of political notables to management positions and directorships in foreign subsidiaries. The European directors of multinational corporations operating in Kenya admitted themselves that such appointments were seen as a form of political insurance. The best example of the symbiotic relationship between the multinational corporations and the political elite in Kenya is that of the appointments of members of the family of the President of Kenya to positions in foreign firms. The President's son-in-law is a director of one of the largest British firms in Africa, which controls mines in both Rhodesia (Zimbabwe) and South Africa. This dynamic businessman, who by all accounts is suited to the job by virtue of his ability and training as well as family connections, not only directs the East African operations of all the subsidiaries of the British firm but also sits on the London board of directors of the parent firm. This firm, through a subsidiary, owns one of Kenya's two daily newspapers (the other is owned by a firm controlled by the Aga Khan), the largest automobile-import agencies, and several plantations and ranches in Kenya. The firm has plans for a £20 million urban redevelopment project in Nairobi. Conveniently, the mayor of Nairobi is the President's daughter. The British mining and trading conglomerate, another British trading firm, and the Kenyan government have recently established a new joint venture which will have a virtual monopoly on automobile import and vehicle assembly in Kenya. The British trading firm mentioned is one of the oldest British firms in Kenya, and at present has the nephew of the President of Kenya as deputy chairman of the Kenyan subsidiary. One of the relatives of the wife of the President is chairman of the Kenyan subsidiary of a tobacco firm which has a monopoly on import and manufacture of cigarettes in Kenya. The total turnover of this firm is among the largest of any firm in Kenya, and a significant portion of the revenues of the Kenyan government are dependent on direct and indirect taxes generated by this firm. The oldest son of the President is a partner in the largest totally African-owned manufacturing firm in Kenya, a firm which makes uniforms for the Kenyan police and armed forces. The same man is also director of a firm which transports refined petroleum products for a foreign oil company from the joint-venture oil refinery in Mombasa to all parts of Kenya. Furthermore, he is director of another firm which has airport handling contracts with many of the foreign airlines which land at Nairobi. The President himself has taken over some of the largest European farms in the highlands, and at present owes a multinational oil firm K£25,000 for petroleum products delivered to the farm, an indirect measure of the President's personal commitment to capital-intensive and energy-intensive farming. Outside the immediate "royal family" in the Republic of Kenya, the friends of the President are also doing well. With help from British and Yugoslav multinational corporations, one of the President's closest friends is well on the way to becoming a millionaire.

Nevertheless, such close links between the multinational firms and the Kenyan political elite may backfire, should the present political regime be discredited. Interviews in London indicated that the head offices of multinational corporations viewed with some misgivings the extreme cliquish nature of the Kenyan political elite and its close identification with a few families belonging to a single sub-national grouping. Moreover, the apparent disregard of the political elite for a more equitable income and land distribution in Kenya might conflict with the desire of the multinational firms for a broader market within Kenya. The manufacturing subsidiaries of multinational corporations, in contrast to plantation subsidiaries, pay workers above the going minimum wage, giving rise to charges of fostering a "labour aristocracy".[80] On the other hand, the commitment of multinational corporations to more equitable distribution of income in Kenya and to increased Africanization at level III tends to be greater at the vocal level in the London offices of directors than at the operational level of the local head office in Nairobi, where European managers, acutely conscious of the fact that it is their own jobs which may be Africanized, drag their feet and speak of Africans in the patronizing tones of the European settlers.

Concluding remarks

By viewing the problem of indigenization from three levels, it can be seen that the process of political de-colonization begun in 1952, culminating in formal political independence in 1964, has led to increased indigenization at level III, the racial division of labour within firms, and at level II, in the form of increased indigenization of ownership of units of production in agriculture and units of distribution in commerce, particularly retail trade, but markedly less progress in indigenization of control of firms in manufacturing, import trade, and banking. On the other hand, the basic structure of the economy remains externally oriented, in part through the continued influence and control of strategic sectors of the economy by multinational corporations. Moreover, there are indications that the political and commercial urban African elite has little motivation to transform the structure of the economy to make it more responsive to domestic human needs, and less dependent on foreign firms.

Notes

[1] This article presents some of the findings from a larger study of the impact of multinational corporations on domestic firms in Kenya and Ghana. Sources for the article include interviews with 33 African and European businessmen in Kenya and with representatives of 15 parent firms in London. Thanks are due to these businessmen for volunteering their time and cooperation. The research was supported by a stipend from the Norwegian Agency for International Development (NORAD); however, the author alone assumes responsibility for the views expressed in this article. Thanks are due to Asbjørn Eide, Rhoda Howard and Apollo Njonjo for valuable comments and suggestions, as well as the Scandinavian Institute for African Studies (Uppsala) for financial assistance in presenting the paper at the IDEP conference on multinational corporations held in Dakar. This article can be identified as PRIO publication no. 27-32 from the International Peace Research Institute, Oslo, and as IDEP publication number CS/2562-26 from the United Nations African Institute for Economic Development and Planning, Dakar.

2 The distinction between formal colonial rule and the imperialism of free trade is discussed in John Gallagher and Ronald Robinson, "The Imperialism of Free Trade", *Economic History Review,* N.S. 6, December, 1953, pp. 1-15.

3 Alison Smith, "The Southern Section of the Interior, 1840-84", p. 267, and D. A. Low, "The Northern Interior, 1840-84", pp. 314-5, both in Roland Oliver and Gervase Mathew (eds.), *History of East Africa,* I, Oxford: Clarendon Press, 1963. The slave trade is discussed separately in J. M. Gray, "Zanzibar and the Coastal Belt, 1840-1884", in Oliver and Mathew (eds.), op.cit., pp 212-51.

4 The Mahiga Kikuyu who traded with the Masai are discussed in Peter Marris and Anthony Somerset, *African Businessmen; A Study of Entrepreneurship and Development in Kenya,* Nairobi: East African Publishing House, 1971, pp. 23-54.

5 Smith-Mackenzie continues to operate in Kenya today as Mackenzie (Kenya) Ltd., part of the Inchcape Group Ltd. Through Mackinnon, the firm was also linked with the ill-fated Imperial British East Africa Company of Zanzibar and Uganda. Smith-Mackenzie were the outfitters of Stanley's expedition into the interior in search of Livingston. The firm's boardroom in Nairobi contains a number of momentos from this period, including the pay-ledger for the 500 porters employed by the Stanley expedition. Other large trading firms such as Dalgety (today merged with Mackenzie), Mitchell-Cotts, and Leslie & Anderson followed later, in the 1920s. There were also a number of independent European traders.

6 Not all the agricultural production ventures by British firms were successful. Cotton, rubber, and wool were among the early failures, sponsored by such firms as the British East Africa Company and the East Africa Syndicate. Much of the material on the colonial economic history of Kenya in this and the following paragraph is derived from C. C. Wrigley, "Kenya: Patterns of Economic Life, 1902-45", in Vincent Harlow, E. M. Chilver and Alison Smith (eds.), *History of East Africa,* II, Oxford: Clarendon Press, 1965, pp. 209-64.

7 For example, Smith-Mackenzie was linked with the British India Steam Navigation Company Ltd. (today part of P&O Lines, associated with the Inchcape Group) and with William Mackinnon & Co. of Scotland. Over the years the firm maintained a primary interest in trade but diversified into tea plantations, sisal plantations and livestock management in the agricultural sector. A large part of the firm's imports today consists of coffee and tea processing machinery.

8 In terms of the balance of visible trade, Kenya has persistently lived beyond its means, relying on the inflow of capital from abroad and on earnings in services to the other East African states to pay for the difference between its imports and exports. Between 1900 and 1945, according to Wrigley, imports always exceeded exports. In the period 1962-71 the net deficit on visible trade ranged between 5.1 and 28.1 percent of the total trade with all nations, averaging 14.3 percent. The ideology of "legitimate commerce" in relation to ending the slave trade is discussed in John E. Flint, "The Wider Background to Partition and Colonial Occupation", in Oliver and Mathew (eds.), *History of East Africa,* I, p. 379.

9 British firms' interests in railway building in East Africa are discussed in E. A. Brett, *Colonialism and Underdevelopment in East Africa; The Politics of Economic Change, 1919-39,* London: Heinemann, 1973, pp. 82-3, 129-32, 296-7.

10 C. C. Wrigley, "Kenya: Patterns of Economic Life, 1902-45", pp. 227, 243.

11 Ibid.

12 African-controlled agricultural production did not recover to the 1925 level until a decade later. See E. A. Brett, *Colonialism and Underdevelopment in East Africa,* pp. 205-6.

13 C. C. Wrigley, "Kenya: Patterns of Economic Life, 1902-45", p. 243.

14 Ibid., p. 250.

15 Ibid., p. 241.

16 For a summary of the European settlers rationale that their incursions benefited the Africans, see Elspeth Huxley, *White Man's Country: Lord Delamere and the Making of Kenya,* I. London: Chatto and Windus, 1953 (1935), pp. 222-3.

[17] Resident Natives Ordinance of 1918.

[18] Asians, who comprised approximately 1.7 percent of the population of Kenya, were absolutely barred from land ownership outside urban areas. Of the total area *reserved* for Europeans, only 18,535 sq.km. (4.6 million acres), or less than one-sixth of that available, was actually occupied by Europeans in 1937. Calculations based on Kenya Colony and Protectorate, *Blue Book for the Year Ended 31st December 1937,* Nairobi: Government Printer, 1938, pp. 210, 475.

[19] There were some exceptions to this generalization. Despite administrative obstacles and discrimination, Africans did enter into competition with European settlers in producing maize and other foodstuffs for the domestic market and, as time passed, gradually entered the production of cotton for export, though hardly on the same scale as African growers in Uganda and Tanganyika.

[20] By contrast, in neighbouring Uganda most African employees in 1938 were found in the agricultural sector, but working for African employers on African-owned farms. See Uganda Protectorate, *Blue Book for the Year Ended 31st December, 1939,* section 23, p. 27.

[21] Data on 1937 distribution of African employment are derived from Kenya Colony and Protectorate, *Blue Book 1937,* p. 479.

[22] Samir Amin, "Underdevelopment and Dependence in Black Africa; Historical Origin", *Journal of Peace Research,* 1972, no. 2, pp. 105-19; also in *Journal of Modern African Studies,* 1972, no. 4, pp. 503-24.

[23] C. W. Hobley, Memorandum on Native Administration, 8th October, 1912, Secretariat Minute Paper (SMP) no. 450/1912, "Native Administration and Provincial Councils", Kenya National Archives, Nairobi.

[24] For example, in 1930 the Labour government in Britain had to intervene in the Kenya Colony's budget to end European obstruction of education and health measures which would benefit Africans. See George Bennet, "Settlers and Politics in Kenya", in Harlow, Chilver and Smith (eds.), *History of East Africa,* II, p. 311.

[25] John Ainsworth, Provincial Commissioner for Nyanza, letter to Chief Secretary, Nairobi, 9th October, 1912, SMP no. 450/1912, "Native Administration and Provincial Councils", Kenya National Archives, Nairobi.

[26] R. T. Coryndon, Governor, speech 14th May, 1924, Colony and Protectorate of Kenya, *Minutes of the Proceedings of the Legislative Council, 1924.*

[27] According to the judgment, "individual ownership of land in Native Reserves cannot be recognised". See Civil Case no. 626 of 1921, Nairobi, File PC/CP. 6/4/2, 1920-23, Kenya National Archives, Nairobi. Individual ownership of land by Africans within the so-called reserves began with title registration in Kikuyu in 1956.

[28] A large number of disputes surrounded alienation of land to church missions operated by Europeans within the Native Reserves.

[29] For more on the unequal distribution of tax burdens and government services among Africans and Europeans, see E. A. Brett, *Colonialism and Underdevelopment in East Africa,* pp. 190-9, which is the source for much of the information in this paragraph.

[30] Ibid., pp. 199-202. See also the often acrimonious debate between the acting general manager of the Uganda Railways and European settler representatives such as Berkely Cole, Lord Delamere and J. E. Coney over extension of the railways to European *v.* African areas, Colony and Protectorate of Kenya, *Minutes of the Proceedings of the Legislative Council,* 17 December 1924.

[31] See S. H. Fazan, Privincial Commissioner, Nyanza Province, "Memorandum Regarding the Marketing of Native Produce Ordinance and the Measures Which Should Be Taken Under It in Nayanza", 10th November, 1937, Ministry of Commerce and Industry, Deposit No. 5, Series I, Box I, 1424, File Trd. 1/6/1 II, item 56c, Kenya National Archives, Nairobi. Although the original impetus behind the bill was the KFA's drive to control African competition in the

cultivation and marketing of maize for domestic consumption, potatoes and other commodities (including even beeswax) were added to the scheduled list. The KFA (Kenya Farmers' Association) was composed of European settlers.

32 C. C. Wrigley, "Kenya: Patterns of Economic Life, 1902-45", pp. 245-6.

33 Ibid., p. 249. Africans were not able to enter pyrethrum production on a large scale until after Independence.

34 Credit to Africans (Control) Ordinance of 1948; An Ordinance to Provide for Controlling the Granting of Credit by Non-Africans to Africans, Chapter 104. Names of the exempted persons were to be published monthly in the Official Gazette by the Registrar-General. The author did not have time to consult this source to see how many Africans obtained exempted status before the ordinance was abolished in 1964. Several of the interviewed African businessmen had obtained exempted status and were of the opionion that exempted status was not difficult to obtain from 1960 onwards. All African businessmen interviewed could recall the ordinance with some bitterness. Few European businessmen had ever heard of it, or claimed it was to "protect" Africans from unscrupulous money-lenders. Such restrictions on credit to Africans dated back to the Credit to Natives Control Ordinance of 1903.

35 Many of these restrictions continue to exist under the Local Government Regulations Act of 1963 and Trade Licence Act of 1967. See Ichirou Inukai, "The Legal Framework for Small-Scale Enterprise Development with Special Reference to the Licensing System", in Frank Child and Mary E. Kempe (eds.), *Small Scale Enterprise*, Nairobi: Institute for Development Studies, Occasional Paper no. 6, 1973, pp. 88-99.

36 One example is the Land Law which prohibits the division of a one-acre plot into 1/16th-acre plots, but allows the division of parts of a larger plot, say a three-acre plot, into 1/16th-acre plots. In the words of an African businessman, "Those laws were passed during the colonial era to keep small poor Englishmen out of business. After all, the colony was run by such fine types as the Duke of York, so you didn't want just anyone setting up a business. Now we're independent and still stuck with these colonial laws."

37 James Russell Orr, speech, 15th September 1924, Colony and Protectorate of Kenya, *Minutes of the Proceedings of the Legislative Council 1924*. Italics added.

38

Education By Race, Kenya, 1937. (Table prepared by author.)

Race	Total number in all schools	Total as percent of race's population	No. in government schools[1]	Government expenditure per pupil in gov. schools
African	82,105	2.5	4593	Shs. 106/85[2]
Asian	8,960	15.7	4231	Shs.122/93
European	3,151	18.7	1108	Shs.568/—

1 Excludes "government-aided" schools and un-aided schools.

2 Excludes extra-ordinary expenditure at Native Industrial Training Depot (£12,013), which had 330 pupils. If included, figure would have been Shs. 151/49 per pupil. The stimated total African population of Kenya in 1937 was 3,253,700 (probably lower than actual), of whom 82,105 or 2.5% were in school. By comparison, in neighbouring Uganda, the estimated total African population was 3,802,900 in 1938, of whom 309,387 or 8.1% were attending school. See Kenya Colony and Protectorate, *Blue Book, 1937,* sections on population and education; and Uganda Protectorate, *Blue Book, 1938,* p. 138.

39 Interviews with African businessmen in Nairobi and Kiambu turned up several instances in which the businessman's shop had been closed by the colonial authorities during the Emergency, and the owner either fled to hide in the forests or was taken into detention. Marris and

Somerset's work on African businessmen in Kenya virtually ignores such historical barriers and views detention camps in a favourable light, since many detainees used the opportunity to learn skills from each other and to form political and business relationships which helped them later on in life. See Peter Marris and Anthony Somerset, *African Businessmen,* p. 209. While it is evident from my own interviews that African detainees were indeed resourceful and resilient under the hardships of detention camps, no credit is due the colonial regime for any indirect benefits detainees derived from the experience. Moreover, such glorification of the detention camps ignores the fact that the detainees' lives were interrupted for two or more years, careers interrupted or businesses ruined, and that many detainees died in the camps. The views of Marris and Somerset exhibit a paternalism bordering on racism, as in the following statement:

> So, for instance, businessmen deeply committed to the Mau Mau movement later accepted as a model the civilization they had so stubbornly resisted.
>
> Marris and Somerset, op. cit., p. 102.

[40] Walter Elkan, "The East African Trade in Woodcarvings", *Africa,* 28 (October, 1958), as cited in Ichirou Inukai. "The Legal Framework for Small-Scale Enterprise Development with Special Reference to the Licensing System", in Frank C. Child and Mary E. Kempe (eds.), *Small Scale Enterprise,* Nairobi: Institute for Development Studies, University of Nairobi, 1973, p. 92.

[41] See for example the superficial discussion of credit restrictions faced by African businessmen in the colonial period as found in Marris and Somerset, *African Businessmen,* p. 181.

[42] Interview with African real estate agent, Nairobi, 8th April, 1974.

[43] This "liberalization" was hardly revolutionary, as the *maximum* loan under the scheme was limited to £500. See John Loxley, *The Development of the Monetary and Financial System of the East African Currency Area, 1950-1964* (Leeds: University of Leeds unpublished PhD thesis in Economics, 1966), p. 248. Registration of individual titles to land in "African" rural areas, begun in 1956, has still not been completed.

[44] Although, strictly speaking, the term multinational corporation should be reserved for foreign firms with subsidiaries, associates or management contracts and licensing agreements in 10 or more nations, including Kenya, I often use the more general term foreign firm in this paper. The dividing line between foreign firms in general and multinational corporations is a fuzzy one at best, since through the process of concentration and monopolization, so-called independent foreign firms are increasingly falling under the control of multinational corporations once they attain a certain size or strategic importance in terms of raw materials, products, or markets.

[45] Interview with director of a trading firm with interests in plantations and shipping, London, 17th December, 1973.

[46] Ibid.

[47] The vertical international division of labour is discussed in Helge Hveem, "The Global Dominance System; Notes on a Theory of Global Political Economy", *Journal of Peace Research,* 1973, no. 4, pp. 319-40. The relationship between international trade and the vertical international division of labour is debated by Arghiri Emmanuel and Charles Bettleheim in Arghiri Emmanuel, *Unequal Exchange; A Study of the Imperialism of Trade,* New York: Monthly Review, 1972. The term "international division of labour" dates back to Marx:

> A new and international division of labour, a division suited to the requirements of the chief centres of modern industry springs up, and converts one part of the globe into a chiefly agricultural field of production, for supplying the other part which remains a chiefly industrial field.
>
> Karl Marx, *Capital,* I, Moscow, Progress Publishers, p. 425.

[48] The distinction between *undeveloped* and *underdeveloped* economies is drived from Rhoda Howard, "Development and Underdevelopment in the Gold Coast: Foreign Business and the African Response, 1886-1938", Montreal: McGill University Department of Sociology, mimeograph, 1974.

[49] Ibid. See also E. A. Brett, *Colonialism and Underdevelopment in East Africa,* pp. 165-212. In using the term *dependence* in connection with the Kenyan economy, I accept the definition of dependence given by dos Santos:

> By dependence we mean a situation in which the economy of certain countries is conditioned by the development and expansion of another economy to which the former is subjected.

Theotonio dos Santos, "The Structure of Dependence", *American Economic Review: Papers and Proceedings,* 60 (May, 1970), p. 231.

[50] E. A. Brett, *Colonialism and Underdevelopment in East Africa,* p. 171.

[51] Information derived from a list of branch offices and managers found in Barclays Bank International, *A World of Banking: List of Offices October 1973,* pp. 44-6, 58-60.

[52] Based on data supplied by the public affairs office of Unilever Ltd., London, December 1973. As a rule Unilever requires that a minimum of 10 percent of senior management in any subsidiary anywhere in the world be expatriate. "By employing groups of mixed nationalities we add sparkle", E. G. Woodroofe and G. D. A. Klijnstra (joint chairmen of Unilever group), *Unilever's Role as a Multi-National Business,* speech, 8th May, 1972, reprinted in pamphlet form by Unilever Ltd. Information Division, London, May 1972.

[53] Interview with British director of manufacturing subsidiary, Nairobi, 25th April 1974.

[54] E. A. Brett, *Colonialism and Underdevelopment in East Africa,* pp. 77-8.

[55] Ibid., p. 205.

[56] Dependence on the traditional vertical international division of labour can be expressed in terms of the composition of trade index developed by John Galtung and Knut Hungrø:

$$\text{Trade composition index} \quad \frac{(a + d) - (b + c)}{a + d + b + c}$$

where

a = the value of raw materials imported,
b = the value of raw materials exported,
c = the value of processed goods imported, and
d = the value of processed goods exported.

Using this index, + 1.00 represents an economy which is completely industrialized and whose imports consist solely of raw materials and whose exports consist solely of processed goods. On the other hand, – 1.00 represents an economy which is completely underdeveloped and whose imports consist entirely of processed goods and whose exports consist entirely of raw materials. See John Galtung, "A Structural Theory of Imperialism", *Journal of Peace Research,* 8 (1971), no. 2, pp. 81-117. The problem with the index is that it is very crude with respect to degree of processing and that it relies on trade to infer the internal structure of an economy. Hypothetically a nation could be fairly self-reliant and still have a negative trade composition index.

Using the Kenya Central Bureau of Statistics data on the composition of trade in terms of raw materials and processed goods rather than the even cruder United Nations SITC classification system, the index of trade composition for Kenya stood at —.400 in 1964, and over the next seven years declined to —.461 in 1971. Data source: Kenya, *Statistical Abstract, 1972,* pp. 60, 72. This includes trade with Tanzania and Uganda.

[57] See also the pessimistic assessment of the effects of import substitution on Kenya's foreign exchange in Christopher Davis (National and Grindlays Bank), "Kenya's Key to Economic Success", *The Banker,* September 1973, pp. 1047-52, esp. p. 1051.

[58] Steven W. Langdon, "Multinational Corporations and 'Appropriate Technology'—A Case Study from Kenya", Mimeograph, South Chailey, England, August, 1973. Langdon's study also deals with the relationship between multinational corporations and imported consumption patterns.

[59] One exception was the recent publication of the ILO report, *Employment, Incomes and Equality: A Strategy for Increasing Productive Employment in Kenya,* Geneva, 1972. The strained reception of the ILO report illustrates the reluctance of the Kenyan government to consider alterations in the present economic structure.

[60] Information in this paragraph and the following one comes primarily from "Banking in Kenya", *The Banker,* September 1973, pp. 1059-63.

[61] Both Barclays and Standard were originally off-shoots of British banks in South Africa. The "South African connection" continues in Kenya today through insurance firms such as Old Mutual of South Africa and South African Mutual Life Assurance Society. In addition some apparently British firms in Kenya are in fact wholly or partly owned by South African firms or by South African subsidiaries of British firms. Examples include Leyland Albion (East Africa), which is owned by British Leyland's South African subsidiary, and Twiga Chemical Industries, which is jointly owned by African Explosives and Chemical Industries of South Africa and by ICI of Britain through a holding company. Source: *Who Owns Whom.*

[62] Kenya, *Blue Book, 1926.*

[63] "Banking in Kenya", p. 1059.

[64] Speech by Mr. D. N. Ndegwa, Governor of Central Bank of Kenya, 1st December 1972, as published in Central Bank of Kenya, *Seventh Annual Report; Year Ended 30th June 1973,* p. 63.

[65] Interview with British banker who had previously served as lending officer and branch manager in a rural bank branch in Kenya.

[66] Figures based on data presented by Barry Herman in "Some Basic Data for Analysing the Political Economy of Foreign Investment in Kenya", Institute for Development Studies, University of Nairobi, Discussion Paper No. 112, July, 1971, p. 13. The figures exclude re-investment.

[67] A similar argument is made by Brett, *Colonialism and Underdevelopment in East Africa,* p. 180.

[68] Based on data at the end of one month in 1974. Urban branches are defined as branches in Nairobi and Mombasa. All other branches are considered to be rural branches. The urban branches with the lowest advances/deposits ratios were branches in African areas of Nairobi and Mombasa.

[69] By contrast, the share of loans to agriculture as a percent of total loans by commercial banks was 12.3 percent in 1969. Source: Central Bank of Kenya, *Economic and Financial Review,* 6 (October-December 1973), p. 20. See also Kenya, *Kenya Development Plan, 1970-74,* pp. 560-2, regarding the government's call for increased loans to the agricultural and rural sectors.

[70] Speech by Mr. D. N. Ndegwa, Governor of Central Bank of Kenya, 1st December 1972, op.cit.

[71] Kenya, *Statistical Abstract, 1972,* p. 104.

[72] Ibid., pp. 91, 104. Although the *average* size of holdings has remained approximately the same, the *median* size of large farms has decreased slightly from roughly 350 hectares (860 acres) in 1963 to roughly 250 hectares (620 acres) in 1971.

[73] *East African Standard,* 17th April 1974, p. 5, and *Evening News* (Nairobi), 17th April 1974, p. 3. For more on the background to this plantation project see John Carlsen, "Danish Private Investment in Kenya", Copenhagen: Institute for Development Research, mimeo, 1974.

[74] Kenya, *Statistical Abstract,* 1972, p. 37.

[75] Ibid., p. 97.

[76] Ibid., pp. 97, 220.

[77] Agriculture contributes 21 percent to the *monetary* gross domestic product, wholesale and retail trade, 17 percent. Kenya, *Statistical Abstract,* 1972, p. 37.

[78] Kenya, *Census of Industrial Production, 1967,* pp. 11 and 15. I regard this data as more reliable than the data on ownership presented on p. 443 of the ILO report, *Employment, Incomes and Equality . . . in Kenya.* The census of industrial production data is based on a survey

which had a 75 percent response rate to questions on ownership. The sample was limited to firms with ten or more employees. Coverage of ownership was better for larger firms than for smaller firms. One hypothesis would be that some of these smaller manufacturing firms are owned by Asians who declined to answer ownership questions if they had citizenship applications pending.

[79] See *East African Standard,* 28th March, 1974, p. 1.

[80] Giovanni Arrighi, "International Corporations, Labour Aristocracies, and Economic Development in Tropical Africa", in Robert I. Rhodes (ed.), *Imperialism and Underdevelopment,* New York: Monthly Review, 1970, pp. 220-67.

Peter Neersø

Tanzania's Policies on Private Foreign Investment

Nationalization

The foundations of Tanzania's present policies on private foreign investments were laid in the Arusha Declaration which was issued by Tanzania's ruling party, TANU, in January 1967. The Arusha Declaration called for socialism and self-reliance and declared that the state must have effective control of the major means of production. After the Arusha Declaration, Tanzania began nationalizing a substantial number of foreign-owned banks, trading companies, industrial companies, etc. In many cases only a part of the shares, e.g., 50 or 60 percent, were taken over at first; in most of these cases, however, the rest of the shares have been subsequently taken over.

At the announcement of the Arusha Declaration, the government declared that Tanzania would pay full and fair compensation for the nationalizations. In almost all cases it has been possible to reach an agreement on compensation with the foreign companies, and it seems that, generally, the foreign companies have been satisfied with the compensation agreements.

It was very important for Tanzania to reach compensation agreements which satisfied the foreign companies, since Tanzania did not consider herself capable of running her entire economy without the technological and managerial skills possessed by the foreign companies. Tanzania wanted the foreign managers to stay on in the nationalized companies and run them under management contracts with Tanzania. Furthermore, Tanzania did not want to have a bad foreign-investment image, which might totally preclude future foreign investments in Tanzania.

Tanzania's policies of public control of the economy put a great emphasis on the parastatal holding corporations. These are a kind of development corporation, primarily financed by government funds. They are subject to governmental supervision, but at the same time they enjoy a certain degree of autonomy, among other things, the right to establish joint ventures and to enter into management contracts with foreign companies. The parastatal holding corporations each deal with a specific sector of the economy: National Development Corporation (NDC) deals with most of industry, National Agricultural and Food Corporation (NAFCO) deals with agriculture, including processing of agricultural products, Tanzania Tourist Corporation (TTC) deals with tourism, etc.

Today, many of the nationalized companies have management contracts with foreign companies. In the same way, many of the new companies founded by the parastatal holding corporations have foreign management, and some of them also have private foreign capital participation.

At the time of the Arusha Declaration, some people thought that Tanzania's policy of nationalization would make co-operation with foreign companies extremely difficult and would therefore lead to difficulties in the Tanzanian economy. Co-operation with foreign companies has run rather smoothly until now, however, and Tanzania has been able to attract foreign management and foreign capital for new projects, both in the sector reserved for public control and in the sector totally open to private investment.

Only a few of the foreign companies affected by nationalization have refused to supply Tanzania wih the required know-how. When the British banks in Tanzania were nationalized in 1967, they immediately withdrew their personnel, leaving the Tanzanian banking system in a difficult position. Nevertheless, by recruiting personnel in foreign countries, but especially by giving greater responsibility to local staff, Tanzania put the banking system in good order within half a year. The successful development of local talent in the banking system and similar experiences in other sectors have made a psychological impact in Tanzania and considerably increased self-respect and confidence in the policy of self-reliance.

Although Tanzania has published a list of the industries open to private investment, it is not quite clear which industries the Tanzanian government wants to control through the parastatal corporations. The major means of production, which are to be controlled by the state, are very loosely defined in the Arusha Declaration. In the years after the Arusha Declaration the government has, on various occasions, undertaken nationalizations and thereby placed further sectors under public control.

The general opinion in Tanzania is that in the future the government will place more and more sectors under public control. Thus, virtually all foreign companies in Tanzania must face the fact that one day they may be nationalized, totally or partially. This generally does not prevent the foreign companies from making new investments in Tanzania, however, because they feel confident that should nationalization occur, Tanzania will pay full compensation, so that the money invested will not be lost.

Criticism of the parastatals

We have seen that the Arusha Declaration and the subsequent nationalizations have not prevented foreign companies from wanting to invest in Tanzania and to co-operate with the parastatal corporations through joint ventures and management contracts.

Part of the explanation for this lies in the fact that the socialist principles in the Arusha Declaration have as yet only been carried out to a limited extent. The Tanzanian economy is still more of a market economy than a centrally planned economy, and the private-profitability criterion (as opposed to the social-profitability criterion) has until now been the dominant criterion for economic decisions.

Until recently, the initiative for formulating new projects has to a large extent been taken by foreign companies and not by the parastatal holding corporations, although these corporations are supposed to be the dynamic force in the development of the Tanzanian economy.

Nevertheless, it seems that the initiative for investment decisions has moved from the foreign companies to the Tanzanian parastatal corporations and other Tanzanian bodies. In recent years, the parastatal corporations have considerably increased their planning staff and thus their capacity for project-formulation. Whereas the primary bottleneck for the expansion of the parastatal sector was previously lack of planning capacity, it is now lack of financial resources.

Another factor influencing the initiative of the parastatals is the severe criticism which has been launched against their performance, particularly against NDC.

The parastatals have been criticized for having low profitability, due to bad management and bad project preparation. NDC has also been criticized for having traditional capitalist investment criteria, that is, short-term private-profitability criteria. These criteria have made NDC undertake investments in import substitution industries producing more or less luxury goods (beer, cigarettes, etc.). Instead, its critics say, NDC ought to have socialist, long-term social-benefit criteria and put more emphasis on investments in the production of simple household goods and in basic industries. NDC has also been criticized for preferring large, capital-intensive projects in major cities (Dar-es-Salaam, Tanga, Moshi, Arusha and Mwanza) instead of small labour-intensive projects scattered about in the smaller towns and villages.

Some of the criticism launched against the parastatals is directly connected to their co-operation with foreign companies. The parastatals are accused of putting too much emphasis on foreign managers, who are said to run the companies in an authoritarian, capitalist way, contrary to the interests of the Tanzanian workers and Tanzanian society as a whole. The terms of the management contracts have been strongly criticized for being too generous to the foreign management agents and for not inducing them sufficiently to run the companies in a way beneficial to Tanzania.

The parastatals have also been criticized for being too careless in the selection of foreign partners, some of whom have proved to be dishonest. In some cases a foreign company has persuaded NDC to participate in a joint venture and to buy machinery from that same company at an inflated price.

Its main goal was not to establish a viable project, but to make a large profit on the sale of machinery.

NDC has defended itself against some of these criticisms in various ways. It points to the fact that its statutes say that the corporation shall be profit-earning and finance new investments largely out of its own earnings. Therefore, it is natural that NDC's primary investment criteria is the profitability of the individual project, and the profitability criterion is also a sound one for measuring the efficiency of the running of the parastatal companies. NDC maintains that it pays attention to the economic policies of the government and also lets social-benefit considerations like forward and backward linkages and effects on foreign exchange and employment influence the choice of investment projects.

NDC has declared that it understands the need for social considerations, but that it would be much easier for it to pay attention to them, if the Treasury were to subsidize it whenever the government wants it to deviate from the private-profitability criterion. NDC also points to the difficulty in implementing labour-intensive projects, when the government makes such projects unviable by raising the minimum wage considerably.

NDC admits that many of its subsidiary companies show losses or only meagre profits, but maintains that, to a large extent, this is a consequence of factors beyond its control. Thus, the government has allowed wages to rise without permitting corresponding price increases, so that the profits of the parastatal companies have been squeezed.

Government control of the parastatals

As a consequence of this criticism against the parastatals, the Tanzanian government has taken various steps to secure that the parastatals work efficiently and in accordance with the development strategy of the government. In 1969 a reorganization of the parastatal sector was carried out. TTC and NAFCO were split off from NDC, and the parastatal holding corporations were put under the control of the pertinent "parent" ministries, NDC under the Ministry of Commerce and Industries, NAFCO under the Ministry of Agriculture and Co-operatives, etc.

The parastatals have also been put more closely under the control of the two "general" ministries, the Ministry of Finance and the Ministry of Economic Affairs and Development Planning (Devplan). Thus, all parastatal projects must be approved by Devplan, which checks that they are consistent with the development goals of the government.

The Tanzanian banking system has gradually assumed an important controlling role over the parastatals. The central bank, Bank of Tanzania, has control over the parastatals' use of foreign exchange, *inter alia,* by managing the import licensing system. The Tanzania Investment Bank is an important source of long-term finance for new parastatal projects and checks the efficiency with which the parastatal companies use their investment funds. At the same time, the National Bank of Commerce, which gives short-term loans to the parastatal companies, is increasing its control over the general financial management of the parastatal companies.

The government has placed special attention on the control of management contracts. In 1971 a revision of existing management contracts took place, and at present all new management contracts must be approved by the Economic Committee of the Cabinet. Tanzania now seeks to make the foreign partner accept a contract which clearly specifies the obligations of managing agents (e.g., in relation to training of local staff), and which makes the fee dependent on the profitability of the company, in order to induce the managing agent to run the company in an efficient way.

As described above, the Tanzanian government now has a rather strict control of the activities of the parastatal corporations, including their collaboration with foreign companies. Consequently, the government has the possibility of making the parastatals act in accordance with its development strategy. One basic weakness, however, is that the development strategy of the government has until now not been sufficiently precise to give the parastatals clear guidelines for their activities, e.g., clear criteria for investment decisions.

For instance, the parastatal corporations are to both run at a profit and simultaneously pay attention to social considerations, such as the employment effect of the projects. It is often the case that the profitability criterion points in one direction (e.g., towards capital-intensive projects) and the social criterion points in the opposite direction (e.g., towards labour-intensive projects). In such cases, there is no clear guideline for the weight to be given the various criteria.

In recent years there has been considerable discussion of development strategy and investment criteria in Tanzania. The discussion is still going on, but from various statements by the government and by TANU some new trends can be seen. These trends suggest that in the future Tanzania is likely to put more emphasis on overall planning and on development in the rural areas. Development projects are likely to become more directly productive and more labour-intensive than before. In the industrial sector, priority is likely to be given to processing of local raw materials for local consumption and for export rather than to import-substitution industries using imported inputs. Finally, these trends suggest that in the future industrial projects are likely to be less heavily concentrated in a few large cities.

Some experiments which agree with the above-mentioned trends have already been made in Tanzania. Although NDC, in general, favours capital-intensive projects, some labour-intensive projects have been undertaken in the industrial sector.

One of these is the Chinese-financed Friendship Textile Mill in Dar-es-Salaam, which started production in 1968. The mill was established on the basis of an agreement between the Chinese and the Tanzanian government, and NDC did not have any influence in the investment decision. NDC was not enthusiastic about the labour-intensity of the project and showed its preference for capital-intensity by establishing, at almost the same time, a highly automatized textile mill in Mwanza in partnership with a French company. The two mills have about the same capacity, but the Friendship Textile Mill has much cheaper machinery and employs about twice as many workers as the Mwanza Textile Mill.

NDC has also established projects with widely different techniques in the cashew-nut processing industry. In a number of *ujamaa* villages (i.e., villages with collective farming) cashew nuts are processed with simple tools, and at the same time cashew nuts are also processed in capital-intensive factories in cities.

Experiments with decentralization of industrial development have been carried out for some years. These experiments have been made because the great majority of industrial plants are located in 4-5 large towns, with a heavy concentration in Dar-es-Salaam. In an effort to decrease the concentration in Dar-es-Salaam, the government has decided that new industrial projects shall as far as possible be located in 9 "growth towns", i.e., Arusha, Dodoma, Mbeya, Morogoro, Moshi, Mtwara, Mwanza, Tabora and Tanga.

Until now the decentralization policy has had some success in that, in the last few years, a large number of industrial projects have been located in up-country towns. For a number of joint ventures, both NDC and the foreign partners would have preferred Dar-es-Salaam, but the government decided that they should be located in one of the priority towns.

Nevertheless, the decentralization policy of the government has not been completely successful, as there has been a heavy concentration of new industrial projects in three of the priority towns, i.e., Arusha, Moshi and Tanga. These towns are rather well equipped with infrastructure, and they have easy access to Kenya, which is an important export market for many industrial products. For a typical consumer article, 40-50 percent of the Tanzanian market is situated in the Dar-es-Salaam/Morogoro area, 30-40 percent in the Northern regions and only 10-30 percent in the rest of the country.[1] This means that for most market-based goods, location in Arusha, Moshi or Tanga is almost as favourable in private-profit terms as location in Dar-es-Salaam and much more favourable than location in the other priority towns, especially Dodoma, Mbeya, Mtwara or Tabora.

NDC has had great trouble in finding projects which could be located in the priority towns situated at a great distance from the main markets, especially as some of these towns are very poor in infrastructure and do not have any natural resources in the neighbourhood on which to base resource-based industries. This problem could be solved if the government introduced an efficient programme of incentives for decentralization of industrial development, but such a programme has not been developed as yet.

Some of the above-mentioned new trends in government development strategy are not very favourable to private foreign investment. This applies especially to the policies on labour-intensity of production and intensified decentralization of industrial development. Industrial projects using labour-intensive techniques and located outside the 4-5 largest cities will, in most cases, not be very profitable to the investors, and therefore foreign companies will not be very interested in investing capital in them. Furthermore, in most cases, the machinery and the managerial and technological know-how they can offer are not very well suited to labour-intensive projects.

The Tanzanian government is well aware that the new trends in its development strategy will make it difficult to attract private foreign capital to Tanzania. Nevertheless, the government is not worried, because this strategy is consistent with recent developments in Tanzania's policies on foreign investment.

Tanzania believes that reliance on private foreign capital is a very expensive way of raising capital and that, in the main, the capital necessary for development can be raised by mobilizing internal resources and by receiving foreign development assistance. At the same time, Tanzania is exploring the possibilities of obtaining the technological and managerial know-how possessed by specialists in the developed countries without accepting private foreign capital.

Provision of know-how for industrial projects

Tanzania is looking very actively for alternatives to private foreign investment for her industrial development. In accordance with her policy of self-reliance, she seeks to rely as much as possible on her own forces. This implies that she places emphasis upon training of local people for all kinds of jobs, including the most responsible ones. Tanzanians are often placed in top positions, e.g., in the parastatal companies, although they are less competent than foreign specialists. In the short run this may lead to poor performance, e.g., to production of goods of low quality; but this is accepted in Tanzania as an inevitable consequence of her long-term policy of self-reliance.

In some cases Tanzania uses know-how provided by a development assistance agency as a substitute for private foreign investment. Thus, Tanzania receives experts for industrial projects from multilateral agencies like the United Nations Industrial Development Organization, as well as from a number of development assistance agencies in capitalist and socialist countries. These experts are expected to train local people to replace them on the expiry of their contracts.

Nevertheless, there are certain limitations upon Tanzania's possibilities for obtaining know-how for industrial projects through development assistance. The socialist countries generally offer their assistance as a package deal including supply of machinery, experts, financing, etc., and some of the components of such packages (e.g., prices of machinery) may be unacceptable to Tanzania.

There are also limitations upon Tanzania's possibilities for obtaining industrial know-how through development assistance from capitalist countries. According to conventional thinking in these countries, the industrial sector should be left to private (local or foreign) investors and, therefore, they show some hesitation in giving assistance to public-sector industries in developing countries. There are also various practical problems in the transfer of technology without direct co-operation with a private firm, especially in industries using sophisticated technologies.

In industries using sophisticated technologies the pertinent know-how is most often not vested in a single person, but in a group of persons. In these industries, transfer of technology can only take place through a team of persons whose skills are complementary and who can work well together. It is very difficult for a development assistance agency to recruit an entire such team at the same time; and even if it is possible, such a team is handicapped by not being able to obtain technical advice from a parent company in a developed country.

One additional difficulty is that in sophisticated industries, technological progress is generally rapid in the developed countries, and a specialist who leaves his company to work in a developing country runs the risk of losing contact with that technological progress. This leads many specialists to prefer to stay at home in order to preserve their career opportunities. Yet another difficulty is that the use of sophisticated technologies is often restricted by the existence of patents owned by companies in the developed countries.

Thus, if Tanzania desires to establish projects in industries where sophisticated technologies are the only efficient technologies available, she is likely to do so in some kind of co-operation with foreign companies, since she herself has no specialists in these industries, and her possibilities of obtaining such specialists through development assistance are small.

In some cases export considerations may induce Tanzania to establish an industrial production in partnership with a foreign company even if this production can be made by simple technologies and, therefore, can be established in an alternative way. If Tanzania wishes to export an industrial product, it is important for her to be able to use a well-known trade mark of a foreign company.

Normally, foreign companies are not interested in exports from their subsidiaries or joint-ventures in developing countries. From Tanzania, however, they have duty-free access to Kenya and Uganda because of the East African common market. If they have no production in Kenya or in Uganda, they may be interested in supplying these markets from Tanzania, and well-known trade marks will facilitate such exports.

Management contracts

If NDC decides to acquire technology from a foreign company, it usually uses a management contract. Because Tanzania has had some bad experiences with management contracts, NDC now considers the terms of such agreements very carefully before concluding them.

One thing which is considered very carefully is the way in which the management fee is calculated. It may be a lump sum, a part of the turnover of the project, a part of the profits of the project or a combination of two or three of these factors.

A lump sum fee has the disadvantage for Tanzania that it does not induce the managing agent to pay any attention to productivity. A fee calculated on the basis of the turnover has the disadvantage that it may induce the managing agent to increase turnover regardless of the costs. A fee calculated on the basis of the profits of the project is preferred by Tanzania, but the managing agents are not very enthusiastic about this. They maintain, not without justification, that profitability is not a fair criterion for evaluation of their performance, since it is dependent on factors outside their control, e.g., the wage and price policies of the Tanzanian government. In practice, in most cases, NDC and the managing agent agree on a management fee calculated on the basis of more than one factor, e.g., a lump sum plus a part of the profits. In some cases the managing agent also holds a part of the equity. This, of course, makes him more interested in the profitability of the Tanzanian company.

One thing to which Tanzania pays great attention is the provision for training of Tanzanian personnel in the management contracts. This is clearly a field where the interests of Tanzania and those of the managing agents tend to clash. Tanzania wants a quick replacement of foreign managers by Tanzanian staff, and, in most cases, the managing agents are not interested in efficient training of Tanzanians because this will make them superfluous and thus deprive them of the management fees (which are normally quite high).

A foreign company providing management for a company in Tanzania has various opportunities to run the company in a way which is beneficial to itself and detrimental to Tanzania. It is, of course, the more tempted to do this, the smaller the financial stake it has in the Tanzanian company.

One way of doing this is to manipulate the transfer prices for deliveries between the foreign parent company and the Tanzanian company. Deliveries of capital goods, raw materials, services, etc., from the parent company to the Tanzanian company can be sold at a price above the world market price. In the same way, deliveries of goods from the Tanzanian company to the parent company can be sold at a price below the world market price.

Even in developed countries, the authorities find it difficult to prevent manipulation of transfer prices, because some of the products traded are of a very special kind, and it is therefore very difficult to establish their world market price.

There is a widespread opinion in Tanzania that such manipulation is common in companies having foreign management, but due to a lack of skilled people, there has until recently been very little Tanzanian control of transfer prices. Nevertheless, since such manipulation is believed to cause a serious drain of foreign exchange, the Bank of Tanzania has recently taken steps to check transfer prices. (See below, "Taxation of foreign companies and remittance of profits.")

The Tanzanian government prefers management contracts of a relatively short duration, because this gives Tanzania the possibility of periodical performance evaluations of the managing agents and of removing bad managing agents in a relatively short time. There have been many cases where Tanzania has declined to renew a management contract, e.g., because of insufficient training of local personnel.

Because of the problems in connection with management contracts, Tanzania is considering other forms of co-operation with foreign companies. She is considering the possibility of separating managerial and technological know-how so as to use Tanzanian managers assisted by technological assistance contracts with foreign companies. In the future, when more Tanzanians have managerial skills, Tanzania is likely to substitute such contracts for management contracts, since they are much cheaper and involve a smaller degree of dependence.

Financing of investment projects in Tanzania

As we have already seen, Tanzania is looking actively for alternatives to transfer of technology from foreign companies. She is looking even more actively for alternatives to private foreign capital for financing investment projects, because she believes that this is a very expensive way of financing.

One of the methods used by Tanzania to obtain capital for development projects is mobilization of her own internal resources combined with an import policy giving priority to imports of capital goods. Since Tanzania introduced her policy of self-reliance in 1967 much has been done in this respect.

Tanzania's first five-year plan (1964-69) projected that the total central government development expenditure (including contributions to the parastatal sector) would be T.Shs. 2,040 million of which T.Shs. 1,590 million would be financed by foreign sources and T.Shs. 450 million by local sources. It turned out, however, that Tanzania could not obtain that much external assistance without modifying her foreign policy, and she decided to speed up the mobilization of internal resources. This policy was successful. Out of an actual total expenditure of T.Shs. 1,533 million, external sources accounted for only T.Shs. 496 million, and local sources for as much as T.Shs. 1,037 million, which is more than twice the planned level.[2]

The second five-year plan (1969-74) also placed great emphasis upon mobilization of internal resources. This policy was successful, making very large investments possible, especially in the public sector. Nevertheless, the general opinion in Tanzania is that taxation has now reached such a high level that it cannot be pushed much higher.

Therefore, Tanzania is very interested in obtaining foreign governmental assistance, and at this moment she has much better opportunities of obtaining it on acceptable terms than before. One of the reasons for this is that Tanzania's policy of self-reliance has made a good impression in both socialist and capitalist donor countries. Furthermore, these countries have come to realize that Tanzania stands firm on her principles, so that the threat of cutting assistance to Tanzania cannot be used as a means of changing Tanzania's foreign policy. The Tanzanian government intends foreign loans and grants to account for 54 percent of total development budget expenditure in 1974/75, which is approximately the same percentage as in the four preceding financial years.[3] It is projected that about 75 percent of the total monetary investment for 1975 will be financed by domestic funds.

Many projects in the parastatal sector are partially financed by foreign development loans. The parastatals obtain these foreign loans through the Ministry of Finance and Tanzania Investment Bank (TIB), which may add a loan out of its own funds. It is planned that in the future all large projects in the parastatal sector will be partially financed by loans from TIB, which in this way will gain control of the financial management of the parastatals.

The parastatals normally pay an interest rate of about 9 percent on the loans from TIB. If a project is marginally profitable, but socially desirable, it can obtain a loan with a lower interest rate from special funds managed by TIB.

Thus, a parastatal project which is partially financed by a foreign development loan on soft terms, i.e., containing a grant element, does not automatically reap the benefit of this grant element itself; more often the benefit is reaped by the Ministry of Finance and by TIB, i.e., more or less by the Tanzanian society as a whole.

In general, foreign development loans are a cheaper way of financing parastatal projects than private foreign capital, and more so, the larger the grant element is. Nevertheless, this way of financing projects implies certain problems. Most bilateral development loans are tied to purchase of investment goods in the donor country. Various studies suggest that these ties often involve a price mark-up to the detriment of the recipient country.[4] One case from Tanzania is very illustrative.

In 1968 Tanzania Portland Cement Company, having decided to expand, bought new cement machines from a Danish firm. The machines already in use in the factory were of German origin, and Tanzania Portland Cement Company was offered additional German machines at a price about 11 percent below the price of the Danish machines, which were not considered by the company managers to be better than the German ones.

Nevertheless, since there was a soft (but tied) Danish loan available to Tanzania, but no corresponding German one, the Tanzanian Ministry of Finance ordered the Portland Cement Company to buy the Danish machines. Because of the large grant element in the Danish loan this was probably a rational arrangement for Tanzania under the circumstances, but it caused some problems for the cement company. The company would have preferred to buy the German machines, not only because they were cheaper, but also because purchase of new machines identical to the old ones would have considerably reduced problems of worker training and especially problems of keeping spare parts.

Many projects in the parastatal sector are to a very large extent financed by loans from both external and internal sources in order to limit expensive financing by private foreign capital and to secure majority equity holding by Tanzania. Whereas conventional economic wisdom suggests that the ratio between loan capital and equity capital should not exceed 1:1 for any project, some of NDC's subsidiary companies have a ratio of 5:1 or 6:1, and this may create problems.

If a project has a very high debt/equity ratio, the calculated percentual return on the equity capital may be extremely high, but if the performance on the project turns out to be only slightly less favourable than projected, a large percentual profit may turn into a large percentual loss. Thus, heavy reliance on loan capital makes it difficult to predict the profits of the parastatal companies and thereby causes difficulties for the planning of both the parastatal companies and the holding corporations.

A heavy debt burden is especially harmful to the liquidity of a project in its first years, when it is running at a loss or at a marginal profit. Whereas dividends on shares normally depend on the profit of the project and are not declared until the project is well consolidated, servicing of loans is a fixed amount and starts at the beginning of the life of the project (unless a period of grace is granted).

Supplier's credits are especially dangerous because they normally have high interest rates and are of a very short-term nature, which means that they solve the problem of project financing only in the very short run. Previously, some parastatal projects relied heavily on supplier's credits, but this has now been forbidden in Tanzania.

Despite the problems relating to financing of projects by loan capital, Tanzania generally prefers foreign development loans to private foreign equity capital for the financing of new parastatal projects. The main reason for this is that development loans are cheaper, even allowing for the fact that tying reduces the grant element, corresponding to an estimated increase in the interest rates in the range of 0 to 6 percent, whereas private foreign capital can normally be attracted only, if the expected return is 20 percent or more.

Wage policies

Until 1967, urban wages increased very rapidly, and therefore the gap in living standard between the urban population and the rural population widened. Therefore, the government decided to introduce a national wage policy. By this policy a Permanent Labour Tribunal was established, with the aim of checking wage increases. All wage agreements between employers and trade unions must be approved by the Permanent Labour Tribunal before becoming valid. The national wage policy stipulates that wage increases cannot exceed 5 percent per year and shall only be given if improvements in productivity are taking place.

In the first years of its existence, this policy proved successful in that wages increased considerably less than in previous years. Since 1970, however, the cost of living has increased very rapidly in Tanzania, especially in the urban areas. This has made it impossible to restrict wage increases to the limits set by the national wage policy. Therefore, annual wage increases of more than 5 percent may be granted today, especially for workers with low wages.

The wage restrictions have led to dissatisfaction in parts of the trade union movement, NUTA. Nevertheless, NUTA officially endorses the national wage policy and also accepts government control of its activities, e.g., by appointing its secretary general (normally the Minister of Labour is appointed to hold this post, as well).

NUTA is not very active, but the demands of the workers nevertheless have a certain influence in Tanzanian politics, since a number of influential TANU and government leaders support them. Thus, in 1972 and in 1974 the government decreed increases in the minimum wage. The minimum monthly wage for urban workers thereby increased from T.Shs. 180 in 1971 to T.Shs. 340 in 1974.

The government has also increased the wages and salaries in the public sector for those who earn more than minimum wage, but these wages and salaries have been increased much less (relatively) than the minimum wage. The result is that the differences in urban wages have been considerably reduced. At the same time, the tax rates for high personal incomes have been increased substantially. It is estimated that the government's income and tax policies have reduced the gap in effective purchasing power between a senior public-sector official and a minimum-wage earner from about 75:1 in 1961 to about 10:1 in 1974.[5] Thus, income differences persist in Tanzania, but they are much smaller than in most other African countries.

The increases in minimum wage have been criticized for not being consistent with the development strategy of the government because they widen the gap between the workers and the small farmers, and because they make labour-intensive production less profitable. Nevertheless, use of labour-intensive techniques is still possible in the public sector, although the minimum-wage increases admittedly make this even more dependent on the application of social investment criteria than before.

In addition, the minimum-wage increases have not affected the possibility of establishing labour-intensive production in *ujamaa* villages, like the above-mentioned cashew nut processing. Persons working collectively are considered as self-employed and not as wage earners and can therefore work at an income below the statutory minimum wage.

There is an additional sector which is not directly affected by the increases in the statutory minimum wage. A large number of small enterprises, generally labour-intensive, pay wages considerably below the statutory minimum wage. They can do so because unemployment makes many people accept a low wage, because it is difficult for the authorities and for NUTA to check that small interprises pay the statutory minimum wage, and probably also because it is common knowledge that an enforcement of the minimum wage regulation in this sector would unavoidably reduce employment in this sector.

The wage increases which have taken place in Tanzania have not caused much trouble for most of the foreign companies. Generally, the foreign companies are rather capital-intensive, and wages and salaries represent only a small fraction of total costs. This is especially true if one deducts salaries of expatriate staff, which are not affected by changes in the Tanzanian labour market. Therefore, even a substantial percent increase in local wages and salaries does not add much to total costs.

Labour relations

Concurrently with the elevation of the educational standard in Tanzania, the government urges the foreign companies to replace foreign managers by Tanzanians. In 1972 the government introduced a training levy on companies employing non-citizens. These companies must pay a levy corresponding to 10 percent of the wages and salaries paid to non-citizens, unless they can prove that they have a satisfactory training and replacement programme.

Despite the endeavours of the government, some companies having foreign management have not done much to train Tanzanians to replace expatriates. This may be because the foreign managers do not think that Tanzanians are able to work satisfactorily in leading positions, or because they are afraid of losing the real control of the company, or because they want to make themselves indispensable in order to force Tanzania to renew a lucrative management contract with them.

Because of the complexities of the problems relating to training and replacement, it is often impossible for outside bodies to check that a serious training and replacement programme exists in the companies having foreign management. Therefore, it is natural that the NUTA and TANU branches in these companies are active in this field. Their pressure for rapid Tanzanization is strongly welcomed by the workers. Only a few of them can benefit directly from training and promotion, but most of them have a strong preference for Tanzanian managers: they think that many foreign managers still have colonialistic ideas and show their disrespect for the human dignity of the Tanzanian workers by using abusive language towards them.

In the last few years the self-respect of the Tanzanian workers has increased considerably, and this has led to a number of strikes and other protest actions in companies, mainly in those having foreign management. It is interesting to note that in most cases the main reason for the actions has not been wage demands. The most common reasons have been complaints by the workers that the managers show disrespect to them by not training them to replace expatriates and by using abusive language towards them. In some cases the workers have demanded that one or more of the managers should be dismissed, or even that the company should be taken over by the workers as collective property.

In such cases of spontaneous actions NUTA has been in an awkward position, because it is simultaneously supposed to fight for the interests of the workers and to co-operate with the management in maintaining peaceful industrial relations and discipline among the workers. Because of NUTA's ambiguous position, the workers have preferred not to rely on NUTA and instead to organize the actions themselves, so that the actions have often taken the NUTA branch leaders by surprise as much as the management. Like NUTA, the government has taken an ambiguous attitude towards the protest actions of the workers. In some cases the government has complied with the demands of the workers. In other cases, however, the government has rejected the demands of the workers and has ordered that some of them should be dismissed or even jailed.

Taxation of foreign companies and remittance of profits

In Tanzania all companies pay a corporate income tax of 45 percent on net profits. In addition, companies pay a "withholding tax" of 15 percent on profits remitted to foreign countries and of 20 percent on management and license fees. The withholding tax may have a slight effect on the re-investment rate and on the use of management and license contracts, but its main purpose is to tax payments to companies in foreign countries.

Most products are subject to price control in Tanzania. For some companies, price control has caused squeezing of profits because selling prices have not been allowed to rise in step with the rise in wages and in prices of raw materials.

For certain goods with a high income elasticity and a low price elasticity, such as cigarettes and beer, the government has increased the sales tax and not allowed selling prices to increase or allowed them to increase by only a fraction of the increase in the sales tax. In such cases the increase in sales tax has been wholly or partly absorbed into profits. This is a way of taxing selected companies (some of which are partly foreign-owned) which produce goods with a rapidly increasing demand and which, therefore, have rapidly growing profits.

Unlike many other developing countries, Tanzania does not offer tax holidays to foreign companies in order to attract foreign investments. Tanzania needs all the tax revenue she can get, and a tax holiday would probably be totally inefficient in attracting hesitant investors to Tanzania. Conservative businessmen consider investments in Tanzania insecure because of the socialist policies of the government. Their hesitation is not likely to be counter-balanced by a tax holiday which is important only if the investment is profitable.

Tanzania offers few incentives to investors apart from protection against imported goods. One of the incentives offered is that companies in certain industries can import most of their inputs without paying customs duties. Another incentive is a capital allowance (normally 20 percent) on fixed investments; this allowance implies that fixed investments can be written off at a rate of 120 percent of the investment expenditure.

This capital allowance has been criticized on the grounds that it gives the investor a premium on capital investment and therefore encourages capital-intensive production. Proposals have been made to change it into a kind of labour allowance which would encourage labour-intensive production. A labour allowance entails many practical problems and it has not been introduced as yet.

In 1972, when Tanzania's foreign exchange reserves declined seriously, Tanzania introduced various restrictions on remittance of profits. The most important restrictions were introduced by the Specified Companies Act. This act gives the Minister for Finance power to regulate levels of dividends and uses of cash flows of companies and corporations. The act affects a number of companies and corporations (so-called "specified companies") selected by the Minister for Finance. One of the criteria for the selection of companies is the absolute size of their profits.

The specified companies cannot in any one year declare dividends which make their net worth drop below 115 percent of their paid-up capital. In addition, their dividends cannot in any one year exceed the larger amount of: a) the average of their annual profits in the preceding three years, or b) 80 percent of the profits in the preceding year.

The Minister for Finance can limit the dividends of any specified company even further, if he considers this to be in the national interest. The specified companies are also required to submit their annual cash-flow budget to the Minister for Finance, and he can require the specified companies to invest money in government securities.

Many of the specified companies are completely or partially owned by foreign investors, and any new foreign investment in Tanzania may be placed under this act. It is almost certain that this act will discourage various potential foreign investors from investing in Tanzania. One of the most important conditions for a foreign investor is a large degree of freedom to remit profits, and the power given to the Minister for Finance by this act is especially annoying to foreign investors since it is, in principle, unlimited.

The Tanzanian government is well aware that this act may deter foreign investors from investing in Tanzania, but it considers this act necessary for government control of the economy. Its basic principle is that if foreign investors cannot adapt themselves to the regulations considered necessary by Tanzania, she is better off without their investments.

The introduction of restrictions on remittance of profits has made it even more tempting to the foreign companies to manipulate transfer prices for deliveries between the parent companies and the subsidiaries in Tanzania in such a way as to shift profits from Tanzania to the home countries of the parent companies. In this way, a foreign company can make the Tanzanian restrictions on remittance of profits ineffective; and if the corporate income tax in the home country is lower than the Tanzanian tax (including the withholding tax), then the foreign company also achieves a tax reduction by this manipulation.

Companies and individuals can also export capital from Tanzania illegally by collusion with a foreign business partner. They can sell goods from Tanzania to their foreign partner and receive, e.g., 90 percent of the amount in Tanzania and 10 percent through an account in a foreign country. A similar manipulation can be made when goods are imported into Tanzania. The importing companies and individuals can pay, e.g., 110 percent of the agreed amount and receive the balance of 10 percent from their partner through an account in a foreign country.

The general opinion in Tanzania is that such manipulations commonly occur with both locally-owned and foreign-owned companies. Because the manipulations are considered to cause a serious drain on Tanzania's foreign reserves, the Bank of Tanzania has taken steps to cope with them. In 1972 the Tanzania General Superintendence Company was established in co-operation with a Swiss company. This company inspects shipment of goods into Tanzania in order to check that qualities, quantities and prices are correct. In this way Tanzania hopes to eliminate that part of illegal capital exports which takes place by overinvoicing of imports.

If this control of transfer prices proves efficient, it will be a hard blow to those companies which manipulate transfer prices in order to evade taxes and restrictions on repatriation of profits. Investors who are willing to accept restrictions on remittance of declared dividends, because they feel confident that they can remit an additional amount through manipulated transfer prices, will be discouraged from investments in Tanzania by her attempt to check overinvoicing.

This attempt is one more indication that Tanzania is not making any effort to create a "favourable investment climate". On the contrary, she is determined to make foreign investors comply with her aspirations; and if they are not willing to do this, she is determined to achieve development without their co-operation.

Notes

[1] I. C. Parker, *NDC investment policy and its relation to national industrial objectives.* Economic Research Bureau, Dar-es-Salaam, 1970, p. 24.

[2] John Loxley, *The finance of government spending in Tanzania since Independence,* Rasilimali, No. 1, published by Tanzania Investment Bank, 1972, p. 24-25.

[3] "Budget Speech Presented in Parliament by the Minister for Finance", *Daily News,* June, 14, 1974, p. 4.

[4] See, e.g., *Untying development finance and trade expansion among developing countries.* UNCTAD, TD/B/AC 10/3, 1970.

[5] C. D. Msuya, *Foreign Aid and Tanzania Development,* Rasilimali, No. 4, published by Tanzania Investment Bank, 1974, p. 5.

O. O. Soleye

The Politico-economic Position of Multinational Corporations: A Nigerian Example

Introduction

This paper discusses a single project—a cement factory—jointly owned by a state government and two multinational corporations, in order to highlight the actual working methods of multinational corporations. Admittedly, generalization cannot be based on a single case; my intention, however, is not to generalize, but rather to describe a real situation at a level which is too often neglected—the local community and state level—when discussing multinational corporations. One of the objectives of this paper is to show the development process of the cement company and how the multinational corporations involved in this project have achieved a politico-economic position that ensures their indispensability for some time to come.

Section I is a discussion of the origin and structure of the cement company and the relationships among the partners, drawing out the implications of the agreement which defines the roles and responsibilities of each partner. Some of the issues that divide and unite the partners are then discussed, as well as the way in which they are related to the situation in the factory. The marketing system of the company is discussed in Section II, in order to emphasize the way in which influential Nigerians at various decision-making centres are used. Section III then draws out certain implications from this case-study, in order to highlight the developmental problems which arise from the roles of multinational corporations in a developing economy.

Section I*

The possibility of manufacturing cement in Western Nigeria was first considered by the Western Region Development Production Board (now the Western Nigeria Development Corporation, WNDC) in August 1954.[1] It was

* Throughout this section, I shall quote from certain letters and documents available to me, although I shall not cite the sources, because these were private documents. The quotations should therefore be seen as field data.

at this point in time that the Western Development Corporation (WNDC) first approached the Associated Portland Cement Manufacturers of Great Britain (APCM). Discussions were at first abortive, due to disagreement as regards capital participation. Negotiations were reopened later that year, however, and an agreement covering a geological survey and paving the way for the creation of an operating company—provided the survey results warranted it—was eventually signed in June, 1955.

In August 1955 two officials of the Associated Portland Cement Manufacturers (APCM) visited certain areas of the Western Region (now the Western State of Nigeria) where limestone was known or believed to exist in large quantities. One of these officials recommended that the search be initially restricted to the Ilaro area because of its proximity to road and rail communications. In March 1956, indications of vast quantities of limestone were found. These indications were subsequently proved, and two 'Special Exclusive Prospecting Licences' were taken out. Geological work to ascertain the quantity and quality of the deposits then began.

In the wake of the good results being obtained by the APCM geologists, negotiations were started for the establishment of a factory with a rated capacity of 100,000 tons per annum and costing £2.5 million. In December 1956, the possibility of raising the rated capacity from 100,000 to 200,000 tons was discussed and later approved. The proposal was to cost £ 4.5 million.

A company to operate the factory was eventually formed and incorporated on 26th February 1959, with a share capital of £ 3 million. The company was named The West African Portland Cement Company Limited (WAPCC). The shareholders are: Associated Portland Cement Manufacturers of Great Britain, (APCM), with 51 per cent of the shares; the Western Nigeria Development Corporation (WNDC) with 39 per cent; and the United Africa Company (UAC) with 10 per cent.[2] Construction started in 1959 and the factory was officially opened on Saturday, 3rd December, 1960.

A diagrammatic representation of the relationships between the West African Portland Cement Company Limited (WAPCC), the Western Nigerian Development Corporation (WNDC) and the Western State Government is given below. It is important to understand these relationships in order to appreciate some of the processes discussed later in this section.

A. The Western State Government set up WNDC as a semi-autonomous body to handle industrial and agricultural development throughout the Western State. WNDC is a profit-making corporation, whose initial capital was provided by the Western State government.

B. The WNDC invited APCM to participate in establishing a cement factory. APCM suggested that the United Africa Company (UAC) be invited as a partner because of UAC's long experience in industrial and commercial enterprises in Nigeria. This suggestion was accepted by WNDC so that we arrive at situation C.[3]

C. The three became partners in the cement company.

D. The West African Portland Cement Company Limited (WAPCC) was formed by the three partners: WNDC, APCM and UAC. The head office of the company is in Lagos, where the general administration of the company and cement sales take place.

E. The cement factory is situated at Ewekoro and is owned by the WAPCC.

In a joint venture of this nature, allocation of roles is necessary for the efficient operation of the enterprise. It is also required by law before the company can be registered. Allocation of roles was particularly necessary in this situation because each of the three partners is itself subject to a higher authority. WNDC is responsible to the Western State Government; UAC is an associated company of Unilever, whose headquarters is in London; and APCM is also a branch of a large firm with headquarters in London (Blue Circle Group).

An agreement between the partners was signed in London in May, 1957. The part of the agreement relevant for the present analysis is that which allocated different roles and responsibilities to the partners. Under the agreement, APCM was to arrange for the planning and supervision of the construction of the factory, as well as for any possible subsequent additions or extensions to it; it was to provide all necessary engineering and technical services in connection with the construction of the factory and of any additions or extensions to it; it was to be responsible for the acquisition and technical control of raw materials and the manufacture of cement and cement products; it was to provide a general manager for the cement company either by secondment (from APCM in the UK) or by direct recruitment, and to recruit all other technical staff, whether supervisory or otherwise, necessary for the efficient operation of the factory.

WNDC was to arrange for the company to secure from the Federal Government of Nigeria the rights to mine and quarry; to give advice on mining rights and rights to grind clinker, and on relations with the governments of the federation.

UAC was to establish commercial and administrative divisions under the control of a Commercial General Manager who was to be provided by UAC; it was to advise on commercial, accountancy, legal and secretariat matters; it was to provide—either by secondment or recruitment—a Commercial General Manager for the Cement Company as well as all other non-technical staff deemed necessary or desirable; it was to purchase all goods required by the commercial and administrative divisions of the company; and it was to purchase goods for the technical division when required to do so.

The agreement also provided for APCM to appoint *three directors,* one of whom would be the managing director; for WNDC to appoint *two directors*; and for UAC to appoint *one director* who was to be the commercial director

(Commercial General Manager).

Some of the main implications of this agreement were as follows. Firstly, it prevented WNDC from exercising any influence on recruitment, which was to be shared only by APCM and UAC. In a way, this violated governmental and public expectations that WNDC was created to provide employment for Nigerians. Secondly, the agreements prevented WNDC from taking part in the purchase of materials for the company in which it was the second largest shareholder. While it was incumbent on APCM to purchase technical equipment, UAC had the responsibility of purchasing all goods required by the commercial and administrative divisions. Thirdly, neither of the two directors representing WNDC was to have a post in the company, whereas one of APCM's nominated directors was to be the managing director, and the one nominee from UAC was to be the commercial director. Fourthly, the functions of WNDC were ones which reflected its awkward position. For example, it had consistently supported the applications of the management of the WAPCC to the government for employing expatriates in the cement factory in accordance with the duty assigned it in the agreements. Yet one of the primary purposes for which WNDC had been established was to provide employment for Nigerians. If, however, WNDC were to oppose the recruitment of expatriates into the cement factory, it would be seen by the other partners as failing in its duty and hindering the progress of the company, for recruitment of expatriates was often justified by the other partners on the grounds that this was necessary for efficient factory operation, as the expatriates recruited were men of high skill and not available locally.[4] WNDC has consistently opposed the government's proposal to start another cement factory by another company in Western State Why did WNDC oppose the government on this issue? WNDC had been established to foster economic development through industrial and agricultural projects, and was also expected (by the government) to be a profit-making and self-supporting corporation. Nevertheless, it was not given a monopoly on establishing industrial and agricultural projects in the state. (Other agencies and individuals could set up industrial projects.) WNDC was therefore not protected from competition, although, like any other business concern, it wanted to discourage competition. Furthermore since the cement factory is one of the most profitable enterprises in which WNDC participates, it desires to protect it from competition. WNDC has thus had to redefine its primary objective to being that of making a profit, even if this means opposing the establishment of another factory by another company which might well be profitable, as well. The opposition of WNDC to the establishment of another cement factory is thus understandable in terms of its interest, but in relation to the purpose for which it was established, its position is anomalous.

On one occasion WNDC was forced to defend WAPCC from a charge of having a "monopolistic tendency" in the following words:

> We do not feel that the case of monopoly has been established against the company . . . it will be better for our existing company to expand as [the] market dictates than to set up a rival company in this State. New programmes of expansion are at present being studied by the Board of Directors.[5]

The position and functions of WNDC described above were sources of dissatisfaction to its personnel. The nature of this dissatisfaction can be readily appreciated if we analyse certain contentious issues among the partners. The higher management structure of the cement company is depicted below as a background for understanding the issues and the relation of WNDC to the other two partners.

The first issue is *Nigerianisation.*[6] It is the policy of all levels of government in Nigeria whenever practicable to replace expatriates with Nigerians in all spheres of employment as quickly as possible. In spheres of employment controlled directly by the federal and state governments—the civil service and the statutory corporations—Nigerianisation was virtually complete by the time of this study. In foreign-owned commercial and industrial enterprises, however, Nigerianisation is largely controlled by the expatriate owners, although the government imposes indirect control by limiting the number of expatriates allowed into the country. A foreign-owned company must show that there are no qualified Nigerians to fill a particular post before it is allowed to recruit expatriates. As mentioned earlier, it fell to WNDC to show that there were no qualified Nigerians before supporting applications by the cement company (WAPCC) for the employment of expatriates. On one occasion, WNDC wrote to the government, explaining that a charge of anti-Nigerianisation levelled against the cement company (WAPCC) was not justified. "Nigerianisation in the Company (WAPCC) seem[s] slow on account of the technical nature of their operations. WNDC's (nominated) directors (in WAPCC) are looking into it."

Yet it was on the very issue of Nigerianisation that WNDC constantly quarrelled with APCM and UAC. On another occasion WNDC wrote to APCM, suggesting the appointment of a Nigerian as a Deputy Managing Director, but APCM replied in the following terms:

> The senior managerial set-up in the Company consists of . . . [See Diagram 2] In this set-up we are afraid there would simply be nothing for a deputy managing director to do.

APCM then went on to make an alternative proposal, at which point the process of bargaining began:

> The present Secretary/Accountant, an expatriate official seconded by the United Africa Company, is due to retire in . . ., and our suggestion is that he should be replaced by a Nigerian. To this extent the United Africa Company

are agreeable to release one of their Nigerian officials who, it is considered, would be suitable to take up the appointment, and we on our part would provide him with an initial period of training in the United Kingdom ...

APCM then concluded:

We hope you will feel that these proposals, within the present framework, are further evidence of the acceptance by the sponsors of the Company of the principle of Nigerianisation. We are confident that in the course of time it will be possible to proceed further with the implementation of this policy but I am sure you will agree that in the case of this Company, which is still of recent origin, and which is operating an industry entirely new to Western Region and is still expanding, it would be unwise and, in fact, detrimental to the interests of all concerned, including Nigerians, to proceed with undue haste.

WNDC then replied, suggesting that the 'schedule of the executive hierarchy' be altered so as to allow the managing director to gradually pass some of his responsibilities to the deputy:

It is our understanding that Nigerians will take over the management of the company eventually and we therefore feel that the time has come when a deputy managing director should be appointed who would understudy the managing director. Unless concrete steps are taken to train and groom a Nigerian as deputy managing director, it will be difficult to find a suitable Nigerian to take over as managing director.

Although WNDC insisted on having a deputy managing director, it accepted the alternative proposal to appoint a Nigerian as the Secretary/Accountant. On the other hand, WNDC rejected the idea that UAC should nominate the Secretary/Accountant, on the grounds that a substantial number of UAC's staff had already been released to work in the Cement Company, whereas none of WNDC's staff had been asked to work there.

APCM gave a final reply, which was also the final decision:

Apart from the fact that there would be little for him to do, both APCM and UAC are of the opinion that it would be injudicious to introduce someone, irrespective of nationality, as a deputy managing director, without his having had considerable practical experience over the years of the cement industry. I think it will be agreed on all sides that considerable progress has already been made in the implementations of the policy of Nigerianisation and I am sure the partners will proceed with this policy with due regard to the prosperity and welfare of the Company, of whose record I feel we can all be justifiably proud. This, I would suggest, is in keeping with the *spirit*[7] [my emphasis] of the Agreement into which the partners entered when they decided to set up the West African Portland Cement Co. Ltd.

In regard to the appointment of a Nigerian Secretary/Accountant, APCM reminded WNDC that under the agreement, it was the duty of the UAC to provide the necessary administrative staff either by secondment from UAC itself, or by direct appointment made by UAC on behalf of the cement company.[8] In the end no deputy managing director was appointed, and the Nigerian secretary/accountant appointed was UAC's nominee.

A second major disagreement over Nigerianisation arose out of WNDC's suggestion to the Chairman of the WAPCC that the cement company should appoint "an indigenous auditor" to work with the firm of expatriate auditors. The Chairman of WAPCC discussed the issue with the firm of expatriate auditors, who rejected the idea for the following stated reasons: that their audit did not lend itself to a division of work; that the combined fee for joint auditorship would almost certainly exceed the fee being charged at that time; that their firm had Nigerians below the level of principals and hoped soon to have Nigerians at the level of principal. (In effect the expatriate auditors were suggesting that they too were Nigerianising their staff).

In writing to WNDC and agreeing with the expatriate auditors, the Chairman of WAPCC said: "... it would be unwise and also unnecessary to bring in an indigenous firm to act jointly".

WNDC answered by rejecting the reasons given by the firm of expatriate auditors for not wanting to associate with a firm of Nigerian auditors, WNDC argued that the auditing work was divisible and that the fee need not increase, since the volume of work would remain the same.

The chairman of the cement company, in his capacity as APCM's representative, consulted UAC and both agreed to appoint a firm of Nigerian auditors. WNDC was informed after the Nigerian auditors were appointed. WNDC welcomed the appointment but protested that it was not consulted before the appointment was actually made. It is clear that WNDC would certainly not have nominated the particular firm appointed, but it had to accept the joint decision of APCM and UAC, since this partially met its demand. These two disagreements over Nigerianisation illustrate the power of multinational corporations and also the processes of bargaining and negotiation inherent in the relationships between the three partners.

Nigerianisation was not mentioned in the Agreement governing the relationship, but it had major national implications which could have led to the collapse of the cement company if not carefully handled. Since the general issue was not governed by any specific rules, every specific incident had to be negotiated.

When WNDC initially raised the issue of Nigerianisation in a tone that suggested that it had the legal right to do so, it was reminded by the other two partners that such an issue was only "in keeping with the spirit" of the agreement. Bargaining took place on this basis and APCM and UAC agreed to the appointment of a Nigerian Secretary/Accountant. It was in the interest of APCM and UAC to negotiate because WNDC had the power to prevent recruitment of additional expatriates. In pursuing their respective interests, the partners had to bargain if their joint relationship was to persist. There were, however, situations in which bargaining did not take place. When WNDC insisted that it should nominate the Secretary/Accountant, it was reminded that according to the *letter* of the agreement, it was UAC's responsibility to appoint an official of that status. Thus the agreement that was interpreted in its *spirit* on one occasion was interpreted in its *letter* on another. The particular agreement, and the rules in general, did not in effect specify or define relationships in any rigid way, since the same rules could be interpreted differently. The rules could therefore be seen as resources which were subject to continuous negotiation and manipulation, according to the changing way in which the relationship between the partners was perceived. The view taken here is that in a situation of this type, where relationships are supposedly specified by rules and are therefore thought to be predictable, they may in fact be unpredictable and may not *necessarily* be either stable or unstable.

The second issue relevant to understanding relations among the partners is the government proposal to establish another cement factory "to break the monopolistic tendency" of WAPCC. All three partners were solidly united against the government on this issue. They argued that on economic grounds it was better to expand the factory at Ewekoro than to have another factory in the state.[9] (The peculiar position of WNDC on this issue was discussed above.) While the partners were divided over Nigerianisation, they were united in their opposition to the government on its proposal to open another factory.

The third issue related to the discipline of workers in the factory. It was common for workers disciplined or dismissed to make representations to WNDC when they felt they had been treated unfairly. On each such occasion WNDC made representations to the chairman of WAPCC, sometimes asking for an explanation of the management's action. WNDC never succeeded, however, in making WAPCC change a decision. The significant questions to pose are: why did the workers at the time look to WNDC for protection? why did WNDC take on the role of defending the workers against its partners?

The answer to the first question seems to be that the workers thought of WNDC as the owner of the factory. They perceived WNDC as effectively occupying position B in Diagram 1, whereas the position of WNDC in relation to the factory is at level C. At this level, WNDC was less powerful than the other two partners not only because it did not have the controlling shares, but also because the responsibilities allocated to it under the agreement were less 'powerful' than those allocated to the other partners separately and collectively. The workers' ignorance of the true position of WNDC was widespread, and it led them to the belief that WNDC had the power to act in their favour against the management, whom they regarded as 'foreigners'. Another reason was the relative inactivity of the trade union at that stage. It was not until early in 1968 that the Union became effective in handling workers' grievances. Yet again, it was not till the middle of 1968 that a personnel department was established in the factory.

In this section, I have briefly referred to the history of the company and especially the way in which the functions of the three partners had crucial implications tending to isolate WNDC from other two partners—APCM and UAC. WNDC had conflicting and incompatible roles to perform and this fact initially affected its relationship with the other partners. This situation, however, is predictable from the allocation of functions in the Agreement, which shows the power of APCM and UAC. It did not appear that WNDC and the state government which set it up have the power—economic or otherwise—to confront APCM and UAC. Since it was preoccupied with the establishment of a factory to provide jobs for Nigerians and to produce cement for development, the government accepted the terms of operation of those who were to provide the capital and technical know-how.

The issue of Nigerianisation which later arose touches on the problems of economic independence and national sovereignty inherent in foreign investment. The sporadic disputes on Nigerianisation and the ways they were resolved emphasize the power of APCM and UAC and their willingness to compromise to achieve their overall economic objective.

Section II

In this section, the marketing system is discussed, in order to further emphasize the way in which the cement company strengthened its position. The product of the company is sold through about 75 distributors. Stocks are allocated each month to the distributors who then sell them through ATCs issued to consumers. The consumers then present the ATCs at the factory or at either of the two depots and collect their stock. The advantage of this system for the cement company is that it need only deal with seventy-five or so distributors instead of the general public. The advantage of the system for the distributors is that they need not store cement physically: what the distributors sell is a piece of paper; it is the consumer who pays the cost of transport.[10] The very high demand for cement, its inadequate supply at home and stringent restrictions on import have all ensured a very lucrative business for the company and the distributors. The competition to be a distributor of the company's product is therefore very high. It is estimated that only about 5-10% of those applying for distributorship stand any chance of success.

The way in which the company selects its distributors is the crucial point for this paper. Although one stipulated condition for being a distributor is a successful business—particularly in building materials—the selection clearly shows politico-economic considerations at all levels. At the local community level near the factory, the distributors are *powerful* local community leaders—the real decision-makers—whose past and present politico-economic roles are known beyond the borders of their local community. In other parts of the country, the distributors include traditional rulers, national political figures, current leaders of business, and relations of very highly-placed government functionaries. The other category of distributors are expatriate firms—some of which are subsidiaries of UAC.

This distribution arrangement necessarily ensures that the company enjoys some amount of goodwill among those who make decisions not only at the national level but also at the state and community levels.[11]

What has hitherto emerged from this paper are the ways in which the cement company has attempted to control its environment. At the inception of this company the third partner (WNDC) was given functions which guarantee the supremacy of APCM and UAC. Secondly, the company has always shown willingness to compromise on issues that do not really disturb the balance of power among the partners. Thirdly, the company has built up tremendous good-will among decision-makers at all levels in the country. The net effect of all this and the efficient management of the factory is the company's increasing success profit-wise.[12] The company has now been authorised to start two new cement projects in Nigeria. When these are completed, the company will control three of the seven cement factories in Nigeria, and will account for well over half the total production of cement.

Section III

This section discusses the role of multinational corporations in the development of African societies within the framework of two questions posed for this conference:

a. Do provision of capital and the transfer of technology reduce the dependence of the underdeveloped countries upon the developed ones, or do they intensify such a dependence and at the same time increasingly integrate the underdeveloped economies into the present, highly uneven world economic order?

b. What are the alternative strategies which African economies can adopt to confront multinational corporations?

The first question raises the issue of the economic independence of developing countries, the issue of national sovereignty and the overall objective of economic development. The case described above is hardly a sufficient basis for answering the question; certain points in this case study are nevertheless pertinent to understanding the process by which the MNCs adjust their positions to changing circumstances. First, it must be admitted that the primary objective of the cement company is to make a profit. In pursuit of this, it establishes a factory, based on modern technology, in an area that ensures its success. It exploits the eagerness of the state government to have a cement factory by securing favourable conditions which ensure success profit-wise and power-wise. Secondly, in spite of this initial advantages, the cement company—spearheaded by APCM and UAC—was not complacent about its position, but played politics at all levels to maintain its position. Thirdly, where conflict arose, the company has shown willingness to compromise. All these are indications that the multinational corporations change tactics and strategies as the situation demands.[13]

In this connexion, the issue of economic independence and national sovereignty of developing countries should also be viewed within a time-perspective and situationally. There are times when national sovereignty will be traded off —even if the myth of sovereignty is openly maintained—for pure economic development, as well as situations where national sovereignty takes precedence over economic development. It seems to me that the real problem of development is how to balance these objectives at *appropriate times.* The success of developing countries in this direction depends on a clear-cut socio-economic objective which recognizes the inevitability of international involvement in development and the need for investment diplomacy. It can be argued that the ease with which multinational corporations penetrate developing countries is due, *inter alia,* to lack of *specific* national (socio-economic) objectives. Multinational corporations therefore do not find it difficult to present their own objectives as invariably consonant with national objectives.

Strategies for confronting multinational corporations must therefore rest primarily on a clearly-defined and articulated set of objectives. Since developing countries are technologically and economically powerless and must take account of the existing international environment, the first option is confrontation on an "ideological" basis. By this is meant a clear-cut plan as to which direction the developing countries wish to move in. This will mean bargaining from a particular position. In the absence of such a clear-cut position and sense of direction, developing countries are likely to continue trying various measures which only make for hazardous participations in their economy. Such haphazard measures as indigenisation, capital participation, foreign exchange and profit-repatriation restrictions, and nationalistic company legislations can only be successful if they are set within a coherent national objective. Otherwise, some of these piecemeal measures will run counter to others. It is perhaps significant that the power of multinational corporations in Africa has not declined despite the various measures mentioned above.

Nevertheless, a coherent national objective as a means of confronting multinational corporations can only be effective if that objective does not include the belief that multinational corporations are indispensable means for economic development. The evidence so far points to such a belief. Official decision-makers tend to rely on multinational corporation; this position is understandable because, for a company, to be multinational is a sign of success, and it is safer to rely on companies with proven success than on others. This *belief* in the indispensability of multinational corporations must change if and only if it is desirable to curtail their powers. It has already been pointed out that the APCM/UAC-dominated cement company in Nigeria will soon start operating two other large projects. The question then becomes: is it more prudent economically for the government to allow the same company to start other cement factories and thereby strengthen that company (and MNCs) than to support another company for the new projects? This seems to me a choice between two evils, since the other company will inevitably be foreign. Successful confrontation is therefore possible only if decision-makers' belief about MNCs change.

If we accept the view that multinational corporations are part of the international business environment with which the developing countries must cope, a permanent strategy for coping with that environment is the development of native manpower sophisticated enough to cope with the intricacies of 20th century technology. In this connexion, there should be no consideration of either East or West (politically) but a vigorous exploitation of international resources in pursuit of this objective. In the final analysis, it is men and their ideas—not a sudden and unexpected wealth—that can sustain real socio-economic development.

Notes

[1] WNDC has been reorganized, and now bears the name "Industrial Investment and Credit Corporation" (IICC). In this paper, I shall use the old name WNDC.

[2] In conformity with a recent decree, the government shares increased to 40%, and that of UAC decreased to 9%.

[3] WNDC does not have a monopoly of industrial and agricultural projects. Private companies and individuals can set up their own projects. The Government can even invite firms (indigenous and foreign) to establish projects without consulting WNDC. It should be noted that the cement factory is just one of the *many* projects in which WNDC participates.

[4] It is still a subject of bitter public argument whether the jobs to which expatriates are recruited could not be filled by Nigerians. Some take the view that expatriates are recruited not because Nigerians with the appropriate skills cannot be found, but because the effective owners of industrial and business concerns in Nigeria are expatriate firms who are unwilling to surrender total control to Nigerians. Consider, for example, the following statement:

"The whole of the production function at Ewekoro is now in Nigerian hands, but the specialist engineering functions are in expatriate hands and the problem is this—how far can one put the maintenance and engineering of some £8,000,000 of plant at risk by too early Nigerianisation?"—From the speech of an APCM official at a seminar in London on "Nigeria Now", 9th April, 1970.

[5] From a *confidential* letter. The government's proposal to establish another factory stemmed from complaints by the public that the price of cement was too high and that WAPCC was charging high prices because it had no competitor; the cement factory was unable to meet the demand for cement, although it was in operation twenty-four hours a day. Another cement factory controlled by the same company (WAPCC) is to be built between 1975 and 1976 in the Western State. A third factory to be built by the same company was announced as this paper was being prepared.

[6] For a concise discussion of "Nigerianisation", see Taylor Cole: "Bureaucracy in Transition", in Tilman, R. O. and Cole, Taylor, *The Nigerian Political System* (Duke University Press, 1962). The Government's position on Nigerianisation of business activities is stated in Decree No. 4 (1972), Nigerian Enterprises Promotion Decree.

[7] There was nothing in the agreements signed by the partners about 'Nigerianisation'. It therefore became an issue that had to be negotiated not according to the *letter* of the agreements, but in the *spirit* of the agreeements.

[8] In the case that the *letter* or 'workings' of the Agreement were to be adhered to.

[9] The same company has, however, agreed to establish two other factories in Nigeria.

[10] An arrangement modifying the system is now well under way. This involves *inter alia* appointment of distributors and sub-distributors, the cement company now bearing transport costs. The proposed changes do not affect my argument.

[11] For a detailed description of the relationship between the MNCs and the national bourgeoisie, see Claes Brundenius: "The Anatomy of Imperialism: the case of the multinational mining corporations in Peru." *Journal of Peace Research,* pp. 189-207, No. 3, 1972.

[12] Since the company was formed just over a decade ago, the labour force, production, sales and profit have doubled. The company has previously declared a dividend of 50%.

[13] This has been referred to as controlling "*investment climate*", which consists of *economic, social, administrative and political climates.* See: Litvak, Isaiah A. and Maule, Christopher J., (eds.): *Foreign Investment: The Experience of Host Countries.* (Praeger Publishers, 1970), Chapter 12.

DIAGRAM 1. The relationship between the Government, WNDC and the Cement Company

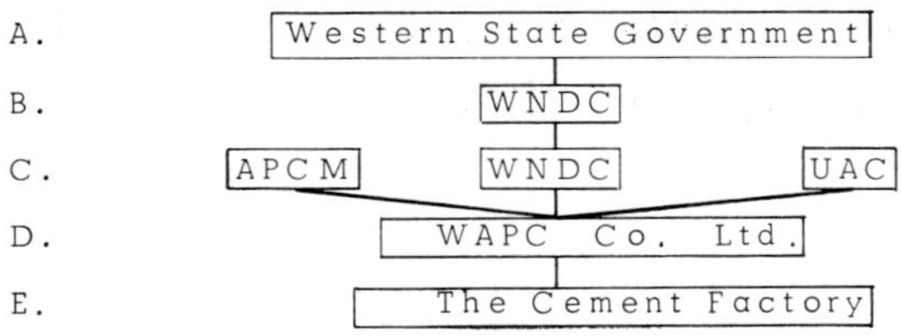

WNDC - Western Nigeria Development Corporation
APCM - Associated Portland Cement Manufacturers of Great Britain
UAC - United Africa Company
WAPC Co. Ltd. - West African Portland Cement Company Ltd.

DIAGRAM 2. Top management structure: WAPC Co. Ltd.

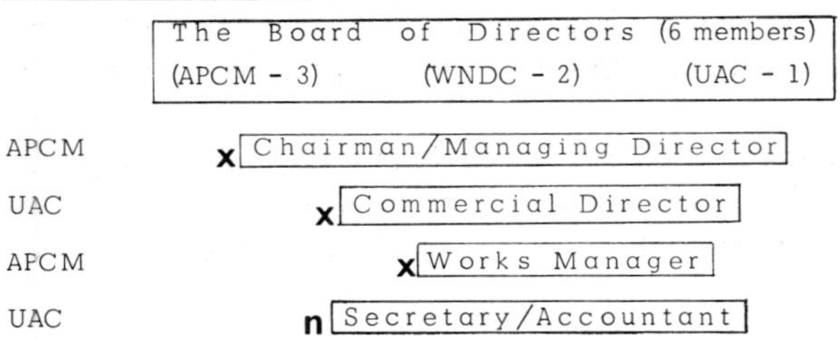

x - Expatriate
n - Nigerian

Ikenna Nzimiro

The Political and Social Implications of Multi-National Corporations in Nigeria*

Objective

The principal objective of this paper is to demonstrate the thesis that where foreign multinational corporations invade a country, and where this invasion is accepted by a ruling class that is predisposed to the capitalist ideology of the bourgeoisie who control these corporations, such a country faces political and economic insecurity. A corollary to this is the axiom that the national interest is subsumed under foreign interest. This axiom is played down by the liberal ideologists, who try to camouflage the interests of the defenders and beneficiaries of foreign investors (the multinational corporations) as those of the host country.

Such an attitude gains ground where the prevailing ruling class plays the compradoral role. Using their media of mass control, they consistently fool the masses into believing that what these leaders are doing is for the benefit of the "fatherland".

The approach

We shall examine the nature of MNC penetration in Nigeria and discuss two leading such institutions—the United African Company and the Shell BP Oil Company.

We shall show how in collaboration with the colonial regime, the UAC manipulated the working class, i.e., the Amalgamated Union of UAC African Workers Union, so as to perpetrate the exploitation of the working class in order to make huge profits through the expropriation of the labour power of its workers.

We shall further illustrate how other multinational corporations pierced through the Nigerian economic curtain and how this led to the development of a new social class that became an ally of these multinational corporations.

* This paper is derived from my book—*Classes and Class Struggles in Nigeria*—now with the Monthly Review Press for consideration.

We shall also discuss, in summary form, the type of social classes that emerged within the decades during which these companies penetrated into Nigeria, so as to identify that very class which is being used by these monopoly octopuses to distort the investment patterns of our economy, leading to the creation of economic inequality in the Nigerian society, and eventually to class contradictions that create instability in the economic and political structures of Nigeria.

Lastly, we shall show the dangers of the multinational corporations in Nigeria—nay, in Africa as a whole.

Introduction

Nigeria today occupies an important position in the continent of Africa. Its human and natural resources, sophisticated class structure and abundant population place it in a good geo-political status *vis-à-vis* the large nations.

It is made up of different ethnic nationalities which were brought together by the British under one colonial administrative political unit after decades of piecemeal conquests of the various areas now defined as the Nigerian geographical entity.

Beginning from the South, the British explorers, after the Landers and Mungo Park had discovered the mouth of the Riber Niger, began the invasion of that part of Africa by the Chartered Trading Companies who, by the middle of the last century, had grown fat from the slave trade that depopulated many parts of Africa. The profits of this trade provided the capital formation which enabled the merchants later to invest in the so-called legitimate trade, to draw raw materials from the African continent and to feed the industrial machines of England and North America.

We all know the great profits of the famous triangular trade, ably spelt out by Eric Williams in his work *Capitalism and Slavery* (London, 1947). We all know that this profit stimulated the industrial development of Europe and the Americas. The trade itself set in motion what Keynes styled 'the multiplier effect' in the whole industrial revolution of England. Nigeria was created as one of the consequences of the affluence enjoyed by the British Companies that took part in this trade.

Evidence about the role the Royal Niger Company played in the trade is not lacking (Williams 1967, p. 9), and from that time until 1900, this company dominated the entire economy of Nigeria. As it grew in the metropolis, it became part of the giant octopus we shall now examine. Nigeria became one large vineyard for the Uniliver Concern. Let us examine its development and involvement in Africa.

Uniliver as an Octopus*

In 1885, William H. Lever, on the Merseyside (near Liverpool), established a soap-manufacturing industry. The need for soap in order to attack industrial dirt was vital and the discovery by the French scientist Chevreu that palm oil was a vital help for the manufacture of soap transformed the entire trade, commerce and industry. The manufacture of soap by Lever was thus a very vital industrial beginning which was to grow into a large concern. The soap he made had the brand name Sunlight; African Red Family ably described the growth of this company into a monopoly in these words:

> On the Merseyside, near Liverpool, England, a certain William H. Lever began to make soap in 1885. He branded his soap "Sunlight" and the little township came to be known as Port Sunlight. Within ten years, the firm was selling 40,000 tons of soap in England alone, and was building up an export business as well as factories in other parts of Europe, America and British Colonies. After Sunlight, came Lux, Lifebuoy, Vim. By 1905 they were selling 60,000 tons in Britain and had factories in Canada, USA, South Africa, Switzerland, Germany and Belgium. For raw materials they required palm oil, palm kernel oil, ground nut oil and copra. So in 1902 Lever sent out explorers to Africa to investigate raw material resources. They reported suitability in the Congo and Lever got the necessary concessions from the Belgian Government.
>
> To extend its control of raw materials, in 1910 Lever bought W. B. Maclear in Nigeria and two small companies in Sierra Leone and Liberia which dealt in palm products. In 1920 they bought the Niger Company and in 1929, the African and Eastern and formed the United Africa Company, UAC. During the 1st War, Lever, using the same raw materials as soap began to make margarine. Meanwhile, Lever had been eliminating competitor after competitor by buying them off, in, as it were, preparation for the grand merger in 1929 between the Dutch firms and Lever, creating Unilever Ltd. (registered in Britain) and Unilever N.V. (registered in Holland), with the same board of directors.
>
> The United Africa Company is Unilever's supplier of raw materials. On its side it also keeps growing. In 1933 UAC bought G. B. Ollivant, and in 1936, it bought the Swiss Trading Company on the Gold Coast. By this time it had organised plantations for growing palms. Factories in USA drew their raw materials from the Congo. Today, UAC is the world's largest International trading company and now concentrates on development in cars, engineering, and pharmaceuticals, while Unilever is a world wide force, making detergents, margarine, lard, ghee, cooking oils, canned foods, candles, glycerine, oil cake, toilet preparations, toothpaste, etc.
>
> As soap making required large quantities of caustic soda, in 1911, Lever bought land in Cheshire for manufacturing the alkali. When they needed abrasives, they bought a lime stone mine in Bohemia, when they needed

* The following three sections are drawn from Chapters 3 & 4 of my book: *Classes and Class Struggles in Nigeria: 1900-1966.*

Table 1. *Industrial investments of the UAC*

Company	Product	Year of start
African Timber & Plywood	Timber & Plywood	1948
Nigerian Breweries	Beer and minerals	1948
Taylor Woodrow	Building contractors	1953
Nigerian Joinery	Woodwork and Furniture	1953
Prestress	Prestressed concrete	1954
Nipol	Plastic products	1957
Vehicle Assembly Plant	Bedford lorries	1958
Raleigh Industries	Cycle assembly	1958
Mina Farm	Pigs	1959
Northern Construction Company	Building contracts	1960
West African Trade	Sewing thread	1961
West African Portland Cement	Cement	1961
West African Cold Storage	Meat products	1961
Walls	Ice cream	1961
Vono Products	Bed mattresses	1961
Cement Paints	Cement paint	1962
Guiness	Stout	1962
Fan Milk	Reconstituted milk	1963
The Nigerian Sugar Company	Sugar and by-products	1963
Narspin	Cotton yarns	1963
Pye	Radio assembly	1963
Vitaform	Foam rubber products	1963
A. J. Seward	Perfumery and cosmetics	1964
Bordpak	Fibre board cartons	1964
Kwara Tobacco Company	Cigarettes	1964
Associated Battery Manufacturers	Vehicle batteries	1965
Crocodile Machetes	Machetes	1965
Textile Printers	Printed textiles	1965

Source: *Industrialisation in an Open Economy,* Kilby, p. 69.

wrapping paper, they bought a paper mill. For transport, they launched ocean-going vessels including bulk-carriers of palm oil, for distribution they own chains of grocery stores etc. Unilever is not only master in politics, the stock exchange and in the tropical plantations. It is also master in the kitchen and toilet and a close acquaintance of the housewife.[1]

United Africa Company

Let us examine the degree of control of property that the UAC exercises ten years after Nigerian Independence. In a recent publication, Peter Kilby documents the following industrial and commercial institutions owned by the United Africa Company (see Table I).

In his work on the ethnographic study of the Naraguta ethnic group in the Jos plateau, Professor Diamond, analysing the colonial economic structure in which the Naraguta have become a part, examines in detail the patterns of UAC involvement in and control of the Nigerian economy. In the table reproduced on page 243, he showed that the UAC of Nigeria, the branch of the great gigantic octopus (Unilever) is split into three: (1) the Lever Brothers, Limited, (2) the Plantation Group, handling rubber, banana and oil palm plantations, and (3) the Van den Berghs and Jurgens Limited, handling margarine. The UAC industrial group is made up of nine major industrial groups handling various items of industrial products: merchandise, for the import and sale of all types of merchandise; produce, for the purchase of all types of produce, either as agents for the statutory marketing boards or as principals; petroleum products, as distributing agents for Mobil Oil Nigeria, Ltd.; hides and skins, for purchasing, processing and export; the citrus juice factory, for the extraction and export of orange juice; Lloyds Agency; the insurance agency, Northern Assurance Company, Ltd.; Niger Rivers Transport, part ownership of Burutu and river transport.

The Company has also the following eleven subsidiaries that constitute the UAC Group: Kingsway Stores Ltd., department store and supermarket; Kingsway Chemists, Ltd., wholesale pharmacy; African Timber and Plywood (Nigeria), Ltd, for production and export of logs, sawn timber, and plywood; UAC Technical, Ltd., for agricultural, earthmoving, and electrical equipment, and construction material; Anchor, Ltd. deals with shipping agents for Barber West Africa Line; West African Cold Storage, Ltd., handles refrigeration and cold storage, food-stuffs; Palm Line, Ltd., maintains an ocean fleet; G. B. Ollivant Ltd. (under separate management), import and sale of merchandise, purchase of produce either as principals or as agents of marketing boards; G. Gottschalck and West Africa, Ltd., same functions as G. B. Ollivant.

Besides these eleven other companies, UAC has part interest in seven other companies: Bulk Oil of Nigeria, Ltd., Nigerian Breweries, Ltd., Nigerian Plastics, Ltd., Nigerian Prestressed Concrete, Ltd., Taylor Woodrow (Nigeria), Ltd., and Nigelec, Ltd.[2]

Both Kilby and Diamond give the names of the products and the companies associated with them, and Kilby gives the dates that these companies were formed, while Diamond breaks them into their subcomponents, revealing the interlocking relationship that makes us dub the UAC a monopolistic combine.

If we examine the products that they manufacture, we find that the manufacturing companies under their control are the replicas of the companies that Unilever controls at the home industrial base. We know that some of these products manufactured in Nigeria are products for which Unilever subsidiaries have controlling interest at home. J. P. Coasts, the makers of thread in the United Kingdom, have a monopoly patent for the manufacture of thread, and this implies that they could also dominate the colonial market where they have exclusive interests.

The second point to observe is that most of the produce-buying companies have ceased to operate since the government controlled by the Nigerian bourgeoisie came into power and allowed only the indigenous middle men to be dealers in produce. The net effect was that the companies had to switch to import substitution industries and accept the pledge by the rulers of the First Republic that they would not tamper with these industries. By this promise, the then Federal government enacted the Pioneer Oil Industries Act (1952), which granted the foreign companies such inducements as enabled them to switch easily and to control the industrial sector, a fact which the military regime now views with some sense of moral indignation, as expressed by the passing of the Indigenization decree.

As it became increasingly clear to the company that it was facing competition from the local indigenous entrepreneurs who were now being patronized by the political class, the switch became inevitable and the dates given by Kilby show that while only two industries were established in 1948 and seven in the 1950s, the other nineteen industries were established between 1960 and 1965. Thus, between 1956 and 1964, UAC diversified its industrial plans in four major sectors—distribution, industry, transportation and agriculture.

While investments in the distribution and industrial sectors increased, those in transportation and plantations decreased, making the switch to the market-oriented industries quicker, as the following table indicates:

Year ending Sept. 30	Distribution	Industry	Transportation	Plantations
1956	1,186	519	296	100
1957	1,624	552	209	172
1958	953	563	263	334
1959	955	563	263	334
1960	1,074	1,224	40	479
1961	1,403	736	82	124
1962	1,386	1,267	48	2
1963	1,293	3,018	37	51
1964	742	1,558	303	74

Source: Kilby, p. 68.

The analysis based on the figures quoted above indicates that the United Africa Company has not by any means relinquished the control of the economy which its earlier parent companies obtained as far back as the latter part of the 19th century. National independence has indeed been a benefit to the Company and even though the gates of Nigeria have been opened to other foreign companies from Europe, America and Asia, the United Africa Company has entrenched its roots so deeply into our economy that

> the governments of the First Republic believed that such deep roots into our economy was the normal role that private enterprise should play in the so-called economic development of the country. More sorrowful is the fact that the products that are manufactured are mere consuming products and are not industries that can generate greater productive factors in the economy. They are deflationary consumer goods and the company gains by manufacturing locally the products that were formerly imported because local production would be profitable in terms of the use of existing cheap labour which the companies exploit. Moreover, the fact that the company was dealing with a bourgeois class interested in sharing the market with the company but willing, in this process, to play the subordinate role of compradorship was another advantage, for the bourgeoisie used such a role as a means of strengthening their economic position. With time, they could eventually oust the company in certain areas by legislation and thereby reserve for themselves, in the name of the national interest, those industries which they feel competent to run, thereby sharing the market with the company.[3]

John Holts

John Holts became a subsidiary of the United Africa Company, but it maintained its administrative independence and therefore continued to function with interests in the following manufacturing companies.

Industries owned by John Holts and Co. Ltd.:

Company	Description	Year founded
Coastains	Construction	1948
Holts Tanneries	Construction	1949
P. S. Mandaides	Gin crushing	1960
Holts Rubber Company	Rubber creping	1962
Thomas Wyatt	Stationary	1948
Nigeria Breweries		1949
Nigerian Canning Company	Corned Beef	1956
Crital Hope	Metal doors, etc.	1956
Asbestos Cement Products		1960
Nigerian Enamelware Co.		1961
Hoco	Perfumery & plastics	1963

Source: Peter Kilby, p. 71.

Other formerly commercially-oriented companies joined in this venture and began to modify their trading policies by switching into industrial manufacture.[4]

The social implications of this exploitation

The century of exploitation of the Nigerian economy by the United African Company brought untold sufferings to the workers under its employment.

UAC was Nigeria and Nigeria was UAC. The country continued to pay the Royal Niger Company, the big brother of the association, a certain annual royalty for handing over the territory to the British Crown in 1898. The Company drew so large an amount that in 1948 the Nationalist Parties were compelled to protest against such continued payment. What acually saved the country from being totally purchased was mere the (accidental) foresight of the ruling British officials, who prohibited an effort made by Unilever to purchase all of Northern Nigeria as a plantation vineyard. In fact, this deal could have been settled, because it coincided with the plan that led to the wholesale purchase of the Congo from King Leopold.

Plantations established in the South led to the creation of a rural proletariat. Huge plantations were set up at Ikot Mbo, Ajegbodudu, Sapoba; many of them enclosed the richest palm, cocoa and rubber plantations; and the peasants were invariably dispossessed of their land. Huge chunks of land were converted, not for food production, but for the production of raw materials worked by the cheap labour of the peasants.

When it was involved in the produce trade, the Company created chains of middlemen and their subagents, who purchased the peasant palm oil and kernel at prices that the Company fixed. The Company removed these products to England and the Netherlands, and turned them into manufactured products, which were again sent back and sold to the consumers at prices determined by the Company. Hence the Company dealt with all types of economic activities (as enumerated), with the result that it had its hand in the Nigerian economy to a point where it became, at one stage, the largest employer of labour in the private sector.

Labour unionism

Trade union organization did not come to the giant establishment for many years. It was only in 1948 that a serious effort was made: Mr. Nduka Eze took over the Union organized by a right-wing liberal unionist, Adio Moses. Nduka Eze gave this union an organizational strength which threatened the Octopus and shook it severely. Before that, the UAC had dominated the policy of the colonial government, which was the protecting arm of the Company.

Burutu shooting—1945

Before the formation of the Union, the Company workers at the Port town of Burutu had agitated against the abominable slave labour that was their lot for many years. They lacked an organized body, a front and leadership, but sporadically, as their woes reached the breaking point, they went on strike and were met with such brutality that it echoed throughout the country. They were fired upon by the colonial police and several were seriously wounded and many died.

The matter was raised in Parliament, and after 'satisfactory explanation' by the Colonial Secretary, an explanation supplied by the Colonial Government through the Colonial Office in London, a Commission was set up as a palliative and there the matter died. Many of the workers lost their jobs and forfeited whatever rights had accrued to them. Since few rights did accrue, what the workers demanded was nothing but the right to return to their jobs-which they never obtained, and which the Colonial Government was adamantly against. The blood of the Burutu workers was wasted so that UAC might continue to reap the huge profit accruing from that port.

Apapa Soap Company strike—1947

In 1947, the workers of the Apapa Soap Company, an ancilliary of the UAC, went on strike, demanding better service conditions. As usual, these workers were sacked *en masse* by the Company. The colonial regime first assisted the Company by sending its Fascist-trained police to batter down the striking workers and break up their resistance. The dismissal of these workers drew considerable comment in the nationalist press; imperialism, however, does not understand the language of peace, merely that of violence being met with violence. Since the workers were overpowered by the colonial police, they lost their jobs and all benefits from the services they gave to the Company for several years.

The UNAMAG class struggle—1950

The greatest historic struggle of the workers employed by this Octopus was waged after years of consistent organization. As pointed out above, Mr. Nduka Eze, in taking over the Union, brought in all the sections of the gigantic Octopus into one fold. The Amalgamated Union of UAC African Workers Union (UNAMAG) embraced all Clerical, Technical, Agricultural, General, and all sorts of workers employed in those establishments under the Company.

This sort of organization gave the Union strength, for the workers in the technical wing had special skills and thus protected the weak clerical and general labour side. The agricultural workers in the plantations derived their strength from their brother workers in the cities. So, for the first time, this Octopus that commanded the economy of Nigeria faced one of the best-organized trade uions in the country. For Eze, organization was the only answer to the problem of working-class unity. But it was more than that. It was organization based on a defined ideology, and that was nothing but Marxism. It was this Union that gave the Nigerian working class the ideological influence that still persists among the left-wing trade unions, particularly the Nigerian Trade Union Congress.

All paid secretaries were recruited for the entire plantation, and the union organized around the bureaucratic structure of the Company, so that regional, sub-regional, and city secretaries were recruited. Within each establishment were also shop stewards, a sure guarantee that the socialist doctrine was consistently spread.

After years of organization the Union presented a comprehensive memorandum presenting the case of the workers and demanding:

(i) minimum wages for all the workers in the company;

(ii) leave with pay, which had never existed for thousands of the workers;

(iii) adequate housing schemes for the plantation workers and those in Burutu and other areas where housing was very difficult to obtain;

(iv) medical facilities for the workers;

(v) accident compensation while at work;

(vi) payment for sick-leave for thousands of the workers that never had such social benefits;

(vii) pension and retirement gratuity for the workers.

It submitted the case of the pitiable conditions of many workers who had served the Company for fifteen to twenty years or more, and yet were on daily paid wages of not more than two shillings per day, and who never had increments for more than ten to fifteen years of their labour for the Company. The memorandum presented the case of all workers in the entire UAC establishment.

The Union gave the Company notice of "Trade Dispute" as specified by the Colonial Labour Code, which actively protected the Company against sudden attack by the workers. The Company was adamant, and the Union called the entire working force out on strike on August 15, 1950. It was an historic struggle and workers mounted picket lines all over the establishment. This response was a triumph of leadership, organization and ideological education.

The colonial sabotage—political implications

The strike was called off in the usual way after the Labour Department intervened and the Union agreed to an Arbitration Tribunal.

The Colonial Government appointed one Justice Berman, himself British, and it was revealed that his relatives had shares in the Unilever. He was assisted by a lawyer, a Nigerian one for that matter, who also was the UAC Attorney. In other words, those that were appointed to settle the dispute were themselves declared friends and associates of the Company, showing the interrelationship and the economic tentacles the Company had in society. The Union nominated two representatives but these could not influence the outcome.

The Tribunal was a colonial one, and its justice was nothing short of Colonial Justice, framed to serve the interest of the large corporations that dominate the English Parliament, the Civil Service, and all facets of British life and institutions known as the Establishment.

The tribunal sat. The workers presented their case and since they could not afford to hire attorneys to present their case, a situation which was odd indeed, for wage claims were determined as if crimes had been committed against the Company.

The Awards came. They did not favour the workers at all, for only 4 of the 11 points were awarded enough to palliate certain sections and to appease them, while giving the Company leeway to reorganize its strategy to check the rising tide of the working class—socialist cries that echoed throughout the class struggle.[5]

Management tactics

In order to immobilize the Union and destroy its leadership, one thing that the Management of the Company (through its Chief Officer, one Mr. H. Porter) did was to refuse to recognize the General Secretary of the Union, Mr. Nduka Eze, as the representative of the Union in matters concerning negotiations between the Union and the Management of the Company.

Mr. Porter argued that Mr. Eze was a Communist and that the Company would not tolerate him any longer. The Company aim was to make the workers wonder whether they could not have previously achieved a lot if a "Communist" had not been the head of their organization. But Eze was too entrenched in the Union to be "snuffed off" by Mr. Porter.

The second tactic was to split the Company establishments into different units, thereby creating quasi-independent structures, each being registered separately as a separate Company. While this was done to evade a future government probe into the Octopus activities and to conceal the ramifications of the Company in the economy of the country, thereby diverting the attention of the new government that was being groomed for a handover in 1952, yet the aim was also to check such a strong and powerful, organized union in the establishment. By so doing, the Company was able to split the units that made up the Union and to safeguard itself from undue attention by a rising bourgeois government which afterwards became friendly to foreign entrepreneurs and threw wide the gates of Nigeria to other companies from other countries.

Adventurism and Mercantile Union—December 1950 strike

But what immobilized the Union to greater extent was the lack of tactics on the part of the leadership, which goaded the workers, in conjunction with other Mercantile Unions that were not well organized, lacked discipline, an ideological base, and leadership, into a strike. In many cases these small mercantile bodies were bought up by the UAC as it sought for take-over bids of those companies that it out-competed in the market, doing so to face the coming competition of other firms coming from Europe and America.

This ill-planned, ill-timed adventuristic December Strike of the Mercantile Workers Union, comprising the Unions in other establishments, weakened the Union. The colonial police came out in its most brutal and Fascist manner to break the strike. Many workers' heads were broken and in Lagos the picket line was smashed as the police escorted workers into the offices, while insidious telegrams were dispatched by the right-wing saboteurs, who told the provincial workers not to strike.

The Colonial regime and the Company triumphed and since 1959, the United Africa Company and its ancilliary bodies as enumerated have enjoyed industrial peace and huge profits. They were all the more helped by the policies of the bourgeois government of the First Republic, which were a carry-over of some of the sins perpetrated during the Colonial regime. As these continued, the Company was able to gain support among the ruling class during this period.

A recent conflict—Federal Government v. bottling companies

In 1972, the Military Government had to face open confrontation with the Brewery over the issue of bottles. The matter reached its zenith when the Company, one of the UAC offshoots, did not want to obey the regulation which affected the control that the Government desired to have over certain products involving beer brewing. A university don, Mr. Ola Oni, sued the Bottle Companies for flouting the law decreed by the Government, but his suit was thrown out on legal grounds.

The deductions we may draw from these brief examples are two:

First, that in a neo-colonial economy where the principle of self-reliance is considered a "Communist principle", the economy is subjugated to consistent looting by foreign companies.

Second, that such a situation weakens the political position of any government; since it depends on the control the foreigners have on the economy, the political base of such a government is therefore shaky. Such a government is prone to numerous pressures, to the extent that its legal process can be perverted even by those to whom the state has entrusted the right of defending her political sovereignty.

Shell BP Company[6]

Let us turn to oil: the Shell BP of Nigeria. The marketing of petroleum products in Nigeria started in 1927. Four of the world octopus companies—Shell, Mobil, Texaco and British Petroleum—were established during this period and were in charge of marketing. When oil was discovered in commercial quantity by Shell BP, the other old-world oil companies joined in the exploration and exploitation of oil resources in the country. Total joined in 1957, Esso in 1958 and Agip in 1963. They are the subsidiaries of the international oil consortium.

The Nigerian golden age of oil was then marked by the influx of these oil companies in the task of prospecting, producing, marketing and processing. By the end of the decade eight oil companies had become established—Shell BP, Nigeria Gulf, Nigerian Agip, American Overseas, Tennessee Nigeria, Mobile Exploration Nigeria, Safrap Nigeria and Philips Nigeria. The presence of these major oil companies created numerous dimensions too difficult for a regime that is not sophisticated in the economic intricacies of oil production, marketing and management to unravel.

The oil companies are attached to ancilliary industrial concerns that handle contracts, supplies and technical jobs. Most of these deal with certain activities connected with those companies, activities that the indigenous companies are incapable of handling, with the result that investment in oil has also brought about the investment in those service industries for which the oil companies have financial interests. For example, payments made by the oil companies in Nigeria in 1966 amounted to 62.2 million Nigerian pounds, including the direct payment to the government of 18.18 million in the form of rent, royalty, premium and profit. Of the 62.2 million, 26.098 went to contractors. These are the subsidiary companies that have been referred to above, the bulk of which are owned by foreign companies. The control of oil by these foreign companies deserves serious attention by well-meaning Nigerian patriots.

International implications of oil

Twentieth-century capitalism is dependent on oil for its mainstay in this age of atom and nuclear know-how. This age is characterized by the global control of the important mineral on which the wheels of modern scientific technology depend. That mineral is oil. Oil is the grease of modern industry. It is the hub of all that support the sources of power necessary to generate all modern industries. Jets depend on it. Atomic reactors and industries developing instruments of human destruction need oil to grease their wheels. Modern communications and all forms of technological innovations rest on its use. A country that possesses oil is on the international map and in the whirlpool of international power politics.

In the capitalist world there are over 100 major operating companies, all of which are controlled by the seven oil octopus-combines: (1) Standard Oil of New Jersey, (2) Royal Dutch/Shell, (3) Texaco, (4) Gulf, (5) Mobil, (6) Standard California, and (7) British Petroleum. The order in which they are written is the order of their general control of the world oil industry. Of these seven world oil octopuses, five are United States controlled. All these have their branches scattered all over the capitalist world and in the countries of Asia, Latin America and Africa. These seven gigantic industrial combines command a greater share of world industrial finance. According to the *Royal Dutch/Shell Information Handbook for 1966/67,* "Over 500,000 million is the estimated cost of the property, plant and equipment used in the oil industry today (leaving aside the communist countries) to meet the demand of 3,000 million tons of oil". "This property", the *Handbook* continues, "plant, and equipment, of which over half is in the United States, comprises oilfields, refineries, pipelines and marketing facilities. Between them, they man over a third of the industry, property, plant and equipment and meet more than half the demand for oil products. Capital expenditure (investments and assets) by these seven majors in 1965 amounted to 1,873 million. Dividends distributed to ordinary shareholders [note: the institutional shareholders invest more and get more dividends] amount to 185 million, representing 52.2 percent income."

The *Handbook* further indicates that the "oil industry's total annual capital requirements are about equivalent to the new capital raised annually by all business in the money markets of North America and Europe".

Nothing is so staggering as this information. The seven oil octopuses, with widespread tentacles in the various gigantic world enterprises,—banks, other minerals, other companies, insurance, iron and steel industries, huge distribution companies, transport—air, land and sea, chemical industries, war industries, etc., have settled in Nigeria, entrenching themselves firmly there, and using their influence to manipulate men and create events favourable to their existence, but unfavourable to our existence. The last civil war in Nigeria was a case in point.

Of these companies, Shell BP has the dominant control of the Nigeria oil—about 85 percent and it is this Octopus that has reluctantly, after great pressure, allowed the Federal Military Government an only 35 percent share in the industry.

The one we (Nigerians) deal with

As stated, the Royal Dutch/Shell group of companies is the second largest oil consortium in the world. It is this octopus which operates in Nigeria.

The Royal Dutch/Shell group of companies is made up of two principal companies: (1) The Royal Dutch Petroleum Company Netherland, (2) The Shell Transport and Trading Company, Ltd. (English-controlled), both of which own the investments and assets of a large number of companies known as the Royal Dutch/Shell group of companies.

The Royal Dutch, a Netherlands company, has 60 percent interest in the group, and Shell Transport, an English company, has a 40 percent interest. They are known as the largest companies and do not themselves form part of the group.

Royal Dutch and Shell Transport do not themselves take part in the oil or chemical business. They own the shares in the two principal group holding companies—Bataafse Petroleum Maat Schappy NV. (BPM), a Netherlands company, and the Shell Petroleum Company, Ltd., an English company. The two group holding companies in their turn hold shares directly or indirectly in over 500 companies engaged in the various branches of the oil and chemical industries in more than 100 countries.[7]

Other multinational corporations

We have discussed the interlocking nature of the multinational corporations found in the Unilever arm, the United Africa Company, as well as briefly discussing Shell. We have singled out these two companies because of their dominance in the Nigerian economy and their precedent over other multinational corporations. The Unilever, we must realize, is one of the largest British firms with a world-wide turnover of 2,500 million pounds sterling annually and is deeply intertwined with the history of Nigeria. Its main subsidiary, UAC, is the descendant of the Royal Niger Company which with the assistance of Sir George Taubman Goldie and Lord Lugard, laid the foundation for what later became Nigeria.

Shell BP was the first to win an oil exploration concession in the country, and being the largest British company, the fourth largest in the world, the impact of these two national corporations in the history of Nigeria is therefore staggering.

But these were not the only ones. Others came into the scene—America, the Netherlands, West Germany, France and to some extent the Lebanese were also there, as the table below shows, although the British interest continued to dominate. This is understandable, for no ex-colonial power has handed over power to a predetermined elite in order to lose its grip on the former colonial economy which it organized around its own industrial production and distribution:

Country	1962	1963	1964	1965	Percentage
United Kingdom	136.6	184.1	181.4	202.9	53.8
USA	19.4	24.0	39.0	57.7	15.3
Netherlands	23.4	26.5	37.9	39.3	10.4
France	3.8	14.5	9.5	13.1	4.5
Germany	1.4	1.9	2.2	2.7	0.7
Lebanon	—	—	2.6	—	—[8]

Source: *Other Side of the Nigerian Civil War*, p. 10

Distorting investment

One way the multinational corporations distort investment patterns of a neo-dependent economy is the shift from the basic industrial foundation of the country under exploitation to what benefits the corporations themselves. This may be observed in a drastic shift in the investment patterns of these companies to areas that would be more rewarding to them and not what would benefit the country itself.

With the oil boom and the use of oil in these countries, the shift to mineral exploitation became the dominant policy of these companies, as the figures below also illustrate:

Industries	1950-51 1954-55	Per-centage	1961-66	Per-centage
Mining	13.8	34.7	13.5	53.2
Manufacturing and processing	3.4	8.5	63.0	24.0
Transport and communication	4.7	11.0	2.7	1.0
Trading and services	12.2	30.36	21.6	8.2
Building and construction	2.2	5.6	12.2	4.7
Agriculture, forestry and fishing	3.5	8.8	0.5	0.2
	39.8	100.0	262.3	100.0[9]

Source: *Other Side of the Nigerian Civil War*, p. 10.

Agriculture became relegated to the background and manufacturing industries were not rated high on their priority list. These companies have one cardinal aim, i.e., to exploit any aspect of the economy that profits them most. Industrial investments were aimed at developing such industries as generated mass consumption and not really at making the economy of the neo-colonial society self-reliant.

The class structure

Every social system creates its defenders and apostates. The incursion of capitalist institutions into Nigeria transformed the country into one with a new social system which economic historians have styled the capitalist society. It is an economic and social system which emerges at an historical epoch in the development of human society. It is characterized principally by freedom of the market, free labour (i.e., indiduals who are legally free and economically compelled to sell their labour power on the market) and private means of production by industrial enterprises.

The incursion of the new economic institutions into Nigeria from the colonial to the post-colonial era set in motion a chain of concatinations of economic transformations that invariably created a variety of social stratification different from the sort that existed in the pre-colonial societies that contributed towards making up the present multinational entity known as Nigeria. Capitalist enterprises, commerce, industries, communications-roads, railways, ports, telegraphic forms of communication, all reacted to create urban communities which drew men away from their natural environment of life in the village, (which had placed them directly under natural labour activities) into new forms of economic activities in which men sold their labour power to eke out their existence.

The degree of this capitalist influence in the Nigerian economy was gradually intensified, due to the above-mentioned activities of certain capitalist combines like the UAC and their ancilliaries, the oil companies, and the other enterprises which developed in the post-colonial era, when the ruling class of the First Republic threw open the internal market to the external agents of the world multinational corporations. This they did by passing in 1952 the Aid to Pioneer Industries Ordinance, and the Income Tax (Amendment) Ordinance. In 1958 the Aid to Pioneer Industries Ordinance was superceded by the Industrial Development (Income Tax Relief) Ordinance. Efforts were made to intensify industrialization of the country; earlier, in 1956, the Government had issued a joint policy statement under the title 'Opportunities for Overseas Investment in the Federation of Nigeria'. In 1957, another inducement intended to stimulate industrial growth was introduced by the Industrial Development (Import Duties Relief) Ordinance. In 1959, the government set up the Investment Company of Nigeria Ltd. Okudare reveals that

> the company was formed by the Commonwealth Development Finance Company Limited on the invitation of the Federal Government, and in consultation with leading Nigerian and British business interests and it was to assist enterprises in Nigeria engaged in industrial production, commerce, agriculture and the exploitation of natural resources, by providing finances for their development, modernisation or expansion. In addition, the company was to attract supplimentary foreign investment capital to private enterprises; seek technical and managerial experts; attract indigenous investment; and actively encourage the growth of a local stocks and shares market.[10]

The infrastructure was being rapidly expanded to facilitate industrialization; this primarily meant the rapid attraction of foreign investors, activities that were rigorously pursued by the ruling class in the First Republic.

Certainly this created a defined class structure. Social classes emerged. According to Lenin,

> classes are large groups of people differing from each other by the place they occupy in the historically determined system of social production by their relation (in most cases fixed and formulated in law) to the means of production, by their role in the social organisation of labour, and, consequently by the dimensions of the share of social wealth of which they dispose and the mode of acquiring it. Classes are groups of people one of which can appropriate the labour of another owing to the different places they occupy in a definite system of social economy.[11]

Since the industrialization of the country became a purposeful activity of the ruling class, and since the indigenous entrepreneurs worked hand in glove with the political class that used their legal position to set up laws that stimulated the inflow of the companies owned by these multinational corporations, let us examine summarily the nature of the social classes that developed, so as to describe in detail (in another section) that class which actually participated in these legal laws and the attendant economic activities linked with these multinational corporations.

Briefly, the class structure in Nigeria may be described as follows:

The Bourgeoisie[12]

To what extent do we apply the term bourgeoisie in contemporary Nigeria? Which social class can we label the bourgeoisie in the context of our analysis?

The bourgeoisie should include all those in the following occupational ratings:

(a) Merchants: produce and merchandise, proprietors of trading companies, including the active partners and directors of such companies. Wholesale traders, manufacturers and financiers.

(b) Members of the salaried executives: managers, supervisors of large firms, technical staff employed in the banks: accountants, secretaries, controllers, all in the upper segment of the banking executives (including of course the managers). Those in the higher-salaried occupations of a wide group of institutions, including educational bodies.

(c) The main body of the civil servants and public corporation senior servants; those in the private establishments owned by foreign companies. Secretaries to governments or Judges of high courts.

(d) Members of the principal recognized professions, salaried or otherwise, such as lawyers, engineers, architects, chemists, lecturers and professors, the upper range or middle ranges of writers and journalists, museum staff and artists, religious preachers—(bishops, monsignors, archbishops).

(e) The upper and middle segment of the armed forces, officer corps and the police.

(f) Vice-Chancellors of Universities, senior members of the University administrations, principals of the colleges of technology, advanced Teachers Institutions, and their senior technical staff—accountants, engineers, bursars, controllers, registrars and their senior assistants.

(g) Owners of large shops and hotel keepers, including their most senior staff such as managers, accountants and other officers employed in the joint stock concerns found in such a business category.

(h) Large transport owners and proprietors, such as road haulage transport, urban bus company directors, and the large contractors associated with road buildings, housing construction and supply of materials of high quantity and turnover to state and private institutions.

(i) Urban landlords with a sizeable number of houses in high ratable property areas, such as Government Reservation Areas, formerly occupied by colonial officials, agricultural plantations owners of great acreage and yield, employing hundreds of labourers for large cocoa, ground nut or palm-produce farming undertaken for export.

(j) Upper range of secondary school teachers and officers of the local government holding—social and political workers.

The groups that come within the range of high income and enjoy special privileges that add to their income and emoluments; those groups that are specifically regarded as vital executives in the management of state and private institutions come within the category that we classify as the bourgeoisie.

The classification has its own internal gradations. There are the upper bourgeoise, then the middle bourgeoisie and the lower bourgeoisie, but all come within an annual income turnover of not less than four figures and running up to the income group that deal with very high annual turnover, such as industrialists, merchants, large urban land-lords, large contractors, large transport owners.

The upper segment consists of the groups named above, including major merchants, indigenous bankers, industrialists, urban land speculators, whose tactics have been discussed in chapters 4 & 5 of the author's work, *Class and Class Struggles in Nigeria, 1940-1966.* Most of the people in this category have turnovers ranging from £20,000 to a million. We have millionaires in Nigeria who conceal their money in Swiss banks for fear of revolution which might lead to the loss of their money.

Petty Bourgeoisie

The members of this class are those in the income group below those above. They are covered within varieties of occupations, as classified by the Ministry of Labour.

(a) Small industrialists. Most of these are employers of two to three persons and some are self-employed. Such craft industries proliferate in the urban centres in the country such as:

tailoring, carpentry, shoe-making, shoe-repair, motor repair, welding, battery-charging, blacksmithing, tinsmithing, printing, banking, radio repair, photography, cornmilling, goldsmithing, painters; These are petty-commodity producers.

(b) Traders include those with one-market stalls in the urban markets, or those that rent market stalls for the display of their wares; retailers, who deal with varieties of merchandise purchased from major merchant shops that handle wholesale; small importers of foreign goods, dealers in food products through long-distance trade or retailers of food products purchased from bulk or wholesale buyers. In short, the majority of the independent small entrepreneurs, aspiring to higher entrepreneur positions but limited due to the vagaries of the market, lack of capital, staff competition, and slow development of the economy, leading to low purchasing power of the consumers.

(c) Government and private junior white-collar workers with West African School Certificates or Professional qualifications not earned in institutions of higher learning, such as professions arising from the nature of the work as they affect posts peculiar to state or private institutions—such as teachers, nurses, tax officers, health inspectors, junior technical workers—that is, salaried workers, police officers.

(d) Students in the Universities, Technical Colleges and post-secondary Institutions.

Again, with such social classes, there is also a hierarchical gradation within the petty bourgeoisie class. Some have social aspirations of elbowing with the bourgeoisie.

The Proletariate—the working class

This is made up of the urban and rural working class. They are those who earn their livelihood by selling their labour power to the owners of the numerous industries controlled by the multinational corporations, various other indigenous privately-run establishments, and the state capitalist establishment. Their number and development have been treated in detail elsewhere.

In Nigeria there are now over two million such persons among the working class, as well as millions in the rural peasantry, whose labour power generates the production of commodities for sale to the State Marketing Boards or their Agents and who are not paid commensurate prices appropriate to their production. These are therefore pauperized by the fact that the prices they receive are not by any standards matched with the prices of the essential commodities they need for their daily existence. These are the poor peasants dependent on the vagaries of what happens in the international capitalist-dominated market.

The Lumpenproletariat

These include the army of the less or half employed and the underemployed people who vainly migrate from the rural to the urban societies in search of their daily means of livelihood. Some are driven by the hardship the urban societies caused by lack of available jobs, a lack caused by the distortion of the national economy by the multinational corporations that control the investment policies of Nigeria, thereby making it impossible for the government to manipulate the economy and gear it to a self-reliant structure which can help to restructure industrial development and direct the natural resources to the most productive use aimed at giving employment to the youths of the country.

These youths who leave the schools in large numbers and who can neither continue their education further, nor acquire the necessary skills to be of use to the community, fall prey to exploitation in the urban towns and they become the pedlers of drugs, organized into pickpocket groups engaged in stealing and all sorts of crimes. The girls become prostitutes and the youths perform all sorts of vices they are driven to by the loss of ethics formerly generated by the traditional societies.

The capitalist mode of production, as well, has its own ethical values. Since the individual acquisition of property takes prominence in this mode over the acquisition of property for the use of the millions, the propensity to commit crimes in order to own is more intense. Hence corruption becomes an ethical value of the capitalist system. The system hypocritically criticizes crimes against property only when they affect the property of the exploiting class. The mass of urban youths faced with the difficulties of life become compelled to commit crimes against the property of the exploiting and parasitic class. Lacking any clear purpose in life, lacking, as it were, a class consciousness of a sort, these *lumpenproletariat* have been used for various purposes by the bourgeoisie and their agents.

In Nigeria, this class supplied the thugs for the political rulers of the First Republic, for demonstration against any ethnic group selected by another for extermination, for burning cars of competing opponents in an election, for calling up prostitutes for the members of the bourgeoisie or those entering the port cities from abroad, for breaking the political opponents of the regime, that is, acting as spies to detect potential revolutionaries who are critical of the state and the exploitative tendencies of the ruling class.

The Peasantry

In a previous study,[13] the author has dealt with the structure of the rural societies; summarized, the situation is as follows:

The penetration of capitalism into the rural societies in Nigeria created social classes which can be summed up as follows.

First, the transformation of the traditional systems of land tenure was brought about by the demand for the production of export crops. This led to the rise of new capitalist landlords—the new farmers who had more land than the rest and who invested in the development of their farms for the purpose of selling cash crops to the agents of the metropolitan capitalists who organized, directed and inspired these new agricultural activities.

Second, a new rich class of money-lenders sprang up in many of these areas. These money-lenders used their new position to exploit the peasants, who had to pledge their farm products, and in many cases their land, for the payment of their debts—when these peasants could not redeem their property, they lost it to these money-lenders. Thus peasant indebtedness increased in the rural areas.

Third, among the peasants, the majority became pauperized, in that they could not cope with the growing difficulties arising from the monetized economy. Fluctuations in the price of their products and increases in the price of the goods that they bought made their position quite hopeless. The whole system of communal production and communal help cracked when confronted with the increasing development of individual means of production, as opposed to the old system of communal means of productions.

This break-up therefore increased the number of poor peasants, as could be seen from the example of Poly Hill on the Batagarwar of Katsina area and the situation which we find among many of the peasants in the rural societies throughout the country.[14]

Those who theorize that the peasants in Nigeria are not exploited, that they are self-sufficient in their standards of living—meaning that they can produce their own food, secure materials for building their houses and farm their land merely because there is an abundance of land—are living in an economic fool's paradise. Nigerian peasants are affected by the vagaries of the capitalist world market. The entire peasant economy is a dependent economy and the economic trauma of inflation has made such great inroads into these rural societies that the peasants are not able to grow enough food for their own existence.

Thus there is a consistent shrinking of area under cultivation and internal migrations from poor areas to areas of rich land, mostly due to increases in population, as well as land hunger.

These difficulties, tied to the fact that the cost of farming has become prohibitive, explain the rise of the money-lenders, the consistent efforts of the peasants to eke out their existence in the face of these overwhelming economic difficulties.

The remnant of the old society

In the formerly pre-capitalist states among the Fulani-Habe-Kanuri, Benin-Edo, Yoruba, some Igbo chiefdoms, Jekri and some Urhobo chiefdoms, Efik Society, Nupe, Igala and so forth, there are still remnants of the old society.

We still find these Emirs, Obas, Onogies and Obis Obongs dominating the lives of the rural societies. These feudal representatives of the traditional societies have been used (particularly in the North) for the continued domination of the peasant masses. Their domination is strengthened by the false religious consciousness built around the office of their kings and institutionalized in the rituals of the office, such as coronation rituals, regalia of office, festivals, emblems of office, mortuary rites and such legal and jurisdictional privileges as they enjoy.[15]

In the modern setting, these officials have not completely died out; the bourgeois allied with this class by creating the Houses of Chiefs and, in many cases, marrying into this class—many of their members rushed to their areas to take honorific titles from these kings, thus warranting most of the title holders to adorn their names with Chief (Dr. or Barrister) this or that person.

The formation of the political parties during the First Republic incorporated this 'feudal' ruling class into the system. The Action Group and the Northern Peoples Congress, both in the regions that were feudal-oriented and dominated for many centuries before the colonial conquest, depended on the members of this class for their existence. The Eastern Regional Government under the leadership of Dr. Nnamdi Azikiwe created a House of Chiefs in order to keep on an equal footing with the other regions, even though an anthropologist appointed by his government to advise on the viability of such an exercise advised that such a formation was not vital, since the type of feudal structures that prevail in the North and West are not very spread among people whose traditional political systems are essentially republican and democratic.

The ruling class and the multinational corporations[16]

Having now summarized the class formation in Nigeria, based on the reasons discussed above, let us then identify the class which is used by the multinational corporations for carrying out their tasks. That class we shall label the ruling class. Who, then, belong to the ruling class?

The ruling class are those who make decisions on how the economy should be run, how amenities should be shared, who should enjoy this or that privilege, which major government project should be set up and where, what sort of relationship should exist between the country and foreign governments, how the army should be structured, whether the working class, youths, peasants and women should be mobilized or not, or whether mobilization should start from the top or the bottom depending on how they regard the top and bottom politically and economically, what ideas should be sold to the masses or not.

In other words, the ruling class are those in the commanding heights of the state power.

The three vital groups within this class are the *politicians,* the *bureaucrats* and the *military.* The politicians used their legal and political positions for their own economic pursuits. They failed in the First Republic to mobilize the masses ideologically for the interest of the governing nations, for unity and economic prosperity for all; rather, they concerned themselves with building their own class interest. Because of this, the military ousted them. The bureaucrats and their allies, the military, subsequently together formed an oligarchy controlling the state power and preparing to hand over this power to the civilians again. In other words, the three contending interests are indeed the members of the ruling class but the capacity for any section to win the interest of the masses depends on the programme which they formulate for the country.

Who are those groups that make up this ruling class? They are the (i) representatives of international capital; (ii) leading members of the political parties in the First Republic; (iii) the bureaucratic bourgeoisie; (iv) the bourgeois entrepreneurs; (v) indigenous bureaucratic managers; (vi) lawyers of the upper stratum of the profession, including foreign legal practioners retained by the multinational corporations; (vii) some university dons being used by multinational corporation-funded research institutes and foundations. All these come within the group we have classified as the bourgeoisie.

Grades of the agencies of the multinational corporations

Here we shall break international capital into three agencies. First are those involved in purely economic activities—such as the banks, insurance, industries, mines, commerce and building and contracting, transport and so forth. They are the business group representing the interests of their multinational corporations operating in the country.

The second group are the agencies sponsored by the foreign governments whose capitalists have investments in the country; these agencies operate as economic advisers, sponsor research institutions, make surveys and studies for Federal and State Governments, and are supposed to serve the interests of the 'young' Nation. Such agencies are either international or government-sponsored. On the international plane, we find close to the Universities such agencies as the Ford Foundation, Rockefeller Foundation, Population Councils, UNICEF, USAID, and so forth, where the so-called 'experts', basing their activities on the bourgeois liberal philosophy, posit theories and programmes aimed at maintaining the capitalist social order, which is not different from the social order of the first group, the economic interest group.

Group three represents those international multinational organizations that had joint enterprises with the regional (now state) governments and act as economic agencies.

How the groups interact in the process of decision-making

Interaction with international capital

We have enumerated the seven groups that interact with one another in the course of carrying out their duties as men of power. Let us now examine how they interact within the framework of their organizations, where they make decisions that bind members of their groups either as representatives of their organizations or individually, and most important, as the powerful groups that determine the future of the lives of millions of Nigerians in the urban and rural areas.

Which group or groups interact with the agents of international capital?

The indigenous bourgeoisie

The indigenous bourgeoisie, though vying for the market with the foreign capitalists, do interact with their representatives, because the indigenous bourgeoisie are merely a comprador class and therefore depend on the assistance and services that they render to these foreign enterprises for their (indigenous) survivai.

Their power is limited (as was the case in India) by the fact that foreign capital dominates the major industries. This therefore makes the bourgeoisie subservient to these foreign octopuses, which command the finance capital, the technological instruments and the managerial expertise that they have developed for many countries.

The dependence of the indigenous bourgeoisie on foreign capital was maintained during the First Republic in many ways:

(a) Through being small honourary directors of foreign companies operating in Nigeria in order to make use of their position in politics to further the interests of the companies;

(b) Through patronage (loans, contracts, bank credits, etc.);

(c) Through partnership with foreign investors and using their positions in politics to secure contracts, etc., for such partnerships;

(d) Through becoming landlords to one or other of the many foreign firms flocking into the country;

(e) Through playing the role of business tycoons, contract men and contract brokers extracting ten percent to twenty percent from such brokerage services;

(f) Through becoming representatives, agents and sub-agents of foreign companies;

(g) Through dependencies on the expatriate banks for credit facilities (overdrafts, short terms credit, etc.).[17]

The dependence relationship of the indigenous bourgeois-entrepreneurs was in many cases not very smooth. The task of the leaders of the First Republic was to create a new and powerful capitalist class through the elimination of such obstacles as stood in their way to the attainment of their economic objectives, such as granting of licenses, award of contracts, available loans to them through government-controlled banks—ACB, National Bank, Agbomegbe Bank and the Development Corporations or Finance Institutions created to help the indigenous capitalists develop their enterprises and expand their base.

This did not go far, however, for the bourgeoisie of the First Republic created the incentives that brought these foreign capitalist investors. The Indigenization Decree has to some extent attempted to redress the wrong by granting to indigenous entrepreneurs the exlusive rights to control the industries specified in the Decree.

Nevertheless, the alliance between the indigenous capitalists and international capital cannot be severed without injury to the comprador class and what this class will continue to do is to see to what extent they can use their position, under pressure of the government (whether military or civilian), to control the economy as they begin to accumulate capital, to gain experience in management, and to obtain access to technological instruments of production. They cannot, however, attain a situation of pure independence, for they now own shares in the industries and enterprises of these foreign capitalists. The share of the indigenous entrepreneur in the market nevertheless remains quite low, and since capitalists have no home when it comes to making money, they will continue their alliance with international capital in order to build up their economic positions and to use these positions in many ways to control political power.

The indigenous lawyers

Another group that interacts with the agents of International Capital are the successful indigenous lawyers who act as legal advisers for and preservers of the economic interests of foreign capital. These lawyers, versed in the laws of the capitalist society derived from the legal rules of liberal bourgeois theories, are paid high fees to protect the property and the legal rights of these companies. They are compradors in the sense that they depend on their existence from the fees derived from these services.

State bureaucrats

The third group that interacts with the representatives of international capital are the officials whose duties imply that they deal with these owners or agents of international capital to ensure that the policies of the government are carried out.

These officials deal also with such international agencies as those listed in the second category, that is, international agencies which deal in the granting of loans to government institutions, providing expert advisers to the government, or agencies concerned with economic development in the field of agriculture, industry, development of infrastructure and so forth, as is mostly the case.

These interactions lead to joint agreements between the government and these foreign agencies, granting concessions to such bodies to establish industries or enterprises, as was the case indicated above, when the decision to grant various incentives for the establishment of Pioneer Industries was made by the rulers of the First Republic.

The role of the state bureaucratic bourgeoisie in these activities is very prominent; it was so during the First Republic and remains so under the Military Regime. These bureaucrats, seasoned in the methods of negotiation, and in most cases relying on 'expert advice' of even the foreign agents of these international corporations, often advise the policy-makers on the appropriate lines to take. These policy-makers might reject the advice, but the 'expert knowledge' of some of this bureaucratic bourgeoisie makes the politician or the army ruler helpless in the face of the 'overwhelming evidence', mostly couched in such a way as to indicate that the advice given is for the interest of the nation.

The entire exercise of drafting the legislations that created those facilities and incentives enshrined in the Pioneer Industry Acts and the numerous tax exemptions already noted could not have been done without the aid of these bureaucrats.

In an interview granted by Chief T. A. Odutola to an *Afriscope* reporter, Chief Odutola emphasized the intellectual ideological belief of the bureaucrats when he said that "The Permanent Secretary of the Federal Ministry of Economic Development and Reconstruction in his paper delivered at the 10th National Conference of the Nigerian Institute of Management showed most ably that long before now, as far back as the 16th century, most countries have through laws and regulations safeguarded the interests of their nationals". This statement was made by Chief Odutola to support the contention that the bureaucrats in the Federal Government clearly understood the ideology behind the Indigenization Decree.

This interaction and cooperation with the agencies of international capital or their governments was made common knowledge by the statement of Mr. A. A. Ayida who made this revelation in a statement made at the Conference on National Reconstruction and Development held at Ibadan on March 24-29, 1969:

> As a matter of historical interest, both the World Bank in Washington and the United States Agency For International Development through an appraisal mission led by the late Arnold Rivkin, were given the facilities and the confidential information which enabled them to finalize their assessment of the New National Plan before the data were made available to the public in Nigeria.

A critic of this Development Plan had this to say:

> Neither the planning process nor the resultant plan shows evidence of any serious attempt to make the economic targets and policies represent national goals in more than the vaguest sense. For all practical purposes, the federal plan was drawn up by a limited number of expatriate economists, working virtually in a vacuum so far as detailed direction of consultation with political leaders went, and with only peripheral advisory contact with Nigerian Civil Servants Planners. The social and political perferences of the plan, as was inevitable given this method of preparation, represent what the planners perferred or felt Nigerians ought to prefer, rather any expressed Nigerian preferences.

Angry as this author was, because his own idea of planning did not go through, both his statement and that of Mr. Ayida reveal the nature of the interaction which we are discussing in this section.

University dons

Another group that interacts with international agencies that control the money of the Foundations are the University dons, foreign and indigenous, who are committed to 'advancing scientific knowledge'. This sort of interaction leads to a subservient type of scientism, that is, the quest for 'scientific knowledge', while in fact these are the pipe-lines for maintaining the liberal bourgeois ideology and using this ideology to serve the interests of foregoing governments as well as supplying information to the indigenous bourgeoisie, whose class interests are served by such services.

Many projects designed by the Ford and Rockefeller Foundations, and some of these Foundation Research bodies, including such organizations in Britain as Nuffield, are designed with the purpose of 'fact finding' of data that might be used by the major corporations and secret intelligence of foreign governments concerned with subverting the country or keeping it within the ideological, economic and political orbit of the international capitalist domain as a neo-colonial country.

University scholars or intellectuals of the administration are often the representatives of the federal or state governments in such institutions or agencies and they serve the class interests of the founding fathers of such foreign agencies and institutions.

Indigenous Nigerian managers

The last of these groups serving the international corporations are the indigenous Nigerians who have been made managers in these foreign combines. These managers have been trained to run capitalist enterprises and to devote their loyalties to these organizations. Before these managers reach the managerial grade, they have been tutored and well screened to keep the official secrets, one of the attributes of modern bureaucracy, and they owe their position to their help in maximizing profits and in making sure that in the lower echelons of their enterprises the workers are well manipulated, so as not to upset the labour relations in the industries.[18]

Conclusion of our analysis

What are the overall political and social implications of these multinational organizations in our society?

Many books have been written about the dangers of multinational corporations and the dangers they pose to the continent of Africa and the Third World generally.

Most of these arguments can be summarized as follows:

First, that they create economic problems and disadvantages for the development of the African economy, because these foreign firms are subsidiaries or holdings of parent companies and corporations abroad, and as such, their basic interests cannot be readily identified with African development.

Secondly, that they have in Africa created a neo-colonial economy which for decades will remain a trading economy. By so doing many African countries have remained an export-oriented economy whose industrial units are vertically integrated with the parent industries in the metropoles, with no or very little integration with other industries or sectors of the neo-colony itself![19]

Third, that their existence makes it impossible to develop indigenous enterprises. By nature monopolistic, these multinational corporations swallow indigenous firms in the name of improving the efficiency in production. The Indigenization Decree is aimed at breaking part of this monopoly.

Fourth, that because of their advantageous position in the economy they are capable of pushing the relatively helpless governments of the African countries to grant them such concessions as lead to huge profits which are repatriated back to the metropolis. The government incentives (stated above) are embodied in five Acts—the Industrial Development (Income Tax Relief) Act, 1958; the Industrial Development (Import Duties Relief) Act, 1957; the Customs Duties (Dumped and Subsidized Goods) Act, 1958; the Customs (Drawback) Regulations, 1959, and the Income Tax (Amendment) Act, 1959.[20]

Fifth, that they can shift quickly to mining, when it becomes more prosperous and by so doing can regulate industries and agriculture, thus distorting the patterns of economic development of the given country. This we have already indicated.

Sixth, that having held the neo-colonial economy to ransom, having fooled the politicians and the bureaucratic bourgeoisie predisposed to the capitalist doctrines of the multinational corporations, they may raise the false alarm that investments can be damaged if the current government pursues a progressive policy of reexaming its industrial and agricultural potentialities and trying to limit the power of the multinational corporations by nationalization. This sort of "whitemail" is calculated to scare the progressive section of the masses into silence while the corporations continue to rape the economy to their own advantage. On this issue, the former Finance Minister in this fashion encouraged foreign investors. His main points were as follows: (1) Nigeria was short of technical and managerial skill and to embark on widespread nationalisation would lead us to import many expatriates with skill. The move would therefore be uneconomical; (2) the financial resources of Nigeria were inadequate for her industrialisation needs and the door must not be barred to foreign capital; (3) the country had created a climate favourable to private investment and we might as well exploit the situation; (4) the need of the country essentially is to maintain and improve economic growth and foreign investment was indispensable for this purpose; (5) to convert the existing private enterprises into state concerns would add nothing to the country's productive capacity.[21]

Seventh, that the multinational corporations help to create a parasitic class within the society, a class that is essentially committed to the doctrine of capitalism; through the several ways enumerated above, they can use these mean created according to their own image and likeness to ensure the preservation of the economic mainstay of the multinational corporations.

The case against the ruling class, as presented above, is a pointer to the dangers facing both Nigeria and Africa as a whole.

Eight, that the multinational corporations, by doing this, create a class that is corrupt, and by so doing, the multinational corporations export the sort of political corruption which we find in Britain, the United States and other capitalist countries. We have observed how the indigenous politicians were corrupted during the First Republic.

Ninth, that such a situation defames the democratic process.

An American writer has this to say about multinational corporations and American democracy:

> The giant organizations we now know do indeed invite the regimentation and suffocation of the individual spirit. Modern business civilisation, with its anarchy of irresposible giants and elevation of the small industrial political elite, shows little promise of maintaining an open society of free men. To allow such private power to rule in the name of individual liberty or national security is to thwart political democracy.

In the book, *Class and Class Struggle in Nigeria,* the present author has shown in Chapter 4 the case of Azikiwe and Awolowo and the investigations into their regimes, which reveal this sort of pattern.

Tenth, that multinational corporations, because they desire to maximize their profits, do everything in their power to give false information to any given government about their real economic activities—turnovers, profits and so on. They do this by taking into account that the countries concerned do not have the men trained in the most sophisticated manner and who might successfully probe the intricacies of the economic manoeuvres of these giant long-standing organizations. Chief Awolowo and Dr. Isong of the Central Bank had, in 1970, revealed the ways the oil companies tried to withhold facts from the Government.

Eleventh, that once the multinational corporations get a grip on the nationals of the country, they induce them through social interaction to legislate against trade unions, on the argument that their industrial productivity would decline and that this decline will harm the national economy, as if these metropolitan capitalists were indeed interested in the affairs of the host country. The non-vigilant neo-colonial mentality oriented leaders of the country concerned accept these silly argument, and then proscribe strikes and impose arbitration conditions which might not be in the best interests of the working class. By so doing, the regime that is swindled ideologically and politically becomes the beacon holding the torch for the foreign firms, while mowing down its own nationals in the false emotion of 'national interest'.

In fact, a neo-colonial economy is prone to induce false patriotism because the rulers, now capitalist in their thinking and action, and having been corrupted by these monstrous unethical foreign institutions, might mistake foreign interests for the interests of their own country. The Federal Military Government and its Labour Commissioner would be wise to review all Labour edicts in the spirit of the loftiest patriotism for their own country.

Twelfth, that once this sort of false patriotism holds the ruling class of a country, the multinational corporations can then manipulate the ruling class. They do this in many ways:

(a) by goading one ethnic nationality against the other. Note the internal, regional and ethnic conflicts in the First Republic;

(b) by inducing witchhunts against true patriots of the country, stigmatising them as Communists, so as to stop any agitation by the exploited masses. In 1953, Nnamdi Azikiwe's Eastern Government passed a law prohibiting "Communists" from teaching in secondary schools in the East;

(c) by making use of the university dons in the various disciplines (especially the social sciences) to spread false theories aimed at defending the capitalist system. Such false theories are labeled 'scientific', 'objective', 'detached' and 'empirical'. Any views to the contrary are regarded as 'polemical', 'ideological' and 'false methodology'. Some dons in the universities in Nigeria are gradually becoming agents of foreign international agencies linked with high espionage bodies, which may be unknown to these dons. We should be vigilant;

(d) they use other institutions through which they manipulate the indigenes such as the professional associations, news media, television, cultural attaches, and so forth to "sell" to the populace the idea that capitalism is good, and that capitalist democracy is synonymous with progress and civilization, while secretly they arm the political parties of the bourgeoisie with money and trained secret and espionage agencies, in order to clamp down on the progressive forces of those that create the wealth of the country—the working class and the peasantry. Such phenomena were not absent in the First Republic;

(e) even church groups are used to tie the souls of the people to foreign and outside religious bodies whose ties intertwine with capitalism. We all know the great wealth of the Papacy or that of the other denominations, a wealth which is staggering. These include industries creating world destructive arsenals, or birth control industries in which the Vatican has investment interests.

We could go on enumerating the dangers of multinational corporations in Africa, and especially Nigeria, without end. The way a country has felt them depends on the degree of involvement of these giant octopuses in the country.

We have demonstrated from facts and figures the impact of the two most ubiquitous corporations in Nigeria, UAC and Shell-BP.

The poverty of the Nigerian economy arose from the long-standing exploitation of the UAC. Its annual turnover is in the millions. In the colonial days, its budgets could swallow the entire budget of the colonial government.

Even now the turnover of its subsidiaries is heavy. Having split into components units, it has concealed some of its total profit turnover, since the government deals with the units and not the agglomerate. The same could be said of Shell-BP. No trade union authorities have been allowed to materialize in these oil corporations.

The conditions of service of its workers have never been satisfactory. Laws prohibiting strike or forced arbitration might be well and good if the country controls its own industries and if the wealth of the country is equitably shared, in keeping with the principles of social justice, but otherwise a government that treads on the rights of workers should realize that its action is only a perverse patriotism. As I have said, the Federal Military Government should re-examine its Labour edicts.

The Nigeria-Biafra war is a true proof of the way the multinational corporations can goad an innocent country into a blood-bath.[22]

This is not the place to go into these issues, but all the same, the multinational corporations, UAC and the Oil Companies definitely all had a hand in the internal broil that led to the war.

Notes

[1] *African Red Family,* Vol. 1, No. 3-4, London, 1973.

[2] Stanley Diamond, *The Naraguta.*

[3] Ikenna Nzimiro, *Classes and Class Struggle in Nigeria, 1900-1966,* Chapter 3.

[4] Peter Kilby, *Industrialization in an open Economy,* Cambridge University Press, 1968, p. 69.

[5] R. O. Okundere, *The Economic History of Nigeria,* 1973, p. 373. The author discusses the series of strikes that plagued the country from 1945 into the 1950s. He was a trade unionist at the time, and witnessed the events that occurred during that period.

[6] Nzimiro, Op. cit. For a fuller discussion of the Shell BP in Nigeria, see Chapter 3.

[7] Ibid.

[8] Boston Research Group, *Other Side of the Nigerian Civil War,* Boston, 1970, p. 10.

[9] Ibid.

[10] Okundere, op. cit.

[11] V. I. Lenin, *Selected Works,* Vol. 29, p. 421.

[12] Nzimiro, op. cit. This is a summary of a section of Chapter 10.

[13] Ibid, Chapter 2.

[14] Ibid.

[15] Ibid, Chapter 12.

[16] Ibid, Chapter 14. This is a summary of a subsection of Chapter 14.

[17] S. G. Ikoku, *Nigeria For The Nigerians,* Lagos, 1956, as quoted in Nzimiro, op. cit., Chapter 14.

[18] Nzimiro, op. cit., Chapter 14. This entire section is derived from that chapter.

[19] Shivji, *The Silent Class Struggle.* Note the case of UAC in Nigerian Agricultural Economy. See Samir Amin, *Neo-Colonialism in Africa,* Penguin, London, 1973.

[20] Okundere, op. cit., p. 297.

[21] Nzimiro, op. cit., Chapter 16, quoting Eme Awa, *Ideology and Nigerian Politics.*

[22] Nzimiro, *Class Contradiction in the Nigerian Civil War: A Case Study of Secessionist Biafra,* forthcoming. Here, the present author examines in detail the role of the social classes, particularly the bourgeoisie, in the war.

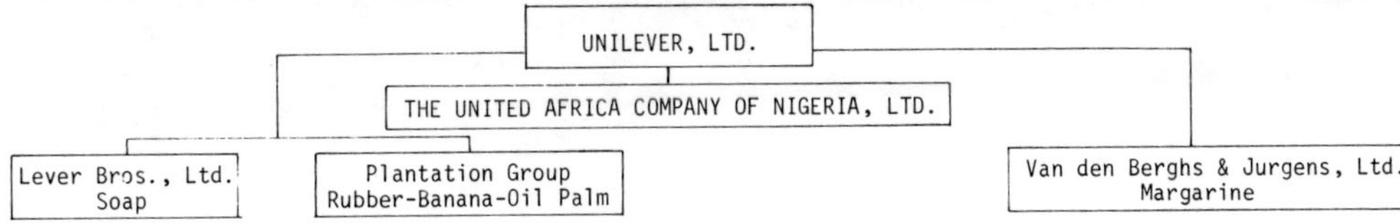

MERCHANDISE	PRODUCE	PETROLEUM PRODUCTS	HIDES AND SKINS	CITRUS JUICE FACTORY	LLOYDS MOTOR AGENCY DEPT	INSURANCE AGENCY	NIGER RIVER TRANSPORT
Import and sale of all types of merchandise	Purchase of all types of produce, either as agents for the statutory marketing boards or as principals	Distributing agents for Mobil Oil Nigeria Ltd.	Purchasing, processing and export	Extraction and export of orange juice	Sale and servicing of vehicles	Northern Assurance Company Ltd.	Part ownership of Burutu and river transport

United Africa Company Group

KINGSWAY STORES, LTD.	Department store and supermarket
KINGSWAY CHEMISTS, LTD. ...	Wholesale pharmacy
AFRICAN TIMBER AND PLYWOOD (NIGERIA), LTD. ...	Production and export of logs, sawn timber, and plywood
UAC (TECHNICAL), LTD.	Agricultural, earthmoving and electrical equipment, and constructional material
ANCHOR, LTD.	Shipping agents for Barber-West Africa Line, Kawasaki Kisen Kalsha, Ltd. & Palm Line
WEST AFRICA COLD STORAGE CO., LTD.	Refigeration and cold storage, foodstuffs
PALM LINE, LTD.	Ocean fleet
G.S. OLLIVANT, LTD. (under separate management)	Import and sale of merchandise. Purchase of produce either as principles or as agents of marketing boards.
G. GOTTSCHALCK AND CO. (WEST AFRICA), LTD.	As Ollivant

Associated companies in which UAC has part interest

BULK OIL PLANTS OF NIGERIA, LTD.	Palm oil storage installation
NIGERIAN BREWERIES, LTD.	Brewery and mineral water boiling plants
NIGERIAN PLASTICS, LTD.	Plastics and household-ware
NIGERIAN PRESTRESSED CONCRETE CO., LTD.	Prestressed concrete building material
TAYLOR WOODROW (NIGERIA), LTD.	Building contracts
NIGELEC, LTD.	Electrical installations

Holdings of the United Africa Company in Nigeria.

Source: Adapted from Stanley Diamond: The Naraguta of Nigeria, Julen A. Steward, editor, University of Illinois Press, 1972 (paperback).

Tetteh A. Kofi

The Role of Multinational Corporations in Cocoa Marketing and Pricing and Economic Development in Producer (African) Countries

Introduction

An aspect of the commodity exchange systems between developing and developed countries since the turn of the century is that the distributive system has been marked by the presence of powerful monopsonies—multinational companies—on the buying side and numerous atomistic sellers on the seller side. There is a *prima facie* case that this affected the equitable distribution of the gains from the international specialization of labor. It is hypothesized here that the monopolistic elements in the vertical price relationships in the different distribution channels has affected the equitable distribution of pure profit margins in favor of the buyers. Thus, levels of capital accumulation in developing countries have been adversely affected; and hence the inequitable distributive system is partly responsible for the lack of the "linkage" effects in developing other sectors of the economy.

The process of underdevelopment, it is claimed in some quarters, arises from low prices for raw materials and relatively low wages in the periphery, while the center reaps excessive profits because the periphery makes excessive payments for technology, finance, and skilled manpower; to the above may be added the institutional constraints that the periphery faces (1, 2, 3).

Questions have been raised as to "why has the growth in exports in these countries not carried over to other sectors and led to more widespread development in the domestic economy?" and "what has limited the 'carryover' from the export sector?" (4, p. 371). Meier examined such questions by analysing the various hypotheses which purported to show that international trade has operated as a mechanism of international inequality. He rejected all these hypotheses, including Prebisch's argument that international market forces have operated in such a way as to transfer income from the poor to the rich countries via a deterioration in terms of trade. Meier sets up an alternative hypothesis: "A more convincing explanation focuses on the differential effects of the various export goods, according to characteristics of their production functions, and on market imperfections and socio-cultural impediments within a poor country" (5, p. 373). Most metropolitan economists implicitly accepted the above thesis and hence most of the literature on the "carryover" problem has dealt with improving "pure competitive" efficiency on the production side. Very little work has been done on improving the producer bargaining power and efficiency in the exchange system.

The purpose of this empirical investigation is to study the role of foreign firms—the multinational corporations—in the distributive sector of the African cocoa-bean economy from farmgate to the manufacturer, their effects on price determination, the distributive share of pure profit margins and hence on capital accumulation, and comment indirectly on their role in the development or underdevelopment of the export-oriented cocoa economies of West Africa. Proposals for equitable pricing are suggested. The present paper uses the historical, social and economic analysis approach so as to capture the role of institutions in price determination and the distribution of gains from international trade. Part I presents a short historical analysis of production and consumption as it pertains to the reallocation of global resources under international specialization of labor. Part II presents a brief summary of the market structure of the world cocoa industry and ends with a brief discussion of vertical channel theory under monopolistic competition and the bargaining power relationships which determine the pure profit margins. Part III presents the empirical investigation into price determination and distribution of profits in the cocoa industry and the reasons why "carryover" has not taken place.

Part I. Cocoa and resource allocation in the world economy

Specialization and the international division of labor

A study of the production, distribution and consumption of cocoa may well provide us one of the best examples of the global process of resource allocation and structuring of the world economy under the international division of labor.

Under worldwide capitalist expansionism—mercantilism, free-trade imperialism, and colonialism—consumption patterns were borrowed and changes in demand, on a global level, generated significant increases in productivity, through geographic concentration. The present underdeveloped countries underwent the most thorough and genuine specialization of labor, from which there emerged the mono-economies of cocoa, coffee, and tea. Nevertheless, the equalization and convergence of the standard of living as predicted by Ricardo and his followers did not happen, although the doctrine of "free trade" and the theory of "comparative advantage" have been, and are still being, fortified by over a century of theoretical work by economists. These theories have been used to explain to the world that the well-being of all nations would be achieved under international division of labor. Furtado (6) points out that the law of "comparative advantage" provided a valid explanation for the existence of trade but concealed the uneven diffusion of technical progress. The structuring of the global process of resource allocation provoked the industrial revolution, generated uneven technological densities, and thereby transformed some economies into the "center"-developed and others into the "periphery"-underdeveloped. The cocoa industry will be examined from this point of view.

From Aztec nobility to European nobility: adoption of consumption patterns

Cocoa is native to Central America. It may well have been the Mayas who first cultivated and used it as a beverage (7, p. 31). The conquering Aztecs believed it was the food of the gods. In those days, the beans were used as a medium of exchange. The beverage, *chocolatl,* prepared from the beans, was consumed by the wealthy. After the conquest of the Americas by Europeans, the conquistadores introduced it to Europe. In 1528 Cortes returned to Spain with samples of the cake and introduced it there. Its use spread in Spain, Italy, Germany and France. Maria Theresa is said to have popularized it in France when she married Louis XIV in 1660. It is said to have become the vogue at Oxford when chocolate drinking spread to England in 1650 (8, Ch. 1).

In the eighteenth and nineteenth centuries, improvements in mechanical grinding reduced costs and product innovation produced milk chocolate, chocolate powder, and chocolate bars; these factors, coupled with rising incomes, led to an increased demand for cocoa beans.[1] Table 1 shows the marked increase in demand. The world supply response via global reallocation of resources is equally interesting.

Changes in world supply response

Cocoa has been the mainstay of many export economies at different points in time—in Mexico, Venezuela, Ecuador, Trinidad, Brazil, and now the West African countries of Ghana, Nigeria, Ivory Coast, and the Cameroons. Table 2 shows the historical dynamics in world supply response under national factor endowments and changing economic conditions.

During the conquest of Latin America, the conquistadores found cocoa so highly regarded by the Aztecs (who had earlier conquered the Mayas) that they restricted it to the ruling classes. Exports of cocoa to Europe started with exports from Mexico to Spain. The manner of conquest of the Central

Table 1. *Estimated average annual world exports from 1830 to 1890 and world net imports for selected years from 1894 to 1937*

Years	Tonnage in thousand long tons
1830/1840	14
1840/1850	16
1850/1860	19
1860/1870	23
1870/1880	31
1880/1890	41
1894	63
1903	22
1912	246
1929	559
1937	737

Sources: The annual averages from 1830 to 1890 are from Anon., *Gordian Essays on Cocoa,* Max Rieck, Hamburg, 1936, as reprinted in Eileen M. Chatt, *Cocoa,* Interscience Publishers, New York, 1953, p. 11.

The annual figures, selected years, are from FAO *Cocoa,* "A Review of Current Trends in Production, Price, and Consumption," FAO Commodity Series Bulletin No. 27, November 1955, pp. 83-86.

Table 2. *Producer shifts in world exports under changing national endowments and economic conditions* (Thousands of metric tons)

	1895	1911	1939	1970
Ghana	—	40.4	285.2	
Nigeria	—	4.5	115.7	
Ivory Coast	—	—	55.2	
Cameroon	.1	3.6	27.6	
São Thomé/Principe	6.1	32.3	10.7	
Brazil	10.8	35.0	132.2	
Dominican Republic	1.7	19.8	28.1	
Ecuador	19.0	38.8	15.3	
Venezuela	7.1	18.0	15.4	
Trinidad	13.6	22.6	7.6	

American states by Cortes and others presumably did not allow the peasants to respond through peasant farming to supply Europe with the commodity, and plantation mode of production was the answer under the ruling social conditions. For example, France began cocoa cultivation in Martinique in 1660.

In the seventeenth century Venezuela became the leading producer. Shipment began there in 1634 and was only surpassed at the turn of the century by Ecuador, Trinidad and Brazil. In the Central Americas production received a setback as a result of a "blast" in 1727 which wiped out most of the plantations.[2] In Trinidad it took thirty years to re-establish production, but in Jamaica as well as other Central American republics it was abandoned until the latter half of the nineteenth century, when high prices made production possible again. The risks involved in cocoa production were high for the plantations—large amounts of capital had to be tied down for 5 to 7 years before the tree bore fruit and then there was no certainty of continued yields, due to diseases and the vagaries of nature. The risks were not so high for peasant farmers whose farms were small and who also lived partly in the subsistence sector. It was only when the African peasant economies started to produce that world supplies increased at unprecedented rates. In 1900 Latin America contributed 85 percent of world production; by 1938 its share had fallen to less than 30 percent and the African peasant farmers' share had increased to 70 percent. The peasant economies with cheap supplies of family labor, low rents, and with one foot in the subsistence economy, found existing cocoa prices attractive, unlike the Latin American plantation owners.[3] The increase in African production was also facilitated by rapid development of cheap and relatively efficient transport costs and, more important, by the traditional mode of organizing for production (9, 10).

Supply response of African peasant economies

Cocoa was introduced into Africa by the Spanish when they planted it in Fernando Po in the seventeenth century. Exports from São Thomé and Principe in Africa in the middle of the 1850s were important. Yet it was when production on the West African mainland started that the center of supply shifted from the Americas to West Africa.

The African countries in 1973 produced close to three-quarters of world cocoa beans: the principal producers are Ghana, Nigeria, Ivory Coast, Cameroon and Togo. Cocoa was first planted in the Gold Coast (Ghana) in 1879 when a Gold Coaster blacksmith named Tetteh Quarshie smuggled some beans out of Fernando Po (11), and started cultivating farms in the Mampong district, which induced other farmers to cultivate cocoa farms. The imperial representatives also encouraged production through the available colonial organizational apparatus—in 1887, Governor Griffith procured pods from Sao Thomé and distributed them among the natives (12). In the case of Nigeria, a native chief named David Henshaw is supposed to have introduced seeds from Fernando Po in 1880. These types of African initiative during the colonial period in which the natives responded to economic challenges has been termed the Ranger Thesis.[4]

In the Ivory Coast,

> . . .it is recorded that a far-reaching French administrator imported cocoa seed and gave it to the Africans but they were unwilling to plant. After much persuasion, however, they planted the seed, but such was their resentment at having to do so, that they used to go out at night and pour hot water on it in the hope of killing it. Nevertheless, some of the seed survived and in due course cocoa became a popular crop (13, p. 14).

Such an uneconomic reason for crop production is untenable; it even defied the Ranger Thesis (see footnote 4). Probably the natives heard of the success in Ghana and started planting it for export.[5] In the Cameroons the Germans tried plantation production; as in Latin America, it could not compete with the peasant mode of production. McPhee examined the reasons as regards the Gold Coast:

> . . . in 1923 Gold Coast exported about 200,000 tons of cocoa, or more than half the aggregate production of the world. This has been accomplished by means of native enterprise, encouraged and directed by the government, apart from the intervention of foreign capital except marketing. The system of cultivation is that of small peasant farmers working on their own resources. The success of the system is peculiar to West Africa. Elsewhere, great exchange cultures have been reared, as in Dutch Java and in the German Cameroons, but they were funded on large plantations, financed by foreign capital and worked by compulsory or semi-compulsory native labor (14, p. 42).

In all the West African cocoa economies production and marketing of cocoa became the leading sectors.[6]

For mono-economies the development process may be viewed as depending principally on "fiscal linkages" and the linkages associated with the distributive sector, i.e., what the country as a whole does with the incomes resulting from the sale of its exports. Capital accumulation out of pure profits is dependent on the share of profits within the distributive channels. It is argued in this paper that the failure of the imperial powers to check the monopolistic elements on the buyer side in the distributive system prevented the export economies from reaping the surplus in the vertical channels to invest in other productive activities. Furthermore, the foreign firms' control of capital and the marketing processes robbed the export economies of the entrepreneural talents and skills which are the externalities associated with marketing.

Hymer (15, p. 441) has surmised that "since the beginning of the industrial revolution there has been a steady increase in the size of manufacturing firms . . . it might almost be formulated as a general law of capital accumulation." The center, by virtue of its more dynamic economy, "sought by an enterprise and/or government to assure the provision . . . of (1) essential raw materials and foods; (2) markets for its manufactured exports; and (3) spheres for the investment of its capital" (16, p. 225). Thus, historically, during the evolution of multinational corporations the imperialistic dimension was always present to ensure a dominant position within the exchange system for the representative firm—Marshallian factory, national corporation or multinational corporation. The above analysis is especially true in the exchange system developed between colonies and the imperial powers in the eighteenth and nineteenth centuries.

A great deal has been written by many metropolitan economists about how market imperfections on the supply side affect development (17, 18, 19). Nevertheless, it seems that monopsony in the distributive channels has worked to transfer income from rich to poor and has stifled the development process in poor countries. (For an analysis of distribution of profit margins, see 28.) Thus it is important for us to examine the role that multinational firms have played in the determination of equitable or inequitable pricing within the distributive channels. To make this analysis we must first study the market structure of the industry.

Part II. Structure of the export markets of West Africa

Character of the colonial trade

A striking feature of the production structure of export economies of West Africa, unlike other parts of the Third World, is that development of the export sectors was based on capital formation out of the then current labor, natural resources, and indigenous ways of organizing for production and trade. One would have hoped that the investment of the surplus generated out of the export sales would lead to cumulative additions to income, employment, capital, technical knowledge, and one thing would lead to another; thus, a dynamic growth would be set in motion. That this did not happen may partly have been because most of the surplus generated out of the distributive system via monopolistic competition was exported out by the metropolitan imperial export and import firms. Thus the surplus investment and related growth via the multiplier effect took place in the metropolis. This proposition we intend to examine empirically.

Ida Greaves gave a vivid economic description of the character of the colonial trade. "A country's export trade", she comments, "is generally regarded as an extension or overflow of the domestic production in certain lines which offer the most advantageous use of its own factors of production. But this is not true of colonial exports" (20, p. 6). Even where indigenous local resources developed the industry, financing of the distributive sector was controlled by the foreign firms. Greaves pointed out that "the system of export agricultures developed in these African territories was that crops produced by native small holders were purchased and shipped by a few external traders with substantial capital at their disposal" (21, p. 5). Greaves continues: "... the credit required by cultivators, middlemen, and exporters is obtained from local branches of British banks, most of which have London offices" (22, p. 6).

We intend to show that for the indigenous African economies the "carryover effects" failed partly because the imperial firms with their superior organizational know-how, backed by administrative power and control, and financial strength, exercised their monopolistic power to maximize their profits and transferred income from poor to rich countries. In such circumstances, the monopolistic exploitation within the marketing channels, leading to gains and losses from trade, was independent of the "terms of trade argument".

Colonial trade and the West African cocoa market structure

Since the turn of the century, and until statutory cocoa marketing boards were instituted, the market structure was one of atomistic sellers (buyers) facing oligopsonistic buyers (oligopolistic sellers) in the export (import) trade. Thus the developing country always faced a monopolist. The prevalence of such a market structure in West Africa has been discussed empirically by many writers, including Bauer (23), and the history of the dominant multinational by Flint (24) and Pearson (25). Table 3 presents some of Bauer's findings. The largest exporter was also the largest importer in both Ghana and Nigeria—the United Africa Company.

Such a market structure must bear adversely on the economic performance of the export economies. Yet some metropolitan economists have spent their entire lives attempting to prove that such market structures do not impede efficient market performance. Mueller, commenting on the work of Bauer and Yamey (26), says in part, "the point they miss is that until some of the commonest causes of monopolistic competition are eliminated, efficient marketing systems are impossible" (27, p. 424). Mueller calls for pure competitive bargaining to ensure marketing efficiency, which does not seem to be possible in the real world. Our disagreement with Bauer and Yamey arises from the fact that they defended concentration on the buyer side but failed to endorse cooperative movements on the seller side to ensure monopolistic or oligopolistic competitive bargaining in price determination within the colonial exchange systems.

Next we present an empirical investigation into imperfect competition in the cocoa market since the turn of the century.

Table 3. *Shares of firms in purchases for export or in exports, Nigeria and the Gold Coast, 1949 or 1950*

	NIGERIA										GOLD COAST
Firms	Total Nigerian non-mineral exports a	Cocoa (1)	Palm kernels (2)	Palm oil (3)	Ground-nuts (4)	Cotton (5)	Timber in logs (6)	Sawn timber (7)	Skins (8)	Hides (9)	Cocoa (10)
	%	%	%	%	%	%	%	%	%	%	%
A	43.3	33.2	48.9	68.2	37.1	48.8	37	69	28	50	38.8
C	9.1	10.9	11.3	5.7	7.8	14.6			8	14	2.7
B	6.5	5.4	7.3	5.4	6.9	8.6			12	15	6.4
E	6.0	8.2	7.1	6.2	4.6	8.3			2	1	1.9
J	3.6	11.7	2.8								13.6
D	2.8	1.4	4.6	5.0	1.3	2.8			7		2.4
K	2.6				13.2						
L	2.3				6.0	15.4			8	6	
M	2.2	8.8									11.7
H	1.6	2.0	1.7		3.4						4.5
N	1.4								24	11	

Source: P. T. Bauer, "Concentration in Tropical Trade: Some Aspects and Implication of Oligopoly." *Economica* (November 1953), p. 312.

West African cocoa market structure: an empirical analysis

I have found it convenient for purposes of analysis to categorize the cocoa market since the turn of the century into four different types of pricing regimes (28):

(1) Pricing without aid of futures markets reflecting local demand and supply conditions—from turn of the contury to 1925.

(2) Pricing under unbalanced or growing futures market regime—pre-World War II, 1925-1938.

(3) Period of administered prices—the war years' commodity control period, 1939-1947.

(4) Era of institutionalized oligopolistic competition, 1948 to present. For an empirical, statistical demonstration of the market periodization using a futures market performance test, see Kofi (29). Qualitative economic analysis may also be used to justify the periodization.

In the first period, before the advent of the telephone, market information was very poor and pricing in the channels reflected only the supply and demand situation in the local market. It was therefore impossible to coordinate prices between overseas buyers and producers. The marketing channel was controlled by a few intermediaries. Marketing during this period was risky. Exporters sought to reduce the level of uncertainty by forming pools, combines and trusts to control information and agree on prices. One such pool, formed in 1925, incorporated the African and Eastern Trading Company and the Niger Company. Producers tried to counteract the collusion by forming the Ghana Farmers Association to combat the oligopsony power of the exporters. The Association sent their leader, Mr. E. V. Akrofi, to try selling direct to buyers in the United States. The reason for this direct contact was that the British buyers (combine) had bid prices down from 75 shillings to 8 shillings per load of 60 pounds weight (30).

In the second period, the shippers' pools dominated the industry by controlling information and regulating supplies, from 1925 until 1938. A shippers' pool was formed under the leadership of the United Lever Concern in 1928 (31). In the cocoa industry effects of the coming depression began to be felt in 1928 when the Accra Pool found itself with large supplies of unwanted cocoa beans (32). Thus the Pools did not have their way all the time, and at times they were forced to withhold information from manufacturers. For example, in January 1930, Elder Dempster Lines (a British shipping firm) refused to give information on shipments from West Africa to the New York Cocoa Exchange.

Marketing during the Depression was a risky business for all, but the group which suffered most were the producers. Their ultimate weapon was to stage holdups of cocoa beans and boycotts of manufactured goods and return to subsistence living while the holdup and boycott lasted. In Ghana there was a holdup strike in 1930-31 which failed. Nevertheless, during the 1937-38 season a successful holdup of cocoa and a boycott of manufactures were carried out by the producers. The British government sent a Royal Commission to investigate the incident. The Secretary of State for the Colonies explained the reasons for the holdup as follows: "Early in November 1937, as a result of Buying Agreements entered into in respect of Gold Coast and Nigeria cocoa by all but one of the important European firms trading in the two dependencies, a general holdup of cocoa, accompanied by a boycott of certain European goods, was started by Gold Coast and Ashanti farmers" (33, p. vii). The Commission's terms of reference, under the Chairmanship of William Nowell, were as follow:

> ... to examine and report on the marketing of cocoa in the Gold Coast and Nigeria, with special reference to the situation which has arisen as a result of the Buying Agreement(s) entered into between certain firms; and to submit recommendations (34, p. vii).

The Commission's report recommended that the buying agreement should be withdrawn and that the marketing of West African cocoa be by a statutory marketing board, an association of producers which would collectively market their produce and represent their interests. At last, a monopoly of producers could face the monopsony of the buyer under bilateral monopoly competitive situation. Before the recommendations could be implemented, however, World War II had begun.

This brings us to the third period, the war years. Peter Ady comments that "one of the more interesting experiments of this war has been the development of bulk purchasing to ensure supplies to the United Kingdom" (35, p. 321). Purchasing and marketing of cocoa was first under the Ministry of Food, and operations began in January 1940. In August 1940 a separate Cocoa Control Board under the Colonial Office was set up. In May 1942 the Board was enlarged to include purchase and resale of commodities such as oil seeds, rubber, groundnuts and palm kernels, Accordingly, the West African Cocoa Control Board's name was changed to the West African Produce Control Board (WAPCB). According to Peter Ady, despite all the name changes, the operations were the same (35, pp. 322-324):

1. Purchasing arrangements on the coast.
2. Arrangements for shipment and sale abroad.
3. Price policy in domestic and foreign markets.

> The actual purchase of the cocoa was handled by the usual buyers and shippers, now acting as agents of the Control and paid upon a fixed schedule of costs plus commision at a standard rate per ton . . . shipment on the coast was left to accredited shippers who claimed repayment of costs incurred from the WAPCB . . . After 1942, however . . . the function of private shipper and seller disappeared, the Produce Control Board taking over the cocoa F.O.B. point, and arranging shipment and sale directly. This reduced the Board's appointed agents on the Coast to the status of buyers . . .

The above quote is necessary to explain the strategy of marketing in the war years. It is surprising that no minimum purchase price to the farmer was guaranteed, since chocolate was an important part of a soldier's ration. Thus, even under the war control period, the atomistic producer still faced the oligopsony exporter firms. It should be pointed out that the British government marketed Cameroonian cocoa on behalf of the French; but the cocoa from Ivory Coast was marketed somehow by local private French interests.[7]

The fourth period, the era of oligopolistic competition, was ushered in after the creation of the marketing boards in the 1947-48 season. Nevertheless, bargaining powers within the channels are by no means equal. On the supply side, Ghana, Nigeria, Ivory Coast, Brazil and Cameroon produce close to 80 percent of the world cocoa beans. On the demand side, Gill and Duffus, A. C. Israel (ACI International), General Cocoa, J. H.

Table 4. *Market shares of multinational firms (middlemen) in industry, their financial strength and degree of vertical integration.*

Company	Countries of operation with subsidiaries	Degree of vertical integration	Index of financial strength[1]	Percentage share of world bean trade in actuals
Dealers				
Gill and Duffus Ltd. London	UK USA Ghana Nigeria Braxil Germany	Middlemen and manufacturers of intermediate products, cocoa butter	£92 million external sales 1969, cocoa share not given	20-30
A.C. Israel (ACLI International) USA	UK USA France	Middlemen	–	20-30
J.H. Rayner USA	UK USA France	Middlemen	–	10-20
General Cocoa USA	Holland USA France	Middlemen	–	10-15
CONTINEF Holland	Holland Ivory Coast Cameroon Gabon	Middlemen Shippers (Ivory Coast, Cameroon, Gabon)	–	5-10
			Total turnover in million dollars; cocoa share in ()	
Manufacturers				
Hershey Foods USA	USA Canada Mexico	Total vertical integration	402 (310)	The manufacturers buy beans from sources whenever they find it profitable; difficult to find a figure for them. Large ones frequently buy beans directly from producers.
Nestle S.A. Switzerland	13 countries	Total vertical integration	3835 (376)	
Cadbury-Schweppes Ltd. UK	6 countries	Total vertical integration	355	
W.R. Grace USA	5 countries	Total vertical integration	1917 (575)	
Rountree-Mackintosh Ltd. UK	10 countries	Total vertical integration	351	

[1] Most of these companies are private and do not report a financial statement.
Sources: Conversations with traders in the market: *Financial Times, Moody's Industrial Manual:* data manufactures from Table 5.2, UNCTAD Report TD/B/C.1/132.

Rayner, and CONTINEF control over 75 percent of world cocoa trade in "actuals".

Table 4 shows the market shares of firms in the industry, as well as their financial solvency.

A review on the state of the theory of power measurement in a distributive system will be helpful for an empirical analysis of profit margin distribution.

Monopolistic competion, vertical channel power and price determination

Orthodox price theory has been written as if the producer sold directly to the final end consumer. The middleman has not been in the picture. Hawkins (36) and Mallen (37) have used the theory of monopolistic competition to examine price determination in the distribution channels.

Theories in price channel competition and market structure

If a channel member is a monopolist and he negotiates with partners in pure competition at another level, vertically, he will reap all the channel's pure profits. Pure profit is defined here as profits over and above the minimum return on capital which will keep a firm in business. In a situation where a channel member faces another in a monopsony-monopoly situation, the agreed price level depends on the relative bargaining power.

As pointed out, in the colonial economies, the few exporters (buying firms) usually faced atomistic sellers; they could, therefore, obtain lower prices than if their level were competitive, and/or faced an ogilopolistic seller. Tables 4 and 5 show the degree of concentration and the theoretical market structure, according to our periodization. The fourth period is a case of oligopsonists facing oligopolists. Our empirical analysis of the market will be undertaken in depth for this period.

It helps to view the distributive channel as a behavioral system, and the marketing strategies involved as a problem in industrial organization. Conceptual models on vertical channel analyses remain in the embryonic stage of development. Part of the reason lies in the difficulty of developing adequate conceptual models of vertical market relationships. Stern has pointed out that we cannot view channels as economic systems alone. "The perspective must be broadened to include social and behavioral variables, for channels are social systems first and then economic systems" (38). In the context of this paper, we must look also at the colonial, social dimension in the vertical exchange, in addition to negotiation skills, market power, demand and cost functions.

Palamountain has observed that the "principal factor differentiating vertical conflict from horizontal or intertype competition is that it is so directly a power conflict" (39, p. 135).

In a recent paper, Curry and Rothchild (40) analysed qualitatively economic bargaining between African governments and multinational companies in which two main variables—demand intensity and impatience—were used in the analysis of power relations in bargaining. In another recent paper, El-Ansary and Stern (41) developed a model on empirically measured power relations in the vertical channels. Their model in mathematical symbols is shown in Appendix A.

In their empirical study, El-Ansary and Stern measured power dependence and power sources by gauging the self-perception of various channel members and the attributions about them by other members. We intend to use the above model structure to analyse qualitatively the power relations in the marketing channels with the aid of a study done by Kofi (42) which quantified the marketing margins in the channel levels. Such an analysis will help us to comment on the original question we posed, i.e., whether income has been transferred from the poor to the rich in the export trade exchange system.

PART III. Empirical analysis of the role of multinational corporations in cocoa marketing and pricing

Comments on market structure

In market structure analysis the characteristics usually emphasized are (1) the number and the size of distribution of buyers and sellers—buyer and seller concentration, (2) degree of product homogeneity, and (3) conditions of entry (43).

Table 5 shows the above characteristics for the four periods. Although the above tables give us ideas about structure and conduct, it is not enough to fully explain performance. Bain (44) has pointed out that market structure and conduct represent only a small part of the determinants of performance. The performance analyses will be undertaken here by referring to market institutions such as futures markets, marketing boards, and the role played by colonial administrators in pricing.

After the war, Statutory Marketing Boards were instituted in Ghana and Nigeria. In the case of Ivory Coast, Cameroons and Togoland, the *Caisse* was instituted in a 1954 legislation and became a commercial concern embracing not only cocoa but all other primary exports in 1964.

Table 5. *Market structure analysis for the four periods (turn of century to 1974): concentration of buyers and sellers, degrees of homogeneity and conditions of entry.*[1]

Period	Suppliers Sellers	Middlemen Buyers	Comment Market Situation
Turn of century to 1925	Atomistic peasant farmers in Africa. Plantations in Americas. Seller side approximates pure competion in Africa. Oligopsony in Americas; bean homogeneity is differentiable.	Few shippers and exporters (combines and trusts).	Atomistic sellers facing monopsonistic buyers (combines). Price determination takes place in local markets depending on demand and supply situation locally; no futures market; shippers control information.
1925-39	Plantations decline. Seller side pure competition; homogeneity improved. Ghana cocoa the standard.	Few shippers and exporters. Shipper pools common. Giant manufacturers; emergence of Hershey.	Futures market aids price determination; Depression – combines, shippers pools increase, market structure same as above. Information control by shippers.
1939-47	Colonial governments control f.o.b. prices; but pure competition at farmgate level; homogeneous commodity.	Few giant dealers operating on behalf of colonial government. Manufacturers-administered competition.	Controlled or administered prices. Competition only at farmgate level.
1948-74	Marketing boards, Caisse de Stabilisation *v.* large exporters. Oligopolistic competition.	Few large dealers and manufacturers. Oligopolistic competition.	Oligopolistic competition in price determination and bargaining; information important in bargaining; information control by Gill and Duffus.

[1] There were rigid entry impediments: institutional impediments (colonial situation) and capital requirements prevented farmers and African middlemen from engaging in cocoa export business. Exporters could not engage in plantation farming because it was unprofitable. Cadbury and Fry set up cocoa plantations in the Cameroons, 1950-1960, but abandoned the project and sold the enterprise to local interests because they operated at a loss. At the Ikiliwindi farm they ran a loss of 4,390 pounds sterling in 1967. (*Source:* Cadbury and Fry (Ikiliwindi) Estate Balance Sheet As At 1st July 1967, mimeo.)

The *Caisse,* unlike the marketing board, does not take possession of the commodity. It remains in the hands of the exporters, who purchase it from the farmers and arrange for transportation, storage and exports on their own account. The *Caisse,* however, fixes an export reference price—an f.o.b. price. If the exporter obtains less than the f.o.b. price in the world markets, he is compensated by the *Caisse*. This arrangement is similar to the marketing of cocoa during the war years by the British government. Thus, multinational corporations—foreign export firms, both French and British—have played a major role in cocoa marketing in West African cocoa economies.

Multinational and market structure

The pre-war, inter-war, and early phases of *statutory marketing boards and Caisses* marketing arrangements in the cocoa industry were hinged on the merchant firms. The exporters advanced capital to intermediaries to purchase the commodity from the farmers inland with instructions on pricing policies. In some countries like Ivory Coast, Lebanese and Syrians became active as brokers.

The cocoa industry registered the highest price instability index (1950-1958), according to a study by Coppock (45, p. 46). Thus, the risk involved in merchandizing is very high. The exporters and manufacturers use the New York Cocoa Exchange or the London Terminal Market for trading purposes to reduce high risks. Farmers in most cases do not use futures markets as adjuncts to their marketing activities. Many reasons are responsible for this: (1) pure farmer ignorance; (2) the colonial situation was such that farmer cooperatives were not encouraged to make their own initiatives towards using the futures market; (3) farmers on their own, especially peasant farmers, do not have the initial capital, the skill and know-how to engage in futures trading.

When the statutory marketing boards were set up, it was decided to trade futures officially, but no attempt was made to do this. Hackman (46, p. 15) examined this issue when commenting on the operations of the Cocoa Marketing Company, a subsidiary of the Marketing Board:

> The operations of the Cocoa Marketing Company (CMC) are limited to the market for physical cocoa and no operation on the Terminal Market is ever undertaken. Since the inception of the West African Companies no attempt has ever been made to use either the New York Exchange or the London Terminal Market to ward off some of the risks of dangerous price fluctuations. It has, of course, to be recalled that the decision to use the New York Exchange was taken at the very outset of the CMC but this never materialized and the whole idea is now comfortably buried in a deep freeze.

It is believed that in 1969 the Ghana Cocoa Marketing Board started trading futures on a modest scale. Nevertheless, the manufacturers and dealers have more resource power over the marketing channel system than the producer organization in these aspects: (1) the vertical integration on the manufacturer-dealer side is higher than on the producer side; (2) dealers have access to more operating capital than producer organizations; (3) the dealers and manufacturers have control over market information; and (4) dealers and manufacturers are much better equipped to use the futures markets as an adjunct to their trading in the actuals market. The above points will be analysed next. The effects of the above market organization structure on producer income will also be examined. Recommendations for equitable pricing will be given.

Table 6. *Estimated linear regression relationship between the spot (cash) price and prior futures price, of the first futures after harvest for cocoa, for various historical periods (1929-1969).*[1,2]

Time Period	Intercept	Slope	r^2	d.w.[4]	Intercept	Slope	r^2	d.w.
	11 months away from contract expiration date				8 months away from contract expiration date			
Period II 1929-38	4.14	.29	.10	2.26	2.97	.51	.19	2.20
	(2.44)[3]	(.32)			(2.53)	(.37)		
Period III 1939-47	-3.02	1.72	.78	2.01	-6.31	2.06	.79	1.88
	(3.45)	(.34)			(3.98)	(.41)		
Period IV 1948-69	16.02	.46	.16	1.50	13.72	.56	.29	1.57
	(7.03)	(.24)			(5.57)	(.20)		
	6 months away from contract expiration date				2 months away from contract expiration date			
Period II 1929-38	1.05	.81	.34	2.03	-.86	1.23	.83	2.05
	(2.67)	(.40)			(1.21)	(.20)		
Period III 1939-47	-.89	1.38	.80	2.05	3.01	.75	.92	2.47
	(2.9)	(.26)			(1.35)	(.08)		
Period IV 1948-69	13.38	.56	.39	1.78	5.03	.83	.70	1.23
	(4.55)	(.15)			(3.69)	(.12)		

[1] The dependent variable—spot (cash) price—is the closing price on expiration of the December contract. The independent variable is the closing futures price of the same future recorded on the last day of preceding months. The variables are measured in cents per pound.
[2] Data Source: *Wall Street Journal,* various issues.
[3] Numbers in parentheses are standard errors of the respective coefficients.
[4] None of the Durbin-Watson Test Statistic results show a significant positive autocorrelation at the 1 percent level.

Source: Tetteh A. Kofi, "A Framework for Comparing the Efficiency of Futures Markets", *American Journal of Agricultural Economics,* Vol. 55, No. 4, Part 1, Nov., 1973, p. 59.

Cocoa market structure, institutions and price determination

Professor Taussig once remarked that actual market prices fall within a "penumbra" and that as market information becomes more complete within the channels—more accurate and timely—the penumbra will tend to narrow (47). The "penumbra" may be said to be relatively narrower on the average for markets with futures institutions than for those without: it has been shown that futures markets are superior to cash markets in price determination, because they provide central market prices established in open competitive bargaining (48).

Table 6 shows the results of the price performance test developed by Kofi (49) to test the efficiency of futures markets, and which was used to periodize the market. It will be seen that the r^2 for the fourth period is much higher than the other periods, indicating that information on supply and demand has improved over the years.[3] Paralleling this improvement, unrelated to market performance, is the bargaining power of producers in obtaining a relatively higher proportion of the spot price, as a result of relatively more timely information available for producers and also due to the creation of monopoly sellers—marketing boards. Analysis of marketing margins over time will help us comment on bargaining in the channels.

Marketing margins are governed by the demand for and supply of service if there is competition. If there is lack of competition, marketing costs and efficiency will be affected, and monopolies and oligopolies will be built up. They may use their power (rings, pools or cartels) to be assured of obtaining a comfortable profit margin. Such cartels are more common where transportation is difficult and sellers cannot shift to competitive markets. This was the problem that the African farmers faced. There were few exporters, for conditions of entry into the wholesale markets (capital requirements) were high. Price formation in the wholesale market is a derived demand; it reflects what wholesalers (exporters) think consumers will pay. At the farmgate point the exporter will offer a price he expects to receive at the consumer end, less an allowance for remuneration (pure profits), and the transport, storage and insurance costs he will incur. Demand for and supply of marketing services are not directly governed by final demand or retail prices; thus, prices at farmgate level normally do not reflect shifts in consumer demand.

Part of the marketing margins computed by Kofi (49) are shown in Table 7. We can deduce from Column 1 that producers were better off in Period 1 than in any other period except in Period 4 if we use the Marketing Board unit average selling price as the price the producer receives (index in parentheses). In this case it may be said that the institutionalization of the monopoly on the selling side (marketing boards) has increased its bargaining power over the dealers relative to its power in previous periods. The producer gross margin

Table 7. *Average ratios of price margins compared to spot price, for periods shown.*

Time period	Producer price as a percentage of spot price[2]	Producer gross margin as a percentage of spot price[3]	Export marketing margin as a percentage of spot price[1,4]	Total global marketing margin as a percentage of spot price farmgate to warehouse overseas[5]
Period I 1913-24	.69	.50	–	.35
Period II 1925-38	.62	.21	.26	.39
Period III 1939-47	.41	-.06	–	.78
Period IV 1948-70	.50 (.83)	.40 (.72)	.46 (.13)	.52 (.19)

[1] Values for Periods I and III are missing because the freight rate index data was not available or was unreliable and not used in these periods.
[2] Spot price, New York Cocoa Exchange prices.
[3] Producer gross margins=producer price—labor cash payments—transportation to buying center.
[4] Export marketing margin=spot price—production price—ocean freight price.
[5] Global marketing margin=spot price—producer price—transport to buying center.

Source: T. A. Kofi, "Vertical Price Relations in the International Cocoa Market and Implications for Ghana's Marketing Policies," in R. A. Kotey, C. Okali, and B. E. Rourke, eds., *Cocoa Conference 1973,* Institute of Statistical and Social Research, University of Ghana, Legon, Ghana.

Data Source: *Annual Reports of the Chamber of Shipping of the United Kingdom,* various issues. Various dissimilar indexes linked and shifted to 1967 base. The rough shipping prices for the period 1920 to 1938 was constructed by multiplying the shipping index by the 1967 average shipping rate quoted by Farrell Lines.

The freight rates for 1945 to 1970 were supplied by Farrell Lines Shipping Company, New York. The figures represent the cost of transporting a long ton of cocoa from Accra, Ghana, to Philadelphia (US).

The link between pre- and post-World War II (1938 and 1948) is entirely based on Kendall's statement that on a 1938 base the new index for 1948 was 330 (*Journal of the Royal Statistical Society*, 1950, Pt. 1, Series A (General), p. 21).

Producer price, labor cash payments and internal transportation costs were obtained from W. H. Beckett (1972), Koransang Cocoa Farm, 1904-1970, Technical Publication Series No. 31, Institute of Statistical, Social and Economic Research, Legon, Ghana; and FAO (1955), *Cocoa,* Commodity Series Bulletin No. 27, Food and Agriculture Organization of United Nations.

(Column 2) follows the interpretations for Column 1. Both cases show that the war years were the worst years for the farmer. F.o.b. prices were fixed by the imperial government; nevertheless, minimum prices for the farmer were not guaranteed. Column 3 explains why the shippers in the second period sought to form rings or combines. The export marketing margins were at

Table 8. *Components of payments for purchases of produce in Nigeria and the Gold Coast*
Percentages based on f.o.b. prices, 1945-6

	Palm oil, Nigeria	Groundnuts, Northern Nigeria	Cocoa, West Africa	Overall average
Total (f.o.b. basis)	100	100	100	100
Less Head Office expenses, profit and tax payable in UK *transferred abroad*	4	3	2	3
Total *retained in Africa*	96	97	98	97

The percentages *retained in Africa* are made up as follows

	Palm oil, Nigeria	Groundnuts, Northern Nigeria	Cocoa, West Africa	Overall average
Transport charges, etc., to port	10	27	7	13
Export duties, etc.	3	3	5	4
Cost of UAC establishment in Africa	14	7	6	7
Paid to producer or trader	69	60	80	73
Total *retained in Africa*	96	97	98	97

Source: Anon., "What the Producer Receives for His Crops," *Statistical and Economic Review,* United Africa Company, March 1948, adapted from p. 11.

times negative. Column 4 shows that during the war years 78 percent of the bean retail price was spent within the marketing margins. This has been reduced to 19 percent as a result of the monopoly power of the marketing boards.

One of the few empirical studies on marketing margins was an official study done by the United Africa Company (50). It was claimed that "roughly three-quarters of the value of produce at the moment it entered the ship's hold actually reached the African producers, or the African intermediaries who are, in fact, the main channel through which purchases are affected." Table 8 shows part of the results of the United Africa Company study. Profit margins were claimed to be 2 percent of f.o.b. price.[8] Our computations from Table 7, however, show that producer gross margin was less than zero for at least part of the war period. The price paid to the farmer was so low that it at times did not cover the variable costs of transporting the cocoa to buying centers. Ady explains why such low prices were paid to the farmer: "... prices paid in West Africa remained at very low levels until 1943 owing to the difficulty experienced in shipping the cocoa purchase ... with the relatively low price being paid by the Board, this low price to the producer was inevitable if the books were to be balanced" (51, p. 327). The wholesale price paid by the manufacturers for cocoa beans was fixed during the war years. Thus it was the farmer who bore the brunt of the price squeeze, since marketing costs were fixed under control conditions and the exporters were given commissions. Thus, the conclusion by the United Africa Company that three-quarters of the value of cocoa was retained by the Africans is misleading.

Chart I shows the diagram of the United Africa Company's buying organization. The Company issued directives up to the farmgate by quoting purchasing prices to its agents. Thus the marketing channel was vertically integrated by the monopsonies in the first three periods, until the companies were phased out by the statutory marketing boards. Nevertheless, in Ivory Coast, Cameroon and Togo the shipper-exporter still operates as before. Even under these old marketing arrangements (still prevailing in former French West Africa), the share of farmers' income in the total value of output has risen, due to greater spread of price information and stabilization schemes. This brings us to the important issue of how control of market information affects price determination via the futures markets.

Cocoa futures markets and the multinationals

Futures markets, as we have pointed out, are superior to cash markets in price determination because they provide a central market place for competitive bargaining. Kofi (52, p. 585), paraphrasing Working's theory of "anticipatory prices" (53), explains that "prices are formed through human decision-making based on available information about supply and demand and past conditions in the market. The theory implies that price fluctuations in the market are due to expert appraisal of the significance of changing economic information in a world of uncertainty ..."

In the cocoa market information on West African yearly supply expectation has a great deal of influence on price swings. Until late 1950 the British government, through the Ministries of Agriculture in the colonies, published estimates on demand and supply. After Ghana's independence, Gill and Duffus, Ltd., more or less filled the role of the British government as the provider of market information for the overseas public. Gill and Duffus Cocoa Market Reports are widely used by speculators and dealers in their day-to-day operations and hence the information in these reports influences

Chart 1. *Diagram of the company's buying organization*

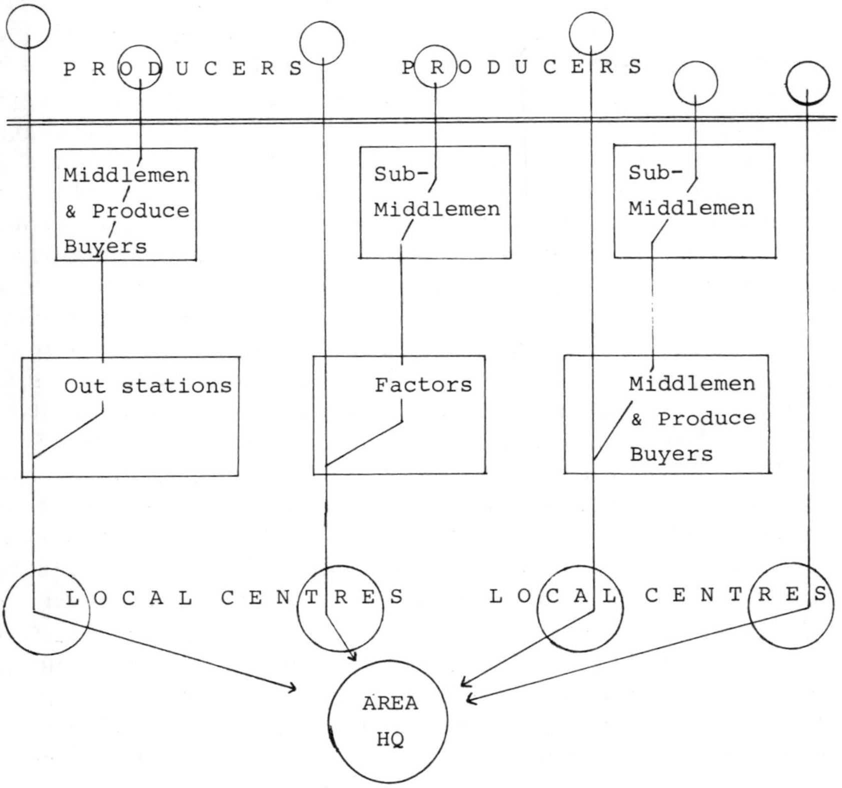

Source: *Statistical and Economic Review,* United Africa Company, Mar., 1949, p. 11.

cocoa futures quotations. In a series of articles Kofi (54, 55, 56) has analysed how Gill and Duffus Cocoa Market Reports affect futures prices. In a recent report the United Nations Conference on Trade and Development (UNCTAD) used the statistical methodology developed by Kofi (57) to show that Gill and Duffus crop forecasts do affect the direction of futures prices. The report said in part, "The concordance between observed and estimated values is sufficiently good to support the view that futures prices are directly and strongly affected by Gill and Duffus forecasts. In this connection, it is relevant to note that these forecasts continue to have an important impact on market sentiment, even when, in the event, they (sic) proved to be substantially in error, as they have in each season since 1968/69" (58, Annex p. 3).

Control of information by the multinational corporation and its effects on bargaining has received little attention in the literature. In this situation a dealer as large as Gill and Duffus, with its corporate power, can maximize monopolistic profits by synchronizing its information control in the futures markets, its purchasing power in the actuals markets, and control of its inventory positions. In this way its control of information gives it a stronger bargaining power, because its forecasts affect the direction of price swings.

From the economic literature, we know that for competition to be perfect the following conditions must hold: (1) the buyers and sellers must be large; (2) the goods they buy and sell must be homogeneous; and (3) the buyers and sellers must have perfect knowledge of the market. The condition that buyers and sellers must have perfect knowledge has not received much attention in the literature. This assumes that buyers and sellers are independent units. Under colonialism, however, producer groups or individual attempts to sell to other markets outside the colonial market areas and institutions failed. Over the years sellers have had relatively less access to information available to dealers. Buyers such as Gill and Duffus, A. C. Israel (ACII), J. H. Rayner and General Cocoa, by virtue of being multinational corporations, have access to a large pool of information, and have facilities to process the information and use it, as well as the finance capital to back their operations, whereas the producer organizations face entry conditions and institutional impediments. Some multinationals have abused their financial power.

The cocoa futures market has witnessed some malpractices in the past few years. The SELIK bank in Switzerland, a subsidiary of United California Bank, tried to corner the market in 1971, with heavy losses (59). Rountree-Mackintosh manufacturers tried to manipulate the market in 1974 and also incurred heavy losses (60). In light of these and other related facts we recommend that the cocoa futures market in New York and London be internationalized—the organization be reorganized, with producers and consumers holding "seats" on the markets so that policing and rule enforcement will represent the interests of producers and consumers and make it possible for farmer organizations to use the market efficiently. This will tend to equalize the control of the market due to institutional advantages on the part of the buyers.[10]

Implications of non-orderly marketing of cocoa in producer economies

The monopsonistic role that multinational corporations (exporters or dealers) have played in price determination has resulted in non-orderly marketing and unequal distribution of profit margins within the vertical marketing channels. This has affected the rate of capital accumulation in the

Table 9. *Percentage share of cocoa export earnings to country's total export earnings*

Major producing countries (West African)	1963-66 average	1967-70 average	1970
Ghana	66.6	64.9	68.0
Cameroon	24.8	—	—
Ivory Coast	17.6	19.9	20.7
Nigeria	15.2	18.9	14.9

Sources: *International Financial Statistics*. 1971; and *United Nations Yearbook of National Accounts and Statistics, 1967.*

Data for Cameroon was not available. It is believed that the percentage share has gone up.

cocoa export economies of West Africa and also the rate of economic development. Table 9 shows the relative importance of cocoa's share in total foreign exchange earnings.

It has been shown that in the first three periods of the cocoa market history, atomistic producers faced monopsonistic buyers and that the buyers used their monopsonistic power unduly by forming cartels and pools or trusts to maximize profits when there were price squeezes in other channels above the immediate producer channel. In the fourth period (post-World War II), the market structure has been one of oligopolistic competition. The bargaining power of producers has increased relative to the first period (see Table 7). Nevertheless, the producer organizations need both to learn to use the futures markets for hedging purposes, and also to find ways and means to regulate their inventories by finding storage places in temperate zones.

The non-orderly marketing of cocoa and unequal exchange has had a more adverse effect on Ghana than on Nigeria, which has a more diversified agricultural base. Curry and Rothchild believe that the strong diversified base of the Nigerian agricultural system helps it in negotiations for equitable oil prices because it need not be forced by the impatience variable to give in easily, whereas this is true for Ghana. "Impatience" to earn foreign exchange from one crop to service vital sectors of the economy usually forces the Ghana Marketing Board to accept lower prices than it would otherwise do. It is only in exceptional cases—where there is an acute shortage of cocoa—for example, in 1954—that the bargaining power of the producer organizations becomes very strong, due to the "demand intensity" variable—pressure on manufacturers to obtain supplies. In this case the buyers' control power is weakened by their "demand intensity". As a result of the price rise in 1954, manufacturers approached the United Nations through their governments to investigate the cocoa pricing problem. A cocoa study group was then organized to draw up an international commodity agreement (which was finally ratified last year).

The price crises of 1964/65 and 1971/72 both led to political instability in Ghana and in both cases the military took over. In the first case, this was due to overproduction, where producers were unable to regulate supplies. In a simulation study, Kofi (61) has shown that if the 1968 International Cocoa Agreement had been ratified, these low prices would have been averted. The 1971/72 price crisis was due to erroneous forecasts put out by the Gill and Duffus Cocoa Market Reports (See 62, Appendix).

The quest for orderly marketing of cocoa within the vertical markets will have to take place in the theory of industrial organization. Producers will have to use marketing techniques and strategies paralleling those of the cocoa multinational corporations. Furthermore, internationalization of the cocoa futures markets, including the institution of proper regulations, will make it easier for producer organizations to hedge. Such institutional impediments to entry of the use of marketing institutions should be removed.

Conclusions

The development of world trade under the international division of labor under mercantilism, free trade in the nineteenth century, imperialism colonialism, and neo-colonialism involved both an international specialization of labor and a complex transfer of resources, and institutional development. A new order of exchange systems was developed. The exchange system between the primary export economies (developing countries) and the developed countries was uneven, because the atomistic producers faced rich advanced corporations aided by their governments and institutions of their creation. In fact, the economic structures in most of the Third World economies (ex-colonial countries) were determined by the imperial governments (63).

This paper has analysed unequal exchange in the cocoa market, with special reference to the multinational (exporter) corporations. It has been argued here that the power and/or control that the multinational monopsonistic corporations wielded over the atomistic sellers, at times with (imperial) governmental sanctions, reinforced and institutionalized the uneven exchange. It was also argued that the unequal exchange has affected capital accumulation and hence development or industrialization in the primary export economies.

The cocoa industry was chosen for this study with reference to the experience of the West African economies. It is suggested that the African farmers of marketing corporations acquire the skills of the multinational corporations, especially in areas of management and marketing skills, so that they can bargain effectively within the imperfect competitive marketing channels, so that pure profit margins may be evenly distributed to ensure capital formation and economic development.

Notes

[1] Cocoa from which two-thirds of the fat—cocoa butter—has been removed produces chocolate powder. The by-product—the butter—mixed with sugar and molded into bars becomes the familiar eating chocolate. Several firms, precursors of the present multinational cocoa companies, were founded in this period. The firm of Van Houten and Zoon was established in Holland in 1815; Cailler was founded in Vevy, Switzerland, in 1819; Cadbury was founded in 1831 in Birmingham, England.

[2] The "blast" of 1727 was reported by C. J. J. Van Hall in *Cocoa,* MacMillan, London, 1914. Because it takes over five years for the cocoa tree to bear fruit, there are no returns on the initial capital outlay during that time. Capitalist farmers have an "entry" impediment, whereas subsistence farmers, with one foot in the monetized economy and the other in the subsistence sector, do not face such an entry barrier.

[3] For a formal treatment of a production cost comparison between peasant and plantation modes of production, see V. D. Wickizer, "The Smallholder in Tropical Crop Production," *Food Research Institute Studies,* Vol. 1, No. 1, November 1960. More work needs to be done to analyse why, historically, under certain conditions the economic and non-economic peasant mode is more optimal than the plantation mode of production.

[4] Identifiable breakthroughs of African economic initiatives during and after the colonial era should not be characterized as a "recovery of African initiative", as Ranger does. The resourcefulness to adapt, adopt and respond to economic and non-economic signals is a continuous historical process. During the colonial times the African societies sought to accommodate to the new challenge. (For the Ranger thesis see Terrence O. Ranger, "The Recovery of African Initiative in Tanzanian History," The University College, Dar es Salaam Inaugural Lecture No. 2, published by the University College, Dar es Salaam, Tanzania, March 1969.)

[5] It is inconceivable that the cocoa industry in Ivory Coast was started by an authoritarian administrator. Monetization and the desire to engage in cash cropping as an adjunct to subsistence living in pre-capitalist African societies long preceded nineteenth century European colonization.

[6] In the case of Ghana, cocoa has been the highest earner of foreign exchange since the beginning of the present century. In the case of Nigeria, cocoa was the highest earner of foreign exchange from 1946 until 1965, when oil earnings surpassed cocoa.

[7] After the fall of France in 1940 the British Government took over the responsibility of purchasing and marketing Cameroonian cocoa to support the economy of Cameroon. "The actual machinery of purchase followed that in British territory, the same merchant firms in many cases acting as Board's agents. Representatives of the Fighting French authorities normally attended meetings of the Board as assessors . . . For various reasons, shipment of Ivory Coast and Togoland cocoa were not in fact effected during the period under review . . . French West African authorities had themselves assumed control of the purchase of cocoa and its handling to the f.o.b. point . . ." (British Command Papers, Cmd 6554, *Report on Cocoa Control in West Africa 1939-1943 and Statement on Future Policy,* September 1944, Section IX).

[8] The performance test was based on the predictive reliability of the futures price being able to predict the spot price at a contract expiration date (see Kofi 49).

[9] It is unfortunate the United Africa Company study did not provide us with a statistical appendix so we could compare its results with similar studies, since their findings are contrary to Kofi's (28) results.

[10] After World War II, market information on cocoa supply conditions was provided by the Ministry of Agriculture in His Majesty's dominions in West Africa. Since these territories accounted for close to 50 percent of world supplies, such market information had a profound effect on the futures markets price swings. In early 1950 Gill and Duffus, a British firm soon to become the biggest middleman in the cocoa industry, began forecasting demand and supply

estimates. After independence, the speculators on the New York Cocoa Exchange and the London Terminal Markets began relying on the Gill and Duffus crop estimates. This is the historical process by which Gill and Duffus came to control the market information in the industry.

The Food and Agricultural Organization (FAO), a United Nations agency, also issues crop forecasts but their reports are always late because the aggregate world forecasts are compiled from individual government estimates which are forwarded to FAO.

The Gill and Duffus monopoly of market information may soon end, since the International Cocoa Organization, with its headquarters in London, will soon begin publishing market information in the cocoa industry.

[11] The cocoa market pricing institutions—futures markets—are regulated by private members of the New York Cocoa Exchange and the London Terminal Markets (whereas the domestic markets in the United States are under the Commodity Exchange Authority (CEA), a government organization which sets rules governing trade). Members on the Exchanges enjoy certain privileges; for example, they do not have to put down an *original* or *variation margin* when they are engaged in *hedging* or *speculating* activities.

Thus, by internationalization of the cocoa market we mean that producer and consumer organizations and members should be represented on the Boards governing the price determination institutions. In this way producers may also enjoy privileges accorded market members and have equal access to market information and *hedging* activities.

Appendix 1

Power as a function of both dependence and sources of power

Power as the dependent variable can also be measured by using both dependence and sources of power as independent variables. This procedure may even increase the accuracy of measurement.

In sum, the basic model underlying the research reported here may be depicted as follows:

	Power of channel member i over member j	*Power of channel member i over all other members, n*
(1)	$P_{ij} = C_{ij}$	$P_i = \sum_{j-l}^{n} C_{ij}$
(2)	$P_{ij} = f(D_{ij})$	$P_i = f(\sum_{j-l}^{n} D_{ij})$
	$P_{ij} = \alpha D_{ij}$	$P_i = \sum_{j-l}^{n} D_{ij}$

(3) $P_{ij} = f(S_{ij})$ $\qquad$ $P_i = f(\sum_{j-1}^{n} S_{ij})$

$P_{ij} = \beta S_{ij}$ $\qquad$ $P_i = \sum_{j-1}^{n} \beta S_{ij}$

(4) $P_{ij} = f(D_{ij}, S_{ij})$ $\qquad$ $P_i = f(\sum_{j-1}^{n} D_{ij}, \sum_{j-1}^{n} S_{ij})$

$P_{ij} = \alpha D_{ij} + \beta S_{ij}$ $\qquad$ $P_i = \sum_{j-1}^{n} \alpha D_{ij} + \sum_{j-1}^{n} \beta S_{ij}$

where:

P_{ij} = power of channel member i over member j.
C_{ij} = control of i over the decision variables in the marketing strategy of j.
P_i = power of i over all other members with whom i is vertically linked.
D_{ij} = dependence of i on j.
α = direction coefficient of dependence: if $D_{ij} > 0$, $\alpha = -1$; if $D_{ij} < 0$, $\alpha = +1$.
S_{ij} = sources of power held by i relative to j.
β = direction coefficient of power sources: if $S_{ij} > 0$, $\beta = +1$; if $S_{ij} < 0$, $\beta = -1$.

Bibliography

1. Raoul Prebisch, "The Role of Commercial Policy in Underdeveloped Countries", *American Economic Review,* Vol. 49, No. 2, May 1959, pp. 251-273.
2. Paul P. Streeten, "The Trade Game", *World Development,* Vol. 1, Nos. 1 and 2, Feb., 1973, pp. 1-2.
3. Stephen S. Hymer, "The Efficiency (Contradictions) of Multinational Corporations", *American Economic Review,* Vol. 60, May 1970, pp. 441-48.
4. Gerald M. Meier, "The 'Carry-over' Problem—Note", in G. M. Meier, ed., *Leading Issues in Development Economics,* Oxford University Press, 1964, p. 373.
5. Ibid.

6. Celso Furtado, "The Concept of External Dependence in the Study of Underdevelopment", in Charles K. Wilber, ed., *The Political Economy of Development and Underdevelopment,* Random House, New York, 1973, pp. 118-123.

7. Ivan Erneholm, *Cocoa Production of South America: Historical Development and Present Geographical Distribution,* Gothenburg, Sweden, 1948.

8. Eileen M. Chatt, *Cocoa-Cultivation Processing Analysis,* Interscience Publishers, Inc., New York, 1953.

9. Polly Hill, *The Migrant Cocoa Farmers of Southern Ghana: A Study in Rural Capitalism,* Cambridge, England, 1963.

10. R. Galletti, K. D. S. Baldwin and I. O. Dina, *Nigerian Cocoa Farmers,* Oxford University Press, 1955.

11. Allen McPhee, *The Economic Revolution in British West Africa,* George Routledge and Sons Ltd., 1926, p. 40.

12. Ibid., p. 44.

13. D. H. Urquhart, *Report on the Cocoa Industry in the French Ivory Coast,* Cadbury Brothers Ltd., Bournville, 1955, p. 14.

14. Allan McPhee, op.cit., p. 42.

15. Stephen Hymer, op.cit., p. 441.

16. Richard D. Wolff, "Modern Imperialism, the View from the Metropolis", *American Economic Review,* Vol. 60, May 1970, pp. 225-230.

17. Marvin P. Miracle, "Market Structure in Commodity Trade and Capital Accumulation in West Africa", in Reed Moyer and Stanley C. Hollander, eds., *Markets and Marketing in Developing Economies,* Richard D. Irwin, Ill., 1968.

18. R. H. Holton, "Marketing Structure and Economic Development", *Quarterly Journal of Economics,* August 1953.

19. P. T. Bauer, "Concentration in Tropical Trade: Some Aspects and Implications of Oligopoly", *Economica,* Nov., 1953, pp. 302-21.

20. Ida Greaves, "The Character of British Colonial Trade", *The Journal of Political Economy,* Feb., 1954, Vol. LXII, No. 1, p. 6.

21. Ibid., p. 5.

22. Ibid., p. 2.

23. P. T. Bauer, op.cit.

24. J. E. Flint, *Sir George Goldie and the Making of Nigeria,* London, 1960.

25. Scott R. Pearson, "The Economic Imperialism of the Royal Niger Company", *Food Research Institute Studies in Agricultural Economics, Trade and Development,* Vol. X, No. 1, 1971, pp. 69-88.

26. P. T. Bauer and B. S. Yamey, "Economics of Marketing Reform", *Journal of Political Economy,* LXII, 1954, pp. 210-235.

27. W. F. Mueller, "Some Market Structure Considerations in Economic Development", *Journal of Farm Economics,* XLI, May 1959.

28. Tetteh A. Kofi, "Vertical Price Relations in the International Cocoa Market and Implications for Ghana's Marketing Policies", in Kotey, Okali, Rourke, eds., *Cocoa Economics Research Conference,* April 5-12, 1973, Institute of Statistical and Social Studies, University of Ghana, Legon, 1974.

29. —, "A Framework for Comparing the Efficiency of Futures Markets", *American Journal of Agricultural Economics,* Vol. 55, No. 4, Nov., 1973, pp. 584-94.

30. *The New York Times,* July 29, 1925, p. 16.

31. —, Aug., 30, 1928, p. 30.

32. Ibid.

33. "Report of the Commission on the Marketing of West African Cocoa" (The Nowell Commission), H.M.S.O., London, CMD 5845, 1938, p. vii.

34. Ibid.

35. P. Ady, "Bulk Purchasing and the Colonial Production", *Oxford Institute of Statistics Bulletin*, Vol. 9, No. 10, Oct., 1947, pp. 322-340.

36. E. R. Hawkins, "Vertical Price Relationship", in Cox and Anderson, eds., *Theory in Marketing,* Richard D. Irwin, Homewood, Ill., 1950.

37. Bruce Mallen, "Introducing the Marketing Channel to Price Theory", *Journal of Marketing,* Vol. 28, July 1964, pp. 29-33.

38. Louis W. Stern, *Distribution Channels: Behavioral Dimension,* Houghton Mifflin Co., Boston, 1969, p. 5.

39. Ibid, p. 135.

40. R. L. Curry and D. Rothchild, "On Economic Bargaining Between African Governments and Multinational Companies", *The Journal of Modern African Studies,* Vol. 12, No. 2, 1974.

41. Adel I. El-Ansary and Louis Stern, "Power Measurement in the Distributive Channel", *Journal of Marketing Research,* Feb., 1972.

42. Tetteh A. Kofi, op.cit. (28).

43. Robert L. Clodius and Willard F. Mueller, "Market Structure Analysis as an Orientation for Research in Agricultural Economics", *Journal of Agricultural Economics,* Aug., 1961.

44. Joe S. Bain, *Industrial Organization,* John Wiley, Inc., New York, 1959, p. 7.

45. J. D. Coppock, *International Economic Instability,* McGraw Hill, New York, 1962, p. 46.

46. U. K. Hackman, "The Marketing of Ghana's Cocoa", *Ghanaian Bulletin of Agricultural Economics,* Vol. 1, No. 2, Sept., 1961.

47. F. W. Taussig, "Is Market Price Determinate?", *Quarterly Journal of Economics,* Vol. XXV, May 1921, pp. 394-411.

48. Henry H. Bakken, "The Factors Favoring a Futures Contract for Live Hogs Outweigh those Against it", in H. H. Bakken, ed., *Futures Trading in Livestock Origins and Concepts,* Mimir Publishers, Madison, Wisconsin, 1970.

49. Tetteh A. Kofi, op.cit. (28).

50. Anon., "What the Producer Receives for Crops", *Statistical and Economic Review,* United Africa Company, March 1948.

51. P. Ady, op.cit. (35).

52. Tetteh A. Kofi, op.cit. (29).

53. Holbrook Working, "A Theory of Anticipatory Prices", *American Economic Review,* Vol. 48, May 1958, pp. 188-99.

54. Tetteh A. Kofi, "World Cocoa Prices and Underdevelopment in Ghana", *The Legon Observer* (Ghana), Vol. VII, Nos. 18, 19, 22, Sept., and Nov., 1972.

55. —, "World Cocoa Prices and Underdevelopment in Ghana—A Rejoinder", *Legon Observer* (Ghana), Vol. VII, No. 24, Dec., 1972, pp. 578-81.

56. —, "World Cocoa Prices and Underdevelopment in Ghana—A Rejoinder", Legon Observer (Ghana) Vol. VII, No. 26, Dec., 1972, pp. 624–31.

57. —, op.cit., (29).

58. *United Nations Conference on Trade and Development,* "Marketing and Distributive System for Cocoa", Report by the UNCTAD Secretariat, TD/B/C.1/132, Feb., 6, 1972, Annex, p. 3.

59. Anon., "Cocoa Futures Leaves a Bitter Taste", Business Week, Sept., 20, 1970, p. 32.

60. Anon., "How the Reckless Chocolate Soldier Got Gobbled Up", *The Economist,* July 14, 1973.

61. Tetteh A. Kofi, op.cit. (29).

62. —, op.cit. (23;).

63. Richard D. Wolff, op.cit. (16).

Biplab Dasgupta

The Changing Role of the Major International Oil Firms

Introduction

No discussion on large international firms is complete without reference to the seven leading firms in the oil industry which are collectively known as "majors" or the "Seven Sisters". Five of these firms have their domiciles in the United States—Standard Oil of New Jersey (or Exxon), Socony Mobil Oil, Standard Oil of California, Gulf Oil, and Texas Oil. Of the other two, one is British (British Petroleum) and the other is jointly owned by British and Dutch interests (Royal Dutch/Shell). A French company, called CFP, is often described as "the eighth major". In addition to these firms, three other types of firms operate in the world oil market: (a) the "minors", mostly American international companies which are quite large by almost any standard other than that of the oil industry (for example, Philips, Standard Oil of Indiana, Occidental); (b) the state-owned companies like Kuwait National Oil Company; some of them (for example, ENI) operate as international firms like "minors"; and (c) the oil firms of East European countries.

Oil-importing countries do not constitute a homogeneous group. For example, the United States is the largest oil-producing country in the world, but because of its high level of demand for oil, it is a net importer. Some of the oil-importing countries (like the UK, Holland or the USA) are to varying extents closely associated with the oil-producing interests, through the operations of the large international oil firms which are domiciled there.[1] Furthermore, one needs to make a distinction between rich and poor oil-importing countries.

The main objective of this paper is to analyse the major characteristics of these firms and the implications of those characteristics for both the oil-producing and the oil-consuming countries in an historical perspective as well as in the light of the current oil crisis. In section II we shall examine the main characteristics of the large international firms. Section III will briefly cover the current oil crisis in an historical perspective. In section IV we shall examine the future role of these firms in the oil-producing and oil-consuming countries, and in section V we shall look at the role of these firms in the three oil-producing countries of Africa. Readers will also find a postscript on the political economy of the current oil crisis.

II. Main characteristics of large international firms in oil

The four main characteristics of these firms are that they are: (a) large, (b) multinational, and (c) vertically integrated organisations operating in an (d) oligopolistic market.

Large

Their vast size and financial resources enable the majors to enter into costly, high-risk, capital-intensive ventures, like finding oil in the North Sea or Alaska. Very few firms outside the oil industry would have the financial resources to commit to such long-term massive investment or to maintain such an enormous budget on R & D as the major oil firms do. Their research activities also help to maintain their technological superiority over non-major rivals. Moreover, very few countries of the world possess the resources, the skilled manpower, and the intimate knowledge of the industry and the world market to bargain on equal terms with these mammoth entities.[2]

Multinational

The "multinational" character of these firms has many interesting implications. Because these firms are multinational, their activities often give rise to serious conflicts between their own *global* objectives and the *national* objectives of the host governments. The history of the oil industry is full of such conflicts. For the oil companies, what matters most is the aggregate profit over all their operations and covering all the countries in which their affiliates and associates are functioning. On the other hand, the national governments are interested in increasing their own revenues from oil exports; or if they are importers and poor, their main concern is to minimise the cost of oil imports through refinery construction, package deals with better prices and terms, and some investment in exploratory activities. Sometimes the national interests of the host governments coincide with the international objectives of these oil firms, sometimes they do not. The following are two typical examples where their interests do not converge:

(a) The amount of crude oil to be extracted from the oilfields of a particular country by a multinational company, which owns oilfields in many countries, depends on a large set of factors, such as the overall crude oil needs of that company, the ownership structure for that particular oilfield (whether it is wholly owned or jointly owned with the government or other companies), as well as the cost, quality and the location of such crude.[3] The amount which the oil company decides to lift may not agree with what the government of the country wants. The latter may want more (to earn more revenue) or less (to conserve its depleting resources) than the companies would consider appropriate on the basis of their global activities. Some of the recent examples of such conflicts of interest are related to the oil companies' practice of acquiring concession rights on a prospective oil-bearing area in order to keep off potential competitors, but with no immediate intention of exploring and producing oil from that area, since its requirements are already being met at a cheaper cost from other sources.[4] There are also instances—as in the case of Iraq in the sixties—where the consortium of oil companies may penalise a host country by offtaking a smaller than usual amount in the event of serious disagreements between them.[5]

(b) Conflicts of interest may also exist over refining crude oil. Many oil-importing countries aspire to be self-sufficient in refinery products in order to minimise costs of imported oil. The conflict arises because the interests of the oil companies may best be served by building fewer and larger refineries (subject to the constraint of transport cost from the refinery to the consumption points), thereby reaping economies of scale and being flexible enough to consume various types of crude and to produce a varying range of output-mix.[6]

One implication of this "multinational" character is that conflicts between the national governments and oil companies become matters of international diplomacy and involve the foreign offices of their mother countries.[7] A good example of this was the series of international political crises following the nationalisation of the Iranian oil industry by Mosadeq in 1951, when both the British and the US governments used their diplomatic influence over other countries to block (successfully) the exports of Iranian oil, which eventually led to the violent overthrow of the Mosadeq government in 1954. More recently (in the sixties), the threat of stoppage of US aid was applied against Ceylon and Peru when they nationalised the oil companies owned by US firms.[8] In return for this support, the major oil companies maintain a close relationship with the foreign offices of their mother countries, and help them in their dealings with the governments of the countries where the companies operate.[9]

Oil being an important material for both war and peace-time economies, the governments of the mother countries of the "majors" are very keen to retain their access to oil reserves through the latter. There are often conflicts between different mother countries for influence in the oil-producing areas, which then lead to the sort of compromise which is reflected in the ownership structure of several oil consortia in the Middle East. Iraq Petroleum Company, whose ownership is shared by British (British Petroleum 23.75%), Dutch-British (Royal Dutch/Shell 23.75%), French (CFP 23.75%), and American (Standard Oil of New Jersey and Socony Mobil jointly 23.75%)

interests, as well as an independent (Gulbenkian 5%), is a good example of the diplomatic involvement of several great powers in the oil industry of the Middle East.

Vertically integrated

A main characteristic of these large, international firms is their participation in all stages of activities in the oil industry, from exploration, development and extraction of crude oil to transporting, refining and marketing. This, combined with the multinational character of their operations, has several important consequences for the economies of the countries in which they operate.[10]

A major consequence of vertical integration is that a great deal of the commercial and trading transactions which take place between countries is no more than intra-company transaction between the affiliates of the same mother company. Hence, the prices charged and paid for those are not the results of 'arm's length deals', but are internal bookkeeping prices, or transfer prices involving various branches of the same corporate body. For example, when the crude-producing affiliate of Exxon in Saudi Arabia sells crude to the Exxon refinery at Bombay, from the point of view of the latter (assuming no interference from the Government), the amount purchased is not dependent on the quoted price.

A corollary of the above is that what matters most to a vertically integrated firm is the overall profit from all its operations, and not the 'profits' shown by its individual constituents. It is possible for such a firm to manipulate the transfer prices for inter-affiliate transactions, and thereby to produce such bookkeeping profits or losses for individual affiliates as are consistent with their overall global objectives. In fact, the tendency for the vertically integrated oil firm is to show a higher profit in crude production, because the latter usually receives more tax concessions than other activities, and to show smaller profit or even losses from downstream activities like refining or marketing.[11]

The profits or losses shown by the affiliates of such a firm for production, transportation, refining and other activities in various countries have no particular significance to the firm concerned, except as a means of tax avoidance and maximisation of aggregate profit over all activities.[12]

On the other hand, the way such prices and profits are shown is highly significant from the point of view of the governments of the countries in which they operate. The larger the price at which the crude-producing affiliate of Company X in Country A sells crude to its refining affiliate in Country B, the higher becomes the foreign exchange cost of oil imports and the lower becomes the government's tax revenue on profit in refining in Country B.

It was not until the sixties that the governments of the poor oil-importing countries came to understand the implications of vertical integration for the crude oil prices which they paid. For example, even in 1961, the Government of India was not aware that the refineries in India, their crude suppliers in the Middle East and a whole range of intermediate dealers who stood between the refinery and the crude supplier, were all merely parts of one and the same corporate organisation.[13] One of the reasons for having so many intermediate organisations was to maintain secrecy about oil prices.

Oligopolistic

The oil industry is a classic example of an oligopolistic market with seven dominant oligopolistic firms and a large number of smaller firms on the fringe. In the 'golden days' of the oil cartel, about four-fifths of crude production, refining and marketing was controlled by the "majors". Even in 1960, the percentages were 84, 74 and 70, respectively, for these three main activities.[14] Even these figures underestimate their influence on the market, since many of the non-major companies are associates of "majors" and are dependent on them for crude supply or for marketing of crude oil or products.

The four basic ingredients of the oligopolistic behaviour in the oil industry are as follows:

World parity pricing system

This is a simple, easily understood, basing-point price formula which is jointly adopted by the oligopolists. Until 1945, the US Gulf was the basing point, and the price of oil anywhere in the world was fixed by adding transport cost from the US Gulf to that consumption point, irrespective of where the oil actually came from. This formula was followed, even when no oil was imported from the United States by a consumption centre, in order to minimise disputes about prices between the oligopolists and the consequent risks of a price war. One consequence of this price policy, from the point of view of many oil-consuming countries, was that they did not benefit from their possible proximity to oil-producing areas, since for the purpose of price fixation it was only their distance from the US Gulf which mattered. For example, the price of oil produced in Burma was cheaper in London than in Calcutta (which was 6,000 miles nearer to Burma) because London was closer to the US Gulf.[15]

After 1945, the Persian Gulf was made the second basing point for the Eastern Hemisphere market. By mutual consent, the "majors" now declared the same 'posted prices' f.o.b. Persian Gulf for crudes of different variety and a wide range of oil products; these were then taken as bases for price fixation in the consumption centres. Even during the sixties, the years of oil surplus when the prices of crude oil and products declined, the f.o.b. Persian Gulf posted prices continued as the base from which discounts in percentage form were deducted.

At one time, the "majors" used to cite the fact that the oil prices were the same everywhere as evidence that the oil market was 'perfectly competitive'; while the reality was (and even now is) that the dominant oligopolists strictly adhered to a commonly-agreed price formula in order to minimise the risks of price wars among themselves.

Market-Sharing Arrangements

The history of the oil industry contains a number of explicit, written, market-sharing agreements between the oligopolists. Sometimes markets were divided up territorially (as in the 1909 agreement), sometimes by percentages (as in the 1928 'as is' agreement), and yet other times by a combination of percentage shares and absolute amounts in a specific market (as in India during 1905-1928). A series of agreements were drawn up during the thirties to regulate the distribution to the rest of the world of Soviet and Rumanian oil, which were not controlled by the "majors", without disrupting the 'world price structure'. Since the forties, written agreements are unknown, because of the fear of US anti-trust legislation, but the behaviour of the "majors" in this respect is influenced by the unwritten code of conduct of the oil industry against encroachment into each other's territory.[16]

Price wars

As distinct from price competition, a price war results in reduced prices only for a short period and, more often than not, is followed by the restoration of prices to the pre-price war level. Like the price-formula and market-sharing agreements, price wars were an interesting feature of the oil industry up to the Second World War. A price war was usually initiated by a company which was dissatisfied with its market share, and was used as a weapon to force its rivals to accept a redistribution favourable to the company initiating the price war.[17]

In many cases, price wars are also initiated when it is thought that some of the provisions of a previous agreement have been violated by a rival (e.g., the price wars of 1909, 1911, and 1928). There was a tendency for these price wars to spread to many markets, and these 'world price wars' caused serious financial losses to all the oligopolists. The 1928 'as is' agreement was an attempt to stop these costly contests, and, since then, except for rare instances of very short-term and highly localised price wars in the petrol trade, price wars between the oligopolists have become a rare phenomenon. Not that competition between them has been completely eliminated: these usually now take the form of non-price competitions, except when selling crude to independent refineries; but even in this case, prices are accompanied by varying credit facilities and freight rates which make them non-comparable.[18]

Since 1928, most of the price wars have been fought between the "majors" collectively on one side, and the newcomers to the oil trade. Before 1959, the competition of "independents" was localised, because of the smallness of their organisations and the virtual absence of non-major sources of crude oil in the Eastern Hemisphere. The "majors" took part in those price wars in order to bring the independents to their knees, and succeeded in either eliminating them from the market, or in forcing them to become appendages to their corporate entities through long-term supply arrangements. Since 1959, such competition is no longer localised, with the entry into the market of a number of large independents, such as Philips, E.N.I., Standard Oil of Indiana, and Occidental.[19]

Organisational interdependence

Apart from explicit or tacit pricing or market-sharing arrangements between themselves, the oligopolists also jointly own a number of important enterprises in the oil industry. In the marketing and refining sectors are many familiar names, like Caltex (jointly owned by Standard Oil of California and Texas Oil), Burmah-Shell (jointly owned by Burmah Oil, an associate of British Petroleum, and Royal Dutch/Shell), Standard-Vacuum (jointly owned by Standard Oil of New Jersey and Socony Mobil, although the partnership was dissolved in the sixties). More important, however, are crude-producing organisations, such as Aramco of Saudi Arabia (jointly owned by four US "majors"), Kuwait Oil Company (jointly owned by British Petroleum and Gulf Oil), Iranian Consortium (where the seven "majors" together own 79%, CFP 6%, and US independents 5%), and the crude-producing organisations of Iraq, Qatar, and Abu Dhabi (where four "majors" and CFP together own 95%, and the rest is owned by a group of American independent companies), where the major companies are jointly involved. In addition, there are several long-term supply arrangements (e.g., between Royal Dutch/Shell and Gulf Oil, under which the latter supplies its entire share of Kuwait oil to the former) and crude—and product—swapping arrangements in order to iron out localised surpluses and deficits of the individual companies without having to arrange long-distance transportation.

As the discussion in Section III will show, the oligopolistic dominance of the oil market by the "majors" weakened after 1959. Until then, however, they were virtually the only suppliers of crude and oil products in the world outside the United States and the Communist countries. Furthermore, as long as they maintained a common front against other competitors and the governments of the oil-consuming countries, it was not easy to argue with them about prices, or to induce them to build refineries where this was not in conformity with their own interests, or to plan for a national, self-reliant oil industry. Not only that, they were hostile to newcomers in the oil industry; the "majors" were in the habit of threatening immediate stoppage of oil supply if the governments of consuming countries attempted to follow a policy which would make them less dependent on "majors". A good example of this was the refusal of the "majors" to refine cheaper crude from the Soviet Union in 1960 in Cuba and India, and another example was their threat to close down their business in India in the following year when the government insisted on a reduction in product prices.

III. The historical background to the current oil crisis

The history of the oil industry can be conveniently divided into the following three phases in terms of the role of the large international firms:

(i) the period until 1959, when the oligopolistic domination of the world market by the "majors" was virtually complete;

(ii) the sixties, when many new competitors arose in the oil market, producing an excess of supply over demand for oil; an era of declining oil prices, which led to the formation of the Organisation of the Petroleum Exporting Countries (OPEC);

(iii) the seventies, when the demand-supply conditions were reversed and prices increased, OPEC became stronger, pushing the major companies into the background in oil negotiations.

One of the important factors in causing this change was the re-entry of Soviet oil exports into the world market in 1958, and on a large scale in 1959. Before 1917, Russian oil was the chief competitor of the American oil in the world market. After the Revolution, Russian oil exports virtually disappeared, except for a brief appearance in the late twenties and early thirties (one of which caused the 1928 price war between the "majors"), until 1959, when a shipment of Soviet crude oil was sold to a Japanese independent refiner. Very soon, Soviet exports spread to Italy, Germany, France, India,

Greece and other countries, and everywhere these were sold at a price lower than world parity price, and often as part of a package deal involving other products under terms favourable to their partners.[20]

A second, and no less important, factor was the emergence of a number of new competitors who succeeded in finding oil in the neutral zone between Saudi Arabia and Kuwait, and afterwards also in Libya. Since they had no ready marketing outlet, these "minors" were prepared to sell their crude at a much lower than prevailing price to the independent refineries of Western Europe and Japan.[21]

Unlike the "majors", who possessed their own marketing outlets, both the Soviet Union (and Rumania, another oil-producing country in the Communist bloc) and the "minors" were in addition prepared to build refineries in partnership with the governments in order to receive priority over their competitors in supplying crude to these markets. They were also willing to help the governments with exploratory activities as contractors or with a minority share in the crude-producing company, terms which were unacceptable to the "majors".

Both of these factors made the oil industry more competitive, particularly from the point of view of the oil-consuming countries, who were now presented with many alternative sources from which they could buy oil. Inevitably, the world parity prices crumbled; in some markets, crude was being sold at prices 30-49% below f.o.b. Persian Gulf 'posted prices'. "Only fools and affiliates pay posted prices", was the popular joke of the time in the oil industry; but even the affiliates were finding it increasingly difficult to pay full 'posted prices', as the Governments of the oil-consuming countries became more aware of the changed conditions of the world oil industry.

The "majors" were as a result forced to reduce 'posted prices' in order to meet this competition. This, however, led to serious conflicts with oil-producing countries, who had been since the early fifties entitled to a half share in the profits from oil, and the decline in oil prices meant for them a lower oil revenue per barrel of oil sold. OPEC was formed in 1960 with the primary objective of halting this decline in oil prices, and they succeeded in their aim to stabilise the 'posted prices'. What this meant in effect was that for the purpose of calculating the tax revenues of the governments of oil-producing countries, 'posted prices' (which were pegged at their 1960 level) were used as the base but in practice the oil companies were selling oil at prices which were lower than 'posted prices'. In other words, while theoretically the profit from oil was split equally between the companies and the governments, in practice, because the realised prices were below posted prices, the host countries received more than half the actual profit.[22]

Two other objectives of OPEC were (a) to induce increases in oil prices, on the grounds that the f.o.b. Persian Gulf price of crude was a small proportion of the price the ultimate consumers paid for oil; and that while the prices of industrial goods had been increasing over time, the oil prices had remained at a very low level for many years; and (b) to secure a greater degree of participation in the oil industries of their own countries.[23]

Their ability to achieve (a) depended on their success in controlling production. Although some attempts were made towards *pro rata* allocation of production, they failed during the sixties. Not all the oil producers were members of OPEC; the Soviet Union was an important outsider. Some of the oil producers like Libya had just begun production, and they were unwilling to accept any *pro rata* arrangements based on existing production shares of the various countries. There were also political problems: Iran could be played against the Arabs; the 'conservative' Arabs (like Saudi Arabia or Kuwait) could be played against the 'progressive' Arabs (like Iraq, and after the coup, Libya). More success was achieved with (b), as the state-owned oil companies were formed which entered into many joint exploration agreements with "minors".

Realised prices were low and declining all through the sixties. New oil fields in Libya, Nigeria, Algeria and Abu Dhabi sustained the condition of an excess of supply over demand, and some experts—notably Maurice Adelman of MIT—confidently forecast a price of one dollar per barrel crude by the seventies. Adelman's argument was simple: the production cost of oil (at 8 to 20 cents per barrel) was too low in relation to the market price of \$1.30 to \$1.60, and he expected that further competition would bring down the latter to a level nearer the 'floor price'. He recognised that the oil market was not that competitive, and that there was a growing pressure from OPEC for higher prices, but thought that the latter would not succeed in uniting and controlling production to effect such price increases.[24]

The changed situation in the seventies has been described in the postscript. The question to ask is, how was it possible for crude-oil prices to increase from about \$1.28 for 24° API[25] in 1970 to \$11.65 per barrel after October 1973? One reason for this is the current fear that oil reserves will be exhausted in another 35 to 40 years. This fear may not be well-founded—the 'proved' reserves are usually conservative estimates, the 'probable' reserves are quite high, and there are possibilities of abundant supplies of non-conventional oil from tar sand, shale and coal. It is the general experience in the oil industry that periods of optimism about future supplies are followed by periods of unfounded pessimism, while the 'proved' reserves continously increase with further exploratory work.[26] What is certain, however, is that whereas a number of large new oil fields were discovered during the sixties, excepting for the North Sea, the record of the seventies has so far not been very impressive, and the production-reserve ratio of most oil fields has been rising. Furthermore, this reduced rate of discovery of 'proved' crude reserves has been combined with an accelerated rate of growth in demand, particularly in the US and Japan. The regulation of crude production by Arab oil producers was now possible for three other reasons:

(a) the Soviet exports were no longer an economically major threat, with the increased demand for oil within that country, which has furthermore been politically close to the Arabs;[27]

(b) the contradiction between new and old producers is not so significant now, since countries like Libya, Algeria and Abu Dhabi have reached their peak production levels;

(c) politically the Arabs were never so united as at present, particularly after the October 1973 war. What needs to be stressed, however, is that prices began rising in 1970, long before the 1973 war, although the war has no doubt strengthened the political will of the Arabs. Whereas OPEC's demand for higher prices failed in the sixties because of their inability to control production, after the 1973 war it has been possible both to increase the price and to regulate production.

Perhaps more remarkable than these price increases is the increasing participation by the governments in running the oil industry. In 1971, Algeria nationalised its oil industry, and Libya nationalised BP. By 1973, the Libyan Government had 51% ownership in other concessions, Nigeria took over 35% of Shell-BP concessions, and Saudi Arabia, Qatar, Abu Dhabi, Iraq and Kuwait took over 25% of equity in oil consortia, and made agreements with the oil companies that by 1982 their share would be 51%. In January 1974, the Kuwait Government acquired 60% of ownership in the Kuwait Oil Company, followed by similar negotiating objectives in Saudi Arabia and Qatar. But the most significant was the nationalisation of the Iranian oil industry in 1973 by the same Shah who overthrew Mosadeq and denationalised the Iranian oil industry in 1954.

The situation as it stands in mid-1974 contrasts sharply with that prevailing in the oil industry two decades ago. Crude prices are no longer fixed by the "majors", this role having been taken over by the oil-producing states. The companies no longer control oil production in the Middle East, and majority ownership has passed into the hands of the governments. Moreover, even in the sphere of marketing—where their dominance was decisive in the clash with Mosadeq—many oil-consuming countries of West Europe and the less-developed world have been busily working out bilateral deals on oil directly with the governments of oil-producing countries, by-passing the companies. Whereas their mother-country governments were so vigorous in the past in defending company interests in the host countries, and often turned a blind eye to their evasion of tax and anti-trust laws, now these governments are often more concerned with maintaining good relations with, and flow of oil from, the oil-producing countries.[28]

What the oil companies are losing in terms of control over the industry is being partly compensated by the lucrative profits they have made, caused by higher oil prices; most "majors" have increased their profit by 60% to 100%

over the past year.[29] Their control over a substantial part of the marketing network and refining capacity should continue to produce good profit figures for them for a long time to come. The nationalisation of their interests has not necessarily jeopardised their access to crude oil; Iran, for example, has agreed to supply crude to the erstwhile members of oil consortia over the next 20 years. Moreover, where the companies' interests have not been fully nationalised, they are continuing to manage the industry; it will take several years before the Kuwaitis, Libyans and Saudis are able to run their own industries independently of the oil companies.

According to one theory, it was Arameo, the US-owned oil consortium of Saudi Arabia, which encouraged its host government in 1973 to press for higher prices, their motive being to gather as much profit as possible from their operation before the eventual nationalisation of the industry.[30] Some even saw the complicity of the US Government with the Sheikdoms in their decision to increase prices, with the objective of making research on non-conventional oil and non-oil substitutes economically viable.[31] There is no way of testing these theories, although two points are clear:

(1) no one has ever suggested that the oil companies voluntarily handed over the control of the industry to the oil-producing countries; and

(2) the demand-supply conditions in the seventies, coupled with the growing stature and effectiveness of OPEC, were the primary causes for oil price increases, although it is not impossible that, once they felt that their days in the Middle East were numbered, the "majors" encouraged OPEC governments to go for further increases.

IV. The future of the large international firms

What is the future role of the large international firms in the oil-producing and oil-consuming countries? From the point of view of the existing oil-producing countries in the Middle East, the 'risk-bearing' function of these companies is no longer of much relevance. The element of 'risk' involved in many exploratory activities is not that high, and in some of these countries, such as Saudi Arabia, Kuwait or Abu Dhabi, the production-reserve ratio is too low to encourage a massive programme for exploration. Moreover, at the present there is no shortage of internal funds for such activities if these countries should decide to go in for intensive wildcat drilling. Nevertheless, the oil-producing countries are still dependent on the foreign interests in three fields: (a) technology, (b) administration, and (c) marketing. For a long time the major oil companies have ignored the local demands for the training of indigenous personnel; the presence of a handful of local personnel in high technical or administrative positions was hardly anything more than symbolic. It was only during the sixties that through the state-owned companies and with the help of international "minors" some progress was made towards the training of local personnel. Even today, although the local personnel are capable of performing the day-to-day routine activities, they lack the confidence and skill to handle breakdowns. The oil-producing countries differ among themselves in their ability to run the industry—from Iran, which has a surplus of technical personnel, to Abu Dhabi, which is almost totally dependent on foreign personnel for high-skilled jobs. With further training of local personnel and a greater freedom of movement of skilled personnel among the oil-producing countries (which is inhibited by political factors, such as the mutual suspicion between Iran and her Arab neighbours), this technological constraint would, one hopes, be removed in the future. But even in the short run the technological dependence on the "majors" is not unavoidable. Unlike the situation 15 years ago, today there are many suppliers of technology in the world market, including the "minors", the East Europeans, the Japanese and the companies like ENI, and equity ownership is no longer a price which must be paid to foreign interests for buying technology.

Perhaps more serious than the technological constraint from a long-term point of view is the marketing constraint. Until very recently an overwhelming proportion of the total crude and refinery production passed through the hands of the "majors", who acted as intermediaries between the oil-exporting and the oil-importing countries. Because they owned many different types of crude, operated refineries with a wide range of product-mix, conducted their business in hundreds of markets with widely varying demand patterns for oil products, and owned tanker fleets to carry oil from a large number of producing areas, it was possible for them to balance the demand and supply for different types of crude and products at the world level, if not singly at least collectively, through long-term supply arrangements and temporary swapping arrangements. In contrast, the governments of the oil-producing countries do not own elaborate marketing networks; because they rely on a limited range of crudes and products, it is not possible for them to satisfy all types of consumers or to meet short-term shortages or surpluses in individual markets. At the moment—with the cloud of oil shortage hanging over the industry—the marketing problem is not so serious; in fact, the buyers themselves are eager to sign up for long-term agreements or to bid enthusiastically for crudes of all varieties which are offered for sale. Nevertheless, this condition may not last indefinitely; with further discoveries of oil and the possibilities of technological breakthroughs in producing non-conventional oil and oil substitutes, in the future it may be necessary for the oil-producing countries to build their own tanker fleet and to strengthen their own marketing arrangements. It is also necessary for various reasons for such marketing activities to be co-ordinated through an agency like OPEC; firstly, because the marketing sector is the stronghold of the large international "majors" and no member country of OPEC would be able to match their strength singlehandedly; secondly, because such co-ordination would make crude supply more flexible from the viewpoint of consumers; and thirdly, because without this co-ordination there is the risk of the member countries following widely divergent pricing policies which are in line with their own individual development programmes.

Coming now to the poor oil-importing countries, their future relationship with the major international oil companies can be considered under three separate headings—crude production, refining, and marketing.

Contrary to the popular view, the large international companies are usually 'risk averters'; this is why an overwhelming proportion of their drilling effort is concentrated on areas with proved oil prospects (like the Middle East) or in or near large Western oil-consuming countries, which are politically stable from their viewpoint. Poor oil-consuming countries with uncertain prospects for oil do not figure highly on their list of priorities. Even when they acquire concessions in those countries and dig a few holes (as Stanvac did in India—taking more than ten years to drill ten wells), the primary motive is to keep potential rivals away, rather than to find oil. With the changed conditions in the oil industry over the past year, it is not unlikely that this attitude of the international oil companies towards exploratory work in oil-consuming poor countries will somewhat change, in order to reduce their dependence on Middle East crude. But the 'political risk' (e.g., nationalisation or the country concerned joining OPEC) of such investment would always be high from the point of view of international companies. This explains the emphasis they place on exploration in Alaska or the North Sea, where the 'political risk' is low.[32]

The reluctance of the major companies to invest in exploration in poor oil-consuming countries, many of whom are now desperate to find at least some oil within their boundaries, may not be a bad thing from the countries' point of view. Unlike the situation 15 years ago, it is now possible to receive technological help from foreign collaborators without conferring equity ownership on them, and there is little justification for thinking that the latter would be any less successful than the "majors" in discovering oil. The history of the oil industry is full of stories of oil explorers with limited means or experience or both; for example, William Knox d'Arcy, who discovered oil in Iran, was a businessman of modest means; Occidental, which has been so successful in finding oil in Libya, had no previous experience in this industry; and the Japanese oil companies are continuing to find oil without much of either. In a large number of cases, after a small explorer has found oil, he has been bought up by a major company. Leaving aside very highly expensive explorations with the most advanced technology, like the North Sea drilling, the success rates of large international firms are not appreciably better than those for the other firms.

The emergence of the OPEC countries as a powerful force in the oil industry has opened up new opportunities for the poor oil-consuming countries, particularly the possibilities of joint exploratory activities both in OPEC and poor oil-consuming countries with the technical help of "minors" or East European countries. From the point of view of the OPEC countries this would be a fruitful investment of their surplus funds in an industry with which they are familiar. It would also be politically effective, both in creating goodwill in poor oil-consuming countries and in diversifying the investment of their oil revenue. Moreover, if oil is found, it would not be competitive with their own production if produced under their part-ownership. From the point of view of the poor oil-consuming countries, whether crude is found in oil-producing countries or within their own territories, this would reduce the impact of the new oil prices on their balance of payments.

In the field of refining four of the strongest arguments usually advanced in favour of the participation of international oil companies (both "majors" and "minors") in equity ownership are as follows:

(a) the latter are able to arrange crude supply on a long-term basis;

(b) they are better able, because of their wide marketing network, to handle 'refinery imbalance', that is, surplus in some oil products (say, petrol) and deficits in some others (for example, diesel), which arises because of the divergence between the pattern of demand for different oil products and the output pattern of the refineries;

(c) they are technically and managerially efficient; and

(d) they can provide the necessary capital and foreign exchange for building the refineries from their own resources.

Of these, (a) is now better secured through direct bilateral arrangements with oil-producing countries, and, as far as (c) is concerned, indigenous personnel in many poor countries—including India—are now able to run their own refinery, once it is installed. If the refineries are built in collaboration with the oil-producing countries, with the arrangement that the latter would provide crude oil and the foreign exchange cost of the project—which is consistent with the OPEC's long-term interest in participating in downstream activities—it would be possible to remove constraint (d) without bringing in the internationals. The constraint (b) is the most difficult to remove in the near future, since neither the oil-consuming countries nor the OPEC countries yet possess the wide contacts with many countries with varying consumption and output patterns.

As the above discussion shows, many of the roles which the "majors" performed in both the oil-producing and the oil-consuming countries can now be performed jointly by these two sets of countries independently of the large international firms. For a long time the major multinationals stood between the oil-exporting and the oil-importing countries as intermediaries. They fixed the prices of crude oil and refined products and arranged their distribution over the whole world. They knew everything there was to know about the oil industry and about the specific requirements and peculiarities of the individual markets, while very few organisations, governments or individuals outside their oligopolistic network were knowledgeable enough to challenge the data they furnished. They decided how much of crude oil to produce from Country A, and how much to sell to Country B, and the governments of these countries, particularly when they were poor and ignorant about the intricacies of the oil business, had very little influence over these decisions. There was no possibility of any direct relationship between Countries A and B, by-passing the "majors". This situation has changed over the past fifteen years, particularly since October 1973. The major oil companies no longer fix oil prices, and the oil-producing countries are now increasingly taking over the role of sellers of their own crude oil through direct negotiations with oil-consuming countries. Moreover, they are increasingly participating in refining and other downstream activities in oil-consuming countries. There is no reason why in the future collaborations in the field of the oil industry could not be extended to oil-based industries (like fertiliser) and other activities which are mutually beneficial to both of these two sets of countries.

How are the large international oil firms responding to this changed situation of loss of power to determine prices and of reduced importance as intermediaries and suppliers of crude oil? It is true that the present high prices of oil are not hurting them financially; but more important than that, from a long-term viewpoint, is their loss of control over the industry and ever decreasing share of ownership of crude oil. A reading of the current literature on oil would point to two alternatives which the majors are likely to follow in the future: one is to find oil in politically safe areas, like the North Sea or Alaska, and the other is to gradually move out of oil and to extend their interests to non-oil and non-conventional oil industries. It is significant that the US "majors" already own 30% of coal reserves and 50% of uranium reserves in the United States. If their research efforts succeed in making a technological breakthrough in producing oil from shales, tar sand or coal at low cost, the balance of power in the energy sector would shift from the Middle East towards North America. The current high oil prices—whether provoked by them or not—is helping them in this respect, both by generating high profits which can be invested in costly exploration programmes and by making research in non-oil energy and in non-conventional oil industries financially worthwhile.

V. Oil-producing countries of Africa

We shall now turn to the three African oil-producing countries, Algeria, Libya and Nigeria, and briefly examine their relatively short experience in the oil industry. In comparison with the Middle East, the oilfields in Africa are smaller, and the oil production cost is higher: 28 cents per barrel in Algeria and 15 cents in Libya and Nigeria, compared to 7-10 cents in the Middle East, according to one estimate;[33] but these differences, although relevant in the pre-1973 period, are insignificant in relation to current oil prices. More important than cost disadvantage are quality and locational advantages the African oil producers enjoy over the Middle East. African crude is lighter and sulphur-free, qualities which are in great demand in the pollution-conscious industrialised consuming countries.[34] In addition, Africa is favourably located in relation to its main consumption centre. The freight advantage is, however, a decreasing function of time, both because of the growth of giant tankers and because with high f.o.b. oil prices the proportion accounted for by transport cost in the c.i.f. price is declining.

The three African countries widely vary among themselves in the pattern of their economies. Before the discovery of oil, Libya's economy was stagnant and poor, with a narrow resource base and a small market of 1.5 million people; Libya was also heavily dependent on the contributions made by the governments of the UK and the USA for the maintenance of military bases, the latter accounting for half the government expenditure in the fifties.[35] The discovery of oil has totally changed the economic landscape of the country, which is now one of the richest countries in the world, with a *per capita* income exceeding 1200 dollars. The resource base nevertheless remains narrow, very little besides oil being produced. In contrast with the desert economy of Libya, Nigeria is predominantly agricultural, rich in the production of cocoa, coffee, palm oil and other crops, and its population is the largest in Africa.[36] Algeria, a desert country like Libya, stands between the two, with large vineyards which traditionally produce wine for the French market, a 3 million ton iron ore production, and several processing industries in steel, chemicals, fertilisers, etc., besides the oil industry itself.[37]

Those countries also vary among themselves in the pattern of ownership of the oil industry. In Algeria, because of its past colonial links with France, the government-owned French companies, rather than the 'majors', dominated crude production until 1971, when the industry was brought under the control of Sonatrach, the Algerian national oil company. The bulk of crude oil still goes to France, and the latter has always paid a higher than normal world price for oil for maintaining its access to 'franc crude'. In Nigeria, until 1973, about 92% of the crude oil production was controlled by majors, while two independents—one Italian, and another French—accounted for 8%. The situation in Libya was historically different from the other two in the sense that the 'minors' or independent US companies played an important role in the development of its oil industry, e.g., Oasis (jointly owned by Amerada, Marathon, and Continental), Occidental, Standard Oil of Indiana, and Philips.

Among these countries Libya was the first to join OPEC, in 1962, but it was not until 1969 that Algeria joined it, and two years later that Nigeria joined.[38] Before the overthrow of the King in 1969, Libya was a strong ally of the West and is one of the three founding members (with Kuwait and Saudi Arabia) of the Organisation of Arab Petroleum Marketing Countries OAPEC), which at the beginning acted as the platform for conservative and monarchial Arab governments. Nigeria, until the 1966 coup, was a 'showpiece' of Western-type democracy in Africa. From the point of view of the oil companies, investment in these countries was secure and profitable because of the quality and location advantages of their oil *vis-à-vis* West Europe. Even Algeria, despite the left-wing character of its regime, and the bitter experience of the liberation movement, maintained close cultural and economic ties with the French.

In all these countries oil was found in the late fifties, but the oil fields were developed in the sixties. The original concessions were drawn up during the colonial period, which favoured the oil companies, so that a great part of the sixties was spent by the governments of these countries in revising those laws. In the case of Algeria, the agreement of 1963 with France—the main consumer and the mother country of its oil companies—was an improvement over the previous concession, but it did not go far enough. It was only after a series of confrontations between the two governments that in 1971, the Algerian Government took over majority control in oil industry. Unlike the Middle East or Libya, Algeria does not play a prominant role in price negotiations or fixation, partly because its production is relatively small and partly because the 'majors' have never been prominant in its oil industry. In Libya the situation was somewhat different from the beginning. The 'minors' working there—who had inadequate marketing facilities—were until 1965 selling crude at a low price to independent buyers, and were paying taxes on profits based on low 'realised prices' rather than according to 'posted prices'. Moreover, unlike the Middle East, where since 1964 $12^1/_2\%$ royalty was 'expensed' from tax calculations, the Libyan independents continued to pay 50% of realised profits as taxes including royalties. In other words the Libyan government was getting about 45 cents per barrel less than its Middle Eastern counterparts because of these arrangements. In 1965 the Libyan Government took the unilateral action of forcing the 'minors' to revise the forms of concession in line with the revised Middle Eastern concessions with the active support of the OPEC and the passive support of 'majors' who also suffered from the competition of low-priced oil owned by 'minors'. Libya was again in the limelight in 1970 when Colonel Godaffi accused the oil companies of producing oil too fast, reduced production by 800,000 barrels a day, and forced the companies to increase oil prices by 30 cents and to agree to a 55% government share in profits, a pattern which was soon followed by the other oil-producing countries.[39]

In the case of Nigeria, as well, the highly unfavourable 'Petroleum Profits Tax Ordinance' of 1959 was not revised until after the 1966 coup, when negotiations with oil companies led to an agreement by the 'majors' to make posted prices the basis for tax calculations and to 'expense' royalties from profits. In 1971, one year after the end of the civil war, the government's share was increased to 55% of profits, and achieved the standards of the other OPEC countries.[40]

As the above account shows, the governments of the oil-producing countries of Africa have largely succeeded over the past decade or so in their efforts to bring the oil industry under their control. As long as the industry remained in foreign hands, its full potential could not be realised. Although the foreign oil companies bore the risk of oil exploration, their main objective was to find an alternative source of oil to the Middle East, preferably nearer the West European market. The oil was produced not for domestic use but to meet the ever increasing energy needs of Europe. Although the technology of oil exploration and production was thus advanced, the local population was denied access to it, and the management remained firmly in the hands of the expatriates. For example, in 1970, of the 12 top management positions in the Shell-BP company of Nigeria, only one was given to a Nigerian, and even his job was marginally connected with producing and marketing oil.[41] The assumption of majority control has enabled the local personnel to learn the technology of oil operations and also to assume managerial responsibilities. In the case of Algeria the French companies threatened withdrawal of all French managing personnel within one month after the 1971 nationalisation, but the Algerians replied by expelling all of them within 24 hours and the refinery and petro-chemical complex at Arzew is now fully operated by Algerian personnel.

Because of its high capital intensity—e.g., £30,000 per employee of Exxon—the oil industry does not provide much direct employment. In a small country like Libya, with a low literacy level, however, oil companies are able to attract the best brains of the country by paying them salaries which constitute a minor component of their total cost, and which force the other branches of the economy—like administration, construction, etc., to offer similar wages, thereby pushing up wages and prices everywhere in the organised sector. Inflation, a distorted wage structure and income inequality are some of the major characteristics of the oil industry in a poor country.

Another important feature of the oil industry, when it is in foreign hands, is the growth of the expatriate sector with a wage level, consumption standard and social life which are different from those of the local population (excepting the local elite which joins the expatriates). For example, in Nigeria in 1967, an average expatriate earned£2,464 plus, while the average earnings of local oil personnel, oil suppliers, and workers in commerce, manufacturing and agriculture were£432,£163,£275,£223, and£102, respectively.[42] The high propensity of the expatriates to import constitutes a heavy leakage of export earnings from oil. According to a report of the Bank of Libya, about 68% of food imports, 89% of beverage and tobacco imports, and 40% of manufactured imports in 1959 were composed of commodities which were either produced or could be produced locally.[43]

Moreover, when the oil industry is run by foreign companies, they tend to rely on foreign imports for supplying various goods needed by the industry. For example, in Nigeria in 1971, the oil companies spent only 11% of their total expenditure on local goods and services and for payment of salaries and wages; and even for 'local purchases' the import content was as high as 60%, and the 'local suppliers' concerned were usually controlled by expatriates.[44]

The assumption of the control of the oil industry by the government makes easier the tasks of integrating this sector with the rest of the economy and minimising the leakages of earnings from oil. It becomes possible to give priority to local purchases for the industry, to reduce the proportion of expatriates and their wages, and to enable local personnel to acquire technological expertise, and to control the import-content of the consumption of the expatriates and the elite. Moreover, instead of only providing the developed countries with a cheap source of energy, it becomes possible to use oil, at low price, for rapid industrialisation of the country.

For a long time Libya and Nigeria were limited by the World Bank advice to encourage the private sector and a free import policy and to confine the state activities to 'normal regulatory functions' of the state. As a consequence, the development of non-oil activities was stifled. Private firms did not come forward to undertake industrial activities, because (a) without protection they had no chance against foreign imports, and (b) they had the alternative of engaging in equally profitable and less risky commercial and trading activities in imported goods. This was a dangerous situation, given the uncertainty of the oil business; developments such as the reopening of the Suez Canal, further reductions in the costs of tanker operation and desulphurisation, and the discovery of large oil fields nearer Western Europe would reduce the comparative advantage of African oil. Moreover, in the long run there is always the possibility of oil being substituted by other forms of energy. A prudent long-run policy is to spend the revenue from oil in developing a viable non-oil sector, to give it as much tariff protection as is necessary at the beginning in the hope that it will eventually be able to stand on its own feet and thereby minimise the country's dpendence on oil.

Postscript

The Political Economy of the Current Oil Crisis

One: Is there an oil crisis?

Is there an oil crisis in the sense that the world oil reserves may very soon become exhausted? The simple arithmetic of the situation is as follows. The 'proved' oil reserve is about 673 billion barrels, which at the consumption rate of 21 billion barrels a year in 1973 would last about 32 years; that is, up to the year 2005. Even this is an optimistic picture, since world oil consumption is not static and until very recently was growing at a high rate: total consumption doubled in the fifties, and doubled again in the sixties, and even in 1973 it grew at an annual rate of $7^1/_2\%$ over 1972. Surely, with higher current prices and the restrictions imposed on oil imports by many countries the consumption will not grow so fast in the future, but even a modest growth would imply that the total stock of 'proved' oil will be exhausted by the end of this century.[45]

That is, however, an alarmist view. In addition to 'proved' reserves, which are rather conservative estimates, there is another 'probable' reserve of 760 billion barrels and 'speculative' reserve of 310 billion barrels, which together should account for about another 50 years of oil consumption.[46] Then there are reserves of oil in shales and tar sands, which are about three times as large as the conventional oil reserve; and by the time the latter is exhausted it would be economically and technologically viable to produce oil from those non-conventional sources, as well as from the huge coal reserves of India, China and South Africa. In fact, we may not need to wait until then; there is always the possibility of producing nuclear power cheaply enough to replace other forms of energy.

If there is an 'oil crisis', this is "due more to political factors than to any physical limitations in petroleum supply". There is no 'world oil shortage', but from the point of view of the Western capitalist countries some uncertainty has been created as regards the security and regularity of its supply, because of the political developments in the Middle East, and Africa, areas which together account for more than two-thirds of the 'proved' reserves, and three-quarters of the international trade in oil, but consume only 5 per cent of the oil produced.[47]

Two: Are the oil-producing countries guilty of blackmailing?

It is true that oil-producing countries of the world have used their command over one of the most strategic materials in the world to attain certain political ends, such as forcing the oil-consuming countries in Europe to adopt a neutralist position during the Arab-Israel conflict and achieving the partial withdrawal of the Israeli forces from occupied areas by pressurising its patron, the United States. Yet, leaving aside the rights and wrongs of that particular political issue, which country does not use its economic power to gain political advantage? What role does 'foreign aid' play in the diplomatic relationship between the donor and the recipient country? It was not very long ago, in 1965, that the Indian government was forced to devalue its currency against all expert advice, liberalise imports, and remove restrictions on the equity ownership and marketing control of foreign monopolies, as a precondition for US aid, particularly food aid.

Three: Is the price of oil too high?

The sudden jump in crude oil prices, from a low $1.30 per barrel in 1970 (for 34° API Saudi Arabian light crude) and after a series of small increases during 1971-1973 (September), to $11.65 in December, 1973, has created the impression that the oil-producing countries are charging a very high price for the precious commodity they own and control by making use of their monopolistic control through OPEC.

The fact is, however, that the oil prices, like the prices of most other raw materials exported from the poor countries, were maintained at a very low level for many decades, and their real values in fact rapidly declined over time, and relative to the prices of manufactured goods which the oil-producing countries imported from the West. Even now the crude-oil prices constitute between one-third and one-fourth of the price the ultimate consumers pay for oil products, the rest accruing to the oil companies, dealers and governments of oil-consuming countries.

Furthermore, these low prices in the past encouraged indiscriminate use of this exhaustible resource in the highly industrialised countries of the world, in the form of big cars and other articles of conspicuous consumption, while in the oil-producing countries themselves, the level of use of this domestic source of energy remained low. For example, in 1973, out of a total world oil consumption (excluding the Communist countries) of 46 million barrels a day, 37.5 million barrels (that is, more than four-fifths) were consumed by the industrialised countries of North America (17.96 million), West Europe (13.96 million) and Japan (4.94 million).[48] Whereas *per capita* oil consumption in North America was 1096 gallons in 1971, and in West Europe it was 556 gallons, the corresponding figures for Asia, Africa, Latin America and Middle East were 87, 33, 159 and 172, repectively.[49] In other words, the cheap price of oil prior to October 1973 largely benefited the Western capitalist countries. The cheap oil prices contributed to the affluence of the

West while the oil-producing countries remained poor and backward, even while their oil reserves were being run down.

Four: How are the poor oil-consuming countries to meet the higher oil cost?

According to a rough estimate prepared by the World Bank, out of the $65 billion additional earnings the oil-producing countries would be making in 1974 over 1973, about $10 billion would come from the poor oil-consuming countries. This is a staggering sum, which has put further pressure on the already precarious balance of payment situation of many of these countries. The hardest hit are the 636 million people of India, Bangladesh and Ceylon; coming next to this group are 90 million people of eleven African countries: Ethiopia, Tanzania, Kenya, Malgasy, Cameroon, Upper Volta, Mali, Malawi, Niger, Rwanda and Somalia. In the short run these countries are frantically trying to arrange oil purchase on a deferred-payment basis, as well as to raise 'soft loans'; but these would not prevent a cut in oil and other imports, thereby reducing the growth rate of the economy.[50] The balance of payment situation is likely to deteriorate for another reason: the amount of grants and loans available from the Western developed countries will now be curtailed, since the latter themselves face balance of payment deficits *vis-à-vis* the oil-producing countries.[51]

It would nevertheless be wrong to put the entire responsibility for the balance of payment difficulties of the poor countries on the oil prices alone. Over the past few years there have been substantial increases in the prices of several raw materials and the price of foodgrains (a great part of which comes from North America) has more than doubled. Those countries which have suffered most from oil price increases are those for which there has been no compensatory rise in their export prices, and who have been forced to bear the burden of all these various types of price increases. The present balance of payment situation is the end product of a whole set of such sectors, oil being only one (though an important one) of them. Moreover, in the case of some countries like India, economic difficulties predate the oil crisis by a long distance.

Within these poor countries the impact of oil price increases is not evenly distributed among the various social classes."The oil price acts like a progressive tax, because the higher the income the higher the proportion of it spent on petroleum products and goods (and services) which are energy-intensive in either their production or use (or both)."[52] For example, in India about half of the total energy consumption comes from non-commercial sources like dry leaf, wood, cowdung, etc.; while the most popular oil product for domestic use is kerosene, which is used as an illuminant by households which cannot afford electricity. A great majority of the population travels very little, or on foot, using bullock cart, bicycles, railways, etc., and so the consumption of petrol is very low; while the rich, who travel by car or air and use synthetic or engineering products would suffer more than proportionately from oil price increases. The rich farmers, who use fertilisers, pesticides, and diesel for operating tractors and irrigation pumps would suffer more than the poorer peasants with limited means. Certainly the poor would indirectly pay for higher transport costs and costs of manufactured products, and lower productivity of agriculture; but, unlike the increase in the price of food imports (which amounted to 4 million tons a year for India and one million tons a year for India and one million tons for Bangladesh), whose incidence is regressive, the increased oil prices would have an egalitarian effect. Moreover, if as a result of this oil price increase the import of cars were prohibited, the highly protected domestic car industry would be closed down, and priorities for transport planning shifted to public transport, not only would a great deal of foreign exchange and other scarce resources be saved, it would also remove the severe traffic bottlenecks and the consequent economic losses in the big cities.

In some countries this oil crisis has created opportunities for the development of indigenous energy sources, like coal in India and hydroelectricity in Nepal; it even makes investment in the costly business of oil exploration look economically attractive. To the extent these countries succeed in using these opportunities, in the long run the impact of high oil prices will not be so severe. Moreover, if the action of OPEC in wrestling control over the oil industry from the hands of the international companies is successfully followed by other primary producing countries,[53] the resulting improvement in their export prices would more than offset the losses through high oil prices. While the poor countries have for many years been complaining about adverse terms of trade, the action of OPEC has shown how the terms of trade can be shifted in favour of the latter. Moreover, the oil crisis, by increasing the cost of synthetics, has created opportunities for the expansion of export trade of commodities like jute or cotton, which have suffered over the past two decades from competition with synthetic-substitutes. Furthermore, if the OPEC countries agree to recycle a good part of their surplus oil earnings to the poor countries by way of investments and loans, not only would this compensate for the curtailment of loans and grants by the Western developed countries, but such a step would also lessen the economic and political dependence of the poor countries on the latter.

Five: The dialectics of Middle East oil politics

Nevertheless, a great deal will depend upon the attitudes of the oil-producing countries towards the oil-consuming poor countries. We have seen in section

IV that the transformation of the structure of the oil industry over the past year has opened up new possibilities for cooperation on a wide range of activities between these two sets of countries. Some of the recent business deals—e.g., those signed by India with Iraq and Iran for crude-oil supply with deferred payment and a soft loan—and the public statements by spokesmen of several Arab countries show that they are not entirely indifferent to those possibilities. So far, however, very little has been done in actual terms in this direction, while the oil-producing countries have devoted more of their efforts towards strengthening their economic ties with the Western capitalist countries.

This is not surprising, and is quite consistent with the class character and the diplomatic position of the regimes ruling in Persian Gulf Arab countries. Some of these are very small artificial entities indeed, e.g., Abu Dhabi with a population of 86,000, and Kuwait with a population of 700,000, half of whom in both countries are non-locals with no citizenship rights. Their larger neighbours are looking for excuses to swallow them; for example, Iran, Iraq and Saudi Arabia have territorial ambitions over Bahrain, Kuwait and Abu Dhabi, respectively. There are no cultural, linguistic and ethnic differences between the tiny populations of thes oil-rich countries and their much poorer Arab neighbours of the Middle East and North Africa. It is inconceivable that these rich enclaves in a poor region of the world should continue for long without the ultimate military and political backing of the Western countries, particularly the United States. Furthermore, these regions—feudal and autocratic as they are—are under the constant threat of revolution; both for fighting revolutionaries and also for securing refuge if the revolution should succeed, they are critically dependent on the former's support. This is true despite the US support for Israel (where the Arab regimes are 'pro-West', it is their misfortune that they are fighting an enemy which is an integral 'part of the West'), despite the last year's threat of US military action against the Gulf States to secure oil supplies (which would have required no more than a small paratroop operation for transferring power to a more loyal and less insubordinate prince—what prevented this military action was the fear of Soviet counteraction—an evidence of the dialectical nature of Middle East politics), and despite occasional militant 'anti-USA' utterances of their princely spokesmen.

As a result of this ultimate dependence of the Arab States on Western countries (which does not rule out the possibility of occasional acts of defiance on the part of the client states), they would never undertake a course of action which inflicts irreparable damage on the Western economic and political order, which is why it is not surprising that the vast proportion of the oil surplus is going back to the Western economies in various forms, and that not much enthusiasm has been shown for supporting the non-Arab poor countries. Their reluctance to invest in poor countries is based on two other considerations—(a) the returns there are relatively low, (b) there is the risk of expropriation by the host governments.

Six: Can OPEC remain united?

We have already noted that the key to the success the OPEC countries had in increasing prices in the seventies was their unity and ability to control production. One important lesson which all the OPEC countries have learnt is that they collectively gain from united action, although the distribution of gain is not necessarily uniform within OPEC. In the short run, given the low elasticity of demand for oil products, they face no problem in holding the price level; conversion to other energy sources is costly and time-consuming. But even in the long run, when substitutes are cheaply produced, it is at least theoretically possible for the OPEC countries to bring down oil prices just below the price of the cheapest substitute through concerted action; given the incredibly low production cost of oil in relation to its current price, such a policy would still leave a sufficiently high profit margin for the oil-producing countries.

Various types of contradictions exist, however, between OPEC countries. One example is the conflict between Saudi Arabia and Iran on crude-oil prices, the former wanting to reduce it while the latter would not mind even increasing the prices a bit more. This conflict mainly stems from the differences between two types of economies—one, which is primarily a desert economy where hardly anything else apart from oil is available, and the other which is a diversified economy with a potential for further diversification and high growth rate. The primary interest of the second type of oil economy is to extract as much revenue from oil as possible within the shortest possible time and then to invest it in other industries, thereby achieving a high economic growth and reducing dependence on oil. In contrast, the desert economies, particularly given their orthodox ‘free enterprise’ views, are unable to spend more than one-third of the current oil revenue, and for them, at a time when inflation is rapid, surplus revenue earned and invested today is no more welcome than oil under the ground and lifted some time in the future. Moreover, since they have very few resources except oil and they feel that their opportunities for industrialisation are limited, these desert countries are more worried about the development of substitutes—due to high oil prices—than the other type of oil-producing countries. The ability of OPEC to maintain prices should largely depend on their success in resolving this contradiction between these two types of economies.

Notes

[1] For a detailed account of the advantages which accrue to the mother countries by way of foreign exchange earnings and access to an important raw material, see Michael Tanzer, *The Political Economy of International Oil and the Underdeveloped Countries,* London, 1969.

[2] For details about their activities see Edith Penrose, *The Large International Firm in Developing Countries: The International Petroleum Industry,* London, George Allan & Unwin, 1967.

[3] Edith Penrose, "Vertical Integration with Joint Control of Raw Material Production", *Journal of Development Studies,* April 1965, pp. 251-268.

[4] Biplab Dasgupta, *The Oil Industry in India—Some Economic Aspects,* Frank Cass, London, 1971, pp. 223-231.

[5] For details, see Edith Penrose, *The Large International Firm in Developing Countries,* op.cit.

[6] Dasgupta, op.cit., pp. 65-68, 113-117.

[7] George Lenezowski, *Oil and State in the Middle East,* New York, 1960.

[8] Penrose, op.cit.

[9] Tanzer, op.cit.; for example, the Vice-President of Standard Oil of New Jersey said in 1966, "Our government has the interest, as well as the means, to promote US investments abroad, in furthering the objectives of our foreign policy". For this and similar quotations, see Zuhayer Mikdashi, *The Community of Oil Exporting Countries: A Study of Governmental Cooperation,* London, 1972.

[10] J. G. Mclean and F. W. Haigh, *The Growth of the Integrated Oil Companies,* 1954.

[11] Penrose, op.cit.; see also "Profit Sharing between Producing and Oil Companies in the Middle East", *Economic Journal,* June 1959.

[12] Penrose, op.cit.

[13] Government of India *Report of the Oil Price Enquiry Committee,* (Damle Committee), 1961.

[14] Penrose, op.cit.

[15] Dasgupta, op.cit., Chapter 4. See also H. J. Frank, *Crude Oil Prices in the Middle East: A Study in Oligopolistic Price Behaviour,* 1966.

[16] Dasgupta, op.cit., Chapter 4.

[17] Ibid.

[18] Ibid.

[19] Ibid.

[20] Harold Lubell, *The Soviet Oil Offensive and Interblock Economic Competition,* 1961, (mimeograph).

[21] Dasgupta, op.cit., Chapters 7 and 8.

[22] Penrose, op.cit.

[23] Based on various papers presented to the World Petroleum Congress during this period. See M. Adelman, *World Petroleum Market,* 1972.

[24] M. Adelman, op.cit.

[25] API is an inverse measure of the specific gravity of crude oil—the lighter the oil, the higher the API reading. Lighter crudes enjoy a price differently based on gravity; for example, during the sixties it was 2¢ per degree API.

[26] *Petroleum Press Service,* July 1973, October 1973.

[27] *Petroleum Economist,* June 1974.

[28] *Petroleum Economist,* July 1974, "Companies Under Fire".

[29] Nevertheless, a great deal of this profit has come from the sale of stocks accumulated before October 1973.

[30] *New York Post,* 10 January 1974.

[31] Counter Information Services Anti-Report, *The Oilfix,* Bertrand Russel Press, 1974.

[32] Dasgupta, op.cit., Chapter 9.

[33] Adelman, op.cit.

[34] The Hassi Messoud crude is rated as 43° API, the Breiga crude of Libya and Meren crude of Nigeria are rated as 40° API, and 39° API, respectively, compared to 31°-35° API rating for the Iranian, Arabian and Kuwaiti crude. API is the inverse measure of gravity. Moreover, the percentages of sulphur in African crude are 0.1%-0.2% compared to 1.3%-2.5% figures for most Middle Eastern crude. See *Petroleum Press Service,* October, 1973.

[35] I.B.R.D., *The economic development of Libya,* 1960; Abdul Amir Q. Kubbah, *Libya, its oil and economic system,* 1960.

[36] Scott R. Pearson, *Petroleum and Nigerian Economy,* Stanford, 1970.

[37] Government of Algeria, *The Algerian Revolution—facts and prospects,* 1972.

[38] Zuhayr Mikdashi, *The community of oil exporting countries,* 1972.

[39] Mikdashi, op.cit.

[40] Terisa Turner, "The political economy of technological transfer to the Nigerian oil industry", 1973 (mimeographed).

[41] See Pearson, op.cit., and Turner, op.cit.

[42] Turner, op.cit.

[43] National Bank of Libya, *Inflation in Libya,* 1963.

[44] Pearson, op.cit.

[45] See *Petroleum Press Service,* October 1972, July 1973, October 1973.

[46] Ibid, July 1973.

[47] British Petroleum, *Statistical Review of the World Oil Industry,* 1972.

[48] *Petroleum Economist,* July 1974.

[49] *International Petroleum Encyclopedia,* 1973.

[50] See Richard Jolly, "A framework for assessing the impact on developing countries and some policy suggestions" in *Bulletin of the Institute of Development Studies,* August-September, 1974.

[51] World Bank Sources.

[52] Dudley Seers, "1974—the opportunity of a real international development strategy", (mimeographed).

[53] See Chris Barker and Bill Page, "OPEC as a model for other mineral exporters", in the *Bulletin of the Institute of Development Studies,* August-September 1974.

M. K. K. Kabala Kabunda

Multinational Corporations and the Installation of Externally-oriented Economic Structures in Contemporary Africa: the Example of the Unilever-Zaire Group

Introduction

In the following study we shall touch upon the essence of the multinational corporation (Unilever) and above all upon its essence in Zaire with respect to the impact of the activities of the Unilever Group on the social, political and economic systems of Zaire.

It would have been possible to present a much more thorough study if we had had access to all the necessary information—information which is difficult to obtain from this corporation. The guidelines which helped us in this work were: world trade, because we known that the market for palm-oil is dominated by Unilever (with 80%) and price-setting is determined by the importance of Unilever; the trends of investments in the world and in Zaire, also difficult to determine; calculation of the rate of general profitability and the importance of Zaire in the refusal or maintenance of the world profit rate—the plantations in Zaire have been determining factors in Unilever's strategy to gain direct access to raw materials and to maintain the monopoly of tropical oil-seeds.

Origin and historical summary

The history of Unilever is intimately linked with that of the industrial revolution and the subsequent economic boom in Europe at the end of the last century. About 1860 two Dutch families, Van den Bergh and Jurgens, were active within the butter trade at OSS in the north of Brabant. In 1869 a Frenchman, Mège-Mouriès, invented margarine, a less expensive product made from oil-seeds. The business was primarily exploited by Dutch firms, which found a ready market among the poorer classes in Great Britain and in Germany. It was at this point that a fierce competition broke out between

Van den Bergh and Jurgens, who had already established subsidiaries throughout Europe. As the family financial means became increasingly insufficient, it was necessary to seek recourse to the capital market by adopting the status of a limited company.

Thus the two Van den Bergh subsidiaries were created—Van den Bergh Limited (England) in 1894 and Van den Bergh Fabricken (Holland) in 1919—as well as M. V. Anton Jurgens Vercenigdi Fabricken Company in 1905.

In order to forestall a price war and to defeat all outside competition, Van den Bergh and Jurgens signed a secret agreement in 1908 to pool all profits. Other agreements were signed which maintained an unsteady truce between the two companies up to the moment when in 1927, after several years of financial crisis, the two houses merged, creating two new companies, the N.V. Margarine Union Limited in Holland and the Margarine Union Limited in England, thus avoiding double taxation and facilitating access to the capital market in both countries.

The history of the European soap industry is parallel to that of margarine. In the case of soap, as in that of margarine, there was a tendency to form associations. During the period when household soap was manufactured in bars, William Lever began to make a soap with an oil base rather than with the traditional tallow. The utilization of technological innovations and of marketing techniques, based on the American model, brought about a rapid growth of the firm. Nevertheless, the problem of financing to cope with the rapidly increasing demand from the mid-19th century induced William Lever to create in 1894 Lever Brothers Limited; by 1906, the firm had at its disposal more than £4 million capital, had an interest in one-sixth of the British soap trade and had expanded to continental North America, Australia and South Africa.

In 1906, however, the soap sector underwent several crises simultaneously, crises which were to have repercussions on the future of the firm, and particularly on its relations with Africa. These crises, due in part to a stabilization of the demand for soap on the British market, can essentially be explained by a sharp increase in the price of raw materials, so that the firm was no longer able to make huge profits; this increase was due to the competition from margarine manufacturers and to the very weak growth of supplies. These two phenomena seriously threatened the expansionist designs of William Lever, who, confronted with this threat, set up trusts in Great Britain, purchasing the businesses of his competitors, rather than battling with them to obtain a larger portion of the market. On the international plane, William Lever fought these crises by increasing his foreign investments in the manufacture and sale of soap in industrialized countries.

The company also sought to acquire its own sources of raw materials in order to enjoy the economy which vertical integration provides, and to increase the growth of the world stock of these materials. It was thus at this point that Lever began the acquisition of concessions, particularly in Zaire.

The merger of the companies described above, giving birth to the Unilever group, was therefore a necessity of the capitalist mode of production. A fall in the rate of profit at the center forces the capitalist firms to greater and greater concentration in their struggle for the market in the center and their attempts to ensure cheap raw-material resources in the countries of the periphery. When William Lever was prevented by the British government from setting up vast plantations in British West Africa (the colonial administration argued that such a system would bring about social unrest and the alienation of enormous quantities of land), he made his request to the Belgian government (which did not have a similar policy), and on April 14, 1911, Lord Leverhulme, Chairman of Lever Brothers Company Ltd., concluded an agreement with the Belgian authorities which gave him the right to choose 750,000 hectares of concessions—reduced to 350,000 hectares by the convention of 1938—in five areas with a radius of 60 kilometres situated in several provinces, thus creating the "Société anonyme des Huileries [oil-crushing plants] du Congo Belge" (HCB). In addition, a convention signed in 1958 granted HCB a monopoly upon the purchase of palm fruit (in the zones of the oil-works) sold by Congolese fruit-pickers.

The oil-works of the Belgian Congo were located successively in Leverville, on the Kwilu (province of Leopoldville), in Alberta near Bumba (province of the Equator), in Elisabetha, near Barumba (Oriental province), in Brabanta near Port-Francqui (province of the Kasaï) and in Flandria, near Ingende (Equator). In 1912 Unilever also installed a large commercial firm in Zaire through an independent subsidiary unconnected with its commercial firms in the Congo (SEDEC). Before assuming an autonomous orientation, this firm was to ensure the importation of goods and the organization of trade stores in the plantation districts. Lastly, another subsidiary of Unilever, the Société des Margarines et Savonneries Congolaises, abbreviated MARSAVCO (the Congolese Margarine and Soap Company), which was created in 1922, manufactures margarine and soap.

This period, as M. Merlier so well notes, must be linked to *primitive accumulation:*

> The plantations and the ranches created the proletariat. Since the conquest, difficulties in recruiting workers hampered colonization: it was necessary first of all to deprive hundreds of thousands of their means of livelihood, then violently to expropriate the peasants from their collective landholdings. Although not well-known, this period of primitive accumulation, the starting point for the capitalist production, lasted about half a century (up to 1930), characterized by reprehensible acts. The system of large Leopoldian concessions and of forced labor . . ., brought about an enormous historical leap in the Congo. Mercilessly crushing the old African agrarian system, the finance

> companies proceeded to make gigantic expropriations, seizing millions of hectares, burning villages, tracking down the population far from the rivers, displacing and deporting them, forcing them to gather plantation crops at the point of a rifle.[1]

This obscure period of accumulation continued into the 1920s.

The activities of the Unilever group in Zaire

The activities of the Unilever group in Zaire are part of a global strategy common to multinational firms, i.e., a "strategy of international valorization of capital, on the basis of the internationalization of capital; this valorization is channelled through the international social extension of the process of capital accumulation—taking into account the specificity and the international differentiation of the accumulation process, the strategy of the firms is different at the center and on the periphery.[2] As part of Unilever's strategy to obtain direct access to the raw materials and to maintain the monopoly of tropical oil-seeds, the plantations of the Congo (Zaire) were determining factors for supplying these raw materials at a very low price.[3]

The oil-works of the Belgian Congo (HCB), which were re-named "Lever Plantations of the Congo" in 1960, then "of Zaire" in 1972, were located successively in the former Leverville (today Lusanga), in Elizabetha (now Dongo), in the former Brabanta (now Mapangu), and in the former Flandria (now Bateka). Eight years after signing the 1911 convention the HCB already owned seven large palm-oil extraction factories. The company worked the "natural" palm-groves first of all but subsequently began planting palm-groves. It expanded its activities at the same time by setting up plantations of heveas, of cacao trees, and of coffee in the Gwaka, Mokaria and Yalingimba districts (see number of PLZ districts (Plantations Lever au Zaire) in 1970 in Appendix 1).

In addition to the plantations, the firm owns about twenty oil-works, two rubber factories, two cocoa factories, a coffee factory, a tea factory, and some autonomous installations for the transport of loose raw materials: tank-barges, pump and reservoir installations in Kinshasa, Matadi, Boma and Port Ilebo. The whole of its fluvial infrastructure opens on the Atlantic from whence the "Palm Line", Unilever's shipping company, conducts its activities on the African coast. The company, through one of its subsidiaries, the "African Animal-Husbandry Company" (CAE)[4] (77,000 hectares of grazing land and 8,500 head of cattle in 1961), also supplies its workers' canteens.

The multinational firm not only exercises control over the production process but is also involved in the circulation process; that is to say, it exercises control over both processes and even includes in its sphere of circulation products from other capital and from other modes of production. This type of linking between the CMP and other modes of production is integrated in the indigenous circulation of economically and socially underdeveloped formations, as will be seen in the present study.

In addition to the plantations, Unilever is represented in the industrial sector by MARSAVCO (margarine, soaps and cosmetics) and in the commercial sector by SEDEC (company for commercial ventures). This sectoral division of Unilever-Zaire is present on the international level, where Unilever includes five sections: Great Britain, continental Europe, territories external to Europe, the United Africa Company group (UAC) and the Plantations-group.

These five sections are also divided into sub-sections: in Zaire we find three subsections:

(a) Overseas committee in charge of industrial activities external to Europe. The margarine, soap and cosmetic firms (MARSAVCO), as industrial firms, are responsible to the overseas committee.

(b) Plantations-Group in charge of agricultural activities in tropical countries. The Lever-Zaire plantations belong to this group.

(c) United Africa Company (UAC) takes care of commercial activities in Africa and the Middle East. The corporation of commercial firms (SEDEC) comes under the UAC.

We shall examine one by one these three sub-sections, beginning with the PLZ, then MARSAVCO and finally SEDEC;

A. The activities of the PLZ cover 47,281 hectares in 11 plantation districts. Having temporarily obtained 750,000 hectares from the colonial government and then in 1958 having definitely obtained 350,000 hectares of private property, PLZ developed only 15.7 percent of its property, and even this cultivated area experienced a regression, falling to 46,400 hectares in 1968. The diagram in Appendix 5, taken from the survey *Plantations Lever Congo* (published by PLZ in 1971), is rather revealing about the volume of the productive activities of this multinational. Taking advantage of the "systems of protection zones" and of the temporary concession of all "vacant lands", Unilever established plantations, as mentioned above, in complete ownership, with the monopoly for the purchase of agricultural products from the peasants at a low price, the monopoly for treatment of these products and the monopoly for recruiting manpower.

The diagram clearly shows that the commodities produced by another mode of production and included in the production as an element of industrial capital are one of the forms of primitive accumulation of capital.

We shall return to that point. In fact, this leads Palloix to say that "the process of accumulation of capital—the processes of creation and realization of surplus value—are only brought about because of a relationship of appropriation of the dominated and exploited modes of production". (*Le procès d'internationalisation du capital,* p. 130). The Lever plantations produce essentially for export. In Appendix 2, we have presented the evolution of PLZ exports of palm products for the years 1964 to 1966. Note, however, that Unilever controls 80 percent of the total international market of oil-seed products. Thus, when the world prices are favourable, the Lever plantations increase their exports and intensify their production activities (investment or purchase from the peasants at higher prices) in order to increase the profit rate. Similarly, they slow down their activities when the price goes down and appeal to the State for multiple exemptions, as was especially evident during the period between 1970 and 1973. Finally, it is the peasants and the State which bear the various costs during a difficult period: the peasants (in the framework of the price monopoly that Unilever enjoys) see that their products are sold less and less or are purchased only at very low prices; the State suffers in the form of reduced tax revenue and diverse exemptions. In order better to understand the importance of Lever Plantations for national exports, we have presented in Appendix 6 a comparative table of palm-oil exports by Zaire-Palm and by the other members of the *entente* of producers. Effectively, the national production of palm-oil (estimated at 168,188 tons in 1972 by the Bank of Zaire) is dominated by a few major producers who have formed a professional association called "the Members of the Entente", which protects the interests of its members and tries above all to preserve its monopoly on all palm-oil exports.

The members of the *Entente* thus form six autonomous groups, including JVL, SIEFAC, CCP, HPK, HEVEA, COREMAN, Madial and Zaire Palm, a cooperative dominated by the Lever group and by far the most powerful member of the producers' *Entente.* In fact, in 1970 the members of the *Entent* marketed slightly more than 170,000 tons of palm-oil out of an estimated 186,000 tons, that is, 90 percent of the industrial branch. That same year Zaire-Palm marketed 78.8 percent of the total of the *Entente* and exported 82.70 percent. Here we should note that these figures clearly indicate the role which Zaire plays in the strategy of direct supply of tropical oil-seeds and other raw materials (coffee, rubber, tea, etc.) for Unilever.

B. The evolution of Unilever's production section of manufactured goods is found in the activities of the margarine, soap and cosmetics company of Zaire, MARSAVCO. It is within the framework of the import-substitution strategy that this branch of Unilever was created in 1922. The margarine, soap and cosmetics company of Zaire has continuously modernized and expanded to become what at present is the most important industry for table oil, margarine and soap in Zaire.

C. SEDEC dominates the entire import market of manufactured products and also possesses some capital stock in the local productive industry, such as Chanimetal, Cyclor, Zaire-Print, Elbema, Nouvelles Huileries du Zaire, etc. SEDEC also represents the General Motors automobile trademark. Therefore, the Unilever group constitutes an economic concentration characterized by a complete circuit running from agricultural exploitation to industrialization and marketing.

The impact of the activities of the Unilever-Zaire group firms on Zaire and on its social, political and economic systems

The evaluation of the impact the activities of the Unilever group have had on Zaire poses an important problem, one concerning the location of essential information on facts relative to the multinational. Given the importance of the problem, we shall here present only certain aspects of the impact of these activities on the Zairois economy and society.

Although for practical analytic reasons we distinguished in the second part of this study between PLZ, MARSAVCO and SEDEC, the Unilever-Zaire group nevertheless constitutes an economic concentration characterized by a complete circuit running from agricultural exploitation to the industrialization of finished products. It is therefore as an integrated group pursuing a single policy (determined in the London/Amsterdam center)—and not as individual units of production—that the Unilever group and the impact of its activities will be considered.

Land expropriations and the proletarization of the population in numerous regions of Zaire

The expropriation of the land belonging to the Zairois population dates back to the period of the Independent State of the Congo (1885-1908), when Leopold II, exercising the right of conquest, appropriated for himself all the lands called "vacant". By virtue of a decree July 1, 1885, the only "indigenous lands" recognized were those which the Zairois population occupied, lived on, cultivated and exploited at that time, as well as those lands which temporarily lay fallow.

All the rest was declared "vacant lands" and the State laid claim to their ownership; the State alone had the right to dispose of these "national" lands, to part with them and to grant concessions there. The Leopoldian expropriations continued to have a speculative nature; they were general and more abstract than real—the granting of concessions usually did not imply an actual takeover of the lands and the forests.

The new colonial State of the Belgian Congo, which succeeded the Independent State of the Congo in 1908, did not suppress the expropriations of landed property, because the Belgian State took over on its own behalf the expropriations of Leopold II, but gave them a new character: the "vacant" lands continued to belong to the State, which expropriated them according to the needs of various firms. To quote Merlier: "The passage from a general expropriation which was relatively abstract to the real expropriation of the best lands reflects the monopolization of raw materials by European trusts, followed by the beginning of primitive accumulation in the Congo and of the proletarization of the peasants." When land speculation ebbed out and the best lands were recognized, their boundaries were then marked out, leading to the expulsion of the local populations, which thus constitute enormous reserves of cheap labour for the trusts.

Nevertheless, in spite of these "mise-en-valeur" (developmental or exploitational) possibilities, by far the greater part of the expropriated lands remained unexploited for a long time. In fact, on April 14, 1911, an agreement was signed between the colony and the Lever Brothers company of Port-Sunlight in England, creating the oil-works company of the Belgian Congo (SHCB). For ten years, this company was to be allowed to select and lease up to 750,000 hectares of the "national" lands bearing Elaeis oil palms in five "circles" with a 60-kilometer radius. In return, the company agreed to install in each "circle" a refinery treating at least 6,000 tons of fruit per year, to set up a clinic services by a doctor, and a school. Finally, beginning in 1945, the lands acquired on lease would become the property of the company upon demand by the company.

The area involved was about one-fourth the size of Belgium. In order to suppress the monopolies and reduce the immense Leopoldian concessions, the colonial administration modified the system of property concessions by henceforth applying expropriation to the best lands and thus to reduced areas.

Lever's choice did not take place immediately and in 1938 a new agrement reduced the total area of concessions granted to 350,000 hectares plus 100,000 outside the zone. This situation posed no problem for the firm, which at that time had not planted even one-tenth of that area. After 1956, these lands became the property of the SHCB. An agreement signed in 1958 additionally granted it the monopoly for purchasing palm fruit in the "oil-works zones" and the responsibility for purchasing all of the fruits presented for sale by the quasi-proletarized population.

In addition to the recruitment and employment of the major labor force which the exploitation of palm-groves (skillfully designated "natural" groves) required, the SHCB had in fact obtained—through certain "tripartite contracts" concluded between the firm and the colony—the right to force the population to sell all their fruits to the firm, except for the fruit required for subsistence. These contracts recognize, on the one hand, that the local population shall "accept" the placing of their lands in joint possession with the "vacant lands" belonging to the State and on the other hand, that the joint possession be managed by the Colony which, by virtue of this right, can lease to Lever a part of the lands in joint possession, a surface equal to that of the "vacant national lands". This article, one suspects, enabled the firm to commit serious abuses, such as ensuring that the best palm-groves still in the hands of the village populations passed into their control and extending limitlessly the zone of the firm's monopoly.

The recruitment of the necessary labour force for the palm groves and the company's oil-pressing brought about the decomposition and destruction of the precolonial societies, due to the prolonged displacement of the populations, the mortality caused by long walks, heavy work, hunger and insufficient housing, the lack of respect for local traditions and the decline of the home regions. In Kwilu the exploitation of the rich southern regions in the lightly-populated zones of Kikwit led the firm to hire fruit-cutters who were Mbunda, Kwese, Pende and even some Angolan workers. Confronted with the population's resistance to working for the firm, the colonial administration assisted the firm both in increasing food production by imposed cultivation, and in forced recruitment of the peasants.

The close collaboration between the colonial administration and the firm concerning recruitment methods (contract, repression and corruption), and especially the fate of the recruits, placed the workers in abominable work conditions beneath that of a free man and above that of a slave. The following figures are quoted for the fruit-cutters recruited for HCB in 1930 and 1931: 356 in 1930 and about 300 for the 5 months of 1931 which preceded the revolt of the Bapende (1932). They were forced (with the help of their family) to bring cases of fruit to the company shed, where trucks came to pick them up.

The season lasts a few months, during which time a cutter can gather about 20 cases of 35 kilos per month. After the great economic crisis which ruined many capitalist plantations, the profits of the company depended essentially upon a reduction in the costs of harvesting and transportation; numerous time studies established the pace of work in a palm-grove; the aim was for a short harvesting cycle, which improves the grade of oil and reduces the time taken to less than ten days, replacing tasks by weight with tasks by area. Even the methods for supervising the workers were made more flexible: an attempt was made to replace the supervisors (called "capitas") by a time-keeper selected by the worker-cutters who were interested in the yield.

The development of the colonial trade system and the extortion of agricultural surplus

In a conventional sense the colonial trade system can be seen as a sale of agricultural products, rubber or palm-kernels by the peasants, who in exchange receive merchandise from manufacturing industries (from the center or locally) and, in the present case, from the distribution circuit of the SEDEC stores.

This type of economy becomes the principle activity of middlemen, European tradesmen who buy the palm-kernels from the population (today the middlemen have been replaced by Zairois).

The oil works of the Belgian Congo had by 1917 themselves created this corporation of commercial enterprises in the Belgian Congo (SEDEC), and whose primary objective—the expansion of a consumption model responsive to the necessities of the capitalist production mode—was to import goods from Europe and to organize trade stores in the plantation districts by buying palm fruit and kernels destined to supply the company. Before 1960 SEDEC sold to the Zairois 20 percent of the products imported into Zaire.

Nevertheless, behind this simple form of exchange of palm-kernels for articles of European origin, it is possible to discern three essential elements of the capitalist production mode during the colonial and post-colonial era.

(1) the extortion of agricultural surplus through price mechanisms from the producers of non-capitalist modes of production;

(2) indirect coercion on the village population to sell their products in order to satisfy the new needs stemming from the domination of the capitalist mode of production;

(3) the palm-nut producers in this case are no longer free producers, for through this sale of nuts, they are in fact selling their labour power. One can refer here to Amin's conclusions at the seminar on agrarian capitalism (Dec. 1973 in Dakar).

The installation of externally-oriented and underdeveloped economic structures

The development of export crops

As has been stated above the company originally devoted its efforts to the exploitation of the so-called "natural" palm-groves. In a second phase beginning in the 1920s, it launched out into significant planting programs; at the end of 1959, 27,000 hectares of palm trees had been planted, as opposed to 15,000 hectares before the beginning of the Second World War; new extension programs brought the total surface of palm plantations to 46,000 hectares, which had been reduced to 33,767 hectares in late 1970.

At the same time as the palm plantations were being extended, the company (beginning in 1944) began to set up plantations of heveas, cocoa and tea. By the end of 1970 it owned 6,370 hectares of heveas in full productivity, 415 hectares of tea in full productivity, a total planted surface of 33,167 hectares of palm trees and 3,766 hectares of cocoa in full productivity.

The company's development of export crops corresponds to a double aim:

(1) to ensure for the European soap industry its own supply sources of cheap fats, enabling it to increase its profit rate in Europe;

(2) to diversify company production by the development of additional crops (rubber, cocoa, and tea) in order not to render the company's economy dependent on a single export crop.

In order to cope with the equalization of the profit rate, the company tried in addition to reduce production costs, particularly the "cost of manpower", by seeking an increased productivity, based on studies carried out in the various Lever-group research centers throughout the world: the improvement of varieties used, the selection and application of fertilizer for tropical soils, work studies intended to increase individual worker industriousness and productivity (based on a more refined organization of operations and a profit-sharing scheme), and finally, new projects for planted surfaces and modernization of factories.

Although the company possesses a certain number of options when confronted with the vicissitudes of the world market, the situation is not the same for Zaire, whose economy—based on the export of raw materials—has become very vulnerable. This is all the more paradoxical because the export price is determined on the world market by multinational firms which produce raw materials in Africa and of which Unilever is the largest representative in Zaire. At the same time one can recognize that any economic independence whatsover is illusionary, since it is this very company which, at a higher level, sets prices, and consequently both the entire tax system of the producer countries and their foreign exchange receipts—i.e., their possibilities for internal accumulation of capital. It is therefore convincing to suppose that if Unilever can accept the "high" taxation of Zaire, it is because Unilever gets something out of it.

Finally, the export of raw materials constitutes a "disaccumulation" of capital on the national level and it is this inability to retain its wealth which constitutes Zaire's underdevelopment. Nevertheless, the national wealth does not leave entirely in the form of goods. It also takes other forms: the importation of modern capital equipment destined to increase production; the repatriation of the salaries of foreign cadres, as well as the importation of consumption goods which the latter cannot do without; the resultant effect on the social stratification (which is more and more marked) and the reinforcement of a consumption model for the newly-emerging social classes.

Industrialization through import substitution

Industrialization through import substitution is, in its widest sense, the creation of local industries to produce goods which were formerly imported. A thorough analysis of this phenomenon should determine: (1) the reasons for transferring to the periphery certain activities formerly situated in the center; (2) the type of products henceforth manufactured locally.

Thus, for the Unilever-Zaire group, MARSAVCO is considered a manufacturing industry geared to the domestic market. We have already described above the activities of this firm, upon which depends the industrialization for the subsidiaries of the Unilever-Zaire group. Contrary to the theoretical model of accumulation (which would have it that on the periphery the fundamental liaison should be established with the sector producing luxury items), in the case of MARSAVCO, it is a question of current consumption goods for the masses: "blue soap" (washing soap) above all, household soap and toilet soap, margarines. The same is true in the textile industry in Zaire, which began with the manufacture of fabrics of low quality destined for the poor working-class masses and peasants: malekani, kaniki, khaki, etc. This clearly indicates the dangers of all generalizing and corresponds to the three phases of industrialization by import substitution:[5]

(1) the easy or euphoric phase, which corresponds to the production of mass consumption goods;

(2) the intermediate phase, with the production of luxury goods;

(3) the maturity phase, with the production of capital goods.

This is logical and corresponds to the evolution of the Zairois society. From colonization to the present day it is in fact possible to distinguish two main phases in the social evolution of Zaire:

The first phase begins with the setting up of wage labour and the formation of a rural and urban proletariat (1910-1930);

The second phase is characterized by two stages: the first, which was characterized by the formation of national junior cadres in the Administration and in the private sector during the 1930s and which up to 1958 created those called "évolués" or "immatriculés", elements whose only requirement was—through diverse cultural and nationalist organizations such as the Cercle des évolués, the APIC, various associations of the former students of such and such a school—attainment of the status enjoyed by whites, and who are characterized by the pursuit of the European style of consumption.

From 1960 to 1967 the elements of the national bourgeoisie originating in the preceding group and the politicians of 1960, no longer content to consume luxury goods, wished to become, as the measures of November 30, 1973 clearly indicate, owners of the means of production belonging to the foreigners.

This is absolutely logical: since the general level of living for the Zairois population was at first very low, it would have been irrational for the capitalist to produce a commodity which he could not sell for lack of a market.

The establishment in Zaire of MARSAVCO in 1922 permitted Unilever to work out and develop in Zaire vertical integration in the soap and edible oils and fats sector. Not only did the company benefit from a local supply of cheap palm oil but it also had the monopoly for the production of soap and margarine in Zaire. A second point justifying the implantation of MARSAVCO consists in the reduction of production and distribution costs, which enabled the firm to sell its products more cheaply, while still making enormous profits. This appeared on the one hand, in the low level of wages distributed within the firms of the Lever group[6] and on the other hand, in the fact that MARSAVCO does not have any warehouses, except for two in Kinshasa and in Lubumbashi. This means that the company does not adopt a formula which would require it to assume distribution of its products by an autonomous network. The distribution of MARSAVCO products is thus ensured by various third-party wholesalers (on condition that a commission, called "administrative charges", be paid)—formerly European intermediaries, today Zairois—known by the vague and confused name of "new acquirers". A third interesting point about the company is tax evasion. The raw materials imported by MARSAVCO for local production escape the import duties on imported products. In the Lever company's system, this policy is not at all new. The company has already had recourse to similar practices from the outset, as described above.

The implantation of MARSAVCO has accelerated the course of the structures of underdevelopment, with its two principal aspects: (1) technological dependency; and (2) insufficient linkage effects.

Analysing the linkage effects of the edible fats and oils industry, J. La Croix wrote, "one can scarcely expect forward linkage effects from an industry concerned exclusively with final demand". As for the backward linkage effects, he writes, "the backward linkage effects are almost negligible as regards the development of raw materials. The palm-oil production obeys the impulses of foreign demand more than that emanating from the local industry." This appears clearly, we think, in the supply difficulties experienced by MARSAVCO, especially in oil for the manufacture of soap, for which it has become necessary to import tallow.

Unlike the backward linkage effects that such an industry can have in developed countries, the local production of goods originally produced elsewhere implies (or more precisely, requires) that adequate machinery produced elsewhere be imported, which from a socio-economic point of view reduces the country to the role of consumer of techniques which it cannot itself produce and therefore forces it to accept the massive outflow of foreign exchange necessary for the purchase of techniques conceived elsewhere and for the payment of manufacturing means and patents.

The colonial trade system and the extortion of the purchasing power of the population

From colonial trade to the constitution and control of a vast internal distribution network for imported or local products, SEDEC has continued to steer its policy within the framework of participation in the industrial firms.

Responding to the objectives of its multinational, SEDEC, created in 1917, had as its primary objective importing merchandise and organizing trade stores in the plantation districts. In the absence of statistics on the quantities imported and exported or even sold on the spot, the analysis of the distribution network and of the associated companies will suffice to show the influence of SEDEC on the economy of Zaire.

In his book, Mandiangu-Bingila gives a precise description of the network, which can be divided into two groups: (1) the commercial network; and (2) the industrial firms.

Commercial Firms

1. The principal one is SEDEC-Trading, whose activities consist of importing in bulk and of distributing the local products. SEDEC-Trading's imports are carried out through the purchasing offices of the United Africa Company (UAC) in Brussels, Paris, London, Manchester and New York, covering quite an array of products: Remington, Aladin, Johnnie Walker, Kodak, Novak and many others. The local products distributed constitute a whole series: the Feltisaf textile products, Zaire-Print, Cotexti blankets, Dux mattresses, Cyclor bicycles, Chanimetal products, FNMA office equipment, MARSAVCO products, etc. The commercial network of the group covers 7 of the 8 administrative regions in the country; Shaba, which is not dependent on this network, is supplied by another subsidiary of the United Africa Company, the United Agencies (UNMAG).

2. The motors division of SEDEC, presently called ACA (Commercial Automobile Agency) has exclusive representation for all the brands and products of General Motors—American, German, and British. It also represents Lester Motors, Frigidaires and Electro-Lux refrigerators and agricultural equipment, as well as having the same network as SEDEC-Trading.

3. The African Pharmacies (PHARMAF), created in 1955, have specialized in chemical, pharmaceutical products and surgical equipment. They include warehouses, dispensaries and a packaging laboratory for products of wide consumption.

4. The G. B. Ollivant Co., specializing in textiles, drinks and hardware, has a clothing workshop with a capacity of more than 12,000 shirts per month.

The industrial firms

In the industrial sphere, the activities of SEDEC developed in the form of participation. Thus SEDEC has interests in:

1. Chanimetal, an industrial company for the construction and manufacture of metal and mechanical items, has a shipyard, a foundary, engineering workshops, and a range of manufactured items, such as oxygen, containers, machetes and hoes.

2. Zaire-Print, a company created in 1969 and specializing in the printing and selling of printed fabrics.

3. Cyclor, a company which manufactures bicycles and motorcycles.

This brief description of SEDEC shows the level attained by this multinational throughout the country on the level of the process of goods distribution, the privileged position in colonial-type trade, and the extortion of the purchasing power of the people. This extortion flows directly from the appropriation of the principal means of production by large-scale-capital.

Conclusions and perspectives

The impact which the multinational has had on the structures of social formation in Zaire has been profound and has contributed greatly to the emergence of new social classes, to the proletarization of the peasants, to marginalization, to the reduction of other pre-capitalist production modes and to the installation of the structures of an underdeveloped capitalism.

The problem which is posed for Zaire as a nation is twofold, and corresponds to two hypotheses:

(a) either Zaire is willing to deal tactfully with the multinational (for as Suzanne de Brunhoff has stated so well in *Le Monde Diplomatique* of June 1974, private capital always needs the existence of a state power) and profit from the awakening of "nationalism" due to the recent measures of Zairianization, in order to open the way for a class of nationals on the executive staff without a notable change in the nature of the firm;

(b) or Zaire breaks relations totally with the multinational and tries to define the ways and means of controlling the multinational's empire. This fact can only be the result of a struggle on the regional level by the whole of the African countries dominated by the multinational. This struggle can only be the result of the internal political struggle and of the ascent of leaders truly committed to the cause of the people.

Notes

[1] M. Merlier, *Le Congo de la colonisation belge à l'indépendence,* Maspero, 1963.
[2] Christian Palloix, *Le procès d'internationalisation du capital,* Maspero, 1970, p. 181.
[3] M. Merlier, op. cit., p. 63–64.
[4] Mandiangu, *Un trust au Congo—Le Groupe Unilever Congo, 1960–67,* ENDA, 1969.
[5] Hector Michelena, comment at the Ouagadougou Seminar, November, 1973.
[6] Cf. Appendix 7, Distributed wages.

Appendix 1

Number of PLZ districts in 1970

	Name	*Principal activities*
1.	Kinshasa	Harbor installation
2.	Lusanga (Kwilu)	7300 hectares palm-tree exploitation, natural palm-groves, 10 palm-oil factories, 1 refinery
3.	Bongimba (Oshwe)	820 hectares palm-trees
4.	Ingende	2513 hectares palm-trees, 2 palm-oil factories
5.	Ngwaka	3986 hectares heveas 1117 hectares cocoa-trees 1 rubber factory and installations for processing cocoa
6.	Brabanta	5431 hectares palm-trees, 1 palm-oil factory
7.	Yalingimba	9156 hectares palm-trees, 600 hectares cocoa trees, 1 palm-oil factory
8.	Mokaria	2535 hectares heveas 2074 hectares cocoa trees 1 rubber factory, cocoa-processing installations
9.	Basoko	7000 hectares palm-trees, 3 palm-oil factories
10.	Bumba	4400 hectares palm-trees 2 palm-oil factories
11.	Muene	349 hectares tea-plants

Source: Secrétariat Général of PLC

Appendix 2

Evolution of PLZ Exports (in Zaria) 1964-1966

	1964		1965		1966	
	Tonnage	Value	Tonnage	Value	Tonnage	Value
Palm-oil	39,388	1,271,013	17,537	649,117	30,000	1,025,166
Rubber	6,047	431,765	3,951	281,867	3,689	252,800
Cocoa	324	95,632	602	32,821	725	40,000
Palm-oil	15,674	602,747	11,372	511,212	12,400	497,810
Palm-kernel oil-cakes	18,298	169,124	12,831	138,411	14,700	160,745
Tea	122	7,953	459	26,640	413	31,000
Total	79,854	2,648,232	46,752	1,640,062	62,427	2,007,521
In relative values of the capital	100	100	58.5	62.4	77.9	75.9

Base: 1964 = 100.

Source: Ministère de l'Economie Nationale, Direction des Investissements

Appendix 3

Range of MARSAVCO products

1. *Food Products*
   Blue Band
   Axa, Covo
   Huildor
   Simba

2. *Toilet soap*
   Lux
   Reward
   Très chic
   Tango
   Astral
   Rexona

3. *Household soap*
   Sunlight
   Le Coq
   Eléphant

4. *Toiletries*
   Pepsodent
   Gibbs
   Sunsilk
   Tango
   Delia

5. *Laundry Products*
   Omo
   Vigor

6. *Scouring Products*
   Vim
   Sav

Appendix 4

Statistics on MARSAVCO sales (in tons)

	1960	1961	1962	1963	1964	1965	1966	1967
Evolution	9,288	11,514	14,673	15,731	17,088	15,722	19,535	22,210
Index	100	123.9	156.3	159.1	194.7	157.4	210.2	235.0

Index on base 1960 = 100.
Source: *Revue Marsavco.*

Appendix 5

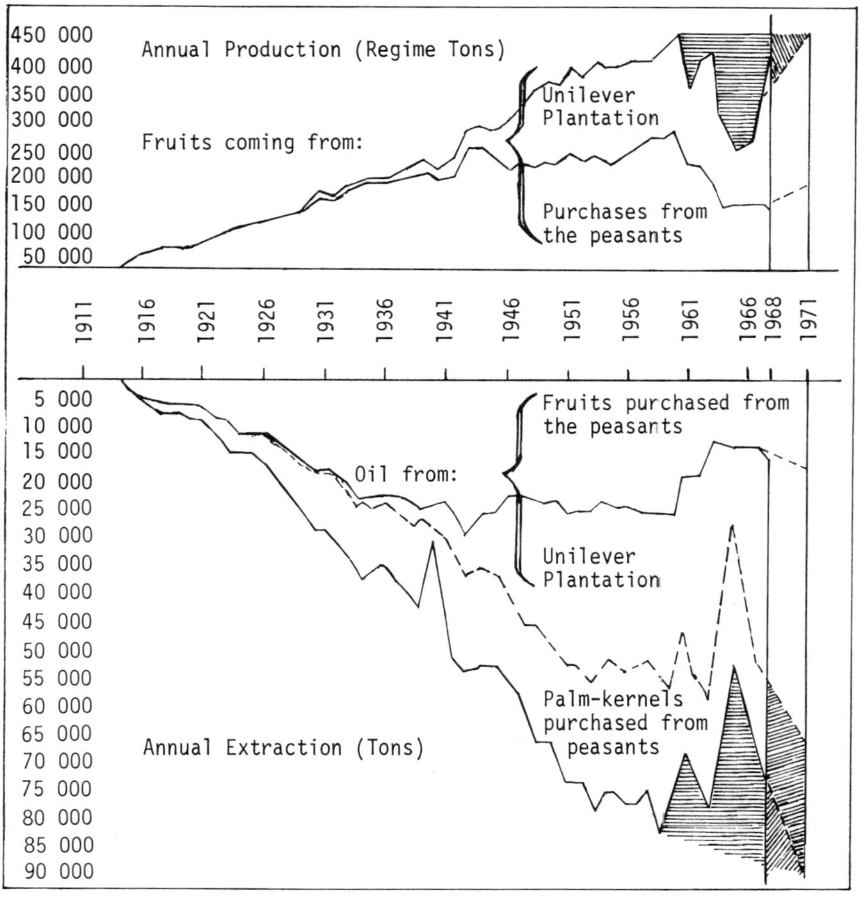

Source: Unilever Plantation in Congo 1971.

Appendix 6

Comparative table

Palm-oil Year	National exports	PLZ exports	%
1965	36,219	11,372	31.3
1966	37,063	12,400	30.7

Palm-kernel oil cakes Year	National exports	PLZ exports	%
1965	40,047	12,831	32.0
1966	41,884	14,700	35.0

Appendix 7

Wages and salaries distributed and PLZ personnel in 1966

Personnel in 1966		%	Wages paid	in Zaria	%
Total personnel	16,105	100	Net total paid	1,250,395	100
Total Congolese	15,976	99.2	To the Congolese	866,031	69.3
Total expatriates	129	0.8	To the expatriates	384,364	30.7

Wages distributed and PLZ personnel in 1967

Personnel in 1967		%	Wages paid	in Zaria	%
Total personnel	20,893	100	Net total paid	1,904,475	100
Total Congolese	20,768	99.4	To the Congolese	1,146,121	60.2
Total expatriates	125	0.6	To the expatriates	758,354	39.8

Source: *Mandiangu Bingila, op. cit.*

Bibliography

Amin, Samir, *Le développement inégal,* Editions de Minuit, 1973.
Bingila, Mandiangu, *Un trust au Congo.* "Le groupe Unilever-Congo 1960-67". Mémoire de fin d'études, ENDA, 1969.
La croissance de la grande firme multinationale, Colloques internationaux du C.N.R.S., Revues 28-30 sept. 1973, Editions du C.N.R.S., 1973.
Firmes plurinationales, Economies et Sociétés, Cahiers de l'I.S.E.A., Tome 11, n° 9, Sept. 1968.
Lacroix, J. L., *L'industrialisation au Congo,* Mouton-Paris, 1967.
Lewin, R. and P. Y., *Les trusts au Congo,* Société populaire d'éditions, Brussels, 1961.
Merlier, Michel, *Le Congo de la colonisation belge à l'indépendence,* Maspero, 1963.
Nicolai, Henri, *Le Kwilu,* CEMMUBAC, LXIX, 1963.
Palloix, Christian, *Le procès de l'internationalisation du capital,* Maspero, 1968.
Plantations Lever au Congo, Revue éditée par l'Unilever à Kinshasa.
Sherrill, Michael, *Unilever et l'Afrique,* Les Cahiers du CEDAF, n° 4, 1973.

The Multinational Corporation in Africa: Strategies for Independence

Clive Y. Thomas

Industrialization and the Transformation of Africa: An Alternative Strategy to MNC Expansion

Part 1: Some aspects of the African industrialization experience

Introduction

A close study of the social forces which have formed the past development of the African economies clearly reveals that the successful industrialization of that continent would require such a quantitative and qualitative upward shift in the level of development of its productive forces, and the approach of its people to material phenomena, that it would be impossible to deal with this issue, as neo-classical economics does, without placing primary emphasis on the *dialectical interaction* between the process of industrialization of Africa, and the development of the social relations which govern production on that continent. Nevertheless, although this situation reflects the objective conditions which prevail in Africa, one must also take into account the fact that at the level of consciousness, in general, almost all economists (irrespective of their ideological positions) would consider most African countries (with perhaps two or three exceptions) as too "small" to engage in successful industrialization, as this term is currently understood. This view, although alarming in its consequences if it were to be true, seems to prevail irrespective of the political nature of the particular state power under consideration.

Similar views have also been expressed about the small, underdeveloped economy on other continents. Thus, writing on Cuba, Huberman and Sweezy observe:

> By committing herself to a program of industrial diversification, Cuba would in effect be condemning herself to industrial backwardness.[1]

Or again, Sutcliffe, in his study of industry and underdevelopment, remarks:

> the size of many, though not all underdeveloped countries is utterly inadequate to support an integrated modern industrial economy. Small economies are perfectly viable as long as they remain in the position of dependent "colonial"

economies largely supplying primary products to the industrialized world. It is only when an industrialization programme is envisaged that their economic size is seen to be inadequate.[2]

Our present contribution obviously cannot attempt to deal with the many issues arising from these considerations. All we shall have space for is to focus on conceptualizing the essentials of an economic strategy for the industrialization of Africa. It should be clearly stated, however, that in our opinion the successful implementation of the strategy outlined here presupposes certain prior developments in the extent to which the workers and peasants in the various African economies are able to dominate the state power, dictate the relationships between classes, and hence determine the distribution of the product and the allocation of the surplus. In pursuit of this major objective of the present paper, we shall first examine some of the broad patterns of recent industrial development in Africa, in order to illustrate the way in which historical circumstances have perverted this process. Secondly, we shall briefly posit an interpretation of the crucial material manifestations of the underdevelopment—size—dependence characteristics of Africa. And finally, on the basis of these analyses, we shall advance the main elements of an industrialization strategy.[3]

The industrial structure of Africa, circa 1960

The early 1960s were a very crucial period for the design of industrial development strategies in many of the African countries. Given the general paucity of statistical data which prevailed at that time, this period was marked by truly massive efforts to assess past and current levels of industrial development, and also by the initiation of a number of manufacturing censuses and surveys aimed at increasing the flow of data on industrial development and prospects in Africa. Much of this work was done through various United Nations agencies working on the continent. It is therefore not surprising to find that United Nations experts have played a significant role in the post-1960 formulation of industrial strategies, which were ostensibly designed to overcome precisely those deficiencies of the industrialization process observed by these experts.

What do these various analyses and assessments around 1960 generally reveal? First, the low overall level of development of the productive forces in industry in Africa was clearly documented. Whereas in 1960 the level of *per capita income in agriculture* in the developed countries was about 2.3 to 4 times that of Africa, in *industry, the level of per capita income* in the developed countries was on the average 20 times greater than that of Africa. Furthermore, the data reveal that, compared with the major industrial

Table 1. *Comparative per capita income in Africa and developed countries 1960* ($US)

Area	Agriculture	Industry	Other Sectors	All Sectors
Developed Countries	120	480	600	1,200
Africa (Total)	41	25	51	117
North Africa	48	22	62	132
West Africa	41	8	25	74
East Africa	31	12	29	72
Central Africa	37	28	38	103
Southern Africa	52	166	271	489

Source: *Industrial Development in Africa,* UN, 1967.

Table 2. *Industrial origin of GDP in Africa circa 1963* (percentage and per capita values)

ctor	Total Africa		West Africa		North Africa		East Africa		Central Africa		Southern Africa	
	$	%	$	%	$	%	$	%	$	%	$	%
riculture	51	37	60	56	64	35	36	47	40	41	42	10
ining	8	6	2	2	10	6	2	3	7	7	52	13
anufacturing	20	14	7	6	25	14	9	12	14	14	106	26
her	58	43	38	36	80	45	30	38	37	38	206	51
tal	137	100	107	100	179	100	77	100	98	100	406	100

urce: *Industrial Development in Africa,* UN, 1967.
he value figures are on a *per capita basis*)

capitalist economies, agriculture in Africa accounted for a relatively large share (37%) of the industrial origin of the GDP of Africa, while the mining and manufacturing sectors only accounted for 20% of the GDP. These data are shown in Tables 1 and 2.

Secondly, the data reveal a considerable degree of diversity in the development of productive forces within Africa. Thus, from the data presented in Table 2, it can be seen that the contribution of mining and manufacturing to the GDP varied from 8% of the GDP in West Africa to 39% in Southern Africa. The value of *per capita* industrial output in Africa also ranged from West Africa $9, East Africa $11, Central Africa $21 and North Africa $35, to Southern Africa's $158. Significantly, much of the diversity in the development of productive forces among African countries was based on

Table 3. *Percentage regional distribution of manufacturing, mining, and population in Africa, circa 1963*

Region	Manufacturing	Mining	Total	Population
North Africa	33.4	30.0	32.4	25.9
West Africa	8.7	7.5	8.4	27.7
East Africa	12.5	10.2	11.8	28.4
Central Africa	7.9	7.9	7.9	10.9
Southern Africa	37.5	44.4	39.5	7.1
All Africa	100.0	100.0	100.0	100.0

Source: Industrial Development in Africa, UN, 1967.

differences in the level of industrial development. The range of variation of *per capita* output in agriculture was, in comparison, relatively narrow indeed, ranging from $36 in East Africa to $64 in North Africa. In this regard, Africa conformed to the universal pattern of sustained rises in *per capita* GDP, this being a function of the level and spread of industrialization.

Naturally, the data also show that most of the manufacturing and mining development in Africa at that time was concentrated among a few countries, and skewed in favour of certain regions. Thus by 1963 Southern and North Africa with 33% of the continent's population accounted for over 70% of its manufacturing and mining output, while East, West and Central Arica with 67% of the continent's population accounted for only 28% of the total manufacturing and mining output (see Table 3).

Although the level of industrial development achieved in Africa by 1960 was very low indeed, official figures nevertheless indicated a very rapid *rate* of industrial growth in Africa. As can be seen from the data in Table 4, the rate of growth of the mining sector in Africa between 1938 and 1960 (3.6%), exceeded the rate of growth of the world's mining sector as a whole (3.4%), as well as that of the industrial countries (3.3%). In the manufacturing sector the rate of growth of output in Africa was even more striking. During 1938 - 1960, manufacture grew at 7.9% per annum in Africa, as compared with 4.8% in both the world as a whole and in the industrial countries. When Southern Africa is excluded from the data on Africa, the recorded rates of growth of industry are generally even more striking (mining 5.1%; manufacturing 8.6%, and total industry 7.4%).

Some observed limitations of pre-1960 industrial growth

As the United Nations experts themselves have observed: "the rapid rate of industrial growth in Africa over the past two decades has, thus far, had

Table 4. *Comparative rates of growth of industry 1938–1960*

Area	Annual compound rates of growth 1938–60
Africa	3.6
Mining	7.9
Total Industry	6.0*a*
Africa, excluding Southern Africa	
Mining	5.1
Manufacture	8.6
Total Industry	7.4*a*
World	
Mining	3.4
Manufacture	4.8
Total Industry	4.6
Industrial Countries	
Mining	3.3
Manufacture	4.8
Total Industry	4.5

Source: *Industrial Development in Africa,* UN, 1967

a up to 1957 only

scarcely any significant effect in bringing about a structural transformation of the African economies."[4] The question which follows, therefore, is why has this occurred? A number of explanations have been put forward by those examining the situation at that time. First, it was pointed out, correctly, that the "rapid" rate of growth was statistically illusory, because of the prevailing small base from which African industrial development was being measured. Secondly, it was pointed out that the industrial structure, as it had developed in Africa, favoured two areas of industry, namely: the preliminary processing of primary output for export (whether minerals or agricultural staples), and the production of light consumer goods and services for the local market, particularly where transport costs warranted it.

Thus, in a study of East Africa, a United Nations team observed:

> Further inadequacies of past and current industrial performance can be seen in the structural characteristics. Production has hitherto centred on: (a) the primary processing of non-ferrous metals, exclusively for export purposes, and greatly limited by adverse transport costs; (b) the processing of agricultural raw materials, such as sugarcane (though very little refining, except in small quantities for local consumption); (c) the production of perishable products, such as bread; (d) the production of goods for which the container is heavy relative to the contents, such as beer and soft drinks; (e) the cheaper end of the

Table 5. *The structure of African industry 1950–1963* (percentage of value added)

	1950					1963				
Sector	North Africa	West Africa	Central Africa	East Africa	Total	North Africa	West Africa	Central Africa	East Africa	Total
Mining and quarrying	20	33	36	34	29	27	27	30	26	27
Agro Allied Industries	31	41	28	30	31	24	45	28	31	29
Light Industries	27	18	11	12	19	24	21	14	16	21
Heavy Industries	22	8	25	24	21	25	8	28	27	23
Total	100	100	100	100	100	100	100	100	100	100

Source: *Industrial Development in Africa,* UN, 1967.

market for such things as textiles and shoes; (f) products which make minimal demands on manufacturing skills; (g) simple essembly operations, and (h) exceptionally heavy or bulky items favoured by transport cost considerations.[5]

The data in Table 5 highlight some of these characteristics of the African industrial structure.

A third deficiency of pre-1960 industrial development in Africa was that many of the heavier consumer goods industries which had been established had a very low domestic value-added content, since they relied very heavily on the importation of "knocked-down" inputs to be assembled locally. Fourthly, it was found that the narrow domestic market for some of the output of these industries created a situation in which optimal scale economies could not be achieved. And worse, the existence of these narrow markets was frequently compounded by the duplication of plants in the different national territories! Thus we had unique combinations of several similar plants, each with idle capacity, the underdevelopment of shift work practices, and output runs of a scale far below optimum requirements.

Fifthly, few of the industries established in Africa by that time had made serious efforts to train skilled African personnel. The reliance on non-African expatriate personnel in some instances accounted for as much as 60 percent of salary and wage bills. Thus in East Africa, in 1963, 6% of the labour force in industry were non-African (i.e., 16,000 out of a total labour force of 280,000). Given pay structures which were derived from the social and political roles these expatriates were expected to play locally, as compared with their African counterparts, this was an additional element in raising unit costs of production in many enterprises.

A sixth major deficiency observed was that the technology in use in some of these enterprises was considered to be too highly capital-intensive, and at the same time made limited use of by-products and wastes of local materials. The result was that continuing industrialization not only failed to raise incomes substantially, but also failed to absorb the growing labour force at anything like a nearly adequate rate. When these were combined with the restrictions on consumer choice, the poor quality of many of the "local" products produced in these factories, the loss in government revenue which accompanied the tax concessions to aid these industries, and the high foreign-exchange content of their capital construction *and* current operations, the harsh verdicts reached on the prevailing levels and patterns of industrialization in Africa could not have been otherwise.

Thus even the bland UN-type verdicts did not hide the disturbing situation:

> On the whole, the current picture of industry in Eastern Africa is far from rosy. First of all, industry has not been able to develop fast enough to meet the growing demand and there has thus been a rapid increase in imports of goods of industrial origin. Secondly the import substitution effort has concentrated on consumer goods and has resulted in a rapid increase of demand for intermediate goods. Little progress has been achieved in capital goods, almost all of which have to be imported. Although the productivity of labour has visibly increased, labour costs per unit of output have also increased, and are one of the factors in the increase in prices of domestically manufactured goods. ... There is no discernible prospect of reducing the absolute level of expatriate employment and progress with respect to the skilled labour supply has been inadequate.[6]

Industrial change and crisis since 1960

Given the picture of African industrialization in the early 1960s as described here, the question we should ask is, what has emerged since then, now that we are at the end of the much-touted Development Decade? In our attempts to answer this question, we shall concentrate on the independent developing countries of Africa which are members of ECA. This permits us to avoid taking up the special problems of South Africa, and the still-colonized parts of Africa.

First, it can be seen from the data in Table 6 that the manufacturing sector still remains a relatively small contributor to African GDP. Most of the expansion in the industrial contribution to the GDP over the last decade has come about through a more than doubling of the contributions of the mining and quarrying sectors. Secondly, as the data in Table 6 also show, regional variations in the size of the industrial sector still remain significant. So also, we might add, do variations in the size of the industrial sectors within regions. Thus we find that of the 41 independent developing countries of Africa, only

Table 6.

Region	Mining and Quarrying		Manufacturing and Electricity		Construction		Total Ind	
	1960	1971	1960	1970	1960	1970	1960	19
North Africa	3.1	14.5	14.7	14.5	6.7	5.5	24.6	34
West Africa	2.5	12.5	5.6	10.4	5.0	5.0	13.1	28.
C. Africa	5.2	7.3	11.7	14.6	4.6	5.2	21.4	27
East Africa	9.9	6.0	7.0	11.1	4.3	5.1	21.2	22
Independent Developing Africa	4.3	11.6	10.1	12.6	5.5	5.2	19.9	29.

Source: *Survey of Economic Conditions in Africa,* 1972.

Table 7. *Manufacturing as a % of GDP*

North Africa		*Central Africa*	
Algeria	9.1	Burundi	3.9
Egypt	21.7	Cameroon	11.4
Libyan Arab Republic	1.7	Central African Republic	10.8
Morocco	12.3	Chad	9.1
Sudan	9.0	Congo, P.R.	12.2
Tunisia	9.8	Equatorial Guinea	3.9
Total North Africa12.6		Gabon	4.7
West Africa		Rwanda	14.0
Dahomey	5.8	Zaire	16.5
Gambia	2.2	Total Central Africa	12.6
Ghana	15.7	*East Africa*	
Guinea	8.3	Botswana	8.9
Ivory Coast	8.1	Ethiopia	6.2
Liberia		Kenya	13.2
Mali	11.4	Lesotho	0.7
Mauritania	2.9	Madagascar	12.3
Niger	6.9	Malawi	12.5
Nigeria	8.5	Mauritius	15.2
Senegal	14.2	Somalia	4.5
Sierra Leone	5.5	Swaziland	14.1
Togo	11.0	Tanzania	10.1
Upper Volta	10.5	Uganda	7.2
Total West Africa	9.3	Zambia	10.2
		Total East Africa	9.7
		Independent Developing Africa	11.0

Source: ECA secretariat.

Table 8. *Share of total value-added by manufacturing in independent developing Africa*
(percentage)

Country	Percentage 1960	1971
Algeria North Africa	7.3	6.6
Egypt North Africa	33.1	27.2
Morocco North Africa	9.7	7.6
Ghana West Africa	2.5	5.7
Nigeria West Africa	9.0	12.5
Cameroon C. Africa	2.3	2.0
Zaire C. Africa	8.9	5.5
Ethiopia E. Africa	2.6	2.1
Kenya E. Africa	2.6	4.0
Zambia E. Africa	1.3	3.0
Total	79.3	76.2

19 countries had by 1971 achieved a GDP structure where the share of manufacturing exceeded 10% (see Table 7). Ten countries, as can be seen from Table 8, account for 76% of the value-added in manufacturing in 1971, as compared with 80% in 1960. Egypt alone contributes over one-quarter of the manufacturing value-added in independent developing Africa. A further feature to note is that the manufacturing sector in Africa maintained a high rate of growth over the last decade—averaging 6.5% per annum, as compared with an overall growth in GDP of 4.3%.

Structurally, the recent industrialization has contributed little to the task of transforming the African economies. With the exception of Egypt, and to a lesser extent Algeria, very little thrust has been directed towards heavy industry for the domestic economy.

Mining still predominates in several economies; the foreign domination of this sector, plus its very exiguous internal linkages (due to emphasis on the production of nearly crude or for exports), ensure that the task of industrialization has not been seriously advanced by these developments. In other African economies the recent thrust has been in the direction of the assembly of consumer goods based on the importation of pre-fabricated inputs.

Thus, from the data in Table 9, we can observe an industrial sector characterized by the familiar emphasis on light industries and small size of establishments. About 70% of the establishments, employing 68% of the manufacturing labour force and contributing 65% of the value-added in manufacturing, were in the category of light industries.

Table 9.

Group	Percentage of total number of establishments	% of persons employed in manufacturing	% of value-added in manufacturing	Number of employees per establishment
Food, beverages & tobacco	25.8	24.3	38.1	75
Textile and clothing	28.8	32.8	19.0	90
wood and furniture	11.3	7.0	4.1	49
Paper, printing & publishing	7.4	4.4	3.4	79
Light Industries	70.3	68.4	64.5	77
Chemicals, petroleum and plastics	6.1	10.5	13.4	135
Non-metallic mineral products	6.2	5.6	4.1	71
Basic metal industries	0.4	2.1	2.8	412
Fabricated metal products, machinery and equipment	13.8	12.3	12.4	71
Other manufactures	3.2	1.1	0.7	28
Heavy Industries	29.7	31.6	33.4	84
Total	100.0	100.0	100.0	79

Source: ECA, *Survey of Economic Conditions in Africa,* 1972.

At the same time heavy industries contributed about one-third of the value-added in manufacturing and a little less than that proportion to total employment in manufacturing. Most of the establishments were, from the labour force angle, small in size, with an average labour force of about 80 persons.

How can we explain the persistence of rapid industrial growth and at the same time the failure of the African economies to move far in the direction of structural transformation? It would be gross naïveté, we believe, to attempt to comprehend the deficiencies and limitations of Africa's recent industrial experience abstracted from the social forces which have determined the role that Africa has historically played in the evolution of international capitalism. The limitations of the recent African industrial experience, just as its much analysed "underdevelopment" and "dependence", can only be fully comprehended as a double conjuncture of, on the one hand, the progressively *objective* socialization of global production which has accompanied the world-wide spread of the capitalist mode of production, and, on the other, the conjunction of productive forces and production relations within African societies.

This is the only *objective* basis for understanding the limited scope of present industrialization, the poverty of African societies with which it must be linked, and the growing inequalities of income and wealth which the world system of capitalist production and exchange continually reproduces. This inequality is seen in the global distribution of wealth, in the pattern of regional development within Africa (i.e., the tendencies of particular countries to act as poles of capitalist influence and so to "grow" relatively faster than others), and within African societies themselves.

Again, this is not the proper forum to take up the wide-ranging issues arising from this situation. What we must indicate here, however, is the background against which we should observe the role of the multinational corporations in the recent industrial growth in Africa. It is furthermore not our task in this paper to analyse the MNCs as such. Other contributions are specifically devoted to this task. Rather, we shall seek to highlight very briefly certain major characteristics of the role of MNCs in African industrialization in order to indicate the logic underlying our subsequent industrial proposals.

Although there is great variation from country to country, most of the important MNC activity in Africa is in the manufacturing sector, including the production of minerals for export. Although there has traditionally been considerable MNC contribution in crop production, their activity in the field of agriculture is decreasing relatively, except in such areas as food processing and the production of important agricultural inputs such as fertilizers. There are a number of alleged advantages which are supposed to flow from these MNC activities in Africa. The MNC being the most advanced organizational form of capitalist enterprise, it has been argued that it should therefore make outstanding contributions to the rapid growth of these sectors in the African economy, because of its inevitable infusions of technology and know-how, capital, and its "unrivalled organizational capacity" in production and marketing.

Actual developments, however, have indicated that this has not been the case and a number of probing questions have been directed towards the operations of the MNCs. One such question is whether the technology transferred to Africa is adapted to, or adaptable to, either the African resource configuration or the prevailing social conditions in Africa. Another concerns the role of patents and licences in promoting the development of an indigenous technology in Africa. Yet another important probing question concerns the true foreign-exchange costs/benefits to the national economy where branches of the MNCs predominate. Some of the answers which have been formulated on the basis of available data indicate the scope of the difficulties which the operations of MNCs present to the African economies.

As regards the first question it should be remembered that it is generally held that Africa is a continent with considerable natural resources. It possesses about one-third of the known and explorable hydroelectric potential and about 10 percent of known petroleum reserves, in addition to having good prospects for solar, thermal, tidal, and geothermic energy. Furthermore, the region has good mineral resources, accounting for about one-third of the total value of world mineral output: "Africa contributes substantially to the world's production of basic minerals. [Its] share in world production of certain selected minerals in 1971 was as follows: gold 81 percent, diamonds 69 percent, phosphate rock 26 percent, lead ore 6 percent, zinc ore 5 percent and coal 2 percent".[7] Most of these minerals are exported, accounting for about one-half of total export earnings.

All this natural resource exploitation takes place on a continent where it is generally conceded that there has been as yet no up-to-date and comprehensive resources inventory. In these circumstances it is clear that whatever technology transfer occurs in the mining sector, it cannot be adapted to local resources in the service of local needs, since, when local resources are the bases of domestic production, such production is for export, and hence really responsive to the needs and requirements of the capitalist centre. When production does take place for the local market, this is invariably based on MNC fabrication and assembly of imported components. Moreover, a great deal of this latter type of production for the "local" market is really directed toward servicing the needs of the relatively small, urban, high-income elite in these countries, an elite which normally consumes along the lines of the metropolitan countries from whence the MNCs have come.

The answer to the second question is equally damaging. The evidence suggests, and this has been confirmed in other countries where this problem has been studied in greater detail, that the licensing and patenting systems in use frequently create a major source of income drain from underdeveloped countries. It has been found that in some circumstances, when technology is sold under these arrangements, it is usually part of a "package deal" which often leads to overselling. Sometimes these arrangements also "lock-in" the domestic purchases to the technology of the patent owner, irrespective of the price at which this technology is available on the market, and the competitive availability of similar technologies.

These arrangements also frequently allow for "commercial lock-ins"; i.e., the African purchaser is tied to the equipment and materials of the patenter, who in turn limits the conditions of production and sale of the output of these enterprises in the local economies.

In addition it has been found that licences and fees usually create a multi-channel source of foreign-exchange drain, because they make transfer pricing possible on a number of items. When this is combined with the evidences of over- and under-invoicing, the operations of management contracts and technical service arrangements, plus the conditions for the repatriation of profits and dividends built in to these contracts, then not only is the rate of return on capital employed often phenomenally higher than the balance-sheet figures show, but the cost in a crucial resource—foreign exchange—is much more considerable than the surface picture suggests.

Evidence on these and many other abuses is available, but the important question we would like to turn to is, how have African governments sought to deal with this rapidly developing situation?

Some marginal solutions to the industrialization impasse[8]

The major features of the multinational corporations operating within Africa are that they are foreign owned and controlled. The basic policy question therefore is, how have African governments responded to the issues of ownership of the local resources which these firms control?

On the question of the ownership structure of the MNCs, there are four basic alternative strategies which have been pursued in Africa. All fall short of nationalization. Indeed, because of this factor, it is often argued that these strategies maximize international capitalistic participation in the national economy, while at the same time they provide precautions with which to minimize the harmful consequences of this. In other words the strategies are supposedly "pragmatic" and are designed to increase the long-run capacity of the country to sustain its own development, by first building up an infrastructure of material production and the requisite skills. These strategies are namely: localization of senior management and administrative staff(e.g., Africanization), requiring foreign firms to raise a substantial part of their capital requirements from the domestic capital market through the issue of local equities, state participation through the establishment of a national institution in competition with foreign enterprise in the same area of activity, and state participation in the ownership structure of foreign capitalistic firms through a majority-share ownership. We shall briefly examine each of these in turn.

Much state activity in all these countries has been directed towards publicizing and pressuring multinational companies into allowing nationals to participate in the higher levels of management. This strategy, it is argued, would not only find opportunities for local skills to be employed, but would also serve to nationalize these companies in their operations and decision-making, through the participation of nationals in the crucial management areas. Often progress is measured simply in terms of the number of foreigners whose jobs have been taken over by local personnel.[9]

There are two basic weaknesses to this strategy. First, it underestimates the social power of these institutions and the degree of their "totality" in the control of individuals. Local persons move into particular institutional structures, with their own ethos, values, life styles, and way of doing things—all of which are derived from the imperative of exploiting local resources for the benefit of metropolitan capital. These nationals therefore work in a situation where there are strong built-in pressures to conform to the values and behavioural patterns of the enterprise. This pressure continues unless the individual leaves. But as this socialization process takes place, instead of the company becoming more and more national, it is in fact the nationals who are likely to become more and more an extension of the exploiting multinational corporation. It is therefore they who become denationalized.

Their confidence and reliance on this acculturation process has therefore encouraged many corporations to welcome nationals into their local operations. This gives them a "national" image without endangering the true nationality of the corporation. Proof of this can be seen from the frequency with which nationals are used at the points where they are most public, e.g., the front office, public relations departments, and as personnel officers. (The latter example also has obvious additional advantages where matters of wage negotiation are concerned!) In every case, therefore, the new strategy can be defeated by the dynamics of cultural and psychological dependence. In the small African economies the sheer weight and power of international capitalism makes it difficult to overcome it in this manner.

The second weakness of this strategy is the phenomenon of organizational substitution which has been made easy through the technological possibilities of virtually instant communications. This process permits the companies to let nationals fill managerial positions nominally, and at the same time empty these managerial positions of any decision-making significance, by simply referring back to Head Office decisions which would normally and routinely have been made locally if they had uncontrolled rights to appoint management. Of course, in so far as the earlier point stands, i.e., local management fits into the corporate structure correctly, the need for this organizationl substitution is therefore an important index of the importance of cultural and psychological dependence in the development of the local managerial petit-bourgeoisie.

The second strategy, i.e., issuance of local equities, also contains a number of equally fundamental limitations. Firstly, the companies usually issue shares in such quantities and in such a way as to avoid putting real control of the company into jeopardy. Secondly, this is reinforced by the tendency for these shares to be taken up by other similarly 'local' enterprises, or a particular clique of local businessmen who specialize in "partnering" local and foreign capital. Thirdly, the local-share issues often serve to raise from the local capital market funds to finance the construction costs of the enterprise, while the remainder of the shares are "exchanged" for patent rights, technical services, etc., from the parent firm.

A fourth objection is that where the enterprise is already a going concern, the issuance of local shares to enable local participation simply provides the firm with funds to invest elsewhere, if the fear of local incursion into its control is taken seriously. In other words it allows these companies to capitalize some of their future claims on the income stream of the enterprise. Finally, the clamour for local participation is often directed only towards foreign capital, although internally many locally-owned firms remain within the uncontested grip of special families and business cliques. This occurs because in general this particular strategy *seeks to create a local bourgeoise to replace the foreign bourgeoise and does not seek to contest the legitimacy of the capitalist structure itself.*

The third strategy, i.e., establishing local, public-owned institutions to compete with foreign enterprises is usually little more than a token recognition of the problem. The waste it involves in duplication, the very futility of seeking to miniatuarize a multinational corporation through peaceful competition often indicates a genuine unwillingness and/or political incapacity to tackle the problem. Despite this it is usually claimed that even if these institutions remain small they have a qualitative impact on the system, since they force the multinational corporations to become sensitized to local needs!

The final strategy, i.e., state participation with a majority shareholding (the 51% formula), is the most ubiquitous among progressively inclined countries. But the truth is that three basic reasons prevent this from leading to any effective control over resources. Firstly, lacking in what they believe to be an "adequate" knowledge of the technical and managerial processes of the firm, participation in ownership has been counteracted by entering into management contracts with foreign capital. This therefore does not diminish the power of *foreign decision-making* in these enterprises. Secondly, these contracts often constitute significant sources of income drain along the lines referred to above. Thus, to take a concrete example, in Tanzania, there are contracts based on the turnover of the firm, and firms with persistent commercial losses are nevertheless forced to carry the income drain of foreign management contract payments since they have been negotiated as a charge on the enterprise before profits.[10]

The really fundamental weakness of this strategy lies in a misunderstanding of what the local expression of a multi-national corporation represents, and in particular the exporting corporation which is so dominant in Africa.

> It is essentially a plant. It is not a firm. It is true that there are titles such as Directors, Managers, Managing Directors etc. But the local expression ... makes no decision as regards prices ... output ... levels of investment, or the markets. All these are done at the Head Office where decisions which normally

define a firm are made. The apparatus which exists locally is just a participation, in a multi-plant firm. Therefore, when we seek meaningful participation, it is not simply to acquire a share in the local apparatus, but to ensure that inroads are made into the decision-making centres, which exist in the North Atlantic.[11]

It is clear from this analysis that these strategies deliberately seek to avoid direct and complete state ownership. Usually this is due either to ideological attachments to free enterprise or the so-called "pragmatic" necessities of politics. We shall not consider the reasonings in these positions in any detail. Instead, we shall enumerate some of the major growth consequences these strategies have had, in an effort to illuminate the complex and multi-dimensional nature of dependence in a small economy and thus the necessity for outright ownership, as a precondition for, and a link with, a strategy of economic transformation, as outlined in Part II.[12]

Despite the high rates of growth of material output, the pursuit of such strategies has led to a number of results which inhibit long-run transformation, as outlined in this paper. Firstly, as we have seen, a great deal of the industrialization has been confined to terminal activities. This is observed in the concentration of production to mining and export of primary materials, or the fabrication of consumer goods imported in a knocked-down condition. The result of this has been on the one hand, the absence of any linkages between changes in final domestic demand and domestic production, and on the other, the domestic value-added created by the low level of this output, which has meant that the gap between domestic resource use and domestic demand, the importance of which we shall underline later, has widened. Where minerals have been produced and exported, the domestically-retained income has been a small proportion of the value of the final product. Moreover, changes in domestic demand for these products are marginal, and therefore incapable of generating any significant changes in the levels of operations of the company. This simple assembly of imported consumer durables has also meant that the bulk of the value-added created by changes in domestic demand, which in this instance is not marginal, accrue to the overseas suppliers of the local firm, usually the parent company.

Secondly, such a development pattern, because it does not link the pattern and rate of domestic resource use to domestic demand, prevents the growth of an indigenous technology which can provide the basis for the necessary organic link between the two. From the viewpoint of the foreign businessmen the local territory usually has no resources. To him resource availability is measured by its availability at internationally traded prices. Furthermore, there is no need to develop a local technological capacity, since investments in *R and D* are already made at the Head Office of his company, where (from the point of view of the multinational corporate structure) the centralization of these investments bring certain obvious economies of scale which a small economy, with a small local turnover, cannot create.

A further consequence of this pattern of industrialization and growth has been that for a complex of reasons the rate of return on capital employed has been very high. Usually this derives from the firm's ability to exert monopoly power in the local market. This monopoly power has been a product of (1) governmental controls on imports offered as an incentive to production, which reduce competition from overseas suppliers, (2) the technical requirements of the optimum size plant, which often require large runs and which equally often even a single firm does not attain, (3) the desire to maximize possible economies of scale in order to maximize the profit rate. In the small underdeveloped African economy these combine to create what is almost a 'natural' monopoly. High profit rates on domestic operations mean that the incentives to find markets beyond the confines of the domestic market are virtually non-existent. Thus, given the high import-content of their operations, this unwillingness to develop an export capacity beyond possibly rationalizing their sales to "neighbouring countries", means that such enterprises contribute neither to raising the low export floor of the country nor to the lowering of its basic import ceiling. Trade therefore remains a manifestation of, and a contributing factor towards, the structural dependence and underdevelopment of the economy.

It is argued that this type of industrialization is inevitable, given the crucial constraint which the size of the national markets represents. It is believed, correctly, that small national markets cannot generate adequate incentives for private capitalism to undertake the industrial transformation of these societies. Because of this, a strategy frequently pursued is to form regional integration arrangements in Africa. Frequently, these arrangements centre on extending the market, by widening the permissive area of "free trade" in goods. The schemes therefore emphasize trade liberalization. They rarely seek to integrate and transform the ownership structure of the MNCs or the planning of the use of the region's resources, and the distribution of its product. Even when this is contemplated, and thus written into the various treaties, as in the East African Community, these clauses frequently remain dead clauses.

It is therefore not surprising that the major beneficiary of the widening of the regional market is the multinational firm. The treaties often do no more than create a framework which allows these firms to rationalize their plant capacity. This follows, despite the national monopoly which they might have had, because the region can be served at a lower unit cost of production and, other things being equal, a higher profit per unit of output, if one plant is made to serve the whole region, and duplication of plants therefore ruled out. The increased profits depend, of course, on the direction and amount of change of the weighted average of restrictions and monopoly power which the firm can command in the region as a whole, compared with the weighted average unit prices of output before integration.

> The direction of this movement is not always certain. Sometimes it may be that in exchange for the entire unified regional market, the firms may have to trade off the level of fiscal and other incentives they can command. In other instances, licences to produce might have already been given to more than one company in the territories to be integrated. Accordingly, the firms will have to negotiate and work out a basis for their competition and their ground rules for market sharing. In these arrangements they also frequently obtain government support, since no territory wants to see any impairment in the level of performance achieved by their industries, before the union takes place.
>
> Success in widening the market in this way, operates as yet another disincentive in seeking to widen their markets the hard way, (i.e., by lowering unit prices, adopting mass selling techniques, or forging a genuine export capacity). The movement toward economic integration becomes but a simple extension of national import-substitution to the region level. It neither aims at, nor is it capable of, generating the market preconditions for spawning the growth of an indigenous capitalism.[13]

A third policy which has recently emerged stems from studies which seek to show that the level of effective protection in African industry (as distinct from nominal protection), is high, and that these high rates of protection favour output in the fabrication and assembly end of industry. This position, it is argued, is further exaggerated by the overvalued foreign-exchange rates of many of the African countries. The policy line recommended and pursued, therefore, is to impose a uniform *ad valorem* tariff on all imports, and to devalue the foreign-exchange value of the currency. The uniform *ad valorem* tariff would be "neutral" in its effect on the industrial structure, while the foreign-exchange price effect of devaluation would favour the export of manufactures.

Such a formulation is, of course, most naïve. It assumes capital is simply available for allocation and will therefore simply follow the direction of local incentives. But when the historical process of African industrialization is fully grasped, it will be seen that what is analysed and interpreted as a "local" strategy of industrialization is in effect a product of changes internal to the central dynamics of industrial capitalism. The growth and spread of the MNC, its dynamically induced changes in investment and marketing patterns, and the nature of the technological transfers which take place, cannot be assessed as "local" phenomena, to be corrected by a more "locally" designed tariff and exchange rate policy. In the whole process, the tariff system is essentially a political product, a point which classical political economy has long recognized:

> Thus whilst . . . protection is of significance to the industrialization process . . . the tariff system is itself a dependent variable, determined by political and

economic factors that are beyond its control, as long as these economies continue to adhere to their present neo-colonial form.[14]

In this form the tariff system becomes one of the many conditions for maximizing the surplus and income drains from the periphery to the industrial centre.

To these three major policies there have been added other subsidiary policies, namely

(i) efforts to encourage the further processing of minerals and agricultural staples in the local economy, in order to capture a higher proportion of the value of the final product;

(ii) export promotion in craft and light-manufacturing industries;

(iii) efforts to encourage the flow of labour-and not capital-intensive technology to Africa;

(iv) efforts to negotiate "technology agreements".

Again, these policies fail to take into full account the true nature of underdevelopment and the dependence of the African economy on the industrial capitalism of Europe, America and Japan.

Part 2. Beyond the MNCs: Towards an industrialization strategy for Africa

Transformation and industrialization

As a consequence of the issues raised in Part 1 of this paper, an appropriate industrialization strategy for Africa must necessarily be informed by the ways in which, historically, the forces of underdevelopment have operated in these economies. In the author's above-mentioned recent study the view was advanced that, historically, there is a crucial significance to the combination of "smallness", which generally characterizes these economies in Africa, and underdevelopment. When put into a dynamic frame, and when expressed in "material" terms, the all-important measure of structural dependence, underdevelopment and economic backwardness of the production process is the lack.

On the one hand of an organic link, rooted in an indigenous science and technology, between the pattern and growth of domestic resource use, and the pattern and growth of domestic demand; and, on the other, the divergence between domestic demand and the needs of the broad mass of the population.

Naturally, this interpretation has both quantitative and qualitative aspects. Together, they show that the elements crucial to the functioning of an economic system, i.e., the linkages among labour-resources-technology-production-demand-needs operate in such a way that these communities have *internalized* "the dynamic of consuming what does not represent the needs of the community, and also, what they do not produce at home, and producing what they do not consume, and also do not need at home". There are therefore "gaps" between both the structure of consumption and output, and the pattern of consumption and needs. Recent industrialization, which has focused on the production of minerals, lightly-processed agricultural staples for export, and also on the assembly of imported "knock-down" consumer goods for relatively high-income elites, reinforces these tendencies, as some African economies pursue the transition from subsistence economy to the neo-colonial mode of production.

The correction to this imbalance has been advanced along the lines of two "iron laws of transformation". One of these "laws" refers to the necessity of planning the convergence of consumption patterns with needs, and the other the planned convergence of consumption patterns with domestic output, based principally on the use of domestic resources. These strategies follow logically if, as we have claimed, the material manifestations of underdevelopment are expressed in terms of the dynamic divergences between domestic resource use, domestic demand, and needs, in the absence of an indigenous technology capable of providing the basis for an organic link between these elements.

The tendency has been for cumulative divergences, notwithstanding recent experiences of industrialization aimed at the domestic market. These can be explained in terms of two factors, both of which are immanent to the structure of international capitalism, and both of which support this as a basic long-term historical trend. The first has been the demonstrated incapacity of these systems to develop an adequate and relevant indigenous technological and scientific capacity. As a consequence of these failures we find that within these economies there is in truth no basis for forging an organic link between resource use and demand. Often domestic resource endownment is not known in even the most rudimentary form. What exists, and what might be said to constitute an inventory of material resources, is frequently not much more than the random search for specific metals by colonial offices, or firms with special licences to search. Thus by the very nature and ways in which the search has been "organized", the full details are often not available to the governments of the host countries.

The second factor has been the long-run historical tendency of global and domestic income elasticities of demand for those types of products which are not produced in the typical small, underdeveloped economy in Africa to be higher than for those produced at home for home consumption, and for export-type commodities. The result is that income changes and its distribution among the population produce changes in demand which reinforce the divergence between domestic resource use and domestic demand. The growth of import-substituting industrialization has not changed this, since as we have seen, what has here been described as industrialization is essentially a process in which multinational corporations, although producing goods with high income elasticities of demand, do so by means of imported knocked-down equipment for simple assembly in the host country. The result is that changes in domestic demand have had limited impact on domestic resource use, because the bulk of the value-added in the production process already lies in the imported knocked-down components. This pattern of high income elasticities of demand for goods which are not produced in the host country, i.e., basically industrial goods, has been a universal phenomenon. It has manifested itself irrespective of the social system which has prevailed. As a result it is inconceivable that at any realistic economic cost to a small economy, these demand pressures can be contained, let alone reversed, seeming as they do to satisfy human needs everywhere. The consequences of this for planning demand are therefore very important.

In view of this it follows that structural transformation, the abolition of poverty, self-sustaining growth, all imply industrialization in the basic sense of the spread of industrial techniques of organization and resource use in the struggle to conquer the material environment. The empirical evidence on industrialization from both capitalist and socialist economies demonstrates that industrialization involves *inter alia* (1) significantly raising the share of manufacturing in total output and the absorption of resources, (2) a qualitative shift in the output of manufactured goods in favour of those which require complex technology and capital-intensive techniques, (3) a substantial upward displacement in the relative output per worker in industry schedule as against primary activity, so that the sectoral shifts in favour of industry raise the national average product per worker, (4) a self-sustained rise in labour productivity occasioned by (i) consistent technical progress, (ii) the continuous enlargement of the market, thereby bringing economies of scale through time, and (iii) through the progressive use of higher levels of capital per worker. As this process occurs, expenditure on manufacturing output shows a high income elasticity of demand:

> Under any social and political system, there can be little question that until high levels of income are reached the demand for the products of the industrial sector as a whole expands more rapidly than real income. This seems to be true of both *laissez-faire* and centrally planned economies, even though the composition of demand for industrial products may be different in these two cases; it seems to be true regardless of the distribution of income.[16]

If as communities develop, their demand structure is transformed in such a way as to lead to an increasing demand for industrial goods, then for this demand to be satisfied, African economies will have to achieve the spread of industry and industrial techniques into all facets of material production. As far as industrialization is concerned, a consistent strategy will have not only to conform to the demands of planned agriculture so as to ensure balance and proportion in the growth and composition of output, but must also lead to the generation of the bulk of material output from industry *per se*. Although this overriding constraint is widely recognized, its basic implications for industrial planning are often disregarded and fudged about under the guise of pressures—real, imagined, and contrived. Naturally, such a constraint has the basic implication that whatever might be the social rate of return of particular projects which together constitute the "Plan", and which have been selected by the use of the usual techniques of project analysis and selection (with the usual time-horizons), the balance of resource flows which follows must decisively favour industry. And, as we shall analyse later, *industry of a particular kind.* If this is not occurring then the problems of a structural transformation are not being confronted, and the plan has no analytical basis in the system of underdevelopment.

One frequently hears many so-called "well-meaning" rationalizations of why development plans in African states cannot conform to this model. Apart from the "Arcadian" view of agriculture implicit in some approaches and the rationalization of further specialization now (i.e., further entrenchment in capitalism) in order to diversify later, the real issue has been the lack of a commanding vision with which to permeate the planning process. Beset by a multitude of foreign experts, advisers, and the bourgeois literature on planning, many policy makers in Africa practice a subtle resignation to what they perceive to be the inevitably enduring nature of poverty and underdevelopment and the rise and spread of MNC activity as the only real countervailing force.

Of course it is not implied here that the industrial imperatives which we can discern in modern history are both mechanical and irresistible. Theoretically they may be resistible, but only at a cost we believe no society wants to, or indeed can afford, to bear. Indeed we believe further, that rather than having occurred *in vacuo,* industrialization is itself a social process which meets the needs of man in mastering the material environment. In this sense the pressures to industrialize cannot be rationally resisted. The industrial imperatives are also not mechanical, in the sense that the flow of resources to industry should follow an equal and unchanging pattern. There are periods of time when resource flows to agricultural or other activities may have to take precedence. Yet unless structural transformation is achieved, these must be construed as temporary expedients created by grave situations, e.g., the *proverbial Acts of God* and their effect on the rural economy, or emergency measures to alleviate social and political strains in the rural economy at certain points in time. Indeed, the latter consideration might very well be the only justifiable rationale behind the pattern of resource flows which has frequently emerged. Nonetheless, the issue has never been truly articulated this way. As a consequence, the consequences of present policies have not been fully appreciated.

The priority of resource flows to industry which has been indicated here neither implies nor presupposes any notion of a 'conflict' between industry and agriculture. Such a way of posing the issue would be to us most artificial. The basic strategy is one of the planned convergence of domestic resource use and domestic demand. All that we are arguing is that it is the industrial component of demand which has the greatest dynamic properties for a policy of planned production geared to satisfy the needs of the community. It is this basic strategy which throws up the priorities of resource flows, priorities which constitute the essence of transformation.

By similar reasoning it follows that this strategy does not presuppose a genuine conflict between capital, or any other 'productive factor' intensity, when deciding on investment priorities. Investment priorities and the choice of technique in our model are determined almost completely by the strategy of transformation and the product choices which this gives rise to. If beyond this there is scope for *de facto* substitutability of resource combinations, and the alternatives are real (in the sense that their social costs/benefits cannot be evaluated on the basis of *a priori* reasoning from the underdevelopment/transformation model), then the choice must be exercised through an evaluation of the alternatives, with reference to resource availabilities and social constraints at the particular time. Our own belief is that choice of technique as it is presented in the literature, i.e., the choice between the intensive use of capital or labour in production, is fairly limited in practice. What might be more important from our standpoint is the choice of raw-material input in making a particular industrial output. On this we shall have more to say later.

Apart from these preliminary observations one further essential point must be immediately conveyed. The investment strategy for industry (and indeed for all activities) cannot be derived on the basis of the micro-applications of choice of techniques to particular projects, in order to determine their "feasibility," so that, having been determined feasible, they are then simply aggregated to give an investment plan. Yet, in actual practice, many plans in Africa have been constructed on precisely this basis. It is usual to find that planning often consists of the application of the so-called objective techniques of micro-economics to a number of individual projects in order to test their feasibility. Depending on the results, these projects are then summated to determine the optimal investment plan. Since these projects all require financing, the cut-off point is then denoted by the amount of investment funds at the disposal of the State. This procedure is made even more complicated by the fact that a significant proportion of the funds "available" to the state derive from foreign sources, often multilateral aid agencies! In practice, the funds provided by foreign sources are closely geared to particular projects. The net effect therefore is that the projects merely constitute a shopping list for aid. As a result, the precise choice of projects, i.e., *the composition of the Plan,* is largely influenced by aid donors. When the shopping list is passed around to private investors, similar influences operate. How can such an exercise constitute planning for structural transformation? How can it be argued that such a process is rooted in an analysis of underdevelopment and the aims of structural transformation?

As if these weaknesses were not sufficient to demolish the idea that present practices constitute planning, there are three major weaknesses *inherent to the techniques* of those project evaluations used, which ensure that they do not have the *logical requirements* for framing an investment programme—whatever other uses they may have as aids to decision-making. The first limitation is that the neo-classical welfare theory on which much of project analysis is based itself recognizes the constraints of second-best theory, which demonstrates that it is impossible to derive an optimal pricing of inputs and outputs in a partial equilibrium situation. As soon as this is conceded, Pareto optimality, which is the implicit aim of the selection techniques, cannot be achieved. Moreover, the extent to which planned pricing deviates from Pareto top-level welfare optimal pricing cannot be either estimated or evaluated, and so the impact on the particular project is not known.

The second limitation is that economic development, no matter how limitedly construed, would require that these techniques should employ general equilibrium analysis. Micro-economic techniques cannot attain this. Thus all direct costs and benefits cannot be measured accurately, both for the reason stated previously, and also because existing techniques have no way of satisfactorily evaluating the qualitative externalities of a project. Finally, there is perhaps the most crucial of the limitations. This follows from the assumption that these techniques are supposedly neutral and objective, because they operate *in vacuo,* i.e., independent of the social system. In fact, they are neither neutral nor objective. Rather than being independent of the social system, they imply that the "system" for which the projects are planned *can generate its own development,* a proposition which is directly contradicted by the realities of these economies.

A proposed industrialization strategy

At this stage we can introduce a more specific delineation of our proposed industrialization strategy. We may best begin by observing that the economic literature generally contains two broad sets of industrialization models. The first, the so-called Russian model, is based on heavy industry in the sense of concentration of resource flows to the production of the machines needed to produce other machines. It is also based on centralized planning of resource use with minimal direct market influences on this. Judging from the short span of time it took for the economy of Russia to be transformed, there is little doubt about the superiority of this model from the point of view of rapidly creating an industrial base. But such a model is applicable only where the volume of the requirements of heavy industry permits feasible development along these lines. Although the starting point of this model is correct, i.e., the limits on industrialization are set by the surplus generated and devoted to industry and *not* the markets for industrial goods, in small dependent economic systems problems of the volume of feasible output become crucial to the social costs of industrialization.

The second type of model to be found in the literature is the one which presently prevails among the African countries, and which is the direct correlate of MNC expansion. This emphasizes light manufacturing industry, mainly the assembly of consumer goods, with the expectation that in time as the market expands this will induce a continuous backward expansion to intermediate and heavy industries. Thus the present MNC participation in the field of simple assembly of consumer goods is seen as a prelude to subsequent heavy industry investments by MNCs.

In Part 1 of this paper, our examination of the consequences of this type of crypto-industrialization process has already illustrated why linkages cannot be successfully forged on this basis. The problems (as we have seen them) are not *technical.* We are prepared to concede here that *technically* the links backward can be made, and in some economies, where the size of the market for intermediate and heavy goods industries justify it on a private calculus, attempts will be made by capitalist enterprises to forge these links. The main obstacles to such a process in the more typical small economies of Africa where the private calculus do not justify it, are *political and institutional.* Indeed, if this were not the case, such a smooth development from consumer goods industries backwards to heavy industries among all Third World economies would undermine the very rationale of MNC participation in these economies. As we have already argued, their imperiatives are to exploit the local market with the *minimum amount of technological transfer,* and the *maximum amount of dependence on imported inputs.*

Although this model is the favourite capitalist one, it is important to note that it does not accord with the historical experiences of such small capitalist countries as Britain and Belgium (which industrialized early), and Australia, New Zealand and South Africa (which are presently industrializing quite rapidly)! This model has often been advocated because to neo-classical economists industrialization plans are, as we have seen, little more than a collection of shopping lists of feasible industries, derived from the application of such neo-classical criteria as the minimization of scarce factor use, the maximization of the wage cost/total cost ratios and so on.

Upon close examination it can be seen that a number of technical weaknesses are evident in these studies, as may be seen in the following examples. Often these ratios are derived as averages of the data of individual firms. The result is that they inevitably tend to mask many important variations in existing practice. The very definitions of industry employed have also often been arbitrary. Thus, we can find the casual separation of tanning and footwear industries from livestock production, or clothing from textiles. Not surprisingly, the results obtained on this basis are often quite misleading, although not generally appreciated as such. In an earlier work this type of analysis was summed up as follows:

> The methods, advanced as they were by some of the empirical and theoretical work of Professors Florence, Kahn and Chenery in the late 1950's and early 1950's may now be more properly elevated to a theory of investment priorities. The logic of this theory is simply that the scarce factor inputs should in aggregate, be minimized per unit of output. In some of the more subtle formulations both input and output have to be measured in social, as distinct from private, values. Thus, less developed countries should minimize, for example, the inputs of capital, fuel and skills and should promote industries with relatively high wage-cost elements, low degrees of localization, small size of operation, low capital-output ratios, low fuel-cost ratios and so on. Only the net result of the various criteria can finally establish the priority, though the adding-up problem has not been left as lucid and amenable to implementation as might be desired.
>
> It must be admitted that this procedure has a strong rationale that is, the incontrovertible fact that the relative scarcity of the factor inputs in less developed countries differs from that of industrial countries. However, the result of these methods has been the recommendation, and in some instances the implementation of a pattern of industrialization which is striking in at least two respects. Firstly, it is the reverse (though not for this reason incorrect) process of the industrial pattern pursued by those nations succeeding Britain's lead, even the more recent ones such as South Africa, Australia, New Zealand. Secondly, the outcome is a structure of industry which has extremely exiguous internal links, low employment and income potential relative to the magnitude of the development problems, and little or no rational continuity with the future course of industrialization. Examples of procedures of this kind may be found in the work of Dr. Bohr, Professor Lewis and the Stanford Research Institute. In this connection it is interesting to note the selection of the industries which were found most suitable in the first two classes, to newly developing areas. (Class 1: Boots, shoes, soap and candles, cooperage, leather goods, bedding and mattresses, jewellery, clothing, paint, hosiery, rubber goods, brooms and brushes, glass, electrical machinery and tanning. Class 2: cardboard boxes, furniture, sheet metal work, cutting and small hand-tools,

> fabricated plastics, steel wire, stoves, ovens, agricultural machinery and implements, textiles dyeing and finishing and earthenware). When we consider the question of industrialization in this way some uncertainty arises about the economic soundness of spreading the available resources over a patchy, loosely linked collection of small scale fabricating industries which, in the aggregate and by the usual critieria may well have a lower priority than the so-called unsuitable industries.[17]

A third model of industrialization of small dependent economic systems can be derived on the basis of our analysis of underdevelopment and the requirements of transformation. It will be recalled that one of the basic strategies of transformation is the planned convergence of domestic resource use and domestic demand. In light of this, the *first point of investigation of a suitable industrialization strategy must be to establish what constitutes the major resource content of demand, and what scope there is for regulating this demand to a country's resource configuration.* An examination of the input/output matrices of industrialized countries would show that despite the innumerable multiplicity of final products, the raw-material content of these products are skewed in favour of a narrow range of basic materials. Two basic materials alone, iron/steel and textiles (natural and synthetic), form the backbone of modern industrial consumption. If to these are added paper, plastics, rubber, glass, leather, cement, aluminium, wood, fuel and industrial chemicals (primarily the alkalis, chlorine, and sulphuric acid), then we can account for the overwhelming bulk of basic materials used in industrial consumption. The bulk of the value-added in industry is derived from this range of industries. As a result it is these industries which constitute the empirically verifiable range of strategic linkages and form the cornerstone of an industrialization programme.[18]

It is not surprising that the widespread ramifications of our observation, and the analysis of its implications for economic transformation have not been pursued in the neo-classical literature. Yet it is clear that given the developments in technology, and the composition of industrial demand in transformed economies, that if these goods are not produced locally, then the organic linkages between domestic demand and output lie abroad in the countries from which these imports are derived. The growth of domestic demand transfers the bulk of value-added abroad. An effective industrialization strategy must therefore seek the vertical integration of the demand structure with domestic resource use. This means that the investment priorities which override all other priorities are the choice of products from this strategic vector of products, and the *intensive* use of domestic resources within this vector of possibilities.

Such criteria for allocation to industry are in direct conflict with the global market incentives criteria which operate with the MNCs in Africa. It is therefore important for us to be clear about the analytical properties of this

Table 10. *Growth elasticities*

Commodity	Growth elasticity
Machinery	2.80
Metals	2.14
Paper	2.69
Petroleum	2.22
Rubber	2.00
Chemicals	1.66
Textiles	1.44
Wood products	1.77
Leather products	1.64
Clothing	1.69
Non-metallic minerals	1.62
Total manufacturing[1]	1.62

Source: H. Chenery, "Patterns of Industrial Growth," *American Economic Review,* 1960, p. 638.

[1] Categories 20–29 on the Standard Industrial Classification.

proposition. Accordingly, the remainder of this section will be devoted to a discussion of the production economics of this pattern of industrialization, particularly as related to the question of economies of scale, since the issue of size is often brought up to preclude rational discussion of any form of heavy industrialization in the typical African economy. It is this same issue of size, however, which is advanced as confirmation of the rationality of investment paths.

At the outset we must be aware that the vector of industries described here, and which has been derived from empirical examinations of input-output data of industrialized economies, meets two important criteria, as far as dynamic demand potential is concerned. These go a long way towards justifying their importance in transformation. Firstly, as we have pointed out, there is considerable empirical data to support the proposition that in the long run the income elasticity of demand for industrial goods is very high. Because of the uniformity and the broad basis of this trend it is taken as indicative of real needs. Nevertheless, although the composition of these goods when finally consumed may vary somewhat, their strategic basic materials content remains broadly stable. Thus it is not surprising that the industries with the highest growth elasticities are to be found in precisely this category. In Table 10 are found data showing the growth elasticities of these industries. The data are derived from Chenery's empirical study of the patterns of industrial growth. As can be observed in all cases cited, the growth elasticities are very high.

Table 11. *Inter-Industry Linkages* (Italy, Japan, USA)

Item	Backward linkages	Forward linkages
Iron and steel	66	78
Non-ferrous metals	61	81
Paper and products	57	78
Petroleum products	65	68
Chemicals	60	69
Textiles	67	57
Rubber products	51	48
Lumber and wood	61	38
Leather and leather products	66	37

Source: H.B. Chenery & T. Watanable, *International Comparisons of the Structure of Production.*

The second criterion which these industries satisfy is that they have high linkages with other activities both backwards and forward. Thus, their planned production can ensure dynamically increasing inter-sectoral linkages and differentiation in the economy. There are, of course, a number of cautions to be applied to the measurement of input/output relationships of this sort. In particular, it should be noted that a great deal of the measured relationships in the capitalist countries may reflect the prevailing structure of industry, e.g., the amount of vertical integration and the degree of monopoly. Despite this, we believe the general impression to be fairly reliable. Stated simply, that impression is that over a range of industrially developed countries the linkages from this set of industries are the greatest. In Table 11 we present data showing the size of inter-industry linkages for certain basic materials sectors in Italian/Japanese/USA industry. Here we clearly observe the strength of inter-industrial transactions.

It is important to understand that in order for the basic materials sector to constitute the critical range of industries in industrial transformation of African economies, *these basic materials must substantially be derived from domestic resources.* It is in this way that domestic resource use may be linked to demand. To plan transformation on this basis, the most elementary and routine requirement would therefore be an up-to-date and reliable inventory of the country's natural resources. Elementary as this would seem, many of the countries of Africa have had years of "industrialization" efforts without attempting the systematic compilation of such an inventory. Often, as we have observed earlier, natural-resource endowment must be estimated from studies initiated during the former colonial administrations. Since only an actual inventory can establish natural resource availability, it follows that the scope for structural transformation will be heavily contingent on the resource configuration which is discovered. *Although this point cannot be overstressed, at least three important technological factors serve to lessen the sheer burden of this constraint.*

First, there is in some cases the possibility of a physical substitutability of one input for another to produce the same product, but with a different material composition. Thus, plastics can substitute for leather, aluminium for steel, cotton for synthetics, wood for glass, etc. Given this physical substitutability *it follows that demand can be planned in such a way as to take account of deficient resource endowments where they exist, as well as to exploit abundant resource availability.* It is for this reason that basic material substitutability can in some instances turn out to be more crucial than labour/capital substitutability. Yet the economic literature has devoted little or no attention to this![19]

The second technological factor which gives rise to flexibility is that in the production of basic materials their *raw material inputs* have some degree of flexibility, giving rise to further flexibility. Thus, charcoal can replace coking coal in iron metallurgy; or power can be fuelled through nuclear energy, oil, coal, or hydroelectricity. It may also be that an abundant unused resource, e.g., molasses or bagasse (by-products of sugar cane), may be used for making a much needed basic output, e.g., making plastics or providing energy, as these two examples suggest.

The third area of flexibility is that technological developments abroad often can be exploited to make up for deficient resources at home. Thus, given the importance of iron and steel, the recent changes in the technology of pre-reduced ore increase the technological options because they open up the possibility for iron and steel manufacture in countries where iron ore supplies may be deficient, as pre-reduced ore may now be imported fairly cheaply. Of course, not all such developments are equally advantageous. Thus, the benefits of iron and steel manufacture at home will be reduced if the industry has a significant import content. Nevertheless, the force of our proposition is that if the alternative is no steel manufacture at home, then reliance on imported inputs for a local steel industry is to be preferred—even though a project evaluation may show that the product cannot be produced at "competitive prices".

The above considerations make two issues abundantly clear. Firstly, the notion of resource endowment cannot be very meaningfully analysed into the broad categories of labour, capital, land, etc., as is the prevailing practice. Specific resource configurations will have to be brought into the analysis. Secondly, the importance of the resource configurations of a country is not independent of the demand structure. The existence of flexibility in the goods demanded, as well as their material input requirements, means that the range of choice permitted, and the planning of demand, are essential to any industrialization programme. In this sense size can in many ways be overcome through correct planning procedures.

In so far as the type of economy we are considering is one partly distinguished by constraints of size, the question of economies of scale inevitably become most crucial, as all of these industries seem to require large volumes of output to be economical. A hazy and casual application of the so-called dictates of this concept has resulted in much confusion when considering the role of industrialization in small economies. Although the concept has been derived from the inverse relation which is said to exist between unit monetary cost of production and the level of output, there is much confusion in interpreting what may be different levels of cost curves, and movements along a given set of cost curves. The consequence of this is that in the literature there is some scepticism about such notions as optimum output levels.[20] Nevertheless, the view predominates that economies of scale are significant.

In strict production terms, economies of scale may be measured as

> . . . the inverse relation between the physical input ratio and the level of physical output, without introducing the distortion of such monetary variables as factor prices. The literature suggests that the major source of purely physical unit cost savings as output is increased derives from the phenomenon of cubic dimensions. This is directly applicable to unit capital cost and indirectly, through its impact on unit variable and depreciation costs, to the unit cost of operation.[21]

The unit cost of operation is also influenced by the length of runs.

In the complex real world of production, many other factors impinge on these considerations. Firstly, when available raw materials are cheap and abundant, industries may be established which do not meet the technological optimum for reaping full economies of scale. Secondly, location and its impact on transport costs often make it worthwhile to establish industries, (e.g., the numerous cement industries around the world) even when the plant size is far below the optimum. Thirdly, variation in factor prices affect the true meaning of unit costs of production. These differences, when added to such factors as the conversion rate of foreign exchange, the degree of monopoly and extent of monopoly pricing, and external economies, result in a situation in which the physical factors may belie the "true" relationship between levels of output and unit production costs. Indeed, the pecuniary factors are so complex that it has been asserted that: "a sufficient volume of empirical documentation has been built up to permit us to conclude fairly confidently that when there is an inverse relation between unit cost and output, the rate of inversion tends to vary along the cost curve."[22]

Such an assertion does not rest on measurement and comparisons of absolute unit cost levels. What the assertion implies is that differences in absolute costs of production between imported products and domestic production of the equivalents are not the crucial factors, even at the technical level, in determining whether to produce the product or not. Furthermore, this point is strengthened when the requirements of disengagement from capitalism are taken into account.

Often there is a difference between costs of production abroad and unit imported prices. This reflects two kinds of distortion. One is the exploitation by firms in the metropolitan countries of different average revenue curves in the home and the overseas market, through systematic dumping. Although dumping can be beneficial to the receiving countries in certain restrictive situations, it can hardly be argued as being so when the purchase of the dumped product leads to the *systematic* distortion of the developmental benefits of producing at home the dumped product. Much evidence exists to suggest that this is a very widespread practice.[23]

The abandonment of pricing policies based on costs of production abroad and/or the import price equivalent in an industrialization programme does not mean that all comparative efficiency considerations are abandoned. It is correct that prices should reflect domestic resource constraints, demand priorities, etc. Efficiency considerations operate in so far as the argument here suggests that the search for the "optimum" scale of operations is *less important than the search for the critical minimum level, i.e., the range over which the rates of inversion of the cost function are greatest.* Fortunately for most of these basic industries, empirical evidence suggests that they operate on an L-shaped cost function. Thus we find that in the production of finished steel an increase in production from 50,000 tons to 250,000 tons reduces the unit cost of production by 36 percent, whereas to treble output beyond 250,000 tons would only lead to a unit cost gain of 25%. In integrated pulp and paper production an increase from 50 to 200 tons a day reduces unit operating costs by 50%, whereas a further increase to 350 tons a day reduces unit operating cost only by a further 20%.[24]

It is clear from such evidence that existing notions of economies of scale are not only confusing, but misleading as to their implications for industrialization policy. As long as the desired (or planned) domestic demand, now or in the near future, for any of the basic industries approaches the "critical minimum" levels as defined above, i.e., the (maximum) point at which the rate of change of average cost with increases in scale is greatest, this product is a candidate for domestic production. This point indicates the level of output where the decreasing social cost function of industrialization is at its maximum slope. The only practical problem which remains is that of sequencing the pattern of industrial establishments in relation to surplus accumulations and foreign exchange availability.[25]

The distinction which exists between unit production costs in the capitalist countries and unit import prices in the African countries are of course, not always evidenced in the one-way direction of dumping. Sometimes monopoly power is exercised to raise prices because the slope of the average revenue makes this profitable. In addition, the development of synthetics also has an impact on raw material prices which the developing countries should correct for when estimating their own social costs of operation, and that implied in the imported price of equivalents. All this represents the second type of distortion and supports the above argument indicating the necessity of disengagement from the present international division of labour wherever possible. Yet the fashionable trend towards imputing world prices into domestic valuation of projects in the Third World countries continues, although merely serving to reinforce the same international division of labour which they should be struggling against.

It would be naïve to deduce from this that the corollary of our industrialization strategy outlined here is that a country seeking transformation should not trade. The point being advanced is that since trade itself is a manifestation of, and a factor reinforcing the structural disequilibrium in the developing countries, the problem must be solved at the structural level. Principally it means that industrialization is necessary (i) to create a domestic capacity to convert domestic savings into investment goods, and (ii) to allow the potential development of an export capacity in industrial goods. Such an export capacity as in the case of, e.g., Japan, makes the pressure of demand and productivity levels operating at home less a constraining factor on earning foreign exchange as compared to primary agricultural exports.

Unless this structural shift occurs, then the country's domestic savings rate is an insufficient indicator—in the absence of an import ability (i.e., foreign exchange)—of the rate of possible expansion of domestic productive capacity. This follows logically from the fact that efforts at expansion of these economies are contingent on their ability to obtain for use goods which *cannot immediately be produceable at home.* The only saving factor is the intensification of the search for local resources and technology implicit in the planning strategy we have advanced. The aim of this strategy is to lessen the range of goods which are effectively not produceable at home.

We can see from this the sort of role trading policies must have in African economies. Such trading policies will have to be evaluated by their contribution towards *increasing inter-sectoral transactions internally.* This can occur through stimulating the use of domestic resources, i.e., by exporting manufactures, or alternatively from integration schemes with neighbouring and/or socialist countries which do not seek merely to liberalize their trade, but to juxtapose and combine resource use and consumption patterns for the planned production of those basic material inputs in which domestic resources or demand may be deficient in their country.

Finally, although we have concentrated on what we have termed the crucial vector of commodities, the production of which is necessary to achieve industrial transformation, certain corollary developments are clearly implicit. One of these—the production of agricultural inputs, e.g., fertilizers, farm tools and so on—was mentioned earlier. The key factor in our approach is that the development and use of these inputs in agriculture leads to transformation in so far as they are produced at home *and are intensive in the use of domestic resources.*

Two other categories of industry are worth brief mention here. One of these is power supplies. It is not insignificant that in the early stages of Russian industrialization, electricity was seen as the "key" to industrial progress. The view was of course mistaken in so far as the availability of electricity was interpreted as a factor leading directly to the revolutionizing of techniques and hence productivity. Instead, historical experience has shown that electricity is a critical complement to an industrialization programme, and not its cause. The same thing can be said for the other category of outputs which we would like to indicate, i.e., transportation. It is clear that both an efficient transportation system and energy supplies are crucial to the achievement of industrial growth. In both cases their capacities and output will have to be planned on the basis of the programme we have discussed here.

If we keep in mind that the industrialization drive is subsumed under the strategy of convergence, then several important implications follow. Firstly, industrialization itself tends to contribute flexibility to the economic system. To this extent it is both more flexible in its resource inputs, as we observed above, and also in adapting to changing demands. Secondly, the organic link between domestic resource use and domestic demand must be rooted in an indigenous technology. But how can this occur if the technology-intensive outputs are imported? Our industrialization strategy seeks to overcome this by internalizing within the economy (through exposure to the *production* of the items and not simply *use*) the dynamics for technological change which have historically been encapsulated in the heavy industry sectors. It is this which provides the material basis for a broadly based drive to transform the society in the widest sense. Finally, concentration on this sector has important spill-over effects, not least of which is into the machine and machine-tools industries. And, as the experience of the US shows, this is neither necessarily a large-scale, nor very capital-intensive industry.

Conclusion

In conclusion, it is necessary to reiterate what has been said at the outset of this paper. This study has focused on outlining an industrialization strategy that takes into account the smallness, the domination of the MNCs, the underdevelopment, and those other historical forces which have shaped the present neo-colonial economies that characterize the African continent. The success of this strategy rests upon the capacity of particular societies to mobilize and allocate resources along the lines indicated. Such success depends basically on political circumstances, and will be a direct correlate of the extent to which the workers and peasants are able to dominate the political, social and economic processes in Africa, and to elevate their class interests to the dominant ones.

That such a development is crucial is obvious, since the real significance of our strategy is that it is the only alternative to continuously developing dependency. Breaking out of the role that Africa has traditionally played in the evolution of international capitalism requires a revolutionary break with the past, i.e., the subordination of prevailing class interests which have dominated the development of African societies to date. No matter how internally consistent our strategy may therefore appear, as with any other strategy it is its *historical* relevance which constitutes the most significant characteristic.

In outlining our strategy we have focused on the essentials of the governmental thrust. Only brief mention has been made of such important industrial topics as energy, construction, and housing. This was not intended to reduce the significance of these factors in industrial development. What we have done was to subordinate them to the requirements of the *thrust to produce the basic industrial materials.* Such a development, given the size and underdevelopment of the African economy, would be inconsistent with the logic of MNC expansion in Africa. It therefore constitutes *the alternative path* to industrialization outside of the multinational corporate path, in Africa.

Notes

1 L. Huberman & P. Sweezy, *Socialism in Cuba,* New York, 1969, p. 74.

2 R. Sutcliffe, *Industry and Underdevelopment,* London, 1971, p. 334.

3 The issues touched on in this introduction are treated in the author's book, *Dependence and Transformation: The Economics of the Transition to Socialism.* Monthly Review Press, New York, Sept. '74. Readers interested in a fuller elaboration and documentation of some of the arguments advanced in this paper are recommended to read this text.

4 *Industrial Development in Africa,* UN, 1967, p. 4.

5 *Cooperation for Economic Development of Eastern Africa,* Part 4, United Nations, 1971, p. 6.

6 Ibid, p. 12.

7 *Survey of Economic Conditions in Africa,* UN, 1972, p. 108.

8 Parts of this and the next section are based on a paper, read to the East African Social Sciences Conference, Nairobi, 1972, entitled "The Transition to Socialism: Issues of Economic Strategy in a Tanzania-type Economy".

[9] The discussion of these points draws from an earlier paper by the author, "Meaningful Participation in Industry: Meaning and Scope, "*Ratoon, Occasional Paper.* Parts are reprinted in a book *The Aftermath of Sovereignty,* (ed.) Lowenthal D. and Comitas L., pp. 351-360.

[10] See the papers by Shivji, "Silent Class Struggle," *Maji-Maji,* and Wells, "The Construction Industry in East Africa", *E.R.B. Paper,* University of Dar es Salaam, May, 1972.

[11] C. Y. Thomas, op. cit., p. 7.

[12] Most of the detailed evidence documenting these consequences of what Rweyemamu calls "perverse capitalist industrialization" can be found in his study, *Underdevelopment and Industrialization in Tanzania,* Nairobi: Oxford University Press. Some of this has previously been released as Economic Research Bureau *Papers.* A similar and earlier extensive documentation is to be found for the Caribbean in Brewster and C. Y. Thomas, *Dynamics of West Indian Economic Integration.* University of the West Indies, 1967.

[13] See Clive Thomas, *Dependence and Transformation,* New York, pp. 108-109.

[14] Op. cit., p. 114.

[15] This part of the paper summarizes the main arguments of Part 2 of the present author's book cited above.

[16] R. B. Sutcliffe, *Industry and Underdevelopment,* p. 245.

[17] *The Dynamics of West Indian Economic Integration,* by H. Brewster and C. Y. Thomas, I.S.E.R, 1967, pp. 141-143.

[18] For an extended analysis of this industrialization strategy, and specific proposals in the Caribbean context see Brewster and Thomas (1967), op.cit. The points made here are based on this earlier study, and the present author's recent book, *Dependence and Transformation.*

[19] Although demands of space preclude our discussing this at length, the significance of demand planning is thus again illustrated here.

[20] See J. S. Bain, *Barriers to New Competition,* Harvard University; and J. Jewkes, "Are Economies of Scale Unlimited", in E.A.G. Robinson (ed.), *Economic Consequences of the Size of Nations,* St. Martin's Press, New York, 1960.

[21] H. Brewster and C. Y. Thomas, op.cit., pp. 57-58.

[22] Op.cit.

[23] See H. W. De Jong. "The Significance of Dumping in International Trade", *Journal of World Trade Law,* Vol. 2, No. 2, March/April, 1968.

[24] See Brewster and Thomas, op.cit, and, *inter alia,* two United Nations Studies, *A Study of the Iron and Steel Industry in Latin America,* New York, 1954; and *Pulp and Paper Prospects in Latin America,* 1955; *Pulp and Paper Prospects in Asia and the Far East,* 1962, *Pulp and Paper Development in Africa and the Near East,* 1966.

[25] Space precludes discussion of the foreign exchange problem. Chapter 7 of the present author's above-mentioned book, however, takes up this issue.

John Carlsen

The Different Modes of Technology Transfer

The rationale of technology transfer

Most developing countries are aiming at a rapid industrial growth, and therefore need a rapid increase in their productive factors.

Industrial development naturally demands large amounts of finance, of which a substantial part must be in foreign exchange to pay for the necessary imports of equipment and technology. Finance is of course not enough. The more crucial factors are industrial technology, managerial and marketing know-how, as well as different kinds of skilled labour.

To some extent, most of these factors of production are available in almost any developing country. But for most developing countries some of these factors must be obtained from abroad—from the industrialized countries. The extent to which this is the case depends on the general level of industrial development, the current economic situation and the specific industrial strategy which is pursued in the individual developing country. Countries like India and Brazil, for example, are less dependent on the importation of these factors than most African countries, because of the experience and resources which have been accumulated in their early industrial development. In both of these countries, a group of skilled managers has developed, and India in particular has herself developed some indigenous technological bases on which a further industrialization can be built.

On the other hand, the balance of payment situation of most developing countries has for many years made it necessary to import foreign capital for the financing of, *inter alia,* the foreign equipment for different industrial projects.

To what extent such importation of foreign capital and in particular foreign technology is necessary depends, however, to a large extent upon the industrial strategy followed by the individual country.

It is very likely that the traditional import substitution policies based upon very unequal distribution of incomes (with the consequent "skew" consumption patterns) which have been followed by most developing countries in the past have lead to excessive importation of foreign capital and foreign technology, compared to more deliberate policies aiming at redistribution of incomes as a base for industrial development with production of labour-intensive mass-consumer goods and simple capital goods.

Nevertheless, no matter which industrial strategy they follow, most African countries will for many years to come still have to import foreign capital, foreign technology and probably also to some extent managerial and marketing know-how for the sake of their industrial development.

In the past, the transfer of these factors of production to African countries has been dominated by the private foreign investments undertaken by multinational companies. Recent studies indicate, however, that the transfer of technology and other scarce resources in a package form within the framework of the multinational corporations has had some negative effects on the local economies of the developing countries.[1]

Private foreign investment characteristically transfers the factors of production in a package form for the purpose of obtaining control[2] while keeping local production; the subsidiaries are operated for profit maximization not in the single venture, but on a world-wide scale, over the whole range of operations of the multinational company. Moreover, many of the private foreign investments in the industrial sector of developing countries have been set up for "defensive" reasons, i.e., they have been undertaken to maintain a foothold in the markets of developing countries after the introduction of import restrictions, which have made further exports from the parent companies to these countries impossible. Export-oriented private foreign investment in manufacture is still not very significant, although a good deal of such investment has been undertaken for the production of labour-intensive components for the sake of exploiting cheap skilled labour, particularly in southeast Asia.

Industrial enterprises set up in this way as part of a defensive strategy tend to have various negative effects on the local economy, as compared to the situation which would most probably have existed, had the investment not taken place.

They tend to produce luxury consumption goods, which often compete with locally-produced products of a more simple nature.[3] When entering the markets of developing countries they often eliminate this competition by taking over local companies.[4] When this is the case local producers find it difficult to survive. The subsidiaries of multinational companies use extensive advertising; in addition, in most developing countries there is a strong xenophile prejudice which values products in descending order of "foreignness". An imported article is *ipso facto* preferable to one made locally and commands a higher price, a foreign brand manufactured locally by a foreign firm is better than the one made by a domestic firm, and so on down the line to purely domestic enterprise.[5] Therefore, local companies find it difficult to compete even when they—as usually is the case—sell at prices below those of foreign subsidiaries.

The foreign companies often use a more capital-intensive technology[6] than their local competitors and consequently the result is that total employment in this industry may be reduced.

Foreign subsidiaries often also have a higher import content and they buy less of their inputs from local companies. Moreover, they are often unwilling to export, as they prefer to cover export-markets from the parent company. This is of course particularly the case of joint ventures and license agreements, as the multinational companies wish to avoid sharing their profits from export with the local partners.

In the same manner, they are reluctant to spread their technical know-how to local firms and very little spread effects result from the training of labour. The labour force is more frequently appropriated from local firms where they have received their basic training: the foreign subsidiaries offer higher wages than the local firms can afford, and the on-the-job training they receive in the subsidiaries is often too specialized to be of much use when they leave for other occupations.[7] Their superior knowledge often gives them excessive bargaining strength when dealing with the local government and they are therefore often in a position to obtain very favourable conditions for their investments, such as tax holidays and high protection against imports and potential foreign producers.

They are therefore in a position to generate higher profits[8] which are remitted in such a way—by the use of transfer pricing and excessive technological payments—that local taxpaying is minimized.

Moreover, within the local economy the foreign subsidiaries make up an enclave which is difficult to control by traditional economic policy. The multinational companies often try to intervene in local politics, as was recently the case of US multinationals in Chile. A large foreign-controlled industrial sector might therefore for political reasons be unwanted by many countries in Africa.

In short, it might for many reasons be unacceptable to governments to import the necessary finance, technology, and managerial and marketing know-how in the package form delivered by multinational companies. Yet what are the alternatives; can their application produce more favourable effects? In other words, is it possible to obtain these foreign-owned factors of production on more favourable terms?

Different models of technology transfer

Obviously, there exist possibilities of splitting the "package" into different elements.

Foreign exchange is in short supply in most developing countries but available from sources other than private foreign investment, i.e., commercial credits, international development banks and corporations and from official assistance. It is quite probable that foreign exchange can be obtained much cheaper from these sources than through private foreign investment.

Managerial know-how has already been developed in many developing countries and it can be supplemented if necessary with official technical assistance and possibly management contracts with foreign companies. Such management contracts have formerly been misused in such a way as to extract almost all the generated profits from the local companies,[9] but if management fees are related to profits, and the prices for trade with the multinational company in question checked, this can probably be avoided. If this is the case, the managerial know-how can probably be obtained cheaper in this way than through private foreign investment.

Nevertheless, marketing skills which are crucial for the development of export-oriented industries are possessed by the multinational companies, who also control a large part of the international trade as intercompany trade.[10] This knowledge can hardly be obtained in other ways than through the multinational corporations, not because the knowledge is very complicated but rather because the multinationals control the world market for many of the potential exportable products. For some products, however, it will probably be possible to overcome this bottleneck by the use of official technical assistance from industrialized countries in this field. Almost the same thing is true for industrial technology. Most of the technology for the kind of products which are produced as a consequence of uncritical import-substitution policies is possessed by a few multinational companies which formerly covered the markets of these countries by export. This technology can therefore only be obtained from these companies and the question therefore becomes one of whether it will be cheaper for the developing countries to itemize the technology package which is transferred through private foreign investment, i.e., by using a combination of alternative sources of foreign exchange, management and license agreement for the industrial technology.

Before this question can be answered fully, we must examine the market for industrial technology, as it has developed since the Second World War.

The market for industrial technology

Industrial production in the world is becoming increasingly technology-intensive. The significant development of industrial production no longer merely takes the form of increased production of existing commodities, but rather consists of a development of new and more efficient processes for the production of existing goods, of a development of new varieties and qualities of existing goods, and also to a large extent of a development of new products (for which the demand is often "produced" in the same scientific way as the product itself).

This kind of industrial development demands large expenditures on industrial research and development (R&D). The consequences for the global control of production and control of the world markets are very important.

Firstly, there are significant economies of scale in R&D, so that very large corporations have important advantages over small business units in developing new techniques, new product qualities and new products. Industrial R&D therefore tends to be concentrated in the hands of a very few large multinational companies; in other words, the important factor of production, technology, is increasingly being monopolized by a few multinational companies.

Secondly, the international law system of industrial property rights—patents and trade-marks—assures that the monopoly on technology becomes a monopoly on production and thereby a monopoly in the world market for the finished products. (This monopolistic tendency is being reinforced by the extensive use of patent and trade-mark cross-licensing between multinational companies.) In this way, the increasing significance of technology in industrial production has strengthened the monopolistic tendencies in world production and world trade and thereby contributed to a concentration of economic and political power in the world.

This becomes particularly evident when one examines this development from the point of view of the underdeveloped countries. 98 percent of all expenditures on R&D are spent in the industrialized countries and only 2 percent in the underdeveloped countries. Moreover, this research is concentrated in a few of the industrialized countries, such as the USA, UK and West Germany, or rather in a few of the large companies originating in these countries. The increasingly uneven distribution of technology between industrialized and underdeveloped countries is reflected in the distribution of patent ownership between local and foreign companies in the underdeveloped countries. In most of these countries 80-90 percent of all patents are granted to foreign companies—a tendency which has been rapidly increasing over the last 25 years.

Thirdly, high expenditures on R&D have significantly increased the fixed cost of production and have therefore made the size of the market an increasingly important factor for determination of the overall profitability of production. Production of technology-intensive products pays only if it can take place on a very large scale, and therefore the control of the world market, which is partly secured by industrial property rights, becomes increasingly important to the large technology-producing companies. Therefore, even the relatively small and insignificant markets for industrial products found in the underdeveloped countries become significant to the overall profitability of the multinational companies, and if these markets cannot be reached by exports (because of restrictive import policies), the foreign companies must set up local manufacturing facilities. But when foreign companies enter into arrangements for "transfer of technology" to underdeveloped countries—whether this takes place as indirect transfers, i.e., technology embodied in commodities and machinery, or directly in technology contracts and as private foreign investment—they therefore have very strong incentives to keep the "core" technology secret, so that the partner does not become technologically independent.

The question of access to foreign technology and of the terms on which it can be acquired thus seems to be important to an understanding of the problems of industrialization of underdeveloped countries. A few characteristics of this process of importing foreign technology are worth mentioning.

Firstly, technology, when commercialized, is usually embodied in intermediate products, machinery and equipment, people's skills, whole systems of production (e.g., turnkey plants) and even systems of distribution or marketing. Thus, know-how represents a part integrated in a larger whole and as a result, the market of the former is not independent of the market of the latter. This market integration for various inputs creates non-competitive conditions for each of them, since they are sold in a package form.

Secondly, in the formulation of the demand for technology, i.e., information on how to produce, as in all other markets, a prospective buyer needs information about the properties of the items he intends to purchase, so as to be able to make appropriate decisions. Yet, in the case of technology, what is needed is information about information, and this may effectively be one and the same thing. Thus, the prospective buyer is confronted with a weakness intrinsic in his position as a purchaser of technology, and with a resulting imperfection in the corresponding market operations.

Thirdly, contrary to the usage of other factors of production, the usage of technology does not in itself reduce its availability, present or future. Thus, the incremental direct cost in the use or sale of an previously-developed technology is very little for someone who has already access to that technology. The opportunity cost, however, can be very significant. From the point of view of the prospective purchaser, however, the relevant incremental cost for developing the same type of an alternative technology with his own technical capacity will usually be several times larger. The market situation is typically that of oligopoly-oligopsony where the final price is determined solely on the base of crude bargaining power.

Whether the package of factors of production can be obtained more cheaply by using alternative sources of finance and management combined with license agreements depends, therefore, to a large extent on the bargaining power of the parties. Developing countries can most probably achieve access to industrial technology on better terms by increasing their bargaining power.

Developing countries and bargaining power for industrial technology

Many developing countries have realized that the cost of importing foreign technology depends on the relative bargaining power of the parties involved. Their governments therefore pay considerable attention to efforts which can improve their bargaining position *vis-a-vis* foreign technology suppliers.

Closer examination would require some analysis of the concept "bargaining power". Only the most significant elements of the concept will be mentioned here. These are (i) the skill and knowledge of the negotiator, (ii) the structure of the market, i.e., the number of alternative buyers and sellers of a given technology and (iii) the attractiveness of the involved parties as operators of the technology in the given country, which again to a large extent depends upon the size of the market.

To illustrate what developing countries can do to increase their bargaining power and to diminish the cost of acquiring foreign technology, the cases of Colombia and India may be mentioned.

The Colombian case[11]

Colombia is now a member of the Andean Common Market, which in 1970 agreed upon various common Andean rules concerning private foreign investment and foreign technology.

The Andean countries considered it appropriate to link trade liberalization and the introduction of common restrictive policies on foreign investment. In the first place, they did not want to give the foreign investors the benefits of trade liberalization without getting anything in return. Secondly, they considered that an Andean common market encompassing about 70 million inhibitants would be an attractive market, so that foreign investors would still keep coming, even if the investment rules were restrictive. Thirdly, they thought it necessary to have common policies on foreign investments, because this would prevent foreign investors who were contemplating investments inside the Andean Common Market from playing the member countries off against each other during negotiations with the Andean governments. To a very large extent the common rules (Decision 24) build upon the experience gained by Colombian authorities in their efforts to decrease the cost of imported technology.

During the early sixties, Colombia experienced considerable balance of payment difficulties, and foreign firms were in part blamed, due to their negative effects on Columbia's foreign exchange.[12] In 1967, the government imposed various controls on the balance of payments and instituted measures for a gradual and continuous devaluation of the peso. As part of the general tightening of exchange controls, a number of regulations and restrictions were also imposed on the inflows and outflows of foreign firms. Thus, Decree 444 of 1967 was clearly motivated by the balance of payment situation, but at the same time it was a deliberate effort to increase the bargaining power of the government *vis-à-vis* foreign firms in vital areas, such as transfer of technology and evaluation of foreign investment proposals. The major issues of Decree 444 were approval of new foreign investment, restrictions on remittance of profits, approval of all contracts concerned with transfer of technology and registration and approval of foreign loans.

While there were no restrictions on the entry or expansion of foreign investment prior to 1967,[13] after the passing of Decree 444 all new investment and major expansion had to be approved by the Planning Department.

Each proposal was required to be evaluated according to a number of criteria,[14] which were fairly sophisticated and complex in theory, even if they have not really been applied in practice.

The restrictions on remittance of profit were imposed as a proportion of a firm's net worth assessed in US dollar terms by the Banco de la Republica, i.e., the figures on foreign corporations' net worth; these figures were updated by agreement between the firms and the foreign exchange office to compensate for the devaluations of the peso. The limit was initially fixed at 10 percent in 1967, but after strong protest from the foreign business sector this was raised to 14 percent a year later. Profits up to this level could either be sent abroad by the firm or reinvested and counted as an addition to the net worth, whereas profits above 14 percent could neither be remitted nor added to the net worth until some later period when they could be accomodated within the specified ceiling.

Somewhat surprisingly for the Colombian government, the actual level of declared profits was substantially below the limit set; in 1968 the average rate was 4.5 percent of net worth, in 1969, 4.8 percent and in 1970, 5.4 percent. On the whole, therefore, the restrictions could not have proved a major inconvenience to foreign investors. Only 34 out of 413 foreign enterprises repatriated the full extent of profits permitted, and new investment continued to flow into the country. The government therefore suspected that the predominant effect of the restrictions on remittance of profits was that foreign investors shifted to other means of repatriation, such as royalties and transfer pricing.

The government therefore began to examine technology contracts and to check on transfer pricing.

Out of the 269 technology contracts examined by the Royalty Committee in the first round of renegotiations in 1968-69, only 98 were approved without any modification of their original terms. 171 contracts were renegotiated by the Royalty Committee, 19 were directly refused, and in 152 cases a reduction in royalties payment was required. If these 269 contracts had not been examined they would have led to an explicit payment of US $12.5 mil. The Royalty Committee reduced this payment to US $7.8 mil.; in other words, the original payment was reduced by 37 percent.

In a second round of renegotiation, a basic improvement was made by the Royalty Committee. No technological payments were allowed between subsidiaries and parent companies within the same international corporation. It was argued that the return on the technological contribution was incorporated in the profits earned by the subsidiary, i.e., the authorized rate of profit remittance, 14 percent, was considered to include royalties and technical fees. Thus, in some cases royalties were allowed but on condition that royalties plus dividends did not exceed 14 percent of the net worth. Such a criterion has been officially recognized in the Andean Pact regulations. With the application of this new principle, the reduction in royalty payments become even higher. By June 1971, 395 contracts were evaluated and the savings increased from US $4.7 mil. to US $8.0 mil. per year.

In addition, the Colombian government has also had some success in stopping transfer pricing, which had been widely used in Colombia, partly because of the government ceiling on dividends and interest payments and the reduction in royalty payments, and partly because of the differential rates of exchange formerly used in the foreign exchange market, the price controls that exist in some industries, and the political desirability of showing a low profitability.

The tax system had furthermore made it advantageous to transfer profit in Colombia in this way rather than declaring it as a dividend. In addition to these incentives, the use of transfer pricing was facilitated by the fact that a very high proportion of Colombian international trade is interfirm trade.[15]

The Import Control Board (INCOMEX) and the Planning Department have found considerable evidence that foreign subsidiaries have been using the transfer pricing mechanism to transfer undeclared profits abroad. A comparison between the actual prices charged by foreign subsidiaries with comparable prices in world markets or in other Latin American countries, with a generous allowance for transportation costs and errors, showed that for a sample of chemical products overpricing was 25 percent, for rubber 44 percent, for electrical and electronic components 54 percent, and for pharmaceuticals 155 percent.

The government then introduced direct controls on transfer pricing in 1971, and it imposed penalties on some pharmaceutical firms which were found guilty of overpricing their intermediate imports. The annual savings achieved in the pharmaceutical sector as a result of the reduction in prices of imported intermediates amount to US $3.3 mil. out of an import bill of US $1.5 mil., but so far no action has been taken against firms guilty of overpricing in other sectors.

According to the Andean Pact, international price divisions in order to control import prices will be set up in each of the member countries, and (provided the information system functions) this will further improve the ability of the member countries to control import prices. Nevertheless, one must of course realize that many of the items traded are highly specialized components and machines for which there is only one supplier and thus for which no world market price exists. It will therefore never be possible completely to prevent foreign investors from remitting their profits by the use of transfer pricing.

The Colombian experience shows, however, that it is to some extent possible to lower the prices of import technology and to limit the outflow of profits. An annual saving of US $8.0 mil. on royalties and US $3.3 mil. on transfer pricing—a total equal to approximately one half of the average annual inflow of new foreign investment in 1967-1971—is not without significance to the Colombian balance of payment.

In addition to the Colombian rules which aim at stopping the outflow of profits—the 14 percent limitation on remittance of profit, the need for approval of interfirm loans, the prohibition against royalties from a subsidiary to its parent, and the check on transfer pricing—Decision 24 goes a step further, in that it forbids the capitalization of imported know-how.

According to Article 21 of Decision 24, import of know-how is compensated for through the payment of royalties by nationally-owned firms to their licensors and through an increase in the profitability of foreign-owned subsidiaries. Decision 24 therefore does not recognize patents, technical services or know-how as part of foreign capital.

In Colombia, the capitalization of know-how has very often been used by foreign companies to gain control of joint ventures, to avoid paying dividends to local shareholders, and to circumvent the 14 percent ceiling on remittance of profit.[16]

In the Chudnovsky sample of foreign companies in Colombia, 16.4 percent of a total investment of US $101.8 mil. was paid in as patents, trade-marks and know-how, but for some of the companies the proportion was much higher and for one company the entire investment consisted of patents, trade-marks and know-how.

There are therefore good reasons to believe that this prohibition against commercialization of technology will be implemented in Colombia. It seems to be well in accordance with the general Colombian policy of diminishing the negative effect of private foreign investment on the balance of payment.

The experience of the Colombian Royalty Committee was also of great importance to the Andean Groups in the formulation of more general policies related to the commercialization of technology.

While initially the Royalty Committee had a very narrow objective, i.e., the reduction of royalty payments in order to improve the balance of payment situation, little by little its scope was enlarged. Restrictive business practices, such as tie-in clauses for purchases of raw materials and export prohibitions, began to be revealed, and action was taken to overcome their negative consequences. The technology involved in the contractual arrangements began to be assessed by means of comparisons between different firms, types of transfer and amounts of payments. Moreover, patents and trade-marks were examined in order to see whether they were actually being applied and for what purpose.

In addition, the problem of commercialization of technology was also studied on an Andean basis. In order to understand the terms of the commercialization of technology, various studies were undertaken on the subject in the Andean countries between 1968 and 1971. These studies included an evaluation of contracts for the purchase of know-how, an investigation of the structure and implications of the present patent system and a financial analysis of the price effects of technology embodied in imported intermediate products.[17]

One of the most frequent clauses encountered in contracts for the commercialization of technology is one prohibiting export. Such restrictive practices generally limit the production and sale of goods produced with the use of foreign technology to the territory of the receiving country, and in some cases also to specific neighbouring countries, because the technology supplier wants to cover exports to other countries either from the parent company, from wholly-owned subsidiaries, or from other licencees.

In Colombia it was found that out of 117 technology contracts for which information was available, 90 contained a total export prohibition and 2 contracts permitted exports to certain areas only. It must be noted that such restrictions need to be formally stated only when the technology supplier does not fully control the activities of the recipient; where such control exists, the restrictions can of course be applied directly. The absence of export restrictive clauses in a license agreement therefore does not necessarily mean that the licensee will be free to export.

As a consequence of this study, the Royalty Committee has prohibited the inclusion of all such clauses in existing and future technology contracts, but this of course does not completely solve the problem. Local companies which are dependent on a steady inflow of foreign technology and perhaps on the right to use foreign brand names will be more than willing to enter into gentlemen's agreements not to export.

A number of technology contracts also contained other types of restrictive clauses. The most important one was the requirement which obligated the purchaser of technology to tie his purchases of intermediate and capital goods to the licensor. This is patently undesirable, in so far as it permits the latter to charge relatively high prices for these goods.

For more than two-thirds of the technology contracts on which information was available in Bolivia, Colombia, Equador and Peru, such tie-in clauses existed. In Colombia, 100 percent of the contracts of foreign-owned subsidiaries and above 95 percent of nationally-owned firms in the pharmaceutical industry included tie-in clauses. In the Colombian chemical industry 60 percent of the contracts had such clauses.

It is interesting to note that throughout the Andean countries it appeared that the pharmaceutical industry, in which the most extreme examples of transfer pricing were found, also had the highest or among the highest percentages of tie-in clauses. It seems that the monopolization of technology is strongest in this sector, and that this situation is being exploited to extract high profits, which are then transferred abroad by all possible means.

In Colombia, the Royalty Committee has attempted to eliminate these clauses and with great success. By 1971, they had succeeded in getting rid of 90 percent of the tie-in clauses. To the extent that there exist alternate suppliers of these products this can contribute to breaking the monopoly situation of the technology supplier, but unfortunately this is rarely the case.

Other types of restrictive clauses, such as the fixing of domestic selling prices, the use of improvements resulting from the licensee's experience with a particular technology, the granting of patents which are not actually used, and so on, have also been eliminated when considered harmful to Colombian interests.

Particular emphasis has been given to the role of patents and trade-marks in the commercialization of technology within the Andean Group.

In a study undertaken by Constantine Vaitsos for the Planning Department,[18] it was found that patents and trade-marks played an important role in the monopolization of technology which made it possible for the technology suppliers to defend their commodity markets and to charge high prices for technology.

In order to understand the effects the patents have on developing countries, it is necessary to stress three aspects.

Firstly, the patents granted in developing countries are almost entirely of foreign origin. If the patents granted by developing countries are weighted by their economic value—for example, by the volume of sales they represent or their value-added—the percentage of patents of national origin will probably be less than 1 percent. Moreover, the trend has been towards more foreign dominance. The patents granted by developing countries have experienced a progressive denationalization during recent periods.[19] That has been the case in Chile, as well as in other Andean Pact countries.

Secondly, patents are increasingly concentrated in the hands of a few large multinational companies, which use patents for their global business policy. In Colombia less than 10 percent of all the firms that have obtained patents in the pharmaceutical industry controlled more than 60 percent of all the patents in the sector in 1970. The same percentages prevail with regard to patents for synthetic fibres and chemicals. The uneven concentration of patents in the hands of a few foreign firms leads to the concentration of production in the respective industries or product-areas, since patents define, sometimes quite exclusively, the firms that can produce (or import) certain goods.

As a consequence of the concentration of patents, it is possible to control the market for the final product so as to maximise the overall interest of a small number of firms, which are owners of industrial property privileges. This market control and monopolistic concentration is reainforced by the system of cross-licensing between companies, which in turn reduces a worldwide oligopolistic structure into a, regionally, monopolistic one.

Thirdly, not only do patents granted by developing countries belong almost entirely to foreign companies, but in addition, almost all remain unexploited in such countries. In Colombia, out of a total of 3513 patents evaluated by the Planning department, only 10 were actually used in industrial production.[20]

The lack of patent exploitation in developing countries is a basic contribution to the preservation of secure import markets for the multinational companies and thereby limits any possible competition from other companies, whether foreign or national. This is due to the fact that the unused patents have a precautionary role. They prevent not only manufacture of the product for which the process is patented, but also importation by other companies. The repercussions of this lack of competitive forces may be significant price increases, with negative income and balance of payments effects on the recipient countries.[21]

As regards trade-marks, it is clearly shown by Chudnovsky[22] that they are complementary to patents. A trade-mark is an artificial device used to distinguish one product from another. Although they do not in themselves involve any technological innovation, trade-marks are therefore important instruments in the product differentiation process characteristic of modern industries, and make it possible for their owners to obtain a monopoly rent. When it is not possible to patent the finished product, but only the process for making it—as has been the case in Colombia since 1967—the trade-mark of the finished product is therefore very important.

The Colombian experience also shows that it is the commercialization of technology (which takes place by secrecy, patent legislation and trade-marks) which leads to restrictive business practices and makes it possible for the technology possessors to acquire a monopoly rent. Patent licensing has provided classic examples of restrictive business practices and violation of antitrust or antimonopoly legislation.

Much of the technology actually imported by developing countries is widely knows and can be acquired from various sources. When it is a question of this type of technology, intelligent national local entrepreneurs can exercise their negotiating power and avoid restrictions in the use of know-how. Patents, on the other hand, carry monopoly control, even if the technology they cover is potentially accessible through various firms. The licensee's negotiating power is, in this case, seriously weakened. Thus, although the role and effects of patents have often been underestimated compared to the non-patented know-how used in developing countries, it remains true that patents may constitute a serious cause of restrictive business practices.

Recent research in Colombia has indicated that a very high percentage of contracts for patent licensing and sale of technology include clauses which put limits on the licensee's business practices. For example, in those contracts in the textile, chemical and pharmaceutical sectors that contained relevant information, Vaitsos found that about 85 percent explicitly prohibited exports by Colombian-owned firms and ventures.

To sum up, the Colombian experience was of great importance in the formulation of the Andean rules for import of technology, because it contributed to a better understanding of the whole process of commercialization of technology. Whereas Colombia only attempts to combat some of the negative effects of the commercialization of technology—high profits and high remittance and various restrictive clauses—the Andean rules additionally focus on the root of the problem: the system of industrial property rights and the lack of industrial research and know-how in the member countries.

Articles 20 and 25 of the Andean Agreement establish for the first time in these countries a legal base for dealing with restrictive business practices that result from the purchase of technology and from the licensing of patents and trade-marks. As in Colombia, export restrictions, tie-in arrangements, control of the size and structure of production, personnel hiring, use of alternative technologies, etc., are now also regulated in the other member countries. Moreover, pursuant to Articles 26 and 54, new legislation was to have been enacted by the end of 1971 to regulate matters relating to industrial property, as the inadequacy of the existing patent system and the international agreements that regulate it had been fully understood by the member countries.

Nevertheless, to touch upon property rights for industrial innovation is a very delicate question. The Andean Secretariat has produced a "White Paper" on the subject, but as yet, no decisions have been taken on a common policy on industrial properties.

A similar "White Paper" has been produced on common policies on the science and technology of the Andean Pact; it is therein stated that in the future the member countries will play a much more active role in the importation of foreign technology by deliberate efforts to support industrial research more strongly, to assist in the "itemization" of the needed technology (which is otherwise usually imported in package form), and by improving mutual communication on alternative sources and conditions for different types of technology. These principles have now been accepted as the basis for policies on science and technology in the Andean Group, but the crucial thing is, of course, how such a policy is implemented.

In this respect, Colombia has some clear advantages over other member countries, due to its experience in dealing with these matters in the Royalty Committee since 1967. The Royalty Committee has in these years obtained results that are far greater than the direct yearly savings of foreign exchange of US $11.3 mil. It has strengthened the Colombian bargaining position *vis-à-vis* foreign firms, and it has established norms for the negotiation of prices for foreign technology in different industries. It has reduced bounds for transmitting profits via technological payments, and has sought to minimize the various restrictive practices that often accompany technological agreements. Its effectiveness has naturally increased as it has gained greater experience and knowledge, and this has also enabled Colombia better to evaluate foreign investment proposals.

The Indian case

The Indian experience goes a bit further than the Colombian. In addition to pursuing a restrictive policy on foreign capital and foreign technology, India is attempting to increase her bargaining power by both supporting local research and development efforts and influencing the market situation for technology in India in a manner favourable to India.

By assisting *local research and development* efforts in the public as well as in the private sector, the government hopes (a) to decrease the need for import of technology, (b) to increase the knowledge of alternative sources of technology, (c) to increase the ability to evaluate the benefits of the alternatives and (d) to improve facilities for the adaption of imported technology. The assistance has been given directly, through the establishing of various national and regional research laboratories, as well as indirectly in the form of tax benefits for research in private industry.

The relative importance of industrial research in the government laboratories is shown below. (Table 1)

Table 1. *Estimated R & D allocations* (Rs Crores)

	1958–59	1965–66	1968–69	1969–70
Central Sector (incl. universities)	26.05	74.89	105.74	118.99
State Sector	1.00	3.51	6.90	8.60
Private Sector	0.15	2.43	7.07	8.13
Total	27.20	80.83	119.71	135.72

Source: Cabinet Secretariat, "Report on Science and Technology", 1969—quoted from ICICI: "Conference on Research and Development in Industry", December 15 and 16, 1970, p. 8.

These data do not, of course, say anything about the quality—the usefulness—of the research undertaken in the government laboratories. Formerly, the research undertaken was of a poor character. There was no mechanism for ensuring that the basic research results were developed into a stage where commercial exploitation became possible and there was very little contact between the laboratories and the industrial companies. Partly as a result of the import substitution policy pursued after the foreign-exchange crisis of 1956, partly because of the Sino-Indian war in 1962, the government laboratories began to put more emphasis on industry-oriented applied research. Before 1962, there were no specific guidelines available to research organizations concerning the priorities related to R & D in India. Since then, however, the research agencies have begun to emphasize defence orientation, import substitution and, lately, export promotion. These are, of course, only very broad guidelines, but have nevertheless had a positive effect on the country's R & D, and as a result, there has been a good deal of process and product improvement and development in the sixties. As may be seen in Table 1, research expenditures increased substantially and the laboratories have been able to take out 1,482 patents, of which, however, only about 150 have been commercially exploited. The commercial exploitation of the research results of the government laboratories is undertaken by the National Research Development Corporation (NRDC), which also provides financial assistance in converting research into pilot plant projects. Even though these technologies are sold to private companies at very low royalty rates, the private companies are reluctant to buy know-how from the government. They argue that the quality of the technology developed at home is inferior to the quality of imported technology, and that the know-how from the laboratories is obsolete. They further argue that it is developed regardless of cost and import content and that laboratories, having no manufacturing experience, could not give as much help as foreign suppliers of technology in solving problems of operating the technology.[23] This criticism should be accepted, but with some modification. Many of the companies have never had any contact with the laboratories and their views are often impressionistic and second-hand. Companies which have accepted technology from the laboratories have a less adverse view of them, although they are by no means uncritical.

The research efforts of laboratories run by associations of industries, such as textiles, and jute, have been more successful in terms of commercial exploitation than the ones run by the state. This seems to be due mainly to their orientation of work to the specific problems of the industries and to their direct contact with the manufacturers. Nevertheless, more important reasons for the reluctance of the Indian companies to use Indian technology are (a) they are not willing to take the risk of using technology which has not shown its commercial viability and (b) they prefer foreign technology because of the possibility it gives for illegal capital export.

This can certainly not be offset by a mere restructuring of research in the public sector.

This reluctance to develop Indian technology in the private sector can also be gauged by the low level of R & D allocations in the private sector (see Table 1.) Industry in India has never incurred any matching expenditure for R & D in order to adapt or further develop the imported technology.

There are two main reasons for this low level of research in Indian companies. As mentioned earlier, research is very expensive and there are considerable economies of scale in R & D. All over the world, most research activity is concentrated in the large firms. This is also the case in India.

In 1969-70, 50 percent of the private sector's research expenditures was accounted for by only 36 companies. Small companies do not use money for research. Indian companies, however, are typically small. More than half the value-added in industry is still accounted for by the small-scale sub-sector, which makes up 92 percent of all companies in this sector. Very few of them can afford to use any money on research. Moreover, a large propertion of the companies technically falling within the medium- or the large-scale sector, are also relatively small by international standards and they seldom have the resources or the incentives to undertake research.

Secondly, there is some evidence that firms which have foreign collaboration tend to rely more on their associates or parent company for research, rather than develop their own independent facilities. Quite often, Indian companies which have entered into foreign collaboration continue to rely upon the know-how of their foreign collaborators and are not interested in supplementing this know-how with new R & D results obtained in India. Moreover, even if they wanted to, it is not always easy, since many foreign collaborators are reluctant to transfer their "core technology", to train Indian engineers not only to "know" but also to know "how", and to support the

Table 2. *Pattern of research undertaken by ICICI sample companies* (No. of companies)

Range of turn-over	Import substi-tution	Product Im-provement and adaption	Process modifi-cation	Product Innova-tion
Up to Rs 1 crore	9	3	2	—
Rs 1–5 crores	22	14	18	2
Rs 5–15 crores	14	13	14	4
Over Rs 15 crores	10	10	10	8

Source: ICICI, op. cit., p. 12.

creation of R & D departments in their affiliates. If Indian companies were to become technologically self-reliant, the foreign companies would lose their license-fees, etc., and—more important—it would be very difficult for them to continue to sell their components and their machinery in India. To protect this market, the foreign collaborators must be very careful not to make themselves superfluous, and they will therefore generally be reluctant to support any steps in this direction. It is often argued that it would be advantageous for the foreign companies to transfer part of their R & D activities to India—which has plenty of qualified researchers—as salaries in India are much lower than in the developed countries. This argument, which neglects the role of R & D in competition, is true only for "peripheral" and "import substitution" technology. Complete sub-contracting in the production of technical know-how will probably only take place when the foreign company has full control over the utilization of technology, i.e., in wholly-owned subsidiaries, and even in these companies the danger of losing trained local engineers to competitors generally makes the foreign companies reluctant to undertake research. These tendencies are supported by the figures available on the pattern of research conducted in the Indian companies (see Table 2). These show that most of their research is of the "import substitution" and adaption type, e.g., research conducted to decrease the import content of the final product and to adapt the imported technology to local raw materials.

Research is only undertaken by the Indian companies when it is unavoidable or necessary for making a foreign technology commercially viable in India.

The Indian government has introduced various fiscal incentives to promote more research in Indian companies and it is now considering whether to include in all collaboration agreements clauses which make the use of some funds for R & D in Indian companies compulsory. Nevertheless, as long as a main motive for choosing to import foreign technology instead of setting up local R & D facilities is the possibility for illegal capital export, no fiscal or other incentives will be strong enough to push companies who have no other motivation to undertake research into doing so.

Except for a few companies like Tata and Birla, who have tried to become self-sufficient in certain fields, efforts to increase the Indian bargaining power *vis-à-vis* foreign companies on matters of technology transfer have come, and will continue to come, from the public sector. Therefore, the more actively the government enters into industrial production and research in the future, the better will be the possibilities of developing Indian technology and the better the chances of improving the bargaining power of India in relation to import of foreign technology.

The Indian government should, however, not be satisfied with this. There are other ways of increasing the bargaining power of a developing country, either by increasing the number of potential suppliers of a given technology or by limiting the number of buyers. The Indian government is attempting to work along both lines.

It goes without saying that the government can invite more foreign companies to submit offers only when the buyer of the know-how is a public sector industry. In the private sector, the government can only influence the outcome of negotiations by approving or disapproving the application for collaboration agreement. Recently, the government has started *to invite more suppliers of a given technology* to participate in negotiations. The aim of this has been to play the companies off against each other so as to obtain a better deal.

The Indian government has also used the *Eastern European countries as alternative suppliers of technology*. Since 1966, there has been a large increase in the number of agreements concluded with these countries. India now realizes that for many of the products relevant to India, i.e., cement-machinery, tractors, etc., the quality of East European commodities is just as good as that of Western products, and that the terms offered by Eastern European enterprises usually are more beneficial to India than the terms offered by companies in the West.[24]

First, the Eastern European enterprises usually ask only for a lump-sum payment, which is usually relatively low.

Second, Eastern Europeans are often less concerned than Westerners about the protection of knowhow: they are willing to train Indian engineers, and the Indian company is usually free to adapt the designs to Indian conditions.

Third, Eastern Europeans do not ask for restrictive clauses on export, which is of course very important for a developing country like India. But from the point of view of the private sector in India, collaboration has one important disadvantage. As India has bilateral, commercial agreements with Eastern European countries, technical agreements cannot be concluded by the private sector. Moreover, some of the important considerations behind technology imports from the West—access to a famous brand name and the opportunity for illegal capital exports—are not relevant for collaboration with Eastern Europe.

The government has attempted to increase its bargaining power and its control over import of technology by taking up discussions of ideas on centralized purchase of know-how.

The idea of a *central agency responsible for all import of know-how for sublicensing* has been put forward. It was thought that the total cost of importing a given technology could be reduced not only because a central agency would be in a strong bargaining position but also because repetitive imports of technology could be avoided.

These plans, which in fact would have meant nationalization of import, met such strong criticism from the private business lobby that they have been given up. It was argued that it was impossible to be certain that such a central agency could obtain a fully operative technology unless the agency was itself engaged in manufacture and unless it tried out the technology. If the agency itself were a manufacturer, however, it would have an incentive to withhold the technology from other companies. Finally, it was argued that there would be no guarantee that the technology would be up-to-date. Whether this criticism is based on firm knowledge and experience of the efficiency of Indian government activities or not, it stresses one very important point: the question of control of technology import is related to the question of industry ownership in the developed countries, as well as in India. Policies which neglect this fact are likely to fail.

Efforts to introduce a "*plural licensing system*", where several potential Indian producers come together in order to buy a specific technology, have not been successful, either. The advantages of "plural licensing" are that the total cost of obtaining a given technology will be lower. But the Indian companies have been reluctant to use this system. Access to foreign technology gives an Indian company a comparative advantage over its competitors, among other things because of the xenophile attitude of the Indian consumer. When an Indian company has found a supplier of a potentially profitable technology, it simply does not want to share this "gold mine" with others. Therefore, "sub-licensing" or "plural licensing" are not very likely to gain momentum in the private industrial sector in India.

We have discussed the different ways in which the Indian government has tried to strengthen the bargaining position of the Indian party in relation to foreign collaboration. Despite its efforts, the government has not succeeded because the private sector has not been willing to cooperate.

The Indian experience therefore shows that to be successful, a policy on import of technology must be related to the question of ownership in industry.

Conclusion

The question as to different modes of technology transfer is difficult and, as it involves evaluation of the impact of private foreign investment, also often considered controversial.

Nevertheless, the examples of Colombia and India clearly show that it is of advantage for governments in developing countries to initiate active policies to obtain the necessary foreign technology in the cheapest way.

Even so, it is very doubtful that such policies can solve the real problems of the developing countries: unemployment and poverty.

Why, then, does industrial development not automatically lead to full employment in underdeveloped countries? One explanation could of course be that the industrial growth rate is not large enough. This, however, is simply not true. Firstly, the industrial sector grows very rapidly in most of these countries. Secondly, even if they employed all available resources for development of industrial production, this would not be sufficient for full employment, given the capital-intensive techniques which are usually applied in industrial production. Even rapid industrial growth does not solve the unemployment problems of underdeveloped countries, mainly because the foreign technology which is used is capital-intensive.

As labour cost is relatively high and has been increasing in the countries where most of the technology imported to underdeveloped countries has been developed, the tendency in R & D has been towards labour-saving technology. In underdeveloped countries, however, labour cost is relatively low and therefore the imported technology is not well suited to the circumstances of the underdeveloped countries.

To utilize the imported technology in an optimal way, it is therefore necessary to adapt it, not only to local tastes and local raw materials, but also to local factor prices.

Nevertheless, very little is generally done to adapt the imported technology to the circumstances of underdeveloped countries. Though this would be very beneficial for them as such (social benefits), it is not always so for the private entrepreneur (private benefit). Even if adaption, i.e., changed factor proportions, would lead to a decrease in cost of production, it is not very likely to take place. The local entrepreneurs are generally reluctant to engage in R & D and as the local market is generally highly protected, the incentives for engaging in a costly, time-consuming adaption process are very few. Moreover, the local entrepreneur is not particularly dissatisfied with the labour-saving character of the imported technology, as the industrial relations between workers and management are often bad. Problems of organizing and controlling a large labour force in companies in the underdeveloped countries have made the managers more willing to accept the labour-saving technology. This holds even for public-owned industries.

(Often when government R & D laboratories are contracted by public companies, they are to develop a labour-saving technology, as in India).

Even if the imported technology were adapted to local factor prices, these technologies would still be relatively capital-intensive. This has to do with the import substitution character of the commodities produced with the imported technology. Most of these commodities are luxury consumption goods for which the brand name plays a very important role. Given the quality, most of these products can only be produced economically in one way, which is usually very capital-intensive. Even if the choice of technique were based on social cost benefit analysis using the most extreme shadow-pricing of factors like wages, interest rates and foreign-exchange ratios, the result would point to the use of the same technique in the underdeveloped countries as in their home country. For many of these import substitution commodities the choice between capital- and labour-intensive technology simply does not exist.[25]

The choice of technique could, of course, be broadened if it were possible to change the quality of these products. This, however, is not very often the case. First, one of the reasons that the technology is bought is that it gives the right to use the foreign brand name. But as the brand name serves as the consumer's guarantee for quality and the technology suppliers are sensitive to the reputation of their brand names, they are not willing to accept any lowering in quality. Therefore, most license agreements which include the right to use the foreign brand name also include a clause on quality control. Second, the high-income groups of the underdeveloped countries (those who consume these luxery items) are not willing to accept a lowering of quality in these products, so that this is not likely to take place. For most of these products, a high quality is tantamount to a high degree of homogeneity which can only be obtained by the use of highly-automatized capital-intensive technologies.

Nevertheless, for certain imported processes, it is possible to substitute labour for capital. This is especially the case for internal transportation of raw materals, components, etc., but also for other processes, such as packing. But the choice of technique for these operations is influenced towards a capital-intensive technology by various distortions of the relative factor prices in the underdeveloped countries, such as capital allowance systems. The relative factor prices are even influenced by the technology import itself. Companies operating a relatively capital-intensive technology are more likely to give in for wagc claims put forward by the workers. Their production costs are not very sensitive to wage increases, as wages only form a minor part of the total cost, and they are willing to pay higher wages to "stabilize" the labour force, as a large turnover of labour or even industrial disputes are much more expensive to companies using capital-intensive technologies. This might have a spread effect to the rest of the economy, so that the import of capital-intensive technologies via increasing wages gives incentives to the use of labour-saving technique. On the other hand, as most of these commodities are sold in highly protected markets, it is doubtful whether the relative factor prices have much influence on the choice of technique in the underdeveloped countries.

As some of the foreign technologies compete directly as well as indirectly with indigenous labour-intensive technologies in the factor market (i.e., the companies using foreign capital-intensive technologies attract the scarce skilled-labour force by offering higher wages) as well as in the commodity market, the effect on employment in some industries may even have been negative. This has probably been the case in the textile industry, where imported synthetic fiber technology is competing with a traditional technology based on cotton, which is often locally produced. Moreover, the structure in the demand for labour differs significantly between capital- and labour-intensive technologies.[26]

To operate a capital-intensive technology, one needs relatively many skilled and semi-skilled workers—which are in short supply—but relatively few of the abundant unskilled workers. By relying on foreign technology, the underdeveloped countries have built up a class of relatively well-off skilled and semi-skilled workers—a labour aristocracy[27]—who may perhaps be more interest in the preservation of the status quo than in radical policies, which can benefit the rural and urban poor.

Thus, equality-oriented industrial strategies cannot rely on foreign investment or import of foreign technology.[28]

Rather, a solution to such strategies should be found in one of the two possibilities mentioned below or in a combination of the two.

Obviously, the scope for choice of technique is wider in some sectors than in other. One way of increasing employment—which has been successful in, for example, Colombia—may therefore be to concentrate on the development of sectors with a large employment potential, e.g., construction. The employment criterion could simply be made the decisive one when considering whether a product should be produced locally or should continue to be imported. (It should perhaps not be consumed at all within the country—from an equality point of view).

The second possibility is to concentrate on production of low-quality mass consumption *and* mass investment goods (like agricultural implements) and to concentrate on R & D for the development of modern labour-intensive techniques for the production of these goods.

In both cases, however, the real problem will be that such policies can be carried through only if the rich are willing to renounce some of their privileges. If that is the case, then there is a chance that the vicious circle—unequal distribution of income, demand for luxury goods, capital-intensive technology, unequal distribution of income—may be broken. But only if that is the case can "reformist", equality-oriented industrial strategies be successful.

Notes

[1] See for example: P. Streeten and S. Lall, *Main findings of a study of private investment in selected developing countries.* UNCTAD, TD/B/C. 3/111, 1973; D. Chudnovsky: *Foreign manufacturing firms' behaviour in Colombia: A study of the influences of technology, advertising and financing upon profitability, 1966-1970,* unpublished Ph.D. thesis. University of Oxford, 1973; M. Kidron, *Foreign Investment in India.* London, 1965; S. Langdon, *Multinational Companies in Kenya,* unpublished Ph.D. thesis. University of Sussex, Brighton, 1974; J. Carlsen, *Danish private investment in Kenya,* Memo, Institute for Development Research. IDR-paper D 73.1, Copenhagen, 1973; J. Carlsen & P. Neersoe, *Transfer of technology to India—A case study of private Danish business activities in India,* Memo, Institute for Development Research. IDR-paper A 73.6, Copenhagen, 1973.

[2] This theory of private foreign investment was first presented by S. Hymer and subsequently developed further by Y. Aharoni, R. Cavels and A. V. Vaitsos.

See S. Hymer, *The international operations of national firms: A study of direct investment,* unpublished Ph.D. thesis. MII, 1960; A. Aharoni, *The foreign investment decision process.* Boston, 1966; R. Cavels, "International Corporations: The industrial economies of foreign investment", in *Economica,* London 1971; C. V. Vaitsos, *Transfer of resources and preservation of monopoly rents.* Development Advisory Service, Harvard University, paper 168, June 1970.

See also Charles Cooper, *The channels and mechanisms for the transfer of technology from developing Countries,* UNCTAD TD/B/AC. 11.5.27. April 1971.

[3] See S. Langdon, op.cit., J. Carlsen, op.cit., and J. Carlsen and P. Neersoe, op.cit.

[4] See D. Chudnovsky, op.cit., p. 162-185.

[5] See S. Langdon, *Multinational Corporations and Appropriate Technology: A Case Study from Kenya,* Appropriate technology Conference, Edinburgh University, Paper PE/E 12, 1973 and M. Kidron, *Pearson on Private Foreign Investment,* Pearson Conference document No. 28. Colombia University, 1970, p. 3.

[6] See S. Langdon, op.cit. 1973 and J. Carlsen, op.cit.

[7] See G. Arrighi, "International Corporation, Labour Aristocracies and Economic Development in Tropical Africa", in R. I. Rhodes, ed. *Imperialism and Under-development,* New York, 1970, and J. Carlsen, op.cit.

[8] Recent studies of the profitability of private foreign investment in developing countries show that they earn very high profits.

See J. Carlsen & P. Neersoe, "Danish Private Investment in Developing Countries", forthcoming; J. Carlsen, op.cit.; D. J. Morgan, "*British Investment in East Africa*", O.D.I., London, 1965; and D. Chudnovsky, op.cit.

[9] When Tanzania nationalized some industries after the Arusha Declaration in 1967 and gave foreign companies management contracts, this was the case.

See P. Neersoe, "Tanzania's Policy on Private Foreign Investment", in *World Development,* Vol. 2, No. 3, March 1974 and this volume, pp. 178–195.

[10] See G. K. Helleiner, *Manufactured Exports from Less Developed Countries and Multinational Firms,* mimeo, 1972 and S. Langdon, *Export Oriented Industrialization through the Multinational Corporation, Evidence from Kenya,* IDR Internal Papers E 74.5. Copenhagen, 1974.

[11] For a more detailed analysis of Colombia's policy on private foreign investment and foreign technology see: J. Carlsen & P. Neersoe, *Peru's and Colombia's Policies on Private Foreign Investment and Foreign Technology,* IDR papers A 74.6. Copenhagen, 1974.

[12] See UNCTAD TD/B/C. 3. (IV)/misc.l, 21 June 1973, *Balance of Payment and Income Effects of Private Foreign Investments in Manufacturing: Case Studies of Colombia and Malaysia.*

[13] There were previous attempts to register foreign capital in 1951 and in 1965, but on both occasions this was subsequently abandoned.

[14] The criteria are the following: net balance of payment effect, employment creations, technical contribution and degree of utilization of domestic raw materials, relations with domestic capitalists (giving preference to joint ventures), improvement of market competition, and contribution to the Latin American integration process.

[15] D. Chudnovsky, op.cit., estimates that as much as 25 percent of Colombian imports are interfirm transactions.

[16] See D. Chudnovsky, op.cit., p. 112-124 and p. 162-185.

[17] See Constantine V. Vaitsos, *The Process of Commercialization of Technology in the Andean Pact,* Lima, October 1971.

[18] See Constantine V. Vaitsos, "Patents Revisited; their function in Developing Countries", in Charles Cooper (ed.), *Science, Technology and Development,* London, 1973.

[19] See *The Role of Patents in the Transfer of Technology to Developing Countries,* United Nations publication Sales No. 65, II B.1.

[20] See Constantine V. Vaitsos, op.cit., p. 39.

[21] Such an example of price increases caused by patents was quoted in *El Tiempo,* June 2, 1970. In 1970, the German-owned firm that controls the patent of a particular pharmaceutical product sold this product to the Colombian government for Col.pesos 700/thousand units. A North American firm without access to the patent offered the same product for Col.pesos 133.50/thousand units. But the Colombian government was forced to buy from the German firm through a court decision based on the patent coverage.

[22] See D. Chudnovsky, op.cit., p. 199.

[23] See National Council of Applied Economic Research, *Foreign Technology and Investment,* New Delhi, 1971.

[24] See Friedmann & Bequin, *Joint International Business Ventures in Developing Countries,* New York, 1971, p. 318.

[25] See Frances Stewart, *Choice of Technique in Developing Countries,* mimeo, Oxford, 1970, and ILO, *Employment, Incomes and Equality—a Strategy for Increasing Productive Employment in Kenya,* Geneva, 1972, p. 133-135 and p. 371-382.

[26] See G. Arrighi, op.cit.

[27] Ibid.

[28] This does not, however, imply that private foreign investment or import of foreign technology should not take place. For numerous products of great importance to the underdeveloped countries, e.g., fertilizers, the technology is the property of multinational companies. For small poor countries, the only or the cheapest way to obtain access to this technology may be to accept private foreign investment.

G. Massiah

Multinational Corporations and a Strategy for National Independence

Introduction

During the past few years, a considerable number of studies have been devoted to multinational corporations. Few economic phenomena have ever been the subject of so much attention, so many case studies and such a volume of quantified data, to which must be added a number of efforts to carry out theoretical analysis.

Let us leave aside the liberal approach to the problem; it has shown its utter inability to go beyond the mere formalisation of descriptive-type analysis, although the importance of some works closely connected with this approach must be stressed. The value they attach to observation and their concern for information provide fitting lessons for those studies verging on theoretical abstraction. The works of Vernon, Dunning, the Boston Consulting Group and the study on American multinational corporations prepared by economists for the US Congress have become standard reference works on such corporations and the development of the whole phenomenon.

Nevertheless, the inability of these liberal studies to provide a valid explanation compatible with the frame of reference of liberal economics and capable of defining the multinational phenomenon within its proper context, coupled with their confusion in the face of the present crisis of imperialism further weaken their dominant ideology by signalling the collapse of the theoretical foundation for the capitalist mode of production.

As far as the Marxist approach is concerned, the debate quickly centered on the fundamental problem, i.e., development imperialism. Imperfect though the tools may be, despite past trial and error, and although modesty is more necessary than ever, events have shown that there can only be one approach to an analysis of this problem.

There have been counter-attacks to the development of multinational corporations. Initially, resistance was linked to the secondary contradictions of capitalism, supported in the United States and Europe by those sections of the bourgeoisie whose power was threatened. There has been a counter-reaction on the part of those trade unions associated with social democracy, perpetually searching for a "counter force", in their endeavors to organise multinational trade unions, as, for example, in the chemical industry (cf. the works of Levinson). The unions affiliated with the World Federation of Trade Unions reacted by strengthening their anti-monopoly alliances (cf. the European Congress of the French CGT and the meeting of West European Communist parties in London), an effort which (although still at an embryonic stage) aims at the co-ordination of spontaneous struggles arising within the subsidiaries of the same group (cf. the examples of Michelin and Air Liquide).

From this wealth of experience, a number of policies have been formulated with regard to proposed actions. An analysis of the present stage of imperialism underlies each of these policies. Only at this level is it possible to arrive at any consistency, to assess the results and to devise a strategy.

The crucial question, therefore, relates to the meaning of this phenomenon: the rise of multinational corporations. Does this phenomenon purely and simply reflect the evolution of capitalism—whether monopoly or state capitalism—or is it tantamount to capitalism's transcendence of some of its own contradictions or even, as some people claim, to calling into question the very nature of the state? The debate, although sound, has sometimes become bogged down. From the withering away of the state to the establishment of a world state, interminable abstract discussions have taken place, diverting the efforts necessary for an exhaustive study of the changes of capitalist organisation and the development of a new phase of imperialism. There already exists a signal danger for the undisputable theoretical advances of Maxist research over the past few years. Our aim is not to refine the conclusions of this research, to seek knowledge for the sake of knowledge, but to understand the world in order to change it. What a wonderful period the past ten years have been for research! The new efforts poured into the building of socialism, the new forms of liberation struggles, the efforts towards national independence, the multifarious forms of the imperialist crisis have all opened a new field of knowledge and offered new prospects for social practice. The facts are there; they are available for anyone who is prepared to couple research with his own participation in the struggles, the proclaimed purpose of which is to control reality in order to understand and change that reality.

In such a limited study as this, it cannot be our intention to launch into an exhaustive treatment of the phenomenon of multinational corporations. While remaining faithful to our proposed approach, we have nevertheless attempted to draw those lessons which in the present state of research could serve to provide a definition of a strategy for national independence from the standpoint of relations with multinational corporations.

The first part of this study relates to the specificity and the development of the multinational phenomenon; we have attempted to define the characteristics of the multinational corporations and to analyse their behaviour.

The second part is devoted to ascertaining the role of multinational corporations within the framework of imperialist strategies and the resulting consequences, particularly from the standpoint of the existing contradictions within the class alliances.

An analysis of the multinational phenomenon, on the one hand, and on the other, the place it occupies within the imperialist strategies makes it possible to define the guidelines for studying the strategy of a given corporation in a given country.

In the third part of this study, we shall inquire into the meaning and some of the characteristics of a strategy for national independence and the implications of such a strategy in relation to multinational corporations. It is obvious that there cannot be a general definition for such a strategy; everything depends on the specific aspects of each of the social formations and, furthermore, the strategy cannot be defined from the outside. It can only be moulded in the heat of battle.

We have restricted ourselves to providing a few indications on some problems which have actually arisen and on the possibilities available for the definition of a strategy with regard to the multinational corporations. Our aim is to draw the necessary lessons from theory, so that those who are involved in current struggles may put them into practice and, conversely, use their practical experience to enrich theory.

Development and analysis of the multinational phenomenon

The specific nature of the multinational phenomenon

We shall begin with the assumption that multinational corporations today represent the most advanced form of the organisation of capital at the present stage of imperialism. From the early colonial trading centres to the sophisticated financial participation of the conglomerates, the history of multinational corporations contains all the forms of organisation which, at every stage, made possible the penetration and expansion of the capitalist mode of production.

These new forms of organisation developed in societies where the capitalist system was most advanced, in the imperialist centres and particularly in the United States. Their intervention was characteristic of the various developmental forms of imperialism, which today consist in:

the internationalisation of capital and the development of the world market linked to American domination;

the extension of the capitalist mode of production in the imperialist social formations through the new development of the sphere of commodity relations (capitalist domination of all aspects of life);

the extension of the capitalist mode of production with new forms of domination of peripheral social formations, through class alliances corresponding to the combination of the capitalist mode of production with other, pre-existing modes of production.

While integrating the main features of the imperialist stage of development, the multinational corporations were able to develop profit strategies adapted to their needs. They endeavoured to control the factors which influence the profit rate, thus intervening in the control of sales (methods of distribution and prices), of circulation (centralised management of all the liquid assets) and of innovation (research and development).

Their highly developed forms of organisation made it possible for the multinational corporations to avoid, or even to benefit from, some of the contradictions that other sections of capital were compelled to confront directly. Diversifying the location of the various stages in the production process enabled them to minimise the threat to their profits posed by possible developments of the class struggle in any given country. The high degree of capital concentration enabled them further to intervene directly on the markets by applying integrated methods of distribution. Market control and price manipulation made them willing partners in the strategy which consisted in giving an inflationist answer to the claims of peasants and workers. Their ties with bank capital, their ability to maintain internal cash generation and to borrow enabled them to implement accumulation strategies regardless of either the tying up of capital in any given sector or of attempts at credit control in any given country.

It has often been said that easy access to the international monetary system is the particular trade mark of the multinational phenomenon. Indeed, apart from the special opportunities for action which these firms have because of their history, their ties with the banking system and their size, one can observe the consistency between their forms of organisations and those of the international division of labour, especially in the world market and the international monetary system. This observation becomes explicitly clear in the superstructures of the world system as exemplified by the International Monetary Fund, the World Bank and the International Finance Corporations.

Thus, the attempt to inject consistency into the system, which is determined by the efforts of the capitalist mode of production to dominate the world, makes it possible to define the specific nature of the multinational phenomenon on the basis of the characteristic features of imperialism in its present stage of evolution. In order to analyse the nature of multinational corporations, it is necessary to take into account the contradictions of the imperialist system and their consequences for the multinational phenomenon.

Evolution of the multinational phenomenon

Although the rise and the specific nature of the multinational phenomenon is relatively recent in history and the entirety of the phenomenon itself has only become apparent since 1958, it must not be forgotten that its characteristics were present from the very beginning of capitalism.

The development of the capitalist mode of production

Long before the 17th century, European companies (Dutch, English, French) were controlling plantations, building warehouses and workshops, and stationing garrisons in their trading centres in Asia (China, Japan, Southeast Asia), Africa and the Middle East. These companies were already engaged in multisectoral activities, operating on the capital markets and simultaneously evolving their own brand of diplomacy.

The development of the capitalist states, the resulting conflicts and the transition to direct control over their territories and colonial exploitation—all this tended to restrict the influence of the large companies and encourage the rise of a greater number of small firms more closely linked to the development of national capitalism. The nature of such firms varied according to the various developments within the capitalist states (France, Britain, Holland, Belgium, Spain, Portugal, Germany). These companies later diversified on the basis of a restructuring of capitalism in their countries and there soon arose companies involved in trading, plantations, agricultural raw materials and mining.

The development of the imperialist stage

From 1870 to 1945, the development of the imperialist stage underlined the strengthening of the new characteristics analysed by Lenin.

The role played by bank capital and its internationalisation laid the foundation for the world superstructures of imperialism: its amalgamation with industrial capital opened up new international prospects and determined the structure and nature of financial capital. This amalgamation also demonstrated the importance of controlling and directing technological progress, and may best be observed in the case of Belgian capitalism with, on the one hand, the example of the Société Générale financing the exploitation of the African colonies and, on the other hand, the development of companies exploiting new innovations from 1870 (gas and water distribution, processing mineral ores using the Coppee process, the activities of the Empain Group in the railway sector, the Solvay group in chemical industries, etc.).

The development of the class struggles and the 1917 Revolution accelerated the trend towards geographical diversification, already well launched by the oil companies before the beginning of the century. Controlling raw materials and securing their investments became a matter of major concern for international companies and imperialist states. Because of this concern, the ties between the states and the international companies were strengthened and as a result, a considerable influence within the national state apparatus was bestowed on the stratum of the bourgeoisie represented by these companies.

Latin America provided a testing ground for American imperialism and a field for experimentation by the major American multinational corporations. After a preliminary period devoted to the elimination of their competitors and the protection of their imperialist sphere, all the direct or indirect forms of intervention, hand in hand with the strategies typical of the recent neo-colonial period, were developed and refined. The excess profits from the oil companies and from the exploitation of Latin America provided the economic basis for the alliance of the classes in the United States, exactly as formalised by President Roosevelt.

In the period between the two world wars, the intense class confrontations and the success of the socialist revolution resulted in the acceleration of the trend towards a fall in the profit rate, adding a new dimension to the inter-imperialist conflicts and paving the way for a very high degree of protectionism in Europe. The development of the domestic market based on the production of new use-values, aided and abetted by advertising, nevertheless provided only a partial answer to this situation. In order to circumvent the protectionist barriers, and considering the need for continuity presupposed these forms of marketing, the manufacturing companies—particularly the American ones—sought to multinationalise, thus initiating the recent trend.

The period from 1945 to 1973

In a previous study on the crisis of imperialism, we distinguished between three stages during the period from 1945 to 1973:

From 1945 to 1956, when American imperialism established itself as the dominant imperialism. The cold war accelerated the decline of French and British imperialisms and conferred upon the United States the role of protector of the interests and supplies of the "free world". During this entire period, international investments were basically public (Marshall Plan) and paved the way for an expansion of the American imperialist sphere.

From 1956 to 1965, when American imperialism may be considered as hegemonic. The USSR agreed to peaceful coexistence as a tactical necessity, the Suez crisis having put an end to the illusions of French and British imperialism and, encouraged by the United States, these countries accelerated the process of decolonisation. From 1957 onwards, the British banks were no longer able to use the pound sterling as a means of settlement outside the sterling area;

The return to the convertibility of currencies in 1958 enabled the development of private international investment and witnessed the beginning of American multinational corporations establishment in Europe, Japan and Southeast Asia. These corporations entrenched themselves firmly in certain sectors (oil, chemical industries, electrical and electronic engineering). This period of a "no-holds-barred" expansion of the American corporations was marked by the birth of conglomerates. In a way, it was the golden age of the multinational phenomenon. Its growth was such that those European and Japanese firms too large to be completely absorbed were invited into certain forms of association. Within the framework of the "Pax Americana", the concept of an international capitalism that was self-reliant and independent of national states became an accepted reality.

In 1965, the rise of secondary imperialism began. In 1963/64, the restrictions of the capital market in the United States brought about the appearance of the Eurodollar market. The lessons taught by the Vietnamese people opened the way for a general radicalisation of peoples' struggles. The collapse of the "Pax Americana" policy led American firms to seek the protection of their government. Increased productivity in Europe and Japan encouraged the beginning of European and Japanese multinational corporations, which sought to compete in the American domestic market and attempted to set up independent imperialist spheres.

During this period, peaceful coexistence became a strategic choice and the multinational corporations, particularly the American ones, established agreements with state-owned firms in the USSR and other East European countries for a share in their production and markets.

Nevertheless, apart from these new developments, further contradictions came to light within the multinational phenomenon. The rise of secondary imperialism had serious repercussions on the monetary market and contradictions between these corporations and individual states, particularly in Europe, began to appear. The intensification of the class struggle and efforts to achieve national independence at times pressured various states into attempting to arrive at a compromise so as to safeguard their class alliances, compromises often detrimental to the interests of various multinational corporations previously established in their countries.

Since 1973, new phases have occurred in the crisis of imperialism which threaten to alter the whole picture. Was the oil crisis a defeat for European and Japanese imperialism, or was it simply a recovery by the United States prior to the establishment of a world with five power blocks? Was the Middle East crisis an occasion for the establishment of new power relations within the framework of peaceful coexistence, or was it simply a series of patchwork operations? Does the rise of the bourgeoisie in certain countries linked to the control of raw materials open up new prospects of class alliances in these countries and on an international scale? Last, but not least, to what extent does the crisis increase the possibilities for certain countries to take advantage of an already existing revolutionary situation?

Analysis of the multinational phenomenon

A study of the development of multinational corporations provides some highly valuable indications for an analysis of their strategies. A distinction must be made between conglomerates and other multinational corporations, even though it is a fact that industrial multinational corporations play a crucial role in the international division of labour.

The conglomerates, limited in number but very powerful—the most notorious of which is ITT—play a central role in the equalisation of the profit rates in every sector and in every country. Their policy is to take over firms with a high potential growth rate but lacking financial resources and firms with a high liquidity surplus or unused borrowing capacity. The profit strategy is solely based on the control and profitability of the capital invested. The problem is to purchase or sell businesses on the basis of interesting transactions and in the meantime to ensure optimal operation of the business. Strictly speaking, there is no general organisational rule for the groups, except at the level of economic return and financial management. Conglomerates form a special category of multinational corporations; they began to develop separately from the international banking system as early as 1960. Thus, although often considered as the most representative among multinational corporations, the conglomerates were not the driving force in the international division of labour. Cumbersome and dangerous though they are, their main concern is the rationality of financial capitalism. They play their part in relation to an equalisation of the profit rates, benefiting from the international division of labour without actually being its real motivators.

For every other type of multinational firm, the nature of the sectors in which they operate becomes highly important. There, they develop sectoral profits strategies based on security of supplies, domination of the market and control of innovations. When any such corporation operates within a number of sectors at the same time, there very often exist a number of autonomous sectoral managements, whereas the financial management is always a single and centralised one.

Such corporations basically operate in a single sector, typically in the oil sector, in automobile engineering, in electrical and electronic engineering or in the chemical and food processing industries. Nevertheless, in most cases the profits strategy of multinational corporations is based on diversification and intervention in two, three or four sectors.

Sectoral diversification depends essentially on the corporation's possibilities and strategic requirements; they tend to adopt one of the following alternatives:

> moving into another sector, where they attempt to control the import substitution market (e.g., razor blades, electric razors, plastic and cardboard packaging)
>
> the utilisation of by-products of the main product (e.g., petroleum, chemical products);
>
> integration of the different stages of the production process;
>
> control of a strategic input in the production process;
>
> production for the same distribution network (e.g., supermarkets, hotels)

The behavioural basis of a multinational corporation may always be explained through the attempts to exercise an indirect domination of competitive capitalism and the tendency towards new monopolistic or oligopolistic forms, which implies the existence of very strong entry barriers to guarantee superprofits. The effort to dominate competitive capitalism implies control over distribution; the entry barriers may be obtained either through control over supplies (and, in the final analysis, over raw materials) or through the control of research and development. In an attempt to explain the importance of marketing, Mr. Agnelli—the boss of Fiat—declared that a company could afford to associate itself with other companies in almost every field, that it could afford to decentralise almost everything, but that, in all circumstances, it should maintain absolute control either over raw materials and their distribution or over research and development and its distribution. Thus, we could attempt a tentative definition of behavioural types of multinational corporations from the point of view of their implantation in any given country, such as defined in a recent study (study on the behaviour of multinational corporations in contrasting international environments, 1973, DATAR study carried out by the Laboratoire de Conjoncture et de Prospectives and the ACT company).

By taking into account the strategies for sectoral diversification, the nature of the country of origin and the host country (whether more or less economically developed than the country of origin), of the existence or absence of a competitive industry, of the reasons for the establishment (natural resources, market, labour), the means of establishment and the nature of the market (competitive, protected, oligopolistic, exploited or not exploited by other multinational corporations), it has been possible to define eight behavioural types, as summarised below:

Behaviour of multinational corporations with regard to their establishment in a given country

Type No. *Corporations*

1 Well-established oil or mining companies with a strategy of "no-holds-barred" control of deposits, a high research-development ratio, huge size, diversified and with a backward (chemicals) or horizontal (other energy sources) linkage, controlling all the stages of production leading to the marketing of the extracted product.
Examples: "Majors" of the oil cartel.

2 The more recent oil or mining companies, occasionally state-owned, which have taken advantage of the discovery of deposits in areas not dominated by the cartel to increase their shares. Smaller in size. Tied to the cartel only at the refinery stage.
Examples: Independent oil companies.

3 The huge manufacturing companies (chemical products, electrical and automobile engineering), where at one stage of production almost unskilled and badly paid manpower (assembly) is employed.
Examples: Chemical or automobile firms established in Brazil; construction firms acting on tenders (temporary multinationalisation).

4 Firms operating in Europe or Japan, exploiting a new product with a wide market—firms with a high research-development ratio—making a quick kill by taking advantage of a very narrow lead over their competitors.
Examples: food processing corporations (e.g., frozen foods)

5 American corporations with a very high research-development ratio, with product cycle and, because of a very strong technological lead, having almost total monopoly of the market.
Example: IBM

6 Firms whose multinationalisation goes hand in hand with sectoral diversification, with a very high liquidity ratio, with a policy of taking over other companies and intervening in complementary sectors, either connected with the market or with the integration of their production process.
Examples: chemical industries operating in the food sector.

7 Firms concentrating on their main sector of activity, but intervening in other markets through establishment and takeover of control.

Examples: American automobile corporations in Europe, or chemical, electrical or food processing companies intervening in other European countries.

8 European or Japanese companies exploiting an outlet in the United States with a high research-development ratio.

Example: Michelin

It is more than likely that at least one of the following four components plays a role in the profits strategy of every corporation: (1) control of sources of raw materials and surpluses; (2) exploitation of the differential costs of labour; (3) control of markets and distribution; (4) control of capital and financial operations.

It is nevertheless true that, according to a company's particular characteristics (the sectors in which it is established, the structure of the market, the size and extent of its establishment overseas, the forms of organisation, the history of the company itself, etc.), one of the four components may be more prominent than the other three, and modify their importance, thereby imposing its own consistency on the company's overall strategy.

For simplicity' sake, and with regard to the profits strategy from the viewpoint of corporation establishment in a given country, we shall therefore distinguish between four types of corporations:

corporations whose profits strategy is essentially based on the control of sources of raw materials;

corporations whose profits strategy is essentially based on the exploitation of the differential costs of labour;

corporations whose profits strategy is essentially based on the control of markets and distribution;

conglomerates, whose profits strategy is essentially based on capital and financial operations.

It is possible to study the profits strategy components that constitute the main feature of each sectorally or regionally diversified corporation by examing the history of that company. They depend, in fact, on the international division of labour and on the international context whose evolution has determined the profits strategy of the multinational corporations. In order to go further, therefore, it is necessary to go back to the development of the imperialist system.

Multinational corporations and imperialist strategies

Being the main representatives of the most advanced section of capital at the present stage of imperialism, multinational corporations are partners in the class alliances of the imperialist centres. The part that they can play depends on the nature of the dominant class alliance, on its internal contradictions and on the compromises made. Several factors must be taken into account when studying the consequences of the multinational phenomenon on the imperialist centres and the resulting contradictions:

the nature of the imperialist centre (principal or secondary) and the imperialist strategy which it develops because of the sharpening of the imperialist contradictions;

the place of the advanced section of capital in the dominant class alliance and the contradictions between firms arising out of their different profit strategies and their consequences for the contradictions of the dominant class alliance.

Our basic assumption is that the development and the behaviour of these multinational corporations will be determined by the evolution and the contradictions of the imperialist system. In effect, any study of the multinational phenomenon necessitates making a distinction between on the one hand, the American and on the other, the European and Japanese multinational corporations.

The American multinational corporations

American multinational corporations provide the clearest example of the characteristics of the multinational phenomenon. It was in fact during the period when American imperialism was establishing its hegemony that the rise of multinational corporations started and that they appeared as the vectors of the internationalisation of capital, propelled by the United States. This was a threefold strategy, each aspect of which gave these corporations a new field of expansion, which in turn gave rise to new contradictions. The three aspects of this strategy were: (a) peaceful coexistence; (b) the subordinated development of Europe and Japan; (c) control of the dominated countries.

As the strategic assumption for the theory of the equilibrium of a world divided into two power blocks, peaceful coexistence became for the United States a way of consolidating, if not preserving, its hegemonic power. The transition from the cold war to peaceful coexistence transformed the part played by multinational corporations, underlining the importance of those which linked to the world market (capital goods, important consumer goods) in relation to those tied up with the military-industrial complex of the

Pentagon and working mostly on exclusive contracts with a high rate of return. Access to those government and the special contacts this required facilitated the development of conglomerates in the fifties. Subsequently, however, the strategy for diversification has made it obvious that multinational corporations were an industrial rather than a banking phenomenon.

The development of peaceful coexistence brought about other contradictions between these corporations. The overture towards China was liable to attract those firms producing capital goods. On the other hand, the rapprochement with the USSR was considered by most of the large corporations as being very promising. The availability of raw materials from the USSR or through triangular agreements, the industrialisation of Siberia, and the development of mass consumption were all matters of direct interest to the American corporations. Joint-venture agreements have already been struck with Soviet state-owned corporations; strong pressure, particularly from Congress, is being applied in order to make the Soviet corporations less dependent on the state machinery. If these attempts were to be successful, which is rather improbable at present, we might witness the development of a Soviet multinational phenomenon.

Although the corporations appear as one of the factors for applying the strategy of peaceful coexistence, it is especially within the framework of relations between the United States, Europe and Japan that their role has been most decisive and that the present characteristics of the multinational phenomenon have been the most fully developed. Furthermore, the development of inter-imperialist conflicts has been the hallmark of the period from 1965 to 1973. Multinational corporations have had a specific role to play at every stage of these conflicts. The corporations involved in the control of raw materials became a driving force in the process of eliminating secondary imperialism from their own sphere of influence (essentially for the Dutch, the British, the French and the Belgians).

The second phase consisted in an attempt to control the European and Japanese economies in the area of high-technology capital goods (electronics) and mass consumer goods (e.g., agricultural foodstuffs). This attempt took on varying forms according to the potential and the reactions of individual countries, the control strategy not excluding the possibility of negotiations and sharing. The degree of penetration varied according to sectors and the nature of the European or Japanese corporations involved. This differentiation is particularly marked at present, since the equalisation of productivity and the setbacks of American imperialism have allowed the secondary imperialisms to hit back vigorously.

In view of this new situation, some of the American firms (energy and raw materials, conglomerates) were prepared to throw their weight into the battle waged by the United States to recover and consolidate its hegemony, whereas other American corporations might be tempted by a compromise solution involving a partnership with European or Japanese corporations. Nevertheless, it is in their role as controllers of the dominated countries that these multinational corporations appeared and played their most consistent part. The role that they played developed hand in hand with the forms of control that they exercised. Their unmitigated exploitation of raw materials at very low prices still occurs, but it has become more subtle and does not constitute their only form of interference. Two new trends became apparent, representing a break with the old forms of domination. First, some countries became privileged bases of operation and constituted imperialist staging posts; this policy was first tried out in Brazil and is being applied in a number of other countries, e.g., Iran, Nigeria, and Indonesia. In these countries, a rapid industrial growth has brought about the intervention of the giant multinational corporations through the establishment of assembly plants and export-oriented industries.

Secondly, the transition from direct administration of colonies to more sophisticated forms of domination necessitated the introduction of new administrative machinery. In some countries, new class alliances were formed and had to be consolidated. New sectors had to be developed in accordance with the new methods of intervention, such as the control of banking and distribution circuits and—especially—intervention in agriculture (marketing and irrigation), in services, and in tourism.

Thus, the strategy of American imperialism determined the nature of the development of the American multinational corporations, as well as to a great extent the contradictions between these corporations. The strategic options largely cross-check with those that sprang up within the dominant class alliance inside the United States and the solutions advocated for its domestic problems. Let us assume that the dominant class alliance in the United States, under the leadership of the fraction of the bourgeoisie which controls the large multinational corporations, includes the new strata of the petty bourgeoisie (technicians, research workers), as well as a section of the working class, and that the strength of this class alliance depends on the existence of imperialist superprofits. Every setback, every weakening of American imperialism will constitute a challenge to the strength of the class alliance, but any development of the various forms of imperialist domination will also tend to modify the power relations within the leading fraction and thereby exercise an influence on the solution of internal problems, such as selecting the price of energy, the policy of high wages, the problems of unemployment, the campaign against poverty, and the integration of the black bourgeoisie.

European and Japanese multinational corporations

The refusal to be restricted to the role of imperialist "staging-posts" led the European and Japanese states to support the development of their own multinational corporations and to bestow upon them an especially important role within their own strategy. The control of strategic investments (energy, supplies, research-development) represented their first line of defense against the intervention of American corporations in Europe. The trend towards an equalisation of productivity levels even made possible the establishment of Japanese and European corporations in certain sectors of the American market. Above all, however, the creation of a European, as well as a Japanese, imperialist sphere enabled these countries to maintain some measure of independence *vis-à-vis* the United States. As a result, the struggle to control the markets and supplies became tougher and competition got stiffer in the periphery of the centres.

Supplies of raw materials and the ability to export were vital for Japan; and because of its difficulties in acting directly at the political level, the Japanese firms became entrusted with the task of implementing these two targets. In their attempts to expand and strengthen their sphere of influence in Asia, the Japanese corporations sometimes found themselves in a position of acute competition with American corporations. Furthermore, in order to maintain a certain degree of discretion in their intervention, Japanese corporations took over the control of a number of Australian companies which were in a position to operate more freely. The Japanese corporations, in their efforts to expand their areas of intervention, found themselves in direct competition with American and European corporations both in the Middle East (the exchange of oil against capital goods) and in Africa, where the Japanese corporations rapidly expanded their activities in South Africa. They are now trying to widen those activities in the former French and British zones, through the operations of Canadian firms which they have taken over.

In all those areas, the Japanese corporations, being highly concentrated and to a large extent controlled by financial capital, have had the firm support of their state. In other areas, however, their activities have been a source of contradiction between the multinational corporations. Some of the corporations established in Taiwan have tended to inhibit moves towards better relations with China, while others have been more attracted by a policy of industrialisation in Siberia. The contradictions between these two opposing trends in Japan are today coming to a head. For some, the time has come to enlarge the class alliance by integrating a wider section of the working class through a policy of higher wages and an increase in domestic consumption. For others, the maintenance of Japan's export capacity means an end to the inflexibility of the employment market and the disappearance of slave labour (workers, domicile, bonuses), pre-requisited for low wages.

In the case of Europe, as well, priority was given to building its own imperialist sphere. The problem, however, became more complex, due to the struggle for control of Europe waged by the bourgeoisies in various European countries. Africa still remains the least-contested European sphere of influence. Efforts to introduce new activities, based on historical associations, were made in the Middle East, in Asia and even in Latin America. Unlike the Japanese, the Europeans were able to operate more directly at the political level and proposed superstructures in support of their sphere of influence (association with the Common Market), based on the idea of preferential markets rather than on direct intervention by European multinational corporations.

The class alliances, however, vary from one country to another. In some countries (France, Italy), the most advanced sections of capital tended to share power with a politically powerfully middle bourgeoisie. In other countries, the contradictions became very acute between the multinational corporations. In Great Britain, for example, the modernist section was made up of those in favour of strengthening the special relationship with the United States, those who acted as spokesmen for the interests of imperial Britain (today very weak) and those advocating a Europocentric development. In the Federal German Republic itself, certain corporations were more attracted by the idea of improving relations with the USSR, in association with the United States, than by the construction of Europe.

In the present situation, and considering the hardening of the class struggle, two main trends of ideas prevail among the European bourgeoisies. Some consider that the construction of Europe's own imperialist sphere must continue and, to that end, rely on support from the bourgeoisies in the oil-producing Arab countries. Others, on the contrary, consider the dangers of such an adventure for too great and prefer to negotiate the best possible position within an Atlantic alliance, where the United States would be predominant but no longer hegemonic. In the final analysis, the contradictions appear most acute within the European multinational corporations.

Multinational corporations and imperialist centres

Generally speaking, all the imperialist states tend to favour those firms exploiting raw materials, particularly Europe and Japan, whose economies depend to a large degree on the supply of energy and mineral ores. These states, therefore, support the establishment of multinational corporations within their own spheres of influence (e.g., BRGM for France in Africa) and require of them that they increase their international range of activities, providing them with every possible assistance (political support, threats of retaliation, etc.) and allowing them a wide measure of discretion (price increase, investment financing, negotiations of contracts involving guarantees and compensation, etc.). This unreserved support gives considerable political weight to the corporations, as evidenced by the well-orchestrated manoeuvres carried out by oil and coal mining corporations over the past three years and which led to the recent crisis in the United States.

The attitude of the imperialist states towards those of their multinational corporations whose strategy is based upon an exploitation of the differential cost of labour is generally rather favourable, for it provides the best method of enhancing and consolidating their sphere of influence. It is mainly those activities which most heavily rely on unskilled labour that are affected by shifts in location, so that, in effect, no serious consequences arise with regard to unemployment in the home state. Nevertheless, such a policy favours higher productivity levels, high wages and a concentration of industries, and as such is opposed by the various strata of the middle bougeoisie in countries where it occupies an important position within the dominant class alliance. The debate now raging in France on the choice between immigration or the establishment of assembly plants overseas—in the automobile industry, for instance—highlights these contradictions.

The situation is sometimes more complex for those corporations seeking mainly to exploit and control a market. On the whole, all the imperialist states are favourable to the idea, the ultimate aim being to extend their sphere of influence; they offer encouragement in the form of credits, tax exemptions, financing of research-development and the establishment of corporations abroad. This trend, however, gives rise to very serious contradictions within the "social democracy" type of class alliance, allowing as it does some firms to escape the constraints of a strategic agreement with the trade unions representing an important section of the working class. The consequences for unemployment (through a lack of new employment opportunities), for price levels (because of the strengthening of the monopoly situation), for currency (because of the deterioration of the balance of payments—a reduction of possible exports) and for the opportunities for speculation have made most of the American trade unions come out against this trend. From the point of view of the host countries in the centres, the level of contradictions here is very high, especially since many of these firms are located in other imperialist centres where income levels are high because of the presence of large markets. These states react in different ways to the establishment of multinational corporations originating from other imperialist centres. In certain sectors in the United States, reactions are particularly sharp against Japanese and European firms. In general, countries concentrating their development policy on a few sectors in which they have well-established firms (Belgium, Holland) view the arrival of these corporations favourably, because of the expected effects (the creation of job opportunities in depressed areas, the effects on prices through import substitution), whereas the countries following a global industrial strategy aimed at independence and the creation of their own imperialist sphere of influence display a more cautious attitude. Great Britain and France have organised their own structures for analysing foreign investment projects, trying—laboriously and without much apparent success, because of the contradictions between this attitude and their global policy—to channel these investments towards high unemployment areas and towards sectors lacking in dynamism.

In fact, one of the main contradictions at present is the clash between the American multinational corporations and the secondary imperialist centres. The European and Japanese states have had to face a number of counteroffensives in their attempts to build an autonomous imperialist sphere. American multinational corporations play an important role in these counteroffensives, as shown by the monetary crisis (currency speculation, circumvention of exchange controls and credit regulations, the importance of the Eurodollar and Asiadollar markets) and the energy crisis (role of oil companies). So far, the American firms have shown themselves better able to play upon the contradictions within Europe (struggle for leadership of Europe, neutralisation of some European multinational corporations) than the European states, which have not been able to exploit the contradictions between the multinational corporations.

An analysis of the imperialist strategies is therefore indispensible in order to understand the behaviour of multinational corporations. The proceeding brief comments enable us to draw a number of conclusions:

> the multinational corporations are generally not autonomous *vis-à-vis* their state or origin. The role played by a multinational corporation is closely linked to the strategy of the "parent" imperialist centre;
>
> contradictions exist between multinational corporations, reflecting reality and the development of inter-imperialist conflicts;
>
> contradictions exist between the multinational firms of one and the same imperialist centre, according to the options available to the dominant class alliance. The fraction of the bourgeoisie which controls these firms is invariably part of the dominant class alliance, but its place and the importance of the role it plays within the alliance may vary and develop at different periods in time.

Some multinational firms may thus find themselves in conflict with their country of origin, insofar as the fraction of the bourgeoisie which controls them does not necessarily dominate the state apparatus at any given time. Furthermore, any corporation may find itself in opposition to certain decisions or certain specific situations and may prefer, in the short term, to adopt a wait-and-see attitude (e.g., towards monetary policies).

Multinational corporations and dominated countries

With regard to the dominated countries, relations between the state and the multinational corporation seem at first sight simpler to understand, although they conceal an infinitely more complex reality. In fact, the role of these corporations cannot simply be reduced to that of foreign economic agents; a study must be made of the part, direct or indirect, played by these corporations in the existing class alliances, as well as the forms of domination they exercise.

From the viewpoint of class alliances, it is true to say that these characteristics typical of the current stage of imperialism are present in all the imperialist centres. Of course, there may be important differences between one country and another, depending on the specific nature of each social formation, on the history of the class struggle and the nature of the imperialist sphere. This alliance may be more or less far-reaching and its cohesion more or less strong; the internal power relations may be different. Nevertheless, in every case the most advanced section of capital is represented by that fraction of the bourgeoisie controlling the multinational corporations of the country concerned. This fraction may play a hegemonic role, a dominant or simply a leadership role in the alliance. It has a more or less free hand to implement its social strategy, which always involves the proletarianisation of the pre-capitalist strata of the population and the petty bourgeoisie (peasants, employees, trades-men), the encouragement of new strata within the technical and intellectual petty bourgeoisie and the division of the working class by offering to a section of this class a form of social integration based on the consumer model and the ideological offensive of capitalism.

In the dominated countries, the nature of the class alliances is thus more varied and in many cases, the transitional stages have hardly begun. The shape and the direction of the alliance very often depends on the strategy of the dominant country (representatives or associates of the corporations from the dominant country, state bureaucracy more or less directly controlled, import-export traders). In some cases, these alliances give more weight to certain older, established strata (feudal or large landowners, the liberal petty bourgeoisie, entrepreneurs, etc.).

The multinational corporations are rarely directly represented within the class alliance; they are too small in number and more often than not have few cadres or really representative national leaders. The multinational corporations, however, tend to support—and often in a decisive way—some of the sections within the ruling class alliance. Therein lies the source of a certain number of contradictions.

The multinational corporations originating in the dominant country, backed by their state, are generally directly supported by the leading section of the alliance, especially through the state bureaucracy. As a counterweight, the multinational corporations originating in other imperialist centres try to support other strata of the society (import-export traders, entrepreneurs) by promoting—with the more or less tacit agreement of their state—policies antagonistic to the existing alliance.

The corporations involved in the exploitation of raw materials tend, wherever they exist, to support the feudal-type sections of the alliance. For them, the reproduction of the production relations clearly remains an ideological matter, and the sharing of ground rent takes precedence over accumulation. Conversely, when the state bureaucracy represents the interests of the bourgeois strata of the population, serious conflicts arise with these corporations, insofar as the latter refuse to apply the rent for the purpose of accumulation. By reason of the power relations and the type of control the corporations have over outlets in backward linkage, these situations may give rise to nationalisation measures or to a renegotiation of the terms for sharing the rent.

The corporations involved in the exploitation of the differential costs of labour are, contrary to what is often thought, not at all in favour of systematic policies of high wages, in which attitude they are very akin to the local entrepreneurs. Nevertheless, contradictions soon appear, insofar as these corporations, unlike the local entrepreneurs, are in a good position to meet wage claims from workers, especially at times of tough bargaining. This is all the more true, since the dispersal of the production capacity over a number of countries may, in certain cases, render the production process more vulnerable. If one of the factories grinds to a halt, the supply to the other factories may be jeopardized.

The corporations involved in market exploitation and control rely, to begin with, for support from certain sectors of the large commercial bourgeoisie, wherever this exists. Their traditional policy of high wages and the search for new markets tends to bring them into conflict with both the local entrepreneurs and the feudal landlords. The need for a certain degree of stability encourages them to support the emergence of new class alliances (petty rural bourgeoisie based on land distribution, vast irrigation programmes and credit development; services linked to distribution and tourism, etc.). They are prepared, in some cases, to support certain projects of the petty bourgeoisie, such as some types of land reform, the extension of educational programmes and infrastructural programmes for the development of a trade economy. This last category of multinational corporations today represents the rationality defended by certain international superstructures, such as the World Bank.

In some countries, conflicts may arise between the multinational corporations themselves, particularly in countries for which the imperialist strategy has not yet been clearly defined. This may apply to conglomerates, whose tit-for-tat policy rests on the manipulation of prices and regulations and on special relations with the political authority, a policy which sometimes leads them to intervene systematically at the level of the state apparatus (a particularly striking example is ITT at the centre). In a more general way, there are two conflicting trends in the present American strategy. Take the example of Morocco, where—to put it schematically—the corporations exercise control over the sources of raw materials, which implies support for the feudal strata responsible for the maintenance of order, while at the same time encouraging the emergence of new strata to provide a wider power base at the cost of only a few reforms. The differences of opinion on this policy (as seen in the CIA on the one hand, and the State Department and the World Bank on the other) are highly revealing.

In addition to the role they play within national class alliances, the multinational corporations carry with them the seeds of a world-wide alliance between bourgeoisies and are highly representative of the main forms of domination. Let us for a moment leave aside the various forms of direct control, which are far from constituting the main aspect of the question. What is essential to bear in mind is that these corporations are the privileged actors in the international division of labour; they express its rationality and control its operations in detail, primarily at the level of the world market (control of outlets and circuits) and secondly at the level of superstructures (monetary and financial).

Even shorn of its most ostentatious aspects (control and plunder of natural resources), the logic of the international division of labour becomes increasingly apparent. The contradictions are more clearly felt, in particular as regards the constraints imposed on the state apparatus and the impossibility of implementing a policy of national accumulation. Thus, the benefits which foreign investments and multinational corporations are traditionally assumed to confer (employment, training and technological innovation, development) are increasingly outweighed by the inherent disadvantages (indebtedness, balance of payments, sectoral imbalance and monopoly situation, tighter credit policy, etc.).

An analytical framework for the strategy of multinational corporations

On the basis of the first two parts of this study, it is now possible to delineate an analytical framework for the strategy of a multinational corporation in a given country:

Study of the characteristics of a multinational corporation

At this stage, the following aspects should be studied:

the origin of the multinational corporation (country of origin);

the type of multinational corporation, according to its profits strategy (raw materials, differential costs of labour, control of markets, conglomerates) and its strategy for sectoral diversification;

sectional establishment (sectors and products, its role within the sector, its size and importance, the nature of competition);

the importance and the role of its regional establishment (host country, type of network, form of control over subsidiaries, etc.);

the history of the corporation and its development (linked to international trends at different periods);

the forms of organisation (structure, research and development, shareholding and financial links, etc.).

At this stage, it should be possible to define the characteristics of the multinational corporations and their role in the international division of labour as well as their ties with the international super-structures (world market, monetary system).

The position of the multinational corporation within the context of the imperialist strategy

At this stage, the following aspects should be studied:

the strategy of the imperialist centres, where the multinational corporation has its origin (the trend of the strategy, policies and existing options);

the role of the multinational corporation in the strategy of the centres (inter-imperialist conflicts, control over dominated countries);

the position of the multinational corporation within the dominant class alliance and its role in the internal contradictions within this alliance.

At this stage, it should be possible to define which fraction of the bourgeoisie of the country of origin represents the multinational corporation and, *ipso facto,* to appraise the degree of autonomy of the corporation *vis-à-vis* its home country.

Strategy of the multinational corporation in a dominated country

At this stage, the following aspects should be studied:

the part played by the host country in the overall stragy of the multinational corporation (sectoral establishment, markets, supplies, etc.);

the part that the dominant imperialist country wants the dominated country to play (imperialist staging-post, first or second periphery, inter-imperialist conflict);

the class analysis within the social formation, including a study of the dominant class alliance and its contradictions, in particular with regard to the international situation (and the part played by the multinational corporation within this class alliance: support of certain strata, emergence of new strata, etc.)

It should now be possible to define the strategy of the multinational corporation in a dominated country as well as the consequences of this strategy, having regard in particular to the social strata which support it and the degree of its autonomy *vis-à-vis* the state of its country of origin.

Multinational corporations and a strategy of national independence

The nature of the class alliances in a dominated country

If we are to attempt to define what the existence of the multinational phenomenon means to a strategy for national independence, we shall first of all have to explore the significance of this strategy. If we assume that the state is the indispensible instrument for the implementation of such a strategy, then we must analyse the nature of that state and, consequently, the nature of the dominant class alliance within the appropriate social formation.

It is obviously not our intension to deal with this problem exhaustively or even comprehensively. We shall restrict ourselves to pointing out those factors which we consider most relevant to our study, and therefore shall examine successively:

the problems posed by the study of the class alliances within the dominated country;

the consequences (at the present stage of imperialism) for these class alliances and the resulting strategic options;

the main problems which lie at the centre of any strategy for national independence.

We have already mentioned a few analytical facts about the class alliances in the dominated countries in connection with the role and the position of the multinational corporations. Undoubtedly, a very searching and exhaustive study will have to be carried out for each social formation, taking as a starting point the formation of its social classes and the development of social contradictions. Here it is possible to put forward some complementary facts for analysis.

In almost every single dominated country, the exploited classes and strata of the population are made up of poor peasants, who often constitute a majority of the inhabitants, of small craftsmen, who usually suffer the first shock caused by the penetration of the capitalist mode of production, of the working class, generally not so numerically strong but frequently with a long history of organisation in the transport (railways, ports), mining, construction and public works sectors (and with great variations between the conditions of workers in highly capital-intensive, often foreign undertakings and workers in small, semi-cottage industries), of the mass of low-income employees both in the public and private sectors, especially in commerce and the services (an important number of which are neutralised as a result of intensive ideological brainwashing, as in the the case of domestic servants or salaried workers in the tourist sector), and, finally, of all those who in increasing numbers come to live in an urban peripheral zone, and who have no stable activity but who are involved in various different activities, sometimes as workers, sometimes as craftsmen, sometimes as peasants. This latter group of unemployed or quasi-unemployed persons is very often wrongly described as marginal.

On the other side of the main contradiction and in spite of serious secondary contradictions, there are the feudal landlords and the large landowners, whenever they exist in significant number, the large commercial bourgeoisie, sometimes of great antiquity, and tied up overseas through their import-export activities, the middle commercial bourgeoisie, when consisting of a single, racial minority or of a foreign community (e.g., Lebanese-Syrians, Chinese, Indians) used by and put in a privileged position by the dominant imperialism and who consider that their privileges, and even their safety, depend on continued foreign domination; the large national industrialists producing for export and tied up with the world market and, in particular, the representatives of foreign firms, the long arm of the dominant imperialism within the country, where they manage the interests of multinational corporations. They draw their support from the technical and administratives cadres, who (under cover of technical assistance programmes) often guarantee the perpetuation and reproduction of the system of domination.

The situation of the other classes, strata or social categories in relation to the main contradiction needs to be more exhaustively analysed, taking into consideration numerous other factors surrounding the formation and the history of these social strata.

An analysis, therefore, cannot be restricted to the recent past; it must include the contradictions of the pre-capitalist modes of production and their transformation as a result of the penetration of the capitalist mode of production. Similarly, such an analysis cannot be made within the narrow framework of national frontiers, as these are often artificial, but must be carried out at the regional level (problems of ethnic or national minorities, workers' migration between dominated countries in the same region, emigration towards European imperialist centres, existence of regional or totally foreign communities or minorities holding special positions in the production or circulation process, etc.). The nature of the main contradiction and domination strategy on the one hand and the history of the class struggle on the other, determine the division of the strata into fractions as a result of cleavages and splits, and further determine whether these fractions belong to the dominant class alliance or to the dominated strata.

Thus, the small industrialists and local entrepreneurs are directly confronted with the presence of the multinational corporations, tied up with the world market and with easy access to the financing circuits and to the state machinery. The small and medium scale traders often must deal with the existence of minorities which are privileged by the old political system. The well-off peasants (small holdings or working on rich plantations or co-operatives) are deprived of direct access to the market and do not control the marketing circuits. The national cadres and technicians, both in the private and public industrial sectors, have to face the problems of foreign control of industries and the presence of foreign cadres and technicians, a fact that contributes in a large measure to making them more radical. The state bureaucracy realises its importance for controlling the levers of the state apparatus. The status of the petty intellectual bourgeoisie (teachers, lawyers, doctors, artists) is jeopardized by foreign domination and, furthermore, students (particularly secondary school pupils) strongly resent the existing contradictions between the proclaimed targets of mass education and development and the hard social reality, which is the total absence of possible outlets. Some social categories are particularly affected by social contradictions and frequently play an important connecting role. A specially thorough class analysis is also needed in order to understand the cleavages and behaviour within the army, among the civil servants and among the representatives of religious institutions.

The analysis of a social formation cannot be static; regard must be had to the way in which the classes confront each other, how they are divided and how they change.

It is also necessary to consider the nature and the place of the state within the social formation. Here, the clue is to be found both in the history of the class struggle and, especially, in an analysis of the transition periods, during which antagonisms uncover the reality of the contradictions and new class alliances are formed. In order to pinpoint these periods of transition, we may refer, as far as the recent past is concerned, to a study of the evolution of imperialism. In fact, at every phase, at every stage in the development of imperialism, very profound changes take place in the nature of class alliances within each social formation. If we understand these, we should be able to retrace the development of social contradictions within each social formation and to define a period scale linking these contradictions to the development of imperialism.

For each period, and depending on the nature of the contradiction, a class alliance may be defined by the nature of the classes and strata of which it is made up, the power relations between them within the alliance, as well as the nature and forms of the leadership of the alliance. It is only on the basis of the political target of the leading fraction within the alliance, of the nature of the alliance, and on the basis of the power relations between the classes within the social formation that it is possible to define the social strategy adopted. A given class alliance cannot willy-nilly adopt any strategy and be consistent. To certain alliances correspond certain types of strategies and it is this dialectical relationship that we must try to understand better.

The first phase through which the class alliance applies this strategy is by taking over the State. We do not wish to probe deeper into this question, for it concerns the definition and formation of a front and of a strategy for taking power, although the way in which this phase is carried out largely conditions the second phase of the social strategy. We shall approach the problem from another angle and, in the case of a class alliance already in control of the state, explore possible strategies, taking into consideration the development of imperialism. We shall also enquire into some of the characteristics of class alliances fundamental to these strategies, in order to be better able to define the vital elements of a strategy for national independence.

International environment and imperialist strategy

At the present stage of imperialism, there are two possible class alliances, controlling state power in a dominated country, which define this strategy: firstly, belonging to a sphere of influence within which there develops an imperialist strategy (dominant imperialism, inter-imperialist conflicts, relations with socialist countries), and secondly, the position and the role, accepted or rejected, of the country within the imperialist system and the international division of labour.

As far as the various imperialisms are concerned, the present period is marked by a new effort to carve up the world, giving rise to very severe struggles. Europe and Japan, wishing to pass the stage of being secondary imperialist centres, are attempting to set up their own separate spheres of imperialist domination. They are both in favour of a balance of power based on a world divided into five power blocks. The USA is trying to consolidate its control by opposing European and Japanese designs and relying on a strategy of peaceful coexistence with the USSR. In fact, the USA tends to lean in favour of three power blocks, within which the rift between the USSR and China would enable the United States to rule alone and re-establish complete hegemony over its sphere of influence and to dominate the whole system. The USSR, for its part, seems to favour a world divided into two blocks—using peaceful coexistence with the USA as a strategic axis—to enable it to consolidate its own foreign positions and thereby arrive at solutions rendered necessary because of its own internal development.

China, being committed to the Proletarian Cultural Revolution and the profound transformation of its social relations of production, appears anxious to break the encirclement with which it is threatened. China will probably refuse—as shown by her stand on Europe and Japan—to take part in a world with five blocks, which would be tantamount to consolidating the imperialist system through the emergence of Europe and Japan as principal centres. Considering the eventuality of a two-block world (the two superpowers) as the most immediate, if not the most serious, threat, China has been inclined to encourage every possible tendency capable of counteracting, or at least contradicting, a consolidation of the present balance of power situation, irrespective of the amount of opposition or even the nature of the regime. This, of course, leads to very serious contradictions. The situation, therefore, is much more complex than during the fifties, when the cold war had made possible the emergence of non-aligned nations and enabled some countries to safeguard a relative autonomy. The antagonisms between the two camps were more directly linked to the general power relations rather than to the preservation of regional balances. Nowadays, belonging to a sphere of influence is much more constricting and has very serious repercussions on the nature of the struggles. Three types of spheres, in line with the nature of existing relations, may be distinguished:

> the centres of the power blocks, whether they be main imperialist centres like the USA, secondary imperialist centres like Europe and Japan or, unlike the imperialist centres, an independent centre without any sphere of domination, like China;
>
> the first peripheries of the centres, i.e., areas controlled either economically or politically by one of the centres. In this connection, although schematically, we find that most of Latin America constitutes a first periphery of the USA, part of Africa the same for Europe, part of Southeast Asia for Japan and Eastern Europe for the USSR;
>
> the second peripheries of the centres, in which there generally exists a dominant centre not exercising complete economic control of the country, struggling against other centres to preserve its own domination and very often coming up against situations favourable to the development of liberation struggles.

Thus, Japan is channelling its efforts towards an economic penetration in Africa (particularly in South Africa) and even in the Middle East. The USA is trying to exercise closer control over certain countries in the European sphere in Africa (Nigeria, Zaire), in the Japanese sphere in Southeast Asia, in the

European, Japanese and Soviet spheres in the Middle East, and in the Soviet sphere in Southern Asia. Europe is trying to disentangle southern Europe and to re-establish itself in the Middle East, going as far as proposing a Mediterranean alliance between the European and Arab bourgeoisies.

To conclude these few remarks, we should like to stress the particularly important position of the countries which, after a liberation struggle, are trying to adopt policies of national accumulation and even of transition towards socialism. One may also emphasize the existence of regions where the contradictions of the imperialist system are particularly acute because of revolutionary wars (Vietnam, Palestine) and intense inter-imperialist conflicts. Such is the case in the Middle East, in Southeast Asia and in Southern Europe.

Within the strategy of each of these centres, a well-defined place and role is assigned to each region and to each country. Knowledge of this place and role, their consequences, the contradictions and the conflicts between different strategies existing within a given country is indispensible for a correct appraisal of possible actions that may be taken by those who control the state. Moreover, this knowledge is also valuable insofar as it makes it possible to analyse the classes by bringing to the fore the relationship between and the support of some social strata. Thus in Africa, the American offensive is carried out in the main by the multinational corporations and those strata of the population closely connected with them. In some countries, these strata are especially well supported and may play a decisive role (Nigeria, Zaire, Morocco, Liberia). The ugly racist domination in Southern Africa is rendered possibly through the active support of the USA, as well as Europe and Japan. In some countries in Eastern Africa—Kenya, for example—the British multinational corporations, often tied up with American corporations, coexist with certain strata of the population established within the commercial circle and relying on a policy of preferential markets as practised by Great Britain. France's intervention is carried out much more at the level of public investments and technical assistance in a number of countries in West and Central Africa, relying for support directly on those strata of the population tied up with the state apparatus. Finally, in some countries, the ideological and technological imperatives of a struggle for national independence confer an important place on the petty bourgeoisie and the officials of public corporations (Algeria, Tanzania, Nasser's Egypt).

International division of labour and national independence

Nevertheless, the internationalisation of capital and the development of the imperialist system have the effect, in the long run, of creating relative differences between the various practices of domination. Even though it is far from being a matter of indifference to any country whether it belongs to the periphery of one centre rather than another, the main feature always remains that of being part of a peripheral area. In the final analysis, the crucial question for a given country is its position within the international division of labour. In the wake of de-colonisation, the pursuit of domination and the establishment of "neo-colonialism" are undeniable facts. In effect, the term "neo-colonialism" covers a multitude of different realities, ranging from the situation of a colonial or quasi-colonial country to that of an imperialist relay station. With regard to the international division of labour, apart from the principal or secondary imperialist centres, four different types of situations may be defined:

the quasi-colonies, victims of the strategy of domination and unable to challenge their position within the international division of labour;

imperialist relay stations, which may hope to benefit from a certain growth rate, giving them a higher rank within the international division of labour;

policies of national accumulation, which may cause certain countries to look for national independence and to refuse the role assigned from them within the international division of labour;

policies of transition towards socialism, which imply the rejection of the whole system of international division of labour.

The quasi-colony

The situation of a quasi-colony is, in fact, the most common; almost all of the dominated countries fall into this category. The hopes encouraged by de-colonisation soon disappeared into thin air, and the great ideological offensive of general development and aid from rich to poor countries could not for long conceal the stark reality. Even the general establishment of a type of neo-colonialism substantially different from the policy of plundering resources and directly exploiting peoples appeared to imperialism a luxury which it could only afford in a very limited number of cases. Everywhere else, the imperialist centres tried to support the class alliance which would ensure the permanence of their domination. These leading class alliances are varied and nondescript; their efficiency varies from country to country; and they are more or less capable of facing the popular uprisings or the militancy of the workers. These alliances frequently include feudal lords and large landowners as well as the old traditional chiefs; they also tend to come into conflict with the small industrialists and national businessmen. The huge foreign corporations exploiting these countries (either directly or through work marketing circuits) do not directly appear, and they restrict their action solely to the profitable sectors.

A semblance of power is conferred on the army or on the bureaucratic strata, who benefit from part of the extorted surplus and who, in fact, play the part of functionaries of imperialism. In a great number of countries, "order" is maintained by strong, direct repression and by currying popular support through the incantation of past traditions. The philosophy of imperialism was illustrated to the point of caricature by the doctrine of Papa Doc in Haiti, who gave voodoo and the "tontons macoutes" to the people, the profits to the foreign corporations, and misappropriation and gratuities to the family and friends of Papa Doc. Such a situation, even when less of a caricature, ultimately leads to a radicalisation of popular struggles—there are spontaneous uprisings as a direct result of poverty and injustice. Other contradictions may then develop and especially those felt by the petty intellectual bourgeoisie and by those strata of the local bourgeoisie for whom foreign domination and the absence of control over the state apparatus have removed any possibility for accumulation.

Imperialist relay stations or "staging-posts"

These contradictions become even more acute by the very fact that objective conditions for accumulation, i.e., a mobilisable surplus, do exist. The struggle to obtain control of the surplus necessarily had repercussions on the dominant class alliance:

> a new and sometimes leading role was conferred on certain sectors of the bourgeoisie which controlled the medium-scale industry, thus facilitating entry into the state apparatus for members of the petty bourgeoisie, sometimes via the army;
>
> this entailed a weakening, if not the abolition, of all the pre-capitalist strata opposed to altered earmarking of the surplus (feudal landlords controlling mineral deposits or agricultural production) and to the freeing of labour (feudal landlords and traditional chiefs in the various "tributary" modes of production);
>
> this entailed a new definition of the colonial pact with the multinational corporations involved in the exploitation of raw materials. The advent of production control with the establishment of national corporations encouraged the emergence of a bourgeoisie tied up with the state (Iran, Indonesia, Venezuela); earmarking part of the ground rent for investments; introduction of new competitors; increased obligations to ensure reinvestment and research, etc. Although diminished, the position of these multinational corporations continued to be very important, especially since they retained control of the foreign marketing circuits. To mention an example outside the oil and mineral ore sectors, this was clearly shown in the case of British corporations operating in Sri Lanka (Ceylon);
>
> this facilitated and encouraged the establishment of other corporations (e.g., differential costs of labour with a view to re-export) which would occupy a central position in the new political power structure.

The new class alliances that appeared in some countries had to look for support from new strata of the local bourgeoisies, which were in a position to claim a larger part of the imperialist profits. This represents, in a way, the transition from the status of functionaries of imperialist domination to that of delegate bourgeoisie, similar to the situation in a private enterprise where a salaried manager is moved to the position of director without control over capital. These bourgeoisies were to be closely connected with and controlled by the multinational corporations, essentially by those exploiting labour and exercising direct control over the market. The political objective of these class alliances was to succeed in financing and controlling the administration by obtaining a better rank within the international division of labour. Their aim was to play the part of an imperialist relay station, as illustrated in Brazil, Iran and Indonesia—which are within the sphere of American imperialism.

Nevertheless, to become candidates for the status of imperialist relay station, the class alliances must fulfil a number of conditions:

the possibility, within the present international division of labour, for extracting and controlling a mobilisable surplus, particularly in the form of ground rent (oil, mineral ores, agricultural raw materials necessary for the imperialist centres), which exclude from the leadership of this alliance those strata opposed to mobilising this surplus for capitalist accumulation;

from the viewpoint of the dominated strata, this condition leads to aggression against the poor peasants and attempts to neutralise the rural middle strata (credit, marketing, etc.);

the presence of a cheap and abundant labour force, making possible the creation of a reserve industrial army, which exludes from the leadership of this alliance the strata opposed to the "freeing" of labour;

from the viewpoint of the dominated strata, this condition leads to anti-working class repression and to a particularly vicious anti-trade union policy;

the presence of an actual or potential captive market, which necessitates a sufficiently large population to allow the possibility of controlling other countries in the region. This leads to a policy of agression towards neighbouring countries;

the assurance of the continuity of domination by the dominant class alliance, guaranteeing the insertion of the country into a geopolitical and military strategy of the dominant imperialism, together with the so-called political stability so cherished by multinational corporations with money to invest. This conditions leads to the adoption of policies geared to the maintenance of the established order, which in practice are often fascist-type policies, and whose victims, apart from the broad masses, include large sections of the intellectual petty bourgeoisie.

We may now put forward some conclusions on the basis of the resulting consequences:

the repression necessary for the implementation of such a political target provides the objective condition for an alliance between peasants, the working class and wide sections of the intellectual petty bourgeoisie. As the working class expands, so the revolutionary character of the ensuing struggles becomes stronger;

in countries where such conditions are not present, the bourgeoisie finds itself deprived of an independent political platform capable of enlisting international support, and a part of this bourgeoisie may become tempted to support, or even to join, the peoples' struggles, which assume the shape of new national liberation struggles;

even in the case of countries where these conditions are present, accession to the imperialist stage is not automatic, in view of the fact that there cannot be more than one imperialist relay station per region. Competition is very stiff, as evidenced by the Middle East situation, where the rivalries between Iran and Saudi Arabia render the situation very unstable. Furthermore, this competition reduces the freedom of negotiation allowed the local bourgeoisie, making concessions to popular demands more difficult, thereby contributing to the radicalisation and the widening of the struggles;

this competition will also bring into conflict those countries playing the part of a relay station within the same region on behalf of two competing imperialism, as for instance, between certain countries in Africa or the Middle East supported by France or Great Britain, in relation to other countries supported by the USA. If a few countries are able to take advantage of this situation in order to increase their autonomy, these relay stations, being the vital support of imperialist strategies, generally become pawns in a particularly serious conflict, thus adding to the overall instability of the system. The action of multinational corporations becomes extremely important in these cases, since these corporations are part of a much more global strategy, defined and controlled by the dominant states, which intervene in many crucial areas: economic, political and, increasingly, military.

Efforts towards national accumulation

Quasi-colonies or imperialist relay stations—both situations are unacceptable to the exploited strata of the population. If, after taking power, the alliance between the exploited classes and the dominated strata succeeds in taking control over the state apparatus, it might (together with the working class and as a leading if not the main force) attempt to implement its own political programme, viz. the building of socialism.

We shall not dwell here on the problems posed by a transition to socialism. In some cases, however, certain dominated strata form part of the dominant class alliance without ever taking over the leadership and without having control of the state apparatus, whereas other exploited strata are completely excluded from the alliance. Such a situation may arise when the struggle for national liberation, gaining its support mainly from the broad masses, has seriously weakened the ruling classes and deprived them of all outside support. This may also occur when the bourgeoisie has been compelled to rely on the people for support to abolish the traditional leading strata of the population.

Pressed by popular resistance, limited in scope by imperialist pressures, such alliances try at all costs to safeguard national independence and ensure a policy of accumulation not immediately determined by the imperatives of the international division of labour. Such class alliances are formed during transitional periods, when contradictions are especially acute. Two main political trends confront each other within the same political state machinery.

Faced with the demands of the broad masses to build socialism, the bourgeoisie must impose the recognition of its autonomy on the imperialist system and negotiate a new position within the international division of labour. To achieve that, the bourgeoisie must use the state apparatus so as to ensure its control over the means of production and demonstrate its ability to dominate the broad masses and ensure the reproduction of the capitalist relations of production. Contradiction then arises because, while trying to alter the power relations in its own favour, the bourgeoisie loses all popular support and weakens its own ability to resist the direct aggression of imperialism. Imperialist aggression is backed by all those who have a vested interest in direct domination or who prefer to arm themselves against the risks of a popular victory in the struggle for power. The failure of a policy of national independence may lead to a fascist-type repression, prepared abroad, with the aim of restoring the country to a situation of direct dependence.

Even if the first stages of national independence (e.g., the liberation of territories and the recovery of national resources) may be brought about by wider alliances, the international division of labour today makes it impossible to imagine national accumulation independent of the imperialist system. Only a development of the productive forces outside the international division of labour would make it possible to achieve these objectives. This does not mean that various efforts already launched should be abandoned, or that all relations with the rest of the world must be broken, but a system of planning should be used which does not allow the law of value inherent in the capitalist mode of production to impose itself through the the world market. Although it is not possible to speak of a national bourgeoisie, let us stress the fact that in certain situations, some sections of the local bourgeoisie may be rallied in opposition to imperialist strategies and in defence of policies of national independence. The participation of these population strata in coherent strategies for national independence is both possible and often necessary. Nevertheless, they cannot assume the leadership of the appropriate class alliance without endangering the prospects of achieving these objectives.

The imperative requirements of a strategy for national independence

For a country which has already freed itself from colonial oppression, national independence represents the opportunity of implementing an accumulation policy not subordinated to the mechanisms of imperialism, whether these take the form of belonging to a sphere directly controlled by an imperialist centre or whether they are the direct consequence of the international division of labour and control by the world market and the international monetary system.

A strategy for national independence, in order to be consistent, must meet certain imperative requirements:

The strength and the nature of the class alliance constitute the dominant element. Such an alliance must exclude the traditional and feudal classes liable to form foreign alliances capable of supporting an anti-popular repression so as to delay their own abolition. Similarly, it must exclude those fractions of the bourgeoisie and of the petty bourgeoisie directly dependent on foreign interests (cadres working for multinational corporations, import-export businessmen, etc.);

through the control of the state apparatus it should be possible to eliminate from it all those who are tied up with foreign interests or who may be open to their pressures. The transformation of the state should bring about a redirection of its policies. This is always difficult, because of the existing historical contradictions and the conditions surrounding the formation of the state. The state apparatus will find itself confronted with difficult tasks and will have limited means. Apart from the problems of a defence against imperialist agressions, the state becomes the main instrument for a policy of accumulation and the focus for resolving all contradictions within the class alliance;

the prerequisites for a policy of national accumulation are the recovery of natural resources, the control of the distribution and production circuits and networks, the installation of transport and energy infrastructures and the establishment of a basic industrial infrastructure. Such a policy will come up against formidable problems in the areas of employment, consumption, the location of production and the financing of accumulation. These options will have immediate repercussions on the nature and strength of the class alliance: development and control of a state bourgeoisie, development of worker and peasant conditions, the position of cadres and technicians, of small businessmen and craftsmen, of the intellectual petty bourgeoisie, consumer problems of the middle strata of the population, etc.;

popular mobilisation represents a pivotal and decisive factor in a strategy for national independence and its development. It guarantees the strength of the alliance and, indeed, provides the only guarantee against foreign agression. It facilitates the solution of contradictions within the alliance and the widening of this alliance to include new strata of the broad masses. It renders control over the alliance's leadership possible and ensures preparedness against any treason by some fractions of the bourgeoisie. It provides the opportunity for transforming the state apparatus by pressing for decentralised institutions, allowing for popular control and avoiding further use of anti-popular repression—through mere force of habit—as the mainstay for the maintenance of order. Finally, it allows for experimentation with new forms of organisation with the enterprises, in the countryside and the city worlds engaged in preparing the transformation of the social relations of production, and preventing the adoption of a policy of accumulation at the expense of the workers. In order to achieve these targets, an ideological offensive is one of the cardinal principles of any strategy for national independence;

a policy of alliances is vital in order to avoid isolation. The first should be a regional alliance to increase the chances of economic resistance and to make more difficult any boycotts and infiltration. Secondly, there should be an anti-imperialist alliance at an international level, to challenge the international division of labour, its rationality and its practices as well as all the superstructures which guarantee its permanence and reproduction.

Multinational corporations and national independence

The relations between multinational corporations and the states of the dominated countries depend on the nature of the dominant class alliance. There are no major problems with regard to the quasi-colonies, except tit-for-tat negotiations depending on existing multinational corporations and the power relations within the class alliance. The problem is better defined when a class alliance in a neo-colonial situation claims the status of an imperialist relay station. In order to reach its political targets, the fraction of the bourgeoisie assuming the leadership of the class alliance:

tries to renegotiate the establishment agreements with those multinational corporations exploiting raw materals. Violent conflicts, often with the support of competitors, will arise with some corporations;

encourages setting up the highest possible number of multinational corporations by conferring a leading role on those prepared to develop export capacity, thus enabling a better integration into the world market.

The problem of national independence takes on a different aspect and is no longer a matter of negotiations strategy. Sooner or later, the state will have to face the whole gamut of multinational corporations. Nevertheless, while it is easy enough to strike an agreement within the class alliance for the control of natural resources and raw materials, it is not always as easy to negotiate with the multinational corporations as a whole. Even though some fractions of the bourgeoisie remain committed partners within the alliance, they do not always take a very clear stand on such issues as nationalisation and compensation, the role and extent of the public sector, foreign trade, distribution, etc. Thus, a strategy against multinational corporations is not always forthcoming *a priori*. Nevertheless, the dynamics of this process, once launched, very soon go into high gear. Forever sensitive to the logic of the process, frightened by the prospect of being overtaken by events, multinational corporations choose caution, proceed with disinvestment and very soon are involved in sabotage, with the effect of making the class alliance more radical.

Thus, even if for tactical reasons—depending on the degree of popular mobilisation, the nature of relations with the country of origin or possible support from world opinion—a conflict initially arises with only one or two multinational corporations, one must always be aware of the fact that any strategy adopted must include the whole multinational phenomenon. Such a strategy may rest on four basic principles:

an analysis of the situation leading to the formation of consistent policies;

the setting up of control mechanisms to facilitate resistance against possible counteroffensives;

the implementation of a specific strategy for every multinational corporation;

the widening of the front for an anti-imperialist strategy.

An analysis of the situation

This analysis must take into consideration those multinational corporations which have the power to exercise a significant influence on the economic situation of the country in question. We must distinguish between:

those multinational corporations already established in the country and controlling the production capacity or the marketing capacity;

those multinational corporations not directly established in the country, but in a position to control or divert export capacity;

those multinational corporations not directly established in the country, but able to control or obstruct the flow of supplies.

The analysis must concentrate on every single multinational corporation and on all the multinational corporations as a body, their interrelationships and their differences. Here we refer to the analytical framework mentioned above (pages 406 ff.).

Such studies should make it possible:

to redefine all the multinational corporations studied in the context of the multinational phenomenon, and in particular those corporations not directly established in a country; to study the possible import substitution policies for production and for supplies (competing multinational corporations, possibility of direct intervention on markets, inter-state agreements, etc.);

to redefine all the multinational corporations studied in the context of the strategy of the countries of origin (the position of the corporations within these strategies, their role in the internal contradictions of the country of origin, interstate conflicts, etc.);

to redefine all the multinational corporations studied in the context of the national class alliances and the part they play within the social contradictions of a country.

This analysis should improve and clarify any analysis of the strategy of the dominant states in relation to the country concerned. It should also allow us to determine the support behind the multinational corporations in the country (fraction of the bourgeoisie, employers' organisations, sectors of the army, etc.), and lead to a more accurate appraisal of the strength of the class alliance.

Let us emphasize that such studies need neither be lengthy nor expensive in comparison to the expected results. There are enough available data, at least to begin an overall preliminary conclusions. Those multinational corporations which actually intervene in a significant way are rather limited in number and, once the analytical framework has been established, a systematic follow-up could provide excellent results with relatively limited means.

Controlling the control mechanisms

We shall now consider the control mechanisms of the economy, without which no policy of national independence is viable. The aim is to avoid having recourse in each instance to theoretical measures—which could easily be stacked up in a corner—while making use of existing mechanisms or else relying for support on the state of origin or on international superstructures (IMF, World Bank).

With regard to comprehensive planning, the measures adopted must at least include:

foreign trade (nationalisation or control over prices, quality, origin and destination of commodities, redirection of trade flows);

monetary policy (exchange controls, the issue of bank notes and various items of the balance of payments);

credit policy and the banking system;

inputs policy (energy and other intermediate consumer goods, investments, repairs and maintenance);

distribution policy (consumption and retail trade).

As we have emphasized earlier, multinational corporations are never independent *vis-à-vis* their country of origin. Is it therefore not in relation to multinational corporations that such a strategy must be devised, but in relation to the imperialist states. This is the only possible way to isolate the multinational corporations and to cut off their support. In the final analysis, it is the stability of the class alliance and the strength of the popular mobilisation which will make the strategic choices work. In every instance, it is by attacking the imperialist policy of the country of origin and by reducing its ability to intervene that the multinational corporations are most weakened.

The first stage in this process involves the mastery of the control mechanisms of the economy. This control must be exercised in relation to the dominant state and to the international superstructures (world market, monetary system). For this purpose, inter-state agreements may be relied upon (regional policy, agreements with other centres of power blocks, exploitation of inter-imperialist conflicts) as well as a policy of alliance against the superstructures (agreements among producing countries, Algiers Conferences, etc.).

The specific strategy for multinational corporations

Once formulated, the policy of controlling the control mechanisms of the economy and the adoption of sectoral planning would require a well-defined strategy *vis-à-vis* the multinational corporations. It goes without saying that one must not wait until control of the economic mechanisms has been obtained before intervening; on the contrary, the strategy adopted *vis-à-vis* multinational corporations would strengthen and clarify the general strategy through the development of contradictions. There will nevertheless be many set-backs unless, before going into action, the precaution has been taken of ascertaining that a consistent framework for action is available.

It is then necessary to consider the angle for attack, to choose the weak link in the chain. In order to decide with which corporation to start, the following factors must be considered:

the position of the corporation within the hierarchy of the established multinational corporations as a whole (does it play a strategic role, are there any contradictions with other corporations, etc.);

the possible consequences on the class alliance of any intervention (one should be very careful about the existing divisions within the working class, a direct result of the wage differential between sectors and firms, and the existence of corporatist trade unions controlled by the multinational corporations; one must also assess the consequences on distribution, prices and supplies);

the existing contradictions within the class alliance of the country of origin and the possibility of making use of them to inhibit any potential action by the state of origin;

the prospects for obtaining international support (structure of the sector, other countries concerned, solidarity of the workers and support of world opinion);

and, more especially, the prospects for mobilising popular support in favour of the intervention (policy and public image of the corporation in the country, the situation of the workers, exploitation of natural resources, etc.)

The definition of a strategy *vis-à-vis* a given multinational corporation must be specific and depends on the history of the corporation and its strategy. We should therefore refer back to the previous studies and analysis. Some indication may be given of the possible strong points of these strategies.

Vis-à-vis those corporations whose profits strategy is determined by the exploitation of raw materials, the main supporting policy should be the creation and the strengthening of the output capacities in the public sector. This may be carried out either through nationalisation or through association agreements with state structures, depending on the structuration of the world market, i.e., the possibilities for agreements between producer countries and agreements with consumer states. The policies implemented generally include control over production and research and an improved effort for reinvestment and vertical integration (utilisation of raw materials, search for new outlets, industrialisation in backward linkage).

Vis-à-vis those corporations whose profits strategy is determined by the exploitation of the differential costs of labour, the main supporting policy should be the social strategy to be implemented (workers' demands, transformation of the social relations of production), but particular attention should be paid to the possible consequences on working class unity and the unity between workers and peasants. Apart from that, the policies implemented generally include facilities for completing the production process (usually only part of this process is assured and most often consists of assembly plants), paying particular attention to problems of maintenance and renewal.

In the case of corporations whose profits strategy is determined by a control of the markets, the main supporting policy should concern distribution circuits, paying special attention to problems of after-sales services, spare parts and technological innovation. The policy implemented generally includes import substitution, barter agreements with other states, regulation of the market and a reorganisation of distribution.

In the case of conglomerates, the main supporting policy should relate to credit and exchange controls. The policy implemented generally includes nationalisation of subsidiaries and their integration within the public sector.

Integration within the framework of an anti-imperialist strategy

Once engaged in a policy of national independence, events begin to move very fast and it becomes very difficult to keep them in perspective. Two main dangers are always lurking: the risk of an imperialist aggression and the risk of a fascist-type anti-popular repression. The class alliance may split, for a fraction of the bourgeoisie may be tempted by the possibility of securing a new position within the international division of labour.

In any case, the implementation of the strategy and the resulting responses would afterwards alter relations within the alliance and put its stability to the test. Reorganisation of production and distribution, redirection of consumption and price control may increase or remove popular support. These measures may also frighten a number of people from different social strata who fear that their short-term interests may become jeopardized. Sooner or later the crucial question will arise, namely that debated between the two schools of thought at the Lo Curro symposium in Chile: is it necessary to consolidate in order to move forward or is it necessary to move forward in order to consolidate? There must therefore always be the means available for assessing the results of a strategy of national independence and one must be in a position to redefine, in the light of the main options, the specific strategies in relation to each multinational corporation.

Let us repeat once more that the logic, i.e., the consistency of a strategy for natinal independence, is determined by its anti-imperialist content. Therein lie both the importance and the contradictions of these policies. Events may cause them to reinforce the anti-imperialist camp, to challenge the international division of labour, to reject the rationality defended by the international superstructures, and to seek to create regional and international alliances capable of helping them to resist.

The multinational corporations represent the most advanced section of capital at the present stage of imperialism. The internationalisation of capital creates new contradictions and provides the objective basis for a new internationalism; it renders predominant the anti-imperialist nature of the struggle for national independence within the dominated countries and symbolises the meaning of socialism for all the peoples of the world.